Lecture Notes in Computer Science

Commenced Publication in 1973
Founding and Former Series Editors:
Gerhard Goos, Juris Hartmanis, and Jan van Leeuwen

Kay Römer   Holger Karl
Friedemann Mattern (Eds.)

Wireless
Sensor Networks

Third European Workshop, EWSN 2006
Zurich, Switzerland, February 13-15, 2006
Proceedings

 Springer

Volume Editors

Kay Römer
Friedemann Mattern
ETH Zurich
Institute for Pervasive Computing
Haldeneggsteig 4, 8092 Zurich, Switzerland
E-mail: {roemer,mattern}@inf.ethz.ch

Holger Karl
Universität Paderborn
Fachgebiet Rechnernetze
Pohlweg 47-49, 33098 Paderborn, Germany
E-mail: holger.karl@upb.de

Library of Congress Control Number: 2005939186

CR Subject Classification (1998): C.2.4, C.2, F.2, D.1.3, D.2, E.1, H.4, C.3

LNCS Sublibrary: SL 5 – Computer Communication Networks and Telecommunications

ISSN   0302-9743
ISBN-10   3-540-32158-6 Springer Berlin Heidelberg New York
ISBN-13   978-3-540-32158-3 Springer Berlin Heidelberg New York

Springer is a part of Springer Science+Business Media

springeronline.com

© Springer-Verlag Berlin Heidelberg 2006
Printed in Germany

Typesetting: Camera-ready by author, data conversion by Scientific Publishing Services, Chennai, India
Printed on acid-free paper   SPIN: 11669463   06/3142   5 4 3 2 1 0

Preface

This volume contains the proceedings of EWSN 2006, the third in a series of European workshops on wireless sensor networks. The workshop took place at ETH Zurich from February 13 to 15, 2006. Its objective was to present, discuss, and explore the latest technical developments in the field of wireless sensor networks, as well as potential future directions.

Wireless sensor networks provide a bridge between traditional information systems and the physical world, with collections of wirelessly networked sensor nodes being deployed in our physical environment to cooperatively monitor real-world phenomena, but also to control aspects of the physical world. In contrast to traditional computing systems which are mostly decoupled from the real world, wireless sensor networks are inherently and closely integrated with the real world, with data about the physical environment being captured and processed automatically, online, and in real time. This paradigmatic change comes with a number of conceptual and technical challenges involving a wide range of disciplines in computer science and electrical engineering, but also material sciences, MEMS technology, and power engineering, thus making wireless sensor networks a multidisciplinary area of research. This workshop series aims at providing a high-level scientific forum to implement the cross-disciplinary exchange of ideas and results that is essential for this type of research area. While based in Europe, the workshop serves as a truly international forum with 40% of the submissions originating from Europe, 38% from Asia and Australia, 20% from the Americas, and 2% from Africa.

Wireless sensor networks has become an active and popular research area, which is witnessed by the 133 submissions we received from authors all over the world. The Program Committee chose 21 papers for inclusion in the workshop. It was a difficult choice, based on several hundred reviews produced by the Program Committee and many outside referees, where each paper was typically reviewed by three reviewers.

In addition to the papers contained in these proceedings, the conference program included a demo and poster track, and a special session on European research initiatives focusing on wireless sensor networks. Karl Aberer (EPFL), director of the Swiss National Competence Centre in Research for Mobile Information and Communication Systems (NCCR-MICS), delivered a keynote talk entitled "Unleashing the Power of Wireless Networks through Information Sharing in the Sensor Internet." Moreover, the workshop offered two half-day tutorials:

- Data Management in Sensor Networks (Samuel Madden, MIT)
- Algorithms for Wireless Sensor Networks (Roger Wattenhofer, ETH Zurich)

In closing, we would like to express our sincere appreciation to all authors who submitted papers. We deeply thank all members of the Program Committee and the external reviewers for their time and effort as well as their valuable input. Finally, we would like to thank Springer for their excellent cooperation, our sponsoring institutions, and the Organizing Committee.

February 2006   Kay Römer and Holger Karl, Program Chairs
                                                    Friedemann Mattern, General Chair

Organization

EWSN 2006, the third in a series of European workshops on wireless sensor networks, took place in Zurich, Switzerland from February 13 to 15, 2006. It was organized by ETH Zurich, the Swiss Federal Institute of Technology.

Executive Committee

General Chair: Friedemann Mattern (ETH Zurich, Switzerland)
Program Co-chairs: Kay Römer (ETH Zurich, Switzerland) and
                      Holger Karl (University of Paderborn, Germany)
Publicity Co-chairs: Nirupama Bulusu (Portland State University, USA) and
                      Thiemo Voigt (SICS, Sweden)

Organizing Committee

Christian Frank (ETH Zurich, Switzerland)
Marc Langheinrich (ETH Zurich, Switzerland)
Matthias Ringwald (ETH Zurich, Switzerland)
Kay Römer (ETH Zurich, Switzerland)
Silvia Santini (ETH Zurich, Switzerland)

Program Committee

Ozgur Akan (Middle East Technical University, Turkey)
Michel Banâtre (INRIA, France)
Christian Bettstetter (University of Klagenfurt, Austria)
Nirupama Bulusu (Portland State University, USA)
Srdjan Capkun (Technical University of Denmark, Denmark)
Erdal Cayirci (Istanbul Technical University, Turkey)
George Coulouris (Cambridge University, UK)
Jean-Pierre Ebert (IHP Microelectronics, Germany)
Eylem Ekici (Ohio State University, USA)
Jeremy Elson (Microsoft Research, USA)
Paul J. M. Havinga (University of Twente, The Netherlands)
Wendi Heinzelman (University of Rochester, USA)
Holger Karl (University of Paderborn, Germany)
Bhaskar Krishnamachari (University of Southern California, USA)
Koen Langendoen (TU Delft, The Netherlands)
Pedro J. Marrón (University of Stuttgart, Germany)
Friedemann Mattern (ETH Zurich, Switzerland)
Amy L. Murphy (University of Lugano, Switzerland)

Chiara Petrioli (University "La Sapienza" Rome, Italy)
Bart van Poucke (IMEC, Belgium)
Hartmut Ritter (FU Berlin, Germany)
Kay Römer (ETH Zurich, Switzerland)
Lothar Thiele (ETH Zurich, Switzerland)
Thiemo Voigt (SICS, Sweden)
Matt Welsh (Harvard University, USA)
Dirk Westhoff (NEC, Germany)
Andreas Willig (TU Berlin, Germany)
Adam Wolisz (TU Berlin, Germany)

Supporting Institutions

Embedded Wisents Project (EU FP6-IST Coordination Action)
ETH Zurich, Switzerland

Table of Contents

Routing

Localization

Platforms and Development

Medium Access Control

Measurements

Data Management in Sensor Networks

Samuel Madden

Computer Science and Artificial Intelligence Laboratory,
Massachusetts Institute of Technology, USA
madden@csail.mit.edu

Abstract. This tutorial will cover recent topics in data management
for sensor networks, focusing in particular on high-level systems and languages for querying stored and streaming data in such networks. We will
begin with a survey of language proposals, including TinyDB, Cougar,
Regions, and other more recent work, and will then examine a range of
implementation issues that arise in such systems, including issues related
to power efficiency, time synchronization, data collection and dissemination, fault-tolerance, and state management. After attending the tutorial,
audience members should have a good understanding of the various systems in this space as well as an awareness of the technical issues that
make building such systems difficult.

K. Römer, H. Karl, and F. Mattern (Eds.): EWSN 2006, LNCS 3868, p. 1, 2006.
© Springer-Verlag Berlin Heidelberg 2006

Algorithms for Wireless Sensor Networks

Roger Wattenhofer

Department of Information Technology and Electrical Engineering,
ETH Zurich, Switzerland
wattenhofer@tik.ee.ethz.ch

Abstract. In recent years, there has been a growing interest by theo-
reticians in wireless multi-hop sensor networks. In this tutorial we discuss
some of the latest pearls of algorithmic sensor networking research. In
particular, we investigate the link layer (e.g., MAC, topology control,
clustering), the network layer (e.g., data gathering, routing), and services for sensor networks (e.g., positioning, time synchronization). We
put a special focus on distributed protocols with practical appeal and on
theoretical (im)possibility results "every sensor network engineer should
know."

K. Römer, H. Karl, and F. Mattern (Eds.): EWSN 2006, LNCS 3868, p. 2, 2006.
© Springer-Verlag Berlin Heidelberg 2006

Unleashing the Power of Wireless Networks Through Information Sharing in the Sensor Internet

Karl Aberer

National Competence Centre in Research for
Mobile Information and Communication Systems (NCCR-MICS),
School of Computer and Communication Sciences,
EPFL, Switzerland
`karl.aberer@epfl.ch`

Abstract. We provide in this presentation in a first part an overview of the research activities of the Swiss National Competence Centre in Research for Mobile Information and Communication Systems (NCCR-MICS) in the area of self-organizing, wireless networks. In the second part we present specific MICS research results from our research group on managing information generated in such networks using self-organizing, logical overlay networks.

Recent advances in wireless communication enable the embedding of sensing and actuation technology into our physical environment at an unprecedented large scale and fine granularity. We show exemplary recent theoretical advances and systems developments on self-organizing, wireless sensor networks and mobile ad-hoc networks achieved in MICS. They provide evidence for the comprehensive scope and high degree of interdisciplinarity required in this area of research. We illustrate the deployment of the resulting technologies in real-world applications. An application class we focus in MICS in particular concerns the monitoring of various typical physical phenomena in the Swiss environment, such as watershed, permafrost, and avalanches.

In the long term, the increasing deployment and application of wireless networks beyond specialized, isolated applications will lead to the production of massive amounts of sensor data requiring further processing support and proper interpretation of data. We argue that self-organizing, logical overlay networks for resource and information sharing will play an important role for achieving this task. Structured overlay networks will be used to support scalable processing of data streams. Semantic overlay networks will be used to overcome heterogeneity in information representation. Finally, social overlay networks will be used to form agreements on meaning and utility of data. We illustrate these developments from our ongoing research: Global Sensor Network, a lightweight implementation of an overlay network for sensor data stream sharing, PicShark, a peer-to-peer image sharing system with support for automated generation and sharing of image annotations, and Semantic Gossiping, a social mechanism based on belief propagation to reconcile heterogeneous annotation schemes.

K. Römer, H. Karl, and F. Mattern (Eds.): EWSN 2006, LNCS 3868, pp. 3–4, 2006.

As a result of these developments, we envision the Internet to develop into a Sensor Internet in which physical reality, information technology and human activity become increasingly intertwined into one common complex system for better understanding and more easily mastering the environment we live in.

Semantic Streams: A Framework for Composable Semantic Interpretation of Sensor Data

Kamin Whitehouse[1], Feng Zhao[2], and Jie Liu[2]

[1] UC Berkeley, Berkeley, CA, USA
kamin@cs.berkeley.edu
[2] Microsoft Research, Redmond, WA, USA
{zhao, liuj}@microsoft.com

Abstract. We present a framework called Semantic Streams that allows users to pose declarative queries over semantic interpretations of sensor data. For example, instead of querying raw magnetometer data, the user queries whether vehicles are cars or trucks; the system decides which sensor data and which operations to use to infer the type of vehicle. The user can also place constraints on values such as the the amount of energy consumed or the confidence with which the vehicles are classified. We demonstrate how this system can be used on a network of video, magnetometer, and infrared break beam sensors deployed in a parking garage with three simultaneous and independent users.

1 Introduction

While most sensor network research today focuses on ad-hoc sensor deployments, fixed sensor infrastructure may be much more common and in fact is ubiquitous in our daily environments even today. Homes have security sensors, roads have traffic sensors, office buildings have HVAC and card key sensors, etc. Most of these sensors are powered and wired, or are one hop from a base station. Such sensor infrastructure does not have many of the technical challenges seen with its power-constrained, multi-hop counterpart: it is relatively trivial to collect the data and even to allow a building's occupants to query the building sensors through a web interface. The largest remaining obstacle to more widespread use is that the non-technical user must semantically interpret the otherwise meaningless output of the sensors. For example, the user does not want raw magnetometer or HVAC sensor data; a building manager wants to be alerted to excess building activity over the weekends, or a safety engineer wants to know the ratio of cars to trucks in a parking garage.

Our paper presents a framework called *Semantic Streams* that allows non-technical users to pose queries over semantic interpretations of sensor data, such as "I want the ratio of cars to trucks in the parking garage", without actually writing code to infer the existence of cars or trucks from the sensor data. The key to our system is that previous users will have written applications in terms of *inference units*, which are minimal units of sensor data interpretation. When a new semantic query arrives, existing inference units can then be *composed* in

K. Römer, H. Karl, and F. Mattern (Eds.): EWSN 2006, LNCS 3868, pp. 5–20, 2006.

new ways to generate new interpretations of sensor data. If the query cannot be answered, the system may ask for new sensors to be placed or for new inference units to be created. In this way, the sensor infrastructure and the semantic values it can produce grow organically as it is used for different applications.

The system also allows the user to place constraints or objective functions over quality of service parameters, such as, "I want the confidence of the vehicle classifications to be greater than 90%," or "I want to minimize the total energy consumed." Then, if the system has a choice between using a magnetometer or a motion sensor to detect trucks for example, it may choose to use the motion sensor if the user is optimizing for energy consumption, or the magnetometer if the user is optimizing for confidence. Finally, our system allows multiple, independent users to use the same network simultaneously through their web interface and automatically shares resources and resolves resource conflicts, such as two different requirements for the sampling frequency of a single sensor. Towards the end of the paper, we demonstrate how this system is used on a network of video, magnetometer, and infrared break beam sensors deployed in a parking garage.

2   The Semantic Streams Programming Model

The Semantic Streams programming model contains two fundamental elements: *event streams* and *inference units*. Event streams represent a flow of asynchronous events, each of which represents a world event such as an object, person or car detection and has properties such as the time or location it was detected, its speed, direction, and/or identity.

Inference units are processes that operate on event streams. They infer semantic information about the world from incoming events and either generate new event streams or add the information to existing events as new properties. For example, the *speed inference* unit in Figure 1 creates a new stream of objects and infers their speeds from the output of sensors A and B. The *vehicle inference* unit uses the speeds in combination with raw data from sensor C to label each object as a vehicle or not. As a stream flows from sensors and through different inference units, its events acquire new semantic properties.

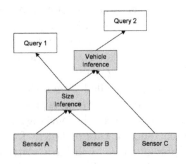

Fig. 1. Programming Model. Events streams feed inference units and accumulate semantic information as they flow through them.

The goal of this programming model is to allow *composable inference*; event streams can flow through new combinations of inference units and still produce valid world interpretations. While composable inference will never infer completely unforeseeable facts, it can be used to answer queries which are slight variations or combinations of previous applications, for example inferring the size of a car using logic that was originally intended to infer the sizes of people. For simplicity, we can assume that all inference units are running on a central server where all sensor data is collected, although it would be straightforward to execute some inference units directly on the sensor nodes.

3   A Logic-Based Markup and Query Language

In order to automatically compose sensors and inference units, we use a markup language to encode a logical description of how they fit together. To ensure that inference units are not composed in ways that produce invalid world interpretations, each inference unit must be fully specified in terms of its input streams and output streams and any required relationships between them. For example, the *vehicle inference* unit in Figure 2 may *create* vehicle events and *need* speed events and sensor C events that are co-temporal and co-spatial.

The Semantic Streams markup and query language is built using SICStus Prolog and its constraint logic programming (real) (CLP(R)) extension. Prolog is a logic programming language in which facts and logic rules can be declared and used to prove queries. CLP(R) allows the user to declare numeric constraints on variables. Each declared constraint is added to a constraint set and each new constraint declaration evaluates to true iff it is consistent with the existing constraint set. For a more complete description of Prolog and CLP(R), see [1].

3.1   Declaring Sensors and Simple Inference Units

Semantic Streams defines eight logical predicates that can be used to declare sensor and inference units. The font of each predicate indicates whether it is a top-level or an inner predicate.

- **sensor**(<sensor type>, <region>)
- **inference**(<inference type>, <needs>, <creates>)
- *needs*(<stream1>, <stream2>, ...)
- *creates*(<stream1>, <stream2>, ...)
- *stream*(<identifier>)
- *isa*(<identifier>, <event type>)
- *property*(<identifier>, <value>, <property name>)

The **sensor**() predicate defines the type and location of each sensor. For example

```
sensor(magnetometer, [[60,0,0],[70,10,10]]).
sensor(camera,       [[40,0,0],[55,15,15]]).
sensor(breakBeam,    [[10,0,0],[12,10, 2]]).
```

defines three sensors of type `magnetometer`, `camera`, and `breakBeam`. Each sensor is declared to cover a 3D cube defined by a pair of $[x, y, z]$ coordinates. For simplicity, we approximate all regions as 3D cubes, although this restriction does not apply to Semantic Streams in general.

The **inference**(), *needs*(), and *creates*() predicates describe an inference unit in terms of the event streams that it needs and creates. The *stream*(), *isa*(), and *property*() predicates describe an event stream and the type and properties of its events. For example, a vehicle detector unit could be described as an inference unit that uses a magnetometer sensor to detect vehicles and creates an event stream with the time and location in which the vehicles are detected.

```
inference( magVehicleDetectionUnit,
    needs(
        sensor(magnetometer, R) ),
    creates(
        stream(X),
        isa(X,vehicle),
        property(X,T,time),
        property(X,R,region) ) ).
```

3.2   Encoding and Reasoning About Space

Sensors have real-world spatial coordinates and, as such, our language and query processor must be able to encode and reason about space. As a simple example, our declaration of the `magVehicleDetectionUnit` above uses the same variable R in both the *needs*() predicate and the *creates*() predicate. This encodes the fact that the region in which vehicles are detected is the same region in which the magnetometer is sensing.

A more complicated inference unit may require a number of *break beam* sensors (which detect the breakage of an infrared beam) with close proximity to each other and with non-intersecting detection regions. One way to declare this is to require three sensors in specific, known locations:

```
inference( objectDetectionUnit,
    needs(
        sensor(breakBeam, [[10,0,0],[12,10, 2]]),
        sensor(breakBeam, [[20,0,0],[22,10, 2]]),
        sensor(breakBeam, [[30,0,0],[32,10, 2]]) ),
    creates(
        stream(X),
        isa(X,object),
        property(X,T,time),
        property(X, [[10,0,0],[32,10, 2]]) ), region) ) ).
```

This inference unit description, however, cannot be composed with break beams other than those which have been hard coded. To solve this problem, we could use two *logical rules* about spatial relations:

- *subregion*(<A>, <B>)
- *intersection*(<A>, <B>, <C>)

The first predicate is true if region A is a subregion of region B while the second predicate is true if region A is the intersection of region B and region C. An example of the first rule written in CLP(R) notation is:

```
subregion(
    [ [X1A, Y1A, Z1A],[X2A, Y2A, Z2A] ],
    [ [X1B, Y1B, Z1B],[X2B, Y2B, Z2B] ]):-
        {min(X1A,X2A)>=min(X1B,X2B),
        min(Y1A,Y2A)>=min(Y1B,Y2B),
        min(Z1A,Z2A)>=min(Z1B,Z2B),
        max(X1A,X2A)=<max(X1B,X2B),
        max(Y1A,Y2A)=<max(Y1B,Y2B),
        max(Y1A,Z2A)=<max(Z1B,Z2B)}.
```

The `objectDetectionUnit` can now be defined to require any three break beams that are within a region R and that do not intersect each other.

```
inference( objectDetectionUnit,
    needs(
        sensor(breakBeam, R1),
        sensor(breakBeam, R2),
        sensor(breakBeam, R3) ),
        subregion(R1,R),
        subregion(R2,R),
        subregion(R3,R),
        \+ intersect( _,R1,R2),
        \+ intersect( _,R1,R3),
        \+ intersect( _,R2,R3) ),
    creates(
        stream(X),
        isa(X,object),
        property(X,T,time),
        property(X,R,region) ) ).
```

Where in Prolog `\+ intersect( _,R1,R2)` is true if regions $R1$ and $R2$ do not intersect. With this logical description, the inference unit will function over any three non-intersecting break beam sensors in any region R.

3.3 Declaring Queries

A query is simply a first-order logic description of the event streams and properties desired by the user. For example, a simple query could be:

```
stream(X), isa(X,vehicle).
```

This query would be true iff a set of sensors and inference units could be composed to generate events X that are known to be vehicles. In many cases, the query interpreter will be able to generate many such inference compositions. To constrain the resulting composition set, we could simply add more predicates to the query. For example, we could query only for car events in a certain region:

```
stream (X), isa (X, car),
property (X, [[10,0,0],[30,20,20]], region).
```

A more sophisticated query might require specific relationships between event streams. For example, a histogram unit may update a histogram with incoming events and generate new events each time it is updated. A query could then request a stream of histogram events Y where the values being plotted are the times of vehicle detection events in stream X. The last line of the query further constrains the plot to only those vehicle events detected in a particular region.

```
stream (Y), isa (Y, histogram),
property (Y, X, stream),
property (Y, time, property),
stream (X), isa (X, vehicle),
property (X, [[10,0,0],[32,12,02]], region).
```

4   Query Processing: A Variant of Backward-Chaining

Once the sensors and inference units of a particular sensor infrastructure are defined, our system responds to queries by automatically composing the sensors and inference units using a variant of the standard backward chaining algorithm. In backward chaining, each unproven predicate of the query is matched with the consequent of a rule or fact in the Knowledge Base (KB). If it is matched with a rule, the antecedents of the rule must be proved by matching with another rule or fact. Backward chaining terminates when all antecedents have been matched with facts, and otherwise fails after an exhaustive search of all rules. Inference unit composition is very similar to backward chaining. The query processor matches a predicate in the query with properties of the event streams created by an inference unit. It must then provide everything that the unit needs using either other inference units or physical sensors. This procedure recurses until the requirements of all inference units are satisfied by physical sensors. The sensors and inference units used to prove the query constitute the inference graph that will provide the desired semantic values specified in the query.

The inference composition engine must ensure legal *flow* of event streams:

- all streams with the same variable name in a query or inference unit description are actually the same stream.
- all streams with the different variable names in a query or inference unit description are actually different streams.
- all streams are acyclic and originate only once.

Many inference units require these global properties of all inference graphs in order to guarantee valid interpretations of their input streams.

A pure backward-chaining approach does not guarantee legal flow, as shown with the following example query:

$stream(X)$, $isa(X$, object).

Pure backward-chaining would prove the first predicate in the query with any inference unit that has an output event stream. It would initially try the first unit listed in the KB, eg. the `magnetometerUnit`. The second predicate, however, does not match any post-condition of `magnetometerUnit` so the inference engine matches it with any other inference unit in the KB that does, eg. `objectDetectorUnit`, and completes the proof. The resulting proof is shown in Figure 2(a), and clearly is not a valid solution to the query because the event stream X originates in two different places, once in each subtree of the proof, and the streams denoted by X in the query are not actually the same streams. This problem is caused by the fact that backward chaining proves each predicate in the query in isolation.

Our composition engine actually *instantiates* a virtual representation of each inference unit in the KB the first time it is used in the proof, and each new event stream originating at that unit is unified with a known constant value. Subsequent predicates are proved by matching against all existing virtual instantiations before matching with any new inference units. For example, in the example query above the composition engine matches the first predicate to the `magnetometerUnit`, as did standard backward chaining, but this time creates a virtual instance of `magnetometerUnit` and assigns a unique ID to the event stream X. Once its preconditions are satisfied (by a magnetometer sensor), the inference engine moves on to the second predicate in the query: $isa(X$, object). This predicate does not match any properties produced by `magnetometerUnit`, and a match to `objectDetectionUnit` fails because the two different inference unit instantiations create different stream IDs and cannot both unify with the same variable X in the query. Thus, the illegal proof in Figure 2(a) fails. The composition engine then backtracks and matches the first predicate to a different inference unit: `objectDetectionUnit`. It then tries to match the second predicate

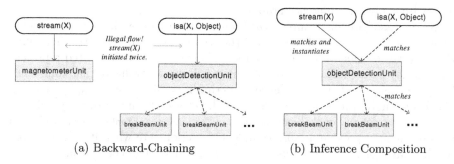

(a) Backward-Chaining   (b) Inference Composition

Fig. 2. Inference Unit Composition. The backward chaining algorithm must be slightly modified in order to yield valid inference graphs; pure backward-chaining cannot guaranteed legal flow.

to the same virtual instance and this time succeeds because this inference graph satisfies legal flow. The resulting legal proof is illustrated in Figure 2(b).

Besides correctness of flow, there are several other benefits to using this variation of backward chaining. First, it is efficient because results from previous proofs are cached and reused; many predicates in a query are likely to be querying the same subtree in a proof. Second, it allows *mutual dependence*, where two inference units each declare the other as a pre-condition. Mutual dependence cannot occur in a pure backward-chaining approach because it would lead to infinite recursion. A third advantage is that, by causing the inference engine to first check which inference units already exist, a query will automatically reuse inference units that were instantiated in response to other queries. If two users run queries that can both be answered with an object detection unit running over three break beam sensors, the unit will only be instantiated in response to the first query; the second query will simply reuse the existing inference units. When the first query terminates, the execution engine removes only those inference units upon which no other units depend so as to not interrupt execution of the second query. In this way, Semantic Streams allows the automatic sharing of resources and the reuse of processing and bandwidth consumption between independent users without requiring them to coordinate with each other.

5   Adding Constraints to Inference Units and Queries

5.1   Quality of Service Constraints

Pure logic queries may be answerable by multiple different inference graphs. In general and especially in a network with many sensors, dozens of similar inference graphs will provide the same semantic information. In such cases, the query processor should be able to choose between comparable inference graphs based on *quality of service* (QoS) information such as total latency, energy consumption, or the confidence of data quality. In this section, we explain how to use CLP(R) notation to define QoS parameters for each inference unit and to define constraints or objective functions in the query that place an ordering on otherwise equivalent inference graphs.

We can associate for example a *confidence* parameter C with each event stream to denote the confidence of the data in the stream. For simplicity, we will assume that C takes a value between 0 and 100, although more sophisticated representations may be used. Each inference unit can derive the value of that confidence from the sensors and other inference units that it is using. For example, we could define a recursive predicate *breakGroup*$(R, [], $ Group$)$ which is proven by unifying Group with a set of break beam sensors. If objectDetectionUnit required such a group, it may provide a more confident detection rate when it is using more break beams for redundancy, as encoded in the following declaration:

```
inference( objectDetectionUnit,
    needs(
        breakGroup(R, [], Group),
```

```
      length(Group,Length),
      Length>=3,
      {C=>Length*20, C=<100} ),
  creates(
      stream(X),
      isa(X,object),
      property(X,T,time),
      property(X,R,region),
      property(X,C,confidence) ) ).
```

A query can then require a specific confidence value on object detections, as shown below. For this query, the query processor would continually try to prove the query until the inference graph provided a confidence value greater than 80, meaning it must include at least 5 break beam sensors (or an alternate object detection unit). Thus, the user does not need to manually specify an inference graph in order to achieve desired confidence; the programmer's logical definition of the QoS parameter allows the user to declaratively constrain the solution to those inference graphs with sufficiently high confidence.

```
stream(X), isa(X,object), property(X, C, confidence), {C>80}.
```

Similar techniques can be used to constrain latency, power consumption, bandwidth or other QoS parameters. For example, an inference unit that requires 10ms to compute the speed of an object will define its own latency to be the latency of the previous unit plus 10ms.

```
inference( speedDetectorUnit,
   needs(
      stream(X),
      isa(X,object),
      property(X,LS, latency),
      {L=LS+10} ),
   creates(
      stream(X),
      property(X, S, speed),
      property(X, L, latency) ) ).
```

Queries can place constraints on multiple QoS parameters as well as declare objective functions over them, as in the following example which minimizes latency subject to constraints on confidence levels:

```
stream(X), isa(X,object), property(X, C,confidence), {C>80},
   property(X, L,latency), {minimize(L)}.
```

To satisfy such a query, the algorithm finds all possible inference graphs that satisfy the confidence constraints and selects the one with the minimum latency. As with all inference in Prolog, the composition algorithm uses exhaustive search over all combinations of inference units, which can be quite expensive. However, composition is only performed once per query and requires minutes or less.

5.2   Runtime Parameters and Conflicts

The previous section assumes that estimates of all parameters are known at planning-time. However, when estimates are not known at planning-time, constraints on CLP(R) variables can also be used at run-time. For example, a sensor that has a `frequency` parameter will not have a predefined frequency at which it must run. Instead, it may be able to use any frequency less than 400Hz and, for efficiency reasons, it would like to use the minimum frequency possible. This unit may be defined as follows:

```
inference( magnetometerUnit,
    needs(
        sensor(magnetometer, R),
        {F<400},
        minimize{F}),
    creates(
        stream(X),
        isa(X,mag),
        property(X,T,time),
        property(X,R,region),
        property(X,F,frequency) ) ).
```

Where `minimize` is a built in CLP(R) function that sets the variable to the smallest value consistent with all existing constraints. Other constraints on its frequency might come from inference units that use this sensor. For example, the `magVehicleDetectionUnit` might require that the sensor be using a frequency that is a multiple of 5Hz.

```
inference( magVehicleDetectionUnit,
    needs(
        stream(X),
        isa(X,mag),
        property(X,F,frequency) ),
        {F1 = 5 * N, N mod 1=0}),
    creates(
        stream(X),
        isa(X,vehicle),
        property(X,T,time),
        property(X,R,region) ) ).
```

When these two inference units are composed, the frequency of the sensor is constrained to be the minimum value less than 400Hz that is a multiple of 5Hz. The resulting constraint set is singular and the planner determines the sensor frequency to be exactly 5Hz. This constraint set (while singular) is passed to the instantiation of the inference unit at runtime through the execution engine.

Because inference unit parameters are represented as CLP(R) variables, parameter conflicts can often be resolved automatically. For example, if another unit were to require that the magnetometer run at a multiple of 12Hz, the resulting constraint set on the variable F would be

- F is an integer multiple of 5.
- F is an integer multiple of 12.
- F is less than 400.
- F is the minimum value satisfying all of the above.

The constraint set reduces to the singular value of 60 which is passed to the magnetometer unit at runtime, and the sensor runs at 60Hz.

When the constraint set is not a singular value, it can be passed to each unit at runtime for what is known as *execution monitoring* and *replanning* in the artificial intelligence literature [2]. For example, the `objectDetectionUnit` from above can be given the constraint set $\{80 < C < 100\}$. When a sensor fails or the nominal confidence values percolating up from the sensors decrease, it may determine that it can no longer meet the required constraints and it signals an error to the execution engine, which asks the query processor for a new inference graph.

6   An Example of Semantic Streams

To provide an example of how the Semantic Streams framework is used, we deployed a sensor network on the second floor of a parking deck on the Microsoft corporate campus. The network consisted of three different types of sensors: a web camera, a magnetometer, and infrared break beam sensors. Both the break beam and magnetometer sensors were controlled by micaZ motes and communicated wirelessly with our microserver, a headless Upont Cappuccino TX-3 Mini PC. The camera and microserver were both connected to the corporate network by Ethernet.

The focus of the network was a 4x5 meter area directly in front of an elevator. All vehicles entering this floor of the parking deck passed through this area, as did most pedestrians using the elevator. We placed 5 infrared break beam sensors in a row across the area, 1m apart and about .5m from the ground, such that the beams were broken in succession by any passing human or vehicle. The camera was also focused on the area and a magnetometer was placed about 10m downstream. The focus area and the arrangement of the six wireless sensors, camera, and microserver is shown in Figure 3.

Although the number of sensors in our deployment is small, they can be used for many different purposes. For example, they can infer the presence of humans, motorcycles and cars as well as their speeds, directions, sizes, metallic payloads and, in combination with data from neighboring locations, even their paths through the parking garage. In this paper, we consider three hypothetical users at Microsoft that want to use the sensor infrastructure described above:

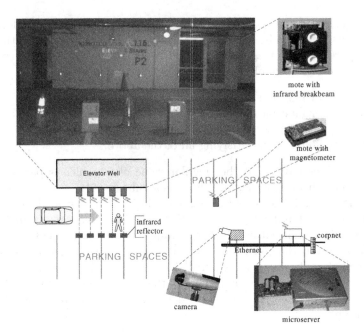

Fig. 3. Sensor Infrastructure. The break beam sensors were laid out in a row on the wall in the focus area. The digital camera was focused on the same area. The magnetometer was placed several meters downstream near the microserver.

- Police Officer Pat wants a photograph of all vehicles moving faster than 15mph.
- Employee Alex wants to know what time to arrive at work in order to get a parking space on the first floor of the parking deck.
- Safety Engineer Kim wants to know the speeds of cars near the elevator to determine whether or not to place a speed bump for pedestrian safety.

All three applications must run continuously and simultaneously using the same hardware. There are several places where conflicts can arise: which nodes are on or off, which program image each node is running, what sampling rates they are using etc. However, all three users are from different organizations within the company and are not be able to easily coordinate. In this example we demonstrate how the system can 1) automatically share and reuse resources between independent users and 2) compose inference units from two different applications to create a new semantic composition for a third application. For brevity, our demonstration does not illustrate how the users optimize QoS parameters.

We assume Pat and Alex are the first users of this sensor infrastructure and must create all of their own inference units. Pat creates units to infer object speeds from break beam sensors, identify them as vehicles, and take pictures of a region triggered by an event. Alex creates a unit to classify objects as vehicles based on magnetometer output and a unit to plot arbitrary values in a histogram. All of these inference units are added to the library associated with

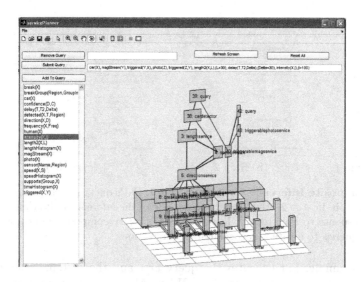

Fig. 4. User Interface. Each user is presented with a 3D rendering of the sensors in the testbed and, on the left, all predicates that are queryable.

the infrastructure and each user is presented with the graphical user interface shown in Figure 4. The interface shows a 3D rendering of each sensor in our garage testbed and the region that the sensor covers. Furthermore, the predicates describing the event streams created by all inference units in the system are listed on the left side of the screen. These stream descriptions are the only predicates that can be used in a query, although variable names may be changed to create new compositions and CLP(R) constraints may be added. Each user selects the appropriate predicates to create their desired queries:

Pat
$stream(X)$,
$property(X,P,\texttt{ photo})$,
$property(X,Y,\texttt{ triggerStream})$,
$property(X,\texttt{speed, triggerProperty})$,
$stream(Y)$,
$isa(Y,\texttt{vehicle})$,

Alex
$stream(X)$,
$property(X,H,\texttt{ histogram})$,
$property(X,Y,\texttt{ plottedStream})$,
$property(X,\texttt{time, plottedProperty})$,
$stream(Y)$,
$isa(Y,\texttt{vehicle})$,

Kim
$stream(X)$,
$property(X,H,\texttt{ histogram})$,
$property(X,Y,\texttt{ plottedStream})$,
$property(X,\texttt{speed, plottedProperty})$,
$stream(Y)$,
$isa(Y,\texttt{vehicle})$,

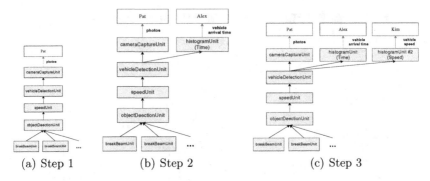

(a) Step 1   (b) Step 2   (c) Step 3

Fig. 5. Composite Inference Graphs. In step 1, Pat's query produces the expected inference graph. In step 2, Alex's query reuses one of the inference units that is instantiated in response to Pat's query. In step 3, Kim's query composes units from Alex's and Pat's queries to create a new semantic composition.

In our example, Pat executes the query first and the system generates the inference graph shown in Figure 5(a). When Alex's query is executed, a new `histogramUnit` is first instantiated. However, it does not use the magnetometer based vehicle detection because another equivalent unit already exists. It uses instead the `vehicleDetectionUnit` instantiated for Pat's application, which is based on break beams. The resulting composite inference graph is shown in Figure 5(b). Alex's application illustrates Semantic Streams automatically sharing resources between independent users.

Kim's query reuses inference units from both Pat's and Alex's applications. The `histogramUnit` from Alex's application can be reused, although a new instance must be created because the existing instance does not match Kim's query (it plots different values). The existing instance of the `speedUnit` from Alex's application, however, can be reused because it is inferring the speeds of vehicle objects. Kim's application illustrates how existing units from the other two applications were composed to create a semantically new application. The final inference graph with all three applications is illustrated in Figure 5(c) and is also seen in the user interface in Figure 4. These inference units can then be instantiated on the server and fed raw data from the sensors as it is received, producing the semantic values requested by the users.

7   Related Work

Semantic Streams adapts ideas from Semantic Web Services (SWS), a movement to semantically describe and automatically compose web services, to the problem of *macroprogramming*, which is the process of writing a program that specifies global sensor network behavior as opposed to the behavior of individual nodes. Sensor networks have previously seen two main classes of macroprogramming: database approaches like TinyDB [3, 4] and functional language approaches such as Regiment [5]. Semantic Streams is similar to these approaches in that the user issues a query specifying global behavior. One main difference is that, in both systems above, the user is required to understand which operations to run over the raw sensor data and how to interpret the meaning of the results. Semantic Streams allows the user to issue queries over semantic values directly without addressing which data or operations are to be used. The advantages of semantic queries are analogous to those of macroprogramming in general: the user of macroprogramming need not specify the best time and place to execute each operation, while the user of semantic queries need not specify which operations to run or which data to run them over. This allows the user to make fewer low-level decisions and allows the system an extra degree of freedom for automatic optimization during execution.

Our inference unit composition algorithm differs from the three main techniques that have previously been used for the automatic composition of Web Services: agent-based, planning-based, and inference-based approaches. Agent-based approaches perform a heuristic search through the set of all Web Services, either simulating or actually executing each of them to find a path to the desired resultant state [6, 7]. This technique does not easily transfer to Semantic Streams because it explicitly assumes a sequential execution model.

A concurrent execution model can be captured by Artificial Intelligence techniques such as Partial Order Planning (POP) and Hierarchical Task Networks (HTN). The problem with these techniques is that the planner performs a rather mechanical matching of post-conditions provided at time t_i with pre-conditions needed at time t_{i+1}; it cannot perform any *reasoning*, which is needed in our system to deal with spatial relationships, quality of service properties, and parameter conflicts, among other things.

Reasoning can be performed by an inference engine as in SWORD [8], which uses an inference engine to automatically compose Web services by converting each one into a set of logic rules which states that its post-conditions will be true given its pre-conditions. The problem with the pure inference-based approach is that all proofs are tree-based while most inference graphs are general directed graphs. Because SWORD does not use virtual representations of inference units during composition, it cannot guarantee legal flow of event streams. Moreover, it cannot represent an inference graph with mutual dependence.

8   Conclusions

The framework presented in this paper provides a declarative language for describing and composing inference over sensor data. There are several benefits to this framework. First, declarative programming is easier to understand than low-level, distributed programming and allows common people to query high-level information from sensor networks. Second, the declarative language allows the user to specify desired quality of service trade-offs and have the query interpreter execute on them, rather than writing imperative code that must provide the QoS. Finally, the framework allows multiple users to task and re-task the network concurrently, optimizing for reuse of services between applications and automatically resolving resource conflicts. Together, the declarative programming model and the constraint-based planning engine in our framework allow non-technical users to leverage previous applications to quickly extract semantic information from raw sensor data, thus addressing one of the most significant barriers to widespread use of sensor infrastructure today.

Acknowledgements

Special thanks to Prabal Dutta and Elaine Cheong for help with the parking garage deployment, and to Nithya Ramanathan for help with the composition algorithm.

References

1. SICS AB: SICStus Prolog 3.12.0 user's manual (2004)
   http://www.sics.se/isl/ sicstuswww/site/documentation.html.
2. Russell, S., Norvig, P.: Artificial Intelligence (Second Edition). Prentice Hall (2004)
3. Madden, S.R., Franklin, M.J., Hellerstein, J.M., Hong, W.: TAG: a Tiny AGgrega-tion Service for Ad-Hoc Sensor Networks. In: OSDI. (2002)
4. Bonnet, P., Gehrke, J., Seshadri, P.: Towards sensor database systems. Lecture Notes in Computer Science (2001)
5. Newton, R., Welsh, M.: Region streams: Functional macroprogramming for sensor networks. In: DMSN. (2004)
6. McIlraith, S., Son, T.C.: Adapting golog for composition of semantic web services. In: KRR. (2002)
7. Carman, M., Serafini, L., Traverso, P.: Web service composition as planning. In: ICAPS. (2003)
8. Ponnekanti, S.R., Fox, A.: Sword: A developer toolkit for web service composition. In: World Wide Web Conference. (2002)

PAQ: Time Series Forecasting for Approximate Query Answering in Sensor Networks

Daniela Tulone[1,2] and Samuel Madden[1]

[1] MIT Computer Science and Artificial Intelligence Laboratory
[2] Computer Science Department, University of Pisa
{tulone, madden}@csail.mit.edu

Abstract. In this paper, we present a method for approximating the values of sensors in a wireless sensor network based on *time series forecasting*. More specifically, our approach relies on *autoregressive* models built at each sensor to predict local readings. Nodes transmit these local models to a sink node, which uses them to predict sensor values without directly communicating with sensors. When needed, nodes send information about outlier readings and model updates to the sink. We show that this approach can dramatically reduce the amount of communication required to monitor the readings of all sensors in a network, and demonstrate that our approach provides provably-correct, user-controllable error bounds on the predicted values of each sensor.

1 Introduction

Wireless sensor networks offer the potential to collect large amounts of high-fidelity information about remote locations. Recent deployments have demonstrated their utility in environmental monitoring [16], agriculture [3], and industrial monitoring [1]. Most of these deployments have a similar character – data is collected at a regular rate to some centralized basestation (or *sink*), where it is stored on disk and analyzed using conventional data processing tools (e.g., databases, mathematical analysis packages, and GIS software.) One major focus of sensor network research has been on building tools to facilitate this collection of data. Researchers have proposed a variety of abstractions to enable such applications to be rapidly built, ranging from database query languages (as in TinyDB [15]) to parallel programming systems (e.g., Regions [22]), to power conserving and failure-masking network layers (e.g., Directed Diffusion [11]).

In this paper we focus on improving the performance of these data collection applications using a probabilistic approach. More precisely, we employ a class of statistical techniques broadly known as *time series forecasting*. These techniques apply to phenomena evolving over time, and use the recent history of readings to predict the most likely future values. In this paper, we propose a general framework to efficiently answer queries at the sink based on a simple type of time-series model called an *autoregressive models* (AR). We chose this model because it is computationally tractable on modern-generation sensor networks (unlike the fully general ARMA models, for example [2]) and because, as we

K. Römer, H. Karl, and F. Mattern (Eds.): EWSN 2006, LNCS 3868, pp. 21–37, 2006.

show, it can offer a substantial reduction in communication and improvement in loss rates over existing data collection approaches.

We evaluate our AR model both analytically and through simulation results that show it can properly model physical phenomena and accurately predict future values. We also show that it has low computational cost and memory usage, suggesting its suitability for a wide range of hardware. Our system, called PAQ (for *Probabilistic Adaptable Query system*) uses a combination of AR models to probabilistically answer queries. The model is used both *globally*, at the sink, to predict the readings of individual sensors, and *locally*, at each sensor, to detect when the sensor produces outlier readings or when the model ceases to properly fit the data (allowing the sensor to re-learn the model and notify the sink of the new model parameters.) Our approach has the following advantages over previous deterministic query systems:

- It significantly reduces the amount of communication required to report the value of every sensor at the sink.
- It allows the detection sensor readings that are "outliers", in the sense that they are not consistent with recent history or have malfunctioned.
- It is adaptive to dynamic changes in the distribution of data produced by sensors, and tolerant of missing sensor data.
- It does not require a large amount of training data or a priori knowledge of the distribution of sensor values and can work with any of the previously mentioned abstractions (e.g., TinyDB) for data collection.

There has been some recent interest in applying statistical modeling techniques to sensor network query systems [8, 4]. Our approach is similar to [8] in its general probabilistic approach: the sink answers queries within a user–specified error bound by computing a prediction for those values without communicating with the sensors, thus avoiding message transmissions and sensing operations. However, there are substantial differences between our approach and previous probabilistic approaches to query answering. First, these existing approaches typically build a model *centrally* at the sink, using an expensive learning phase where each sensor transmits many readings to the sink. One reason for this is that these previous approaches have used relatively complex probabilistic models (e.g., multi-variate Gaussians [8] or generalized graphical models) which are too complex to build or maintain on many current classes of sensor network hardware (e.g., Berkeley/Crossbow Motes [7]). These approaches cannot adapt to changes in the underlying distribution of sensor data without re–running this expensive learning phase. In contrast, our framework relies mostly on *local* probabilistic models computed and maintained at each sensor. In order to adapt the local model to variations in the data distribution, each sensor continuously maintains its local model, and notifies the sink only of significant changes. This allows both the sensors and sink to adapt to changes in the underlying distribution without the addition of a complex decision process that tries to decide when to invoke an expensive re-training phase.

We further limit communication from the sink to each of the nodes by exploiting *data similarities* between sensors that are geographically nearby. Our PAQ system relies on *geographic clusters* of sensors that are similar at a given point in time and that are computed by sensors that are near each other. Therefore, the sink maintains only the models (coefficients) of a few designated sensors, called *cluster leaders*, and uses them for prediction.

2   Related Work

There has been some work on the use of probabilistic and time series models in sensor networks. As in PAQ, [12, 5, 13] rely on a combination of local and global probabilistic models which are kept in synch to reduce communication between sensor nodes and the network sink. For instance, Jain et al. [12] propose a query framework based on Kalman filters: both the sink and sensors activate a Kalman filter with user-specified accuracy when a new query is received. However, this strategy does not support multiple queries with variable precision or clustering, and the local models do not adjust to non–linear phenomena. Recent work by Chu et al. [5] is similar to ours in that it also exploits temporal/spatial correlation. However, it has a heavyweight learning phase that does not work well for non-stationary data. Neither work [12, 5] provides a provable bound on the maximum error or on the error probability of answers provided at the sink. The snapshot queries approach proposed by Kotidis [13] is also similar to ours in that it exploits local models and correlations, but it provides weaker guarantees. Cheng *et al.* [4] and Deshpande *et al.* [8] have shown that generative-model based approaches can significantly reduce the communication burden in sensor networks. However, these approaches require a relatively sophisticated user who can describe the appropriate model for his or her domain and usually involve a complex centralized learning phase that must be re-run if the data distribution changes. In contrast, our approach is predicated on lightweight models that can be learned by the individual nodes in the network and rapidly retrained when confronted with non-stationary distributions.

Other work, such as the work by Olston *et al.* [18] shows how to approximate answers to queries in distributed environments with a fixed bound on the error; these approaches, though simple, have the potential to offer far less reduction in communication than model-based approaches such as ours and those discussed above. Han *et al.* [10] show how similar (non-probabilistic) techniques can be adapted to the sensor network domain in an energy efficient way.

Our approach is similar to the one proposed by Tulone [21] for using autoregressive models built at each sensor node to reduce communications in the context of time syncrhonization. That work did not focus on querying or clustering issues, however. Lazaridis and Mehrotra [14] use a different time-series method to create a piecewise linear approximation of signals generated by sensors, and send those approximations out of the network. Their approach differs from ours in that they capture a large time series and approximate it, rather than building a model that can be used for prediction outside of the network. Autoregressive time series models have been widely used outside the wireless sensor network domain as a way to approximate and summarize time series with applications in finance, communication, weather prediction, and a variety of other domains. Brockwell and Davis [2] provide an excellent introduction to time series and their applications.

3   Preliminaries

In this section, we introduce the notation and terminology we will use throughout the paper, and provide an overview of time series techniques.

3.1   System Model

Our network consists of a dynamic set S of sensor nodes and one or more sink nodes. Each node is equipped with some sensing capability, performing readings on m physical phenomena (metrics) $F_1, F_2, \ldots, F_m$ each of which evolves over time. For example, we might say that F_1 =temperature, and F_2 =light. We assume that each sensor performs a reading on each F_i every Γ time units. We have designed PAQ to work with the lowest-end of today's sensor nodes, including Berkeley Motes [7], with just a few kilobytes of memory and slow, 8-bit processors without floating point or dedicated signal processing hardware.

3.2   Queries

Queries are submitted at the sink. In this paper, we focus on queries of the form:

    `SELECT sensorlist WHERE P(`$F_1, \ldots, F_m$`) ERROR` x `CONFIDENCE` k`%`.

where $P(F_1, \ldots, F_m)$ is a predicate over $F_1, \ldots, F_m$ consisting of atoms $F_i \in [a, b]$, $F_i > a$, and $F_i < b$ where a, b are user-specified. For instance, a valid predicate could be $[(F_2 \in [a, b] \vee F_3 \in [c, d]) \wedge F_m > g]$. Here ERROR x indicates that the user is tolerant to a maximum absolute error in the query result, and the CONFIDENCE clause indicates that at least $k\%$ of the readings should be within x of their true value. For example, the user might issue the query "SELECT nodeid, temp WHERE temp > 25°C ERROR .1°C CONFIDENCE 95%", which would report the temperature at each node to within .1°C, a property which would be satisfied by 95% of the readings.

3.3   Time Series Forecasting

In general, a *time series* is a set of observations x_t, each of which is recorded at time t. An important part of the analysis of time series is the description of a suitable uncertainty model for the data. To allow for the possibly unpredictable nature of future observations, it is natural to suppose that each observation x_t is a sample of a random variable X_t (often denoted as $X(t)$).

Definition 1. *A time series model for the observed data* $\{x_t\}$ *is a specification of the joint distributions of the random variables* $\{X_t\}$ *of which* $\{x_t\}$ *is a sample.*

Clearly, if we wish to make predictions, then we must assume that some part of this model does not vary with time. Therefore, an important component of time series modeling is to remove *trend* and *seasonal* components to get a (weakly) *stationary* time series. Informally, a time series $\{X_t\}$ is stationary if it has statistical properties similar to those of the time–shifted series $\{X_{t+h}\}$ for each integer h. More precisely, $\{X_t\}$ is *weakly stationary* if its mean function $\mu_X(t)$ and its covariance function $\gamma_X(t + h, t)$ are independent of t for each h.

Linear time series models, which includes the class of *autoregressive moving–average* (ARMA) models, provide a general framework for studying stationary processes. The ARMA processes are defined by linear difference equations with constant coefficients. One of the key properties is the existence and uniqueness of stationary solutions of the defining equations [2].

Definition 2. *$\{X_t\}$ is an ARMA(p,q) process if $\{X_t\}$ is stationary and $\forall$ t,*

$$X_t - \phi_1 X_{t-1} - \ldots - \phi_p X_{t-p} = Z_t + \theta_1 Z_{t-1} + \ldots + \theta_q Z_{t-q}$$

where $\{Z_t\} \sim WN(0, \sigma^2)$ and the polynomials $(1 - \phi_1 z - \ldots - \phi_p z^p)$ and $(1 - \theta_1 z - \ldots - \theta_q z^q)$ have no common factors.

Here, $\{Z_t\}$ is a series of *uncorrelated* random variables, each with zero mean and σ^2 variance. Such a sequence is referred as *white noise* and denoted by $WN(0, \sigma^2)$. An autoregressive model of degree p, denoted by $AR(p)$, is a particular type of ARMA model with $q = 0$ (i.e., the right hand side of Definition 2 contains just a single term.) Such models are simply referred to as *autoregressive* or AR models. We will adopt this model to predict the value of F_i read at time t by a sensor. This choice is motivated by its simplicity, which leads to lower computational cost and memory requirements, making such models practical on many current-generation sensor networks. We show that AR models, while simple, still offer excellent accuracy in sensor networks for monitoring applications.

4   PAQ System Overview

As mentioned above, we employ a combination of statistical models with live data acquisition. Each sensor in PAQ maintains a local AR model, and samples its values once every Γ seconds. It uses recent readings to predict future local readings. When a reading is not properly predicted by the model, the node may mark the reading as an outlier or choose to re-learn the model, depending on the extent to which the reading disagrees with the model and the number of recent outliers that have been detected. This design is motivated by the need to (1) *monitor* changes in the physical phenomena and detect outliers, and (2) reduce communication between the local sensors and the sink. Except when a node is a *cluster leader* (see below), it does not need to communicate while monitoring the model or during its learning phase, but only when computing and adjusting its cluster, as described in Section 7.2. We discuss local modeling more in detail in Section 4.1 and the process of marking readings as outliers and deciding when to re-learn in Section 5.

Table 1. Notation used in this paper

Parameter	Description
	Parameters Used in Basic Model
α, β, γ	Coefficients of AR(3) model
Γ	Time elapsed between two consecutive readings
ν	Confidence parameter on predicted sensor readings
ε	Error bound on predicted sensor readings; will have error $> \varepsilon$ with probability $1/\nu^2$
	Parameters Used in Dynamic Model
δ	Error threshold above which model re-computation is triggered
a	Fraction of readings that must be wrong before model re-computation is triggered
Λ	Number of readings during the *monitor window* in monitor() algorithm
Δ	Time that cluster leader waits in cluster formation algorithm
θ	Data similarity parameter

The sink maintains one AR model per *geographic cluster*. A cluster is a subset of sensors within communication range of each other whose values differ from each other by at most by a constant value θ. Intuitively, it should be possible to cluster sensors in this way, since we expect that nearby sensors will often produce similar readings. Clearly, clusters are dynamic sets that can vary in number since the local models are dynamic.

One sensor in each cluster is designated the *leader*. It is responsible for communicating with the sink on behalf of its cluster. The leader's AR model, called the *cluster model*, is used to predict the values of all sensors in the cluster with an error of at most θ over the member sensor's local models, and with the same confidence. The sink maintains the coefficients associated with each of the leaders' models and receives periodic readings from them. It also maintains a list of the current clusters. The leaders' models and the cluster sets stored at the sink allow the sink to answer queries over all sensors using just the cluster models. To reduce communications, clusters are computed locally by the cluster leaders and members of each cluster. Each leader is responsible for notifying the sink of changes in its model coefficients or in its cluster members, and for transmitting periodic readings to the sink. Details of the cluster formation and query algorithms are given in Section 7.

4.1 Local AR Model

The probabilistic model maintained by the sensor must be light-weight, in terms of both the computational and storage requirements because of limitations of the sensor. Our local models are designed with these energy restrictions in mind.

Trends and Seasonal Components. Since physical phenomena are typically not stationary, a time series is usually decomposed into a *trend component* that grows very slowly over time, a *seasonal component* with some periodicity, and a *stationary component*. However, maintaining the trend and seasonal components substantially increases the complexity of both learning and adapting the model. In order to simplify our model and ignore trend and seasonal components, we consider an autoregressive model AR(p) with a narrow *prediction window*, such as $p = 3$, similarly to [21]. As discussed in [2], if the time elapsed since the last reading is relatively short, it is reasonable to neglect those components.

However, an AR(p) model is unlikely to be a good fit for non–linear physical phenomena. In particular, we have observed that sensor network data is typically locally linear, but there are periodic non-linearities that are not well-predicted by AR(p) models. To solve this problem, we enhance our linear models with *dynamic updates* that are detected and performed locally – the idea is to detect when the model is no longer a good fit for the data being sensed, and dynamically re-learn the model coefficients when this happens. The efficiency of this approach comes from the fact that learning and updating the AR model is cheap compared to the costs of learning and maintaining a non–linear model.

Multivariate vs. Univariate Models. In sensor networks, each sensor device typically has multiple sensors. To handle multiple sensors, we can compute a multivariate AR model with m components, one for each physical measurement or we can create m univariate models. Clearly, for $m > 2$ the computational cost of learning the multivariate model is higher than the cost associated with m univariate models. For simplicity of presentation we consider only one measurement, F, in the rest of this paper. However, in general, our techniques apply to either multiple univariate models or a single multivariate model.

Sensing Model. We assume that each measurement reads F every Γ time units, and denote the history of these values up to time t as $v_1, \ldots, v_i, \ldots, v_t$. Although our proposal is independent of the size of the parameter vector q, we consider $q = 3$ because it allows us simplify the model and ignore seasonal and trend components, and has low computational and storage costs. Therefore, each sensor S_j models F as a *dynamic* AR(3) time series with Gaussian white noise of zero mean and standard deviation $b(\omega)$. In case of a time series $F(t)$ with non–zero mean η, we study the time series $X(t) = F(t) - \eta$, as in [2]

$$X(t) = \alpha\, X(t-1) + \beta\, X(t-2) + \gamma\, X(t-3) + b(\omega)N(0,1) \qquad (1)$$

with $\alpha, \beta, \gamma \in \mathcal{R}$. Therefore, the predictor $P(t)$ of F at time t is given by its mean η plus a linear combination of the differences between η and the last three readings. More precisely, the prediction at time $t > t_{i-1}$ is given as

$$P(t) = \eta + \alpha(v_{i-1} - \eta) + \beta(v_{i-2} - \eta) + \gamma(v_{i-3} - \eta)$$

Function $b(\omega)$ represents the standard deviation of the white noise. Here, we assume that the distribution of the noise does not vary over time. The following lemma computes the error bound associated with the prediction $P(t)$ of $F(t)$ at time t.

Lemma 1. *Let $P(t)$ be the prediction of F at time t associated with model (1), and let $\varepsilon = \nu\, b(\omega)$, where ν is a real-valued constant larger than 1. Then, the actual value at time t is contained in $[P(t) - \varepsilon, P(t) + \varepsilon]$ with error probability at most $\frac{1}{\nu^2}$.*

Proof. Since $X(t)$ is driven by a Gaussian white noise with zero mean and standard deviation $b(\omega)$, at any time t the prediction error $v_t - P(t)$ is normally distributed with zero mean and standard deviation $b(\omega)$. The proof follows by applying the Chebychev inequality to obtain the prediction error:

$$P(|F(t) - P(t)| \geq \varepsilon) \leq \frac{b(\omega)^2}{\varepsilon^2} = \frac{b(\omega)^2}{\nu^2 b(\omega)^2} = \frac{1}{\nu^2}$$

We choose ν such that the error probability ν^{-2} can be considered negligible; e.g., for a typical value of ν we use 6 or 7. As a result, readings with an error larger than ε are classified as anomalies that are handled specially as described in Section 5.2.

4.2   Learning Phase

In this section we illustrate the steps taken by each sensor to learn its local model as defined by (1).

Data Structures. There are two parameters that principally affect the efficiency and accuracy of the learning phase: the number of readings, N, collected during the learning phase, and Γ, the time interval between two consecutive readings. During our experiments, we study different values of these parameters. Given these parameters, each sensor builds the following data structures during the learning phase:

- a (initially empty) queue V, containing the most recent N readings.
- the coefficients α, β, γ, and the mean η;
- the standard deviation $b(\Gamma)$ of the white noise during Γ time units.

```
learn():

1) ν ← 0
2) for k = 1 to N
3) read value vₖ
4) enqueue vₖ into V
5) wait for Γ time units
6) ⟨α, β, γ⟩ ← solveSys(V)
7) b(Γ) ←compVar(V)
```

Fig. 1. Learning phase

The learning algorithm is illustrated in Figure 1. During the learning phase the sensor performs a reading every Γ time units, and inserts it into V (Figure 1 lines 3–5.) After performing N readings, it invokes the function **solveSys** which computes the mean η from the N readings, and the coefficients α, β and γ. Notice that we do not recursively compute α, β, γ as in the Durban-Levine algorithm [2]), but only at the end for efficiency reasons, as in [21]. The coefficients are computed by calculating the *minimum squared error* between the readings contained in V and the predicted values via least-squares regression.

Least-squares regression works as follows: suppose that $v_1, \ldots, v_N$ are the values read during the learning phase, and that $\bar{v}_1, \ldots, \bar{v}_N$ are such that $\bar{v}_i = v_i - \eta$ for $i = 1, \ldots, N$. Then, α, β, γ correspond to the coefficients of the *best linear predictor* and are obtained by minimizing the function Q,

$$Q(\alpha, \beta, \gamma) = \sum_{i=4}^{N} (\bar{v}_i - (\alpha \, \bar{v}_{i-1} + \beta \, \bar{v}_{i-2} + \gamma \, \bar{v}_{i-3}))^2$$

The coefficients α, β, γ can be computed by setting the partial derivatives of the minimum squared error to zero and solving a linear system of three equations (we omit the details of this computation and instead direct the reader towards a standard linear algebra text, such as [9]).

solveSys computes the solution of these equations. After computing the mean η and coefficients α, β, γ, the sensor computes the variance of the white noise during Γ time units by invoking **compVar**, Fig 1 line 7. This is done by computing the prediction error $e_i = P_i - \bar{v}_i$ for $i = 1, \ldots, N$, and the mean $\bar{e}$ of $e_1, \ldots, e_N$. Hence, the variance of the white noise during Γ time units is $b(\Gamma) = (\sum_{i=1}^{N}(e_i - \bar{e})^2/N - 1)^{-1/2}$. Thus, the parameters $\eta, \alpha, \beta, \gamma$ and $b(\Gamma)$ uniquely describe the AR model for a given set of learning data $\{v_1, \ldots, v_N\}$.

Costs of the Learning Phase. The computational cost of the learning phase is the cost of reading N values, plus the cost of computing matrices A and B of the linear system $A \, X = B$ in 3 unknowns, which involves $12(N - 3)$ sum and product operations, plus the cost of solving the linear system. Therefore, the total cost is equal to $l + (s + 12)N - 36$, with s cost per reading and l cost for solving a linear system with 3 unknowns. In terms of memory, it requires a $(N + 5)$–vector plus a 3×4 real–valued matrix.

5   A Dynamic Local AR Model

As discussed in Section 4.1 the local AR model must be dynamic. Hence, the sensor periodically monitors its local model and updates it as needed. This design offers several benefits with respect to having the sink or another specialized node monitor the validity of the sensor's model.

First, it allows the sensor to detect *data anomalies* with respect to previous history, where a data anomaly is a sensor value that the model does not predict to within the user-specified error bound. These anomalies can be classified into *outlier values*, which are transient mispredictions that the model simply does not account for, or *distribution changes*, which are persistent mispredictions that suggest the model needs to be re-learned, either because of a faulty sensor or a fundamental shift in the data being sensed.

Second, our approach requires no communication during learning and updating (in contrast with the approach taken in BBQ [8], for example). This is possible because of the simplicity of our local model, which requires relatively small learning history and low computational cost and memory storage.

The efficiency of this approach is related to the efficiency of monitoring and updating the AR model, which we discuss in the remainder of this Section. For the purpose of this discussion, we assume that each cluster consists of just one sensor that is responsible for transmitting changes to its model and/or outlier values to the sink. We discuss forming geographic clusters in Section 7.1; once clusters have formed, only cluster leaders transmit their values to the sink.

5.1 Choosing to Re-learn the Model

In order to save energy, we believe the model should be updated only when its readings diverge *consistently* from its model. We classify data anomalies based on the model's *prediction error*. We consider two thresholds: δ and the maximum error $\varepsilon = \nu b(\Gamma)$ (as defined in Lemma 1.) These thresholds are chosen such that if the absolute value of the prediction error falls in $[0, \delta]$, then the model is a good predictor of the data. If it falls in $[\delta, \varepsilon]$ the data is still within the user specified error bound but the model might need to be updated. Finally, if the error prediction exceeds ε, then the data is an outlier because of Lemma 1. Since ν is chosen such that fewer than a fraction ν^{-2} of the values will be mispredicted (if the stationarity assumption holds) a single outlier value can be neglected while still satisfying the user specified confidence bound. However, though this might be an isolated anomaly that requires no action, it might correspond to an abrupt change in the data distribution (signifying that the data was not stationary), in which case the node should update the model and send the updated model parameters to the sink.

5.2 Monitoring Algorithm

We can now describe the algorithm that is used to monitor the quality of the model, based on the considerations in the previous section. The monitoring algorithm is illustrated in Figure 2. Each sensor starts monitoring its model right after the learning phase. It takes a reading every Γ time units and updates its queue V, which contains the most recent N values (see Figure 2 lines 1-2.) If the prediction error exceeds δ it begins monitoring the next Λ readings, if it is not already doing so. While monitoring, the sensor keeps track of the number of times the prediction error is in the range $[\delta \ldots \varepsilon]$ (denoted in Figure 2 by the counter variable upd), as well as the number of times the error exceeds ε (denoted by the variable out).

```
monitor():

1) every Γ time units
2) read v and update V
3) if |v − P(t)| ≥ δ
4)     mark-if-not()
5)     if δ ≤ |v − P(t)| ≤ ν
6)         up++
7)     else if |v − P(t)| ≥ ν
8)         out++
9)         if notify(out)
10)            send ⟨v⟩
11)    if (up > a) || (up + out ≥ a + 1)
12)        change ← true
13)        send ⟨change⟩
14)if (end-of-monitor) ∧ (changes)
15)    solveSys()
16)    send ⟨η, α, β, γ, outlierList⟩
```

Fig. 2. Monitoring algorithm

This is shown in Figure 2 lines 5-8. The sensor sends a notification to the sink as soon as it detects a variation in the data distribution

(Figure 2 lines 11-13). This occurs if out+up exceeds a parameter a, expressed as a fraction of the number of readings during the monitor window, denoted by Λ, (e.g. 50% of the readings performed). The notify() operation alerts the sink of the presence of an outlier, (Figure 2 line 9). After Λ readings, if the sensor has detected variations in the data distribution, it recomputes $\eta, \alpha, \beta, \gamma$ based on the values stored in V (Figure 2 lines 14-15.) Then, it sends the new coefficients to the sink and optionally a list of the outlier values, (Figure 2 lines 16.)

5.3   Discussion

Clearly, the accuracy and efficiency of the dynamic update depends on the parameters N, Λ, δ, ε, and a. N represents the length of the history that is used to compute the model. The computational cost of re–learning increases linearly with N. However, our experiments suggest that the accuracy does not necessarily improve as N grows. For instance, if the data distribution is irregular (e.g., not well fit by a linear model), then a larger value of N will not result in a better fit. The choice of error bound ε presents a trade–off between accuracy and error probability (ability to meet a specified confidence bound) which is inversely proportional to ν^2. Moreover, the choice of ν also impacts on the number of readings marked as outliers (see Section 6.)

Another trade–off between accuracy and efficiency is presented by the threshold δ which defines, along with ε and a, when the model should be updated. Clearly, it is desirable to keep the number of updates low, since updates incur additional learning and communication costs. However, making the interval $[\delta, \varepsilon]$ too small will not result in a energy improvement since the model will not properly fit the data and will thus flag more readings as outliers over time. Finally, the duration of the monitor window, Λ, presents another tradeoff: we want to keep the monitor window relatively short to update the model as fast as possible, but making it too short can result in many frequent updates.

6   Simulation Results

To study the tradeoffs discussed in the previous section, we implemented the PAQ dynamic model and evaluated it on real data. We used a trace of sensor data from the Intel, Berkeley research lab (http://db.csail.mit.edu/labdata/labdata.html), which consists of about a month's worth of light, temperature, humidity, and voltage readings collected approximately every thirty seconds from 54 sensors. In particular, we have focused on the temperature read by 5 sensors with different characteristics: some of them with many high spikes, others with irregularity, and some with a relatively smooth distribution (this corresponds to sensors 6, 7, 22, 32, and 45 in the aforementioned sensor data.) We selected these particular sensors to provide a sense of the performance of PAQ under different conditions. The traces we used from these sensors include a number of missing readings because the Berkeley Motes [7] used to capture the readings were communicating over a lossy radio channel. Overall, about 25% of the 30 second intervals do not have readings associated with them.

We ran experiments where each node used its model to predict its next value, and measured the error, the frequency with which the model needed to be re-learned, and the number of messages that a node would send to the sink during execution. In Section 7.1 we discuss how the sink uses these local models; in that Section we prove that the sink can maintain a centralized model that introduces a user-specifiable constant error over the error bounds shown here.

We varied several parameters throughout our experiments, though we only report on experiments with a small number of settings here due to space constraints. In general, we did not notice a large degree of sensitivity to the settings of various parameters, except in a few cases which we discuss more below.

Figure 3 shows the total number of messages transmitted by the nodes versus the user specified error threshold ν (here, we use communication overhead as a proxy for total energy consumption, as communication tends to be the most expensive aspect of operation in wireless sensor networks [20].) This includes transmissions as a result of learning new model parameters as well as transmission of outliers. In these experiments, approximately 25% of transmissions are a result of outliers being transmitted; transmitting the coefficients accounts for the remaining communication overhead. In our implementation, we transmit all outlier readings; if users are not concerned with receiving every outlier report, our approach could use somewhat fewer messages. The number of times the model is re-learned varies from point to point; at the lowest error rates (.1), the model is re-learned on about 20% of the monitoring windows. Notice that some sensors have a higher cost; these correspond to sensors that have "noisier" signals.

We also compared our algorithm to an algorithm similar to that proposed in [18] which transmits a value to the sink whenever the current sensor value is more than the user-defined error threshold away from the value last transmitted to the sink. To make the comparison fair, we use a version of this algorithm that uses a monitoring window of the same size as in our algorithm, and that transmits new values at most once per monitoring period. We call this method "approximate caching" and show the number of transmissions it requires for two

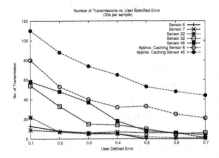

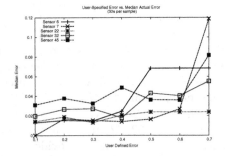

Fig. 3. Figure showing number of messages sent (either outlier or new model messages) for varying error thresholds. Parameters are as in Figure 4.

Fig. 4. Figure showing the actual error rate for different user-input error thresholds. Here, $N = 60$, $\Lambda = 15$, $\nu = 6$, $a = 8$, $\Gamma = 30$, $\delta = 1.8$.

of the sensors in Figure 3. Notice that our approach substantially outperforms the approximate caching approach.

Figure 4 shows how the error varies with the user specified error threshold. Here, the X axis is the value of ε; the confidence is set to 95%. The Y axis shows the average prediction error, which increases slightly with increasing ε but not dramatically since our error bounds are relatively conservative (notice that the actual error is well below the user-specified allowable error line defined by $y = x$). Because all errors are below the user specified threshold, it is not surprising that there is little variation between sensors; for example, even though sensor 45 requires substantially more re-learning phases and outlier transmissions, its average error is still low. We do not show errors for the "approximate caching" method, as it always meets the error bound.

The parameters that most affected our results were Λ, the size of learning window, and a and δ the thresholds that affect when readings are flagged as outliers and when the model is rebuilt. We noticed that the accuracy does not grow with the size of the learning sample N. In most cases it seems that the best prediction error occurs for $N = 60$, or, for sensor 45 (which tends to be "spikier" than the other data) with $N = 120$, while a learning phase consisting of $N = 20$ values implies a high number of model updates. For these reasons we chose to report results where $N = 60$.

Clearly, irregular readings (e.g., sensor 45 in Figure 4) affect the accuracy of the prediction. However, the overall error is not affected noticeably by frequent missing data as shown by our results which are based on real data with a high number of irregular readings, though more irregular sensors do incur a higher overall cost as more outliers must be transmitted out of the network.

With respect to predicting values at the sink, our analysis suggests the maximum prediction error is equal to ν^{-2}; the graphs above suggest, at least for our data set, that this bound does in fact hold. We will see in the next section that this error grows by at most a user-defined constant θ when predicting the values of sensors that are a member of a cluster from that cluster's leader.

7   An Efficient Centralized Model

In the algorithms we have described thus far each sensor sends the sink the coefficients of its local model after the learning phase. However, to use the AR model, the sink requires periodic readings from the sensors, which would require energy-consuming communication on the part of each sensor at every Γ time units. As described above, we can reduce the extent of these communications by exploiting *geographic similarities* between sensors that are within direct radio communication with each other. This is based on the observation that sensors located near each other are likely to have similar readings. Once sensors are organized into clusters, only the leader sends its periodic readings to the sink. Other sensors continue to run the `monitor()` algorithm to update their local models, and detect group membership changes.

7.1 Sensor Clusters

In this section we define data similarity among sensor readings, and show how we can group similar sensors into cluster sets. Let us suppose that θ, the *similarity constant* is a user-provided positive real value.

Definition 3. *Two sensors are similar at time t if their readings differ by at most the similarity constant, θ.*

Using Definition 3, we group sensors that are within communication range of each other and are similar into clusters. Clusters change over time as the AR model is dynamic. Hence, we define a set of clusters $\mathcal{C}(t)$ at time t as follows:

Definition 4. *A cluster set $\mathcal{C}(t)$ at time t is a set of subsets of $\mathcal{S}$ with the following properties:*

1. *any cluster $C \in \mathcal{C}(t)$ contains sensors within radio broadcast range of each other that are similar at time t;*
2. $\bigcup_{C \in \mathcal{C}(t)} C = \mathcal{S}.$

Each cluster C has a *leader*, a specified sensor in C which is elected locally by choosing, for example, the sensor with the lowest ID (or via any other function that can be locally evaluated at each node.) At any time the AR model of the cluster is the same as the local AR model of the current leader. The following Lemma computes the maximum error performed by predicting the value of a sensor in a cluster using the cluster model.

Lemma 2. *The maximum prediction error associated with the value of a sensor in a cluster is at most $\varepsilon + \theta$, with error probability at most ν^{-2}.*

Proof. Suppose we have a cluster C at time t such that $C = \{S_{i_1}, \ldots, S_{i_k}\}$, and node S_{i_1} is its leader. Therefore, the model of C at time t is represented by the model of S_{i_1}. For any sensor S_{i_j} in C, then $|v_t^j - P^{i_1}(t)| \le |v_t^j - v^{i_1}(t)| + |v^{i_1}(t) - P^{i_1}(t)|$ and given Definitions 3 and 4, then $|v_t - P^{i_1}(t)| \le \varepsilon + \theta$. The error probability is at most ν^{-2} because of Lemma 1.

In the next section, we sketch our approach for forming geographic clusters. This protocol relies on the availability of reliable communication and symmetric radio links. We also assume that the round–trip communication time between the sink and any sensor is bounded. Though symmetry and reliability assumptions are not entirely realistic, recent publications suggest that careful neighborhood management and retransmissions can provide loss rates as low as 1-2 percent in static sensor networks [19], which should be sufficient for our purposes.

7.2 Building and Maintaining Clusters

The clustering protocol involves two major steps: first, at the end of the learning phase, sensors compute clusters; second, each sensor monitors and maintains its cluster-membership dynamically. Figures 5(a) and 5(b) present the high-level description of the clustering protocol. Due to space limitations we omit some details.

Building Clusters. At the end of the learning phase each sensor runs a protocol to compute its cluster. The protocol is illustrated in Figure 5(a). Here, id denotes the identification number of the sensor running the protocol, and v is its current reading. The sensor node sets its cluster set CL to its identification number, and its leader L to zero since each id is a positive number (Figure 5(a) lines 1-2.) Each sensor node broadcasts its current value v and listens for Δ time units for other sensor broadcasts in order to detect similarities among its neighbors (Figure 5(a) lines 3-4.) During these Δ time units it listens for broadcasts, for each, and checks if the received value $\bar{v}$ diverges by θ or less from its value v. In this case it inserts the sensor identification into CL. After Δ time units it chooses the sensor with minimum identification number as the cluster leader of CL (Figure 5(a) line 5.) If the sensor has been chosen as the cluster leader, it sends a *leader notification message* that contains the cluster set CL and its model coefficients to its neighbors and to the sink (Figure 5(a) line 6-7.) Figure 5(b) illustrates the steps taken by a sensor when receiving a leader notification. If the sensor belongs to cluster cl and its cluster leader has not been set yet, it sets its leader to l (Figure 5(b) lines 1-2.) Otherwise, it keeps track of the other leaders within its radio broadcast by adding them into list OL (Figure 5(b) lines 3-4.) Notice that since CL is computed locally based on the messages received from its neighbors, a sensor might belong to two different clusters and might receive different leader notifications. The sensor follows the first leader notification. Since data changes over time, the leader periodically transmits its current value to its neighbors (Figure 5(b) lines 8-9.) The other sensors in the cluster verify that their value is θ similar to the leader's value.

Maintaining Clusters. Two factors can trigger changes in the cluster: (1) a sensor in the cluster can become dissimilar from the leadre, and (2) a leader can

---

1) $L \leftarrow 0$	**leader notification:** receive(l, cl)
2) $CL \leftarrow \{id\}$	1) if $(id \in cl) \wedge (L = 0)$
3) broadcast(v)	2) $L \leftarrow l$
4) wait for Δ time units	3) else
upon event receive($\langle \bar{v}, i \rangle$) do	4) $OL \leftarrow OL \cup \{l\}$
if $\lvert \bar{v} - v \rvert \leq \theta$	
$CL \leftarrow CL \cup \{i\}$	**periodic validation:** receive($\langle \bar{v}, l \rangle$)
	1) if $(l = L) \wedge (\lvert \bar{v} - v \rvert > \theta)$
5) $L \leftarrow \min CL$	2) if $(s = \text{nextLeader}(OL) > 0)$
6) if $L = id$	3) broadcast($\langle$join, $s \rangle$)
7) send $\langle$leader, $L, CL, \eta, \alpha, \beta, \gamma \rangle$	4) else
	5) $CL \leftarrow \{id\}$
8) every Γ time units do	6) $L \leftarrow id$
9) send $\langle v, L \rangle$	7) send ($\langle$leader, $L, CL, \eta, \alpha, \beta, \gamma \rangle$)
(a)	(b)

Fig. 5. Clustering algorithm (a) and notification protocol (b)

fail. Let us consider the first case. Upon receiving the leader value, each sensor checks if its current value is within θ units from the leader value. If this condition does not hold, the sensor checks if its value is at most θ units away from the current values of the other leaders within its radio broadcast (Figure 5(b) lines 1-2.) If it detects a leader whose value diverges by at most θ units from its current value, it broadcasts a `join` request, Figure 5(b) line 3. Otherwise, it creates a new cluster and notifies its neighbors and the sink of this change (Figure 5(b) lines 4-7). The leader that receives a `join` request updates its cluster set CL and notifies the sink, while the previous leader removes that sensor node from its cluster set.

Leader failures are detected by sensors listening for periodic sensor value messages. When several broadcasts are missed, a sensor infers that the leader may have failed and computes a new leader based on the remaining sensors in the group. If a sensor detects that it should be the current leader (e.g., because it has the lowest id), it broadcasts a leader-change message as in the initial phase.

7.3 Answering Queries

The sink locally stores the cluster models and the sensors belonging to each cluster. It uses this information to answer queries without additional communication. More precisely, it predicts the sensor values in a cluster using the model of the cluster leader, and verifies if this prediction satisfies the error-bounds associated with the query. Since the correctness of this query framework is strictly related to the validity of the cluster models at the sink, our query algorithm has to take into account the latency occurred in transmitting variations in the cluster to the sink. This is done by delaying the reporting of answers from the sink for a time equal to the maximum network latency. The system must also guarantee the error bound in the case of abrupt changes in the local data distributions at individual sensors. This is ensured by the outlier-transmission protocol described in the previous section. Such notifications are also delayed by at most the maximum latency of the network. Hence, the sink learns of new models and outliers in bounded time and can answer queries with error at most $\varepsilon + \theta$.

Although this approach conserves energy by reducing the amount of communication between the sensors and sink it works well in relatively high density networks since it detects data similarity for sensors which are one–hop away from each other. Second, it can require a many transmissions when data distributions change or nodes fail frequently. We are currently exploring other clustering techniques that are able to overcome these limitations.

8 Conclusions

In this paper, we showed that AR models have the potential to dramatically reduce the amount of communication required to accurately monitor the values of sensors in a wireless sensor network. Compared to existing approaches based on centralized probabilistic models built at the sink, our approach is much lighter weight, allowing sensors to build models locally and monitor their values for significant changes or deviations from the model while still providing substantial communications reductions. This means that our approach is able to detect outliers or fundamental changes in model parameters. We also presented a simple clustering algorithm that allows us to further reduce communication from sensors to the sink while still providing a provable bound on the maximum predicted error at each sensor. Hence, we are optimistic that our approach will be important in future sensor network monitoring systems, and we look forward to extending our work with a complete implementation and evaluation.

References

[1] R. Adler et al. Design and deployment of industrial sensor networks: Experiences from the north sea and a semiconductor plant. In *SenSys*, 2005.

[2] P. Brockwell and R. Davis. *Introduction to Time Series and Forecasting*. Springer, 1994.

[3] T. Brooke and J. Burrell. From ethnography to design in a vineyard. In *Proceeedings of the DUX Conference*, June 2003. Case Study.

[4] R. Cheng, D. V. Kalashnikov, and S. Prabhakar. Evaluating probabilistic queries over imprecise data. In *Proceedings of SIGMOD*, 2003.

[5] D. Chu, A. Desphande, J. Hellerstein, and W. Hong. Approximate data collection in sensor networks using probabilistic models. In *ICDE*, April 2006.

[6] R. Cowell, P. Dawid, S. Lauritzen, and D. Spiegelhalter. *Probabilistic Networks and Expert Systems*. Spinger, New York, 1999.

[7] I. Crossbow. Wireless sensor networks (mica motes). http://www.xbow.com/Products/Wireless_Sensor_Networks.htm.

[8] A. Deshpande, C. Guestrin, S. Madden, J. Hellerstein, and W. Hong. Model-driven data acquisition in sensor networks. In *VLDB*, 2004.

[9] G. Golub and C. Van Loan. *Matrix Computations*. Johns Hopkins, 1989.

[10] Q. Han, S. Mehrotra, and N. Venkatasubramanian. Energy efficient data collection in distributed sensor environments. In *Proceedings of ICDCS*, 2004.

[11] C. Intanagonwiwat, R. Govindan, and D. Estrin. Directed diffusion: A scalable and robust communication paradigm for sensor networks. In *MobiCOM*, 2000.

[12] A. Jain, E. Y. Chang, and Y. Wanf. Adaptive stream management using kalman filters. In *SIGMOD*, 2004.

[13] Y. Kotidis. Snapshot queries: towards data-centric sensor networks. In *Proc. of the 21th Intl. Conf. on Data Engineering*, April 2005.

[14] I. Lazaridis and S. Mehrotra. Capturing sensor-generated time series with quality guarantees. In *Proceedings of ICDE*, 2003.

[15] S. Madden, W. Hong, J. M. Hellerstein, and M. Franklin. TinyDB web page. http://telegraph.cs.berkeley.edu/tinydb.

[16] A. Mainwaring, J. Polastre, R. Szewczyk, and D. Culler. Wireless sensor networks for habitat monitoring. In *WSNA*, 2002.

[17] T. Mitchell. *Machine Learning*. McGraw Hill, 1997.

[18] C. Olston and J.Widom. Best effort cache sychronization with source cooperation. In *Proceedings of SIGMOD*, 2002.

[19] J. Polastre, J. Hill, and D. Culler. Versatile low power media access for wireless sensor networks. In *Proceedings of SenSys*, 2004.

[20] G. Pottie and W. Kaiser. Wireless integrated network sensors. *Communications of the ACM*, 43(5):51 – 58, May 2000.

[21] D. Tulone. A resource–efficient time estimation for wireless sensor networks. In *Proc. of the 4th Workshop of Principles of Mobile Computing, pp. 52–59*, 2004.

[22] M. Welsh and G. Mainland. Programming sensor networks using abstract regions. In *NSDI*, March 2004.

Proactive Context-Aware Sensor Networks*

Sungjin Ahn and Daeyoung Kim

Real-time and Embedded Systems Laboratory,
Information and Communications University (ICU),
119 Munjiro, Yuseong-Gu, Daejeon, Korea, Postal Code: 305-714
Phone: +82-42-866-6811, Fax: +82-42-866-6810
{sungjin, kimd}@icu.ac.kr

Abstract. We propose a novel context detection mechanism in Wireless
Sensor Networks, called PROCON. In PROCON, context decisions are
made in a distributed way, by cooperation of nodes connected through
a context overlay on the network. As a result, the sensor network can
deliver context level information, not low level sensing data, directly
to proper actuators. Moreover, PROCON achieves highly efficient energy consumption compared to the existing centralized context detection
mechanism. The analysis and simulation results show that the proposed
mechanism outperforms the existing centralized mechanism in average
energy consumption, capability of mitigating congestion to a base station, context service lifetime, and reliability.

1   Introduction

Due to its advantageous functional characteristic of monitoring phenomena of
the physical environment with relatively low cost for a broad area, Wireless Sensor Networks (WSN) have been focused and studied as a key infra technology
for realizing context-aware systems. Since in the conventional WSNs [1][2][4][5]
sensor nodes play the role of passive information sources by providing low level
sensing data to a central point (*e.g.,* a base station), it is natural for the central point to make decisions for the desired contexts from the low level data.
However, when a context consists of several "component events", each of which
has different characteristics such as event occurrence rates, locations, and logical
and timing relationships, the centralized approach shows several drawbacks.

First, it consumes too much energy to transmit low level sensing data which is
"useless" in the context decisions. For example, we may want to detect a context
which is satisfied when 1) at least one person is in a room and 2) temperature
of the room is lower than $10\,°C$ to turn a heater on automatically. However,
the difference between event occurrence rates of these two events causes wasted
event notifications when they have to occur while satisfying a timing constraint
between themselves. This shortcoming in turn decreases the lifetime of sensor
nodes by letting them relay useless event notifications and consequently decreases
the lifetime of the context service as well.

---

* This research was supported by the Ministry of Information & Communication, Korea, under the Information Technology Research Center (ITRC) Support Program.

K. Römer, H. Karl, and F. Mattern (Eds.): EWSN 2006, LNCS 3868, pp. 38–53, 2006.

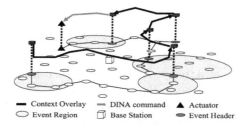

Fig. 1. PROCON architecture

Another drawback is the well-known congestion problem (also known as a *hot spot*) that appears near the BS due to the heavy load of the data relay task. As studied in many of the researches [8], this problem finally results in isolation of the central decision point from the network. In the centralized approach, since the decisions for contexts are performed at a BS, the isolation means the end of the context detection service even though remaining nodes are still sufficiently able to perform the event detection tasks on duty. Moreover, this may come a disastrous result if a critical application such as healthcare and fire detection is served.

To end these drawbacks, we propose a proactive and distributed context detection mechanism for WSN, called PROCON. In PROCON, context decisions are made by cooperating nodes connected through an overlay on the network called a *context overlay*. Along this overlay, "event headers" deliver Event Notification Messages (ENM) to the next event headers, not to a BS and at each event headers partial context decisions are made. This incremental context decision mechanism, called *context fusion*, makes the context decisions from the early stage such a way as to increase the decision level one by one only when a subset of component events has timely occurred. As a result, PROCON significantly reduces the "useless" event notifications, and its "event-to-event" communication model eliminates the congestion problem to the BS. Moreover, it makes *direct in-network actuation* (DINA) possible by letting a normal sensor node send actuation commands to proper actuators. Fig. 1 shows the overall architecture of PROCON.

We make three major contributions in this paper. First, we introduce our context model considering logical and timing relations. Second, we analyze the performance of the two compared context decision mechanisms. From the analytical results, we then obtain the conditions where the distributed context decision mechanism can outperform the centralized one. Finally, we present the designs of PROCON including context descriptors, context fusion, and context overlay construction.

The rest of this paper is organized as follows. In the next section, we introduce our models. In Section 3, we show the results of analytical analysis for both context detection mechanisms compared. Section 4 details the designs of PROCON, and then the performance evaluation results are shown in Section 5. Related works are discussed in Section 6. Finally, Section 7 concludes our work.

2   Models

2.1   Network Model

Our sensor network is, strictly speaking, a sensor and actuator network where actuator nodes are, in addition to the sensors, also an element forming the network. So, actuators can communicate with either sensors or other actuators in a multi-hop way. We also assume that the nodes are location-aware and immobile. The location information can be obtained through GPS in out-door cases [9], localization algorithms [10], or by manual setting in the case of static small-scaled networks. As introduced in the previous section, PROCON requires routing between particular sensor nodes to deliver the event notifications. This routing protocol is not restricted to a specific protocol. It can be any protocol as long as it supports communication between events. Finally, we notice that the main goal of the sensor networks we are considering in this paper is to detect contexts, called compound contexts, that we will introduce next. This means that just collecting low level sensing data continuously to a sink, as is performed in conventional sensor networks, is not of interest here as long as it does not contribute to a condition of a context. For example, a query such as, *"monitor temperature changes of a region for a month"*, is not of interest.

2.2   Context Model

Context and Event. We define *context*[1] as a set of interrelated events (also, called *component event*) with logical and timing relations among them. For example, a context detecting fire occurrence can be detected by inspecting two component events, the temperature and the content of carbon monoxide in the air. An *event* is basically defined by its target area and trigger condition that has to be satisfied for it to occur. Thus sensor nodes, located in the target area and equipped with proper sensor chips, have the duty of detecting the given event. In some cases, detecting an event may need cooperation among several sensor nodes, as in the case of detecting the average temperature event. However, for simplicity we just consider an event as a sensor node, called an *event header* which decides the event. Thus, the cooperation mechanism for detecting an event is not considered in this work.

We classify events into two categories. Consider a sensor node which is periodically awake at every sampling period p to detect an event. In *discrete events*, events detected at continuous sampling periods are considered as separated event instances. In other words, if an event occurs at time t and $t + p$, it is considered that there have been two separate event instances. However, in *continuous events*, event detections at continuous sampling periods are considered as just one event instance. Thus the above situation is, in continuous events, considered as an event instance lasting at least for time p.

---

[1] We also refer to our context as *compound context* to distinguish it from other definitions of context.

Logical Relations. When an event satisfies its required condition regardless of which category it is included, we say it is in a TRUE state, otherwise it is in a FALSE state. *Logical relation* among component events can be defined as a Boolean combination of events. Basically, we support two logic operators between events, "AND (&)" and "OR (|)". Thus, a context can occur only when Boolean operation for the states of all component events results finally in TRUE. For example, given a context C consisting of three component events E_1, E_2, and E_3, which has a logical relation $C = E_1\&(E_2|E_3)$, E_2 or E_3 has to occur, in addition to E_1, to satisfy C in a given timing relation.

We say that a context is a *unit context* when its component events have only AND logical relations. So, we can reorganize a context that contains OR operator into fundamental products form of unit contexts as defined in Boolean algebra. By rearranging the logical relation, above example context is formulated as $C = (E_1\&E_2)|(E_1\&E_3)$, and thus has two unit contexts, $U_1 = \{E_1, E_2\}$ and $U_2 = \{E_1, E_3\}$. This is an important characteristic since occurrence of any unit context, say U_1, of an original context C makes the original context occur regardless of the states of other events, here E_3, which are not elements of the unit context. Thus, a problem of detecting occurrence of the original context is now simplified as detecting occurrence of any unit context. Therefore, algorithms explained from now on focus on detection of a unit context.

Timing Relations. A timing relation $T_{i \to j}$ from E_i to E_j, is defined by *low time bound* $(L_{i \to j})$ and *upper time bound* $(U_{i \to j})$. That is, with E_i as the base event, timing relation $T_{i \to j}$ is defined as follows:

$$T_{i \to j} = (L_{i \to j}, U_{i \to j}).$$

Here, i) $L_{i \to j} < U_{i \to j}$, ii) $\{L_{i \to j}, U_{i \to j}\} \subset \mathbb{R}$, and iii) $\{E_i, E_j\} \subset U_k$.

Given that the base event E_i occurs at time t_i, we say that a timing relation $T_{i \to j}$ is "satisfied" if E_j occurs in a time interval $(t_i + L_{i \to j}, t_i + U_{i \to j}]$. For example, given an timing relation $T_{i \to j} = (-10, +5)$ and $t_i = 30$, E_j has to occur in an interval $t_j \in (20, 35]$ to satisfy its timing relation. From this timing relation model, we obtain several characteristics as follows.

First, given a timing relation $T_{i \to j}$, we can obtain its "reversed" timing relation $T_{j \to i}$. That is, by the definition of a timing relation, if $T_{i \to j} = (L_{i \to j}, U_{i \to j})$, then $T_{j \to i} = (-U_{i \to j}, -L_{i \to j})$. Thus, $L_{j \to i} = -U_{i \to j}$ and $U_{j \to i} = -L_{i \to j}$. We refer to this characteristic as the *reversibility* of the timing relation. A set of timing relations can be represented as a directed graph, called *timing graph*. Here, an event corresponds to a vertex and a timing relation $T_{i \to j}$ makes an edge from vertex i to vertex j. The reversibility makes reversing the direction of an edge possible without loss of the implication of the timing relation.

We now define the feasibility of a set of timing relations. We say a set of timing relations is *feasible* when the probability p_i that an event time instance satisfies the given timing relations altogether is not zero for all the component events. In other words, if there exist one or more timing relations any of whose event time instances is never able to satisfy the timing relations altogether, the set of timing relations is said to be *infeasible*. For instance, a set of timing relations

$\{T_{1\to2} = (+5, +10)], T_{2\to3} = (0, +5), T_{1\to3} = (-5, +3)\}$ is infeasible, since if $T_{1\to2}$ and $T_{2\to3}$ are satisfied, $T_{1\to3}$ can never be done, and if so for $T_{1\to2}$ and $T_{1\to3}$, $T_{2\to3}$ cannot.

With the definitions of the reversibility and feasibility, we now reach a condition of the feasibility: *When an event can have more than one timing relations with other events, but only one for an event, the timing graph of the infeasible timing relation set has a loop.* That is, if a timing graph does not have any loop, the timing relation set is always feasible.

3   Analysis on Context Decision Mechanisms

In this section, we show analytical models for centralized and distributed context decision mechanisms. In particular, we focus on the energy consumption performance modeled by the number of transmissions for a unit time I, and on conditions where the distributed approach outperforms the centralized one.

The notations and assumptions used in this section are as follows. First, for simplicity of modeling, we use the abstracted timing relation model. Here, component events satisfy the timing relation when all of them occur within a unit time interval I. In addition, h_i indicates the number of hops from the event header of E_i to a BS, and H_i does the number of hops from the event header of E_i to that of E_{i+1}. We suppose that all events are discrete events. Then, we define the event occurrence rate λ_i of E_i as the average number of event occurrence during I. Fig. 2 illustrates these models.

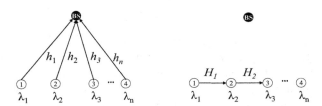

Fig. 2. Models for centralized and distributed context decision mechanism

p_i denotes a probability that E_i occurs during I. Thus, with the assumption that the event arrival process conforms to Poisson process, p_i is:

$$p_i = P\{t_i < I\} = 1 - e^{-\lambda_i}. \tag{1}$$

3.1   Analysis of Centralized Decision

In the centralized case, a basic observation to obtain the expected number of total transmission T_c during I is that, whenever an event occurs, it sends the event notification to a BS. Thus, given n component events, T_c is:

$$T_c = \lambda_1 h_2 + \lambda_2 h_2 + \cdots + \lambda_n h_n = \sum_{i=1}^{n} \lambda_i h_i. \tag{2}$$

To obtain, how much of the portion is actually useful for generating a context among those $\sum \lambda_i h_i$ transmissions, we calculate the effective number of transmissions E_c during I. We say that an event notification is "effective" (or useful) when it finally generates a context together with other component events which have timely occurred. Thus, given n component events, the probability P_n that a context occurs during I, and its occurrence rate r_n are respectively,

$$P_n = \prod_{i=1}^{n} p_i, \tag{3}$$

$$r_n = \lambda_{\min} P_n. \tag{4}$$

Here, $\lambda_{\min} = \min_{i \leq n}(\lambda_i)$. Therefore, since there are $\sum h_i$ transmissions at every context occurrence with rate r_n, E_c is:

$$E_c = r_n \sum_{i=1}^{n} h_i = \lambda_{\min} \prod_{i=1}^{n} p_i \sum_{j=1}^{n} h_j. \tag{5}$$

From Eq. (2) and Eq. (5), we now define the effectiveness ratio R_c of the centralized context decision as:

$$R_c = \frac{E_c}{T_c} = \frac{\lambda_{\min} \prod_{i=1}^{n} p_i \sum_{j=1}^{n} h_j}{\sum_{i=1}^{n} \lambda_i h_i}. \tag{6}$$

From Eq. (6), we first obtain that the effectiveness ratio R_c decreases as $var(\lambda)$ increases, since $\sum \lambda_{\min} h_i \leq \sum \lambda_i h_i$ and $\prod p_i \leq 1$. Second, as I and λ_i decrease, R_c decreases, since in that case p_i decreases. In other words, the centralized approach wastes much energy for transmitting useless event notifications as 1) the differences of event occurrence rates among component events increase; and 2) the probability that an event instance satisfies its timing relations decreases.

3.2   Analysis of Distributed Decision

Before analyzing the distributed decision scheme, we first briefly introduce the distributed context decision mechanism which will be explained later in more detail. The following is the basic algorithm.

There is a chain of component events and E_i denotes i-th ordered event (header) on the chain. Only the header of E_1 can initiate a context decision process by sending an event notification message (here, ENM_1) to E_2. Receiving the ENM_1, E_2 sends ENM_2 to E_3 only when E_2 satisfies the timing relation with E_1. Thus, in general E_i, $i > 1$, sends ENM_i when the preceding events, E_1 to E_{i-1}, satisfy all timing relations among them. If not, the context decision process ends there and then waits for another context decision process. If a context decision process finally reaches to the final event E_n, the context occurs.

According to the above decision mechanism, a basic observation for calculating T_d the expected number of total transmissions during I of the distributed decision, is that there are H_i transmissions whenever E_1 occurs, and H_i transmissions only when a set of events $\aleph_i = \{E_j | j \leq i\}$ satisfies timing relations among them, for $1 < i < n$. Thus, the rate r_1 that E_1 sends ENM_1 to E_2, is equal to λ_1. And the rate that E_i sends an event notification to E_{i+1} is the same as r_i shown in Eq. (4) for all $i > 1$, since the probability that events in $\aleph_i$ satisfy their timing relations is $\prod_{j \in \aleph_i} p_j$, and the rate is governed by $\lambda_i^{\min} = \min_{j \in \aleph_i}(\lambda_j)$. As a result,

$$T_d = \sum_{i=1}^{n-1} r_i H_i = r_1 H_1 + r_2 H_2 + \cdots + r_{n-1} H_{n-1} \tag{7}$$

$$= \lambda_1 H_1 + p_1 p_2 \lambda_2^{\min} H_2 + \cdots + p_1 p_2 \cdots p_{n-1} \lambda_{n-1}^{\min} H_{n-1} \tag{8}$$

$$= \lambda_1 H_1 + \sum_{i=2}^{n-1} \left(\prod_{j=1}^{i} (1 - e^{-\lambda_j}) \lambda_i^{\min} \right) H_i. \tag{9}$$

Now we derive the expected number of effective transmissions E_d and the effectiveness ratio R_d for the distributed case, respectively:

$$E_d = \lambda_{\min} \prod_{i=1}^{n} p_i \sum_{j=1}^{n-1} H_j \tag{10}$$

$$R_d = \frac{E_d}{T_d} = \frac{\lambda_{\min} \prod_{i=1}^{n} p_i \sum_{j=1}^{n-1} H_i}{\lambda_1 H_1 + \sum_{i=2}^{n-1} \left(\prod_{j=1}^{i} (1 - e^{-\lambda_j}) \lambda_i^{\min} \right) H_i}. \tag{11}$$

3.3   Bound Analysis

Now we derive a bound where the distributed decision outperforms centralized one in terms of total transmissions. To do so, the following condition has to be satisfied.

$$\frac{T_d}{T_c} \leq 1. \tag{12}$$

By solving this, we obtain the following theorem. For the sake of simplicity, we assume the events are connected in non-decreasing λ_i order.

Theorem 1. *Given a context overlay which is connected in non-decreasing λ_i order (i.e., $\lambda_{min} = \lambda_1$), T_d is less than T_c when*

$$H_1 \leq h_1 + \frac{\lambda_2}{\lambda_1} h_2, \tag{13}$$

$$H_i \leq \frac{\lambda_{i+1}}{\lambda_{\min} \prod_{1}^{i} (1 - e^{-\lambda_j})} h_{i+1}, \, i > 1. \tag{14}$$

Proof. We prove this using mathematical induction. First, we show the case in which the number of component events n is 2, by Eq. (12),

$$\lambda_1 H_1 \leq \lambda_1 h_1 + \lambda_2 h_2$$
$$H_1 \leq h_1 + \frac{\lambda_2}{\lambda_1} h_2,$$

Then, let us assume that the following is satisfied for all $1 < n < k + 1$,

$$H_n \leq \frac{\lambda_{n+1}}{\lambda_{\min} \prod_1^n p_i} h_{n+1},$$

Now, using the above two results, we prove $n = k + 1$ case,

$$\prod_1^k r_i H_i \leq \sum_1^{k+1} \lambda_i h_i$$
$$\lambda_1 H_1 + \lambda_1 p_1 p_2 H_2 + \cdots + \lambda_1 \prod_1^{k-1} p_i H_{k-1} + \lambda_1 \prod_1^k p_i H_k \leq \sum_1^{k+1} \lambda_i h_i$$

by using using above assumption,

$$\lambda_1 H_1 + \sum_3^k \lambda_i h_i + \lambda_1 \prod_1^k p_i H_k \leq \sum_1^{k+1} \lambda_i h_i$$

by the result of n = 2 case,

$$\sum_1^k \lambda_i h_i + \lambda_1 \prod_1^k p_i H_k \leq \sum_1^{k+1} \lambda_i h_i$$
$$\lambda_1 \prod_1^k p_i H_k \leq \lambda_{k+1} h_{k+1}$$
$$H_k \leq \frac{\lambda_{k+1}}{\lambda_1 \prod_1^k p_i} h_{k+1}.$$

From Eq. (14) of the above theorem, we obtain that as the number of hops h_is from event headers to a BS and the variance of event occurrence rates $var(\lambda)$ increase, the bound for the number of hops between event headers H_i, within which the distributed decision outperforms the centralized one, increases. In other words, the distributed decision becomes more efficient than the centralized decision as 1) h_is increase, 2) H_is decrease, and 3) $var(\lambda_i)$ increases.

4   PROCON: Proactive Context-Aware Sensor Networks

In this section, we present the main algorithms and designs of PROCON implementing the distributed context decision upon the analytical results shown in the previous section. The topics covered in this section include the context descriptor, the construction of context overlay, and the distributed context decision.

```
Context Descriptor {
    cid: 1
    ucid: 2
    Event {
        eid: 1
        type: temperature
        condition: ≤ 10 °C
        area: [(-50,-30), (-10,10)]
        timing: 2, (-5 sec, +5 sec)
        next: 3, [(10,-10), (30,-40)]
    }
    Action {
        id: 4
        location: [(-50,20), (-40,10)]
    }
}
```

Fig. 3. Context Descriptor

4.1   Context Descriptor

A user, who wants to automatically make an actuation when a certain context occurs, generates *context descriptors* through an interface device such as a base station, a PDA, or a laptop which is connected to the sensor network. With information given from the user or sensor network profile being provided by the interface device, context descriptors are generated automatically. An example context descriptor is shown in Fig. 3.

This example context descriptor is for a component event which has *id* 1 (*eid*) and is an element of unit context 2 (*ucid*) of context 1 (*cid*). The *timing* field indicates that the event has a timing relation $T_{1\to2} = (-5, +5]$, and the *next* field indicates the *id* and the *area* of next event (*i.e.,* the area to which ENM is delivered) in order of the context overlay chain. The *Action* field is used for directly invoking an actuation when the context occurs. We call this *direct in-network actuation*. The context descriptors generated for each component event are then delivered to sensors placed at each target area using geocasting [13].

4.2   Context Overlay Construction

A context overlay is a chain of events along which event notification messages (ENM) are delivered. So each event has its own *order* on the chain. Therefore, constructing a context overlay means to assign an order to each event of a unit context. Note that by the reversibility of the timing relation we can assign any order to each event regardless of its timing relation. An interface device calculates the optimal order with an ordering algorithm from those we present next, when a user configures a context. Then, the order is put to the *next* field of each context descriptor. By delivering the context descriptors to corresponding event headers, event headers conduct context detection based on the initial context overlay.

The ordering algorithm is used to find an optimal order of events that minimizes a given objective function that is basically derived from T_d shown in Eq. (9). The optimal solution can be obtained using an optimization tool such as Linear Programming. We employ two items of information to generate the objective function, event occurrence rates and the distance between event headers indicating how many hops an ENM has to be transmitted in which frequency. We now present three ordering algorithms derived from T_d.

Rate-Based Ordering is a simple algorithm which orders events from low event occurrence rate to high event occurrence rate. This is obtained by solving the following object function assuming H_is are equal to a constant C:

$$T_d' = (n-1)C \sum_{i=1}^{n-1} r_i. \tag{15}$$

Note that T_d' is minimized when $\sum r_i$ is minimized. And by the definition of r_i given from Eq. (4), it is in turn minimized when $r_1 = r_{\min}$ and the other events are connected in non-decreasing λ_i order, since in that case P_n is minimized. This algorithm is thus suitable for cases in which the differences of distances between events are small, but the differences among event occurrence rates are large. However, the event occurrence rate information is sometimes not obtainable at the time the context descriptors are generated. Thus, this algorithms can be applicable only when users can estimate or learn the event occurrence rate.

Distance-Based Ordering can be employed when we cannot obtain event occurrence rate information. The objective function of this algorithm is obtained by assuming that the event occurrence rates are all equal to λ. Thus, as differences of event occurrence rates are small, it performs efficiently. Setting λ is up to applications. However, since it is actually difficult to obtain the number of hops information H_i as well, we replace it by geographical distance D_i between two events. Thus, the objective function of Distance-Based Ordering becomes:

$$T_d''(n) = \lambda P D_1 + \lambda P^2 D_2 + \cdots + \lambda P^{n-1} D_{n-1}. \tag{16}$$

Here, λ denotes a constant indicating arbitrary occurrence rate and $P = 1 - e^{-\lambda}$.

Hybrid Optimal Ordering. When we are able to obtain both items of information, we use the Hybrid Optimal Ordering algorithm, which returns an optimal order that reflects both the occurrence rate and the distance between events. The objective function is T_d itself shown in Eq. (9) excepting that H_i is replaced by D_i as is in the Distance-Based Ordering.

4.3   Distributed Context Decision of PROCON

Once the first order event E_1 occurs, PROCON initiates its decision procedure, called a *decision round* (DR), by sending an ENM_1 to E_2. Note that other events except E_1 cannot initiate any DR. Instead, they determine whether or not to let the current DR progress. Only when a *timing validity test* (TVT) for its preceding events succeeds does it progress the current DR by sending an ENM, indicating that the preceding events have all timely occurred. Thus, the fact that E_k receives an ENM_{k-1} from E_{k-1} means that a set of event instances from E_1 to E_{k-1} all satisfy their timing relations for the current DR. We call this *context*

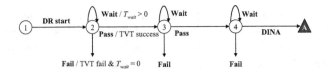

Fig. 4. State Transition Diagram of a DR

fusion in the sense that it conceptually derives high level (context) information by inspecting and aggregating several events and quantitatively reduces the size of packets to be transferred. Finally, when the timing validity test succeeds at E_n the last event header, a context instance for the current DR is considered as occurred. Then, E_n in turn actuates an actuation corresponding to the detected context by sending a DINA command packet to a proper actuator referred by the *Action* field of the context descriptor.

An ENM contains the information required for event headers to examine timing validity. The event information includes identities of context, unit context, and events, event occurrence time, category of event, and so forth. In addition, an ENM includes the DR sequence number. The event information of a current event is appended to the receiving ENM before it is passed to the next. An event header receiving an ENM from a continuous event considers that the previous event is currently in TRUE state, until it receives another ENM notifying that it is now in FALSE state.

Each event header manages a cache, called an *event history cache*. So once detecting an event, it stores its occurrence time in the event history cache during a time T_{cache}. Thus, upon receiving ENM_i, E_{i+1} checks its cache to look up an event history which satisfies the timing relations of the preceding events from E_1 to E_i. If it exists, E_{i+1} sends ENM_{i+1} to E_{i+2}. Otherwise, either the current DR ends there, or E_{i+1} stores ENM_i in the cache during a time T_{wait} since, by the definition of the timing relation model discussed in Section 2, there may be a remaining time during which the timing relation can be satisfied as E_{i+1} occurs. However, if the desired event does not occur even during the additional time T_{wait}, the current DR ends there. Fig. 4 shows a state transition diagram of a DR of a context consisting of 4 component events.

5   Simulations and Results

In this section, we demonstrate our analytical models and performances of PRO-CON compared with the centralized decision scheme by conducting extensive simulations using ns-2. The following performance metrics are considered in the simulations.

1. *Overhead* in terms of energy dissipation is the average of remaining energies of all nodes.
2. *Congestion to BS* is compared by showing the relative energy dissipation pattern of all nodes, based on the nodes' locations.

3. *Context Service Lifetime* is a time taken until a context cannot be detected
any more, starting from the initialization of the network.

5.1   Simulation Model

In our simulations, we use a $50m \times 50m$ sensor field with 100 sensor nodes
including a base station. The base station is placed at a corner of the rectangular
sensor field and other nodes are randomly and uniformly deployed. We take
MICA2 as a sensor node model.

The configuration variables of a context includes:

- $|C|$: the context size, i.e., the number of component events.
- R: variance of λ_is. Given $R = r$, each component event randomly and uniformly chooses its λ_i in an interval $(0, r]$.
- D: average distance of component events to a base station.
- P: geographical proximity of component events. Given $L = 10$, component
  events are located in a square with an edge length 10. We define $P = 1/L$.

Additionally, we notice that the event occurrence process follows the Poisson
process with mean arrival rate λ_i. We use a timing condition $I = 1$ for all
simulations. As a routing protocol for the centralized decision scheme, we use
min-hop routing as MICA supports, and AODV [14] is used for PROCON to
deliver ENM to the next event. In the min-hop routing, nodes frequently consume
a little energy in updating their routing tables and in AODV nodes consume
energy for route discovery[2]. These overheads are included in the results. We use
the Hybrid Optimal Ordering algorithm for context overlay construction.

5.2   Average Remaining Node Energy

To obtain the overheads of both schemes, we measure the average remaining
energy of nodes as time goes by. During these experiments, we also validate the
effects of R, D, and P stated by Eq. (14) for a few context sizes.

Fig. 5 and Fig. 6 show the effect of varying R for the $|C| = 2$ and $|C| = 8$
cases. The component events are uniformly and randomly deployed to the entire
sensor field. We conduct experiments for $R = 10, 50$, and 200. As shown in
the figures, PROCON consumes significantly less energy in data transmission
than the centralized one. And we can see that PROCON's energy consumption
is decreased as R increases and is not much affected by how many component
events a context has. The reason for this is that in PROCON the frequency of
which a decision round is initiated is usually governed by the λ_{min}, and definitely
it is likely for λ_{min} to became smaller as $|C|$ increases. The fact that the overhead
of $|C| = 8$ for $R = 50, 200$ is smaller than that of $|C| = 2$ illustrates this well. In
contrast, centralized decision consumes more energy as the number of component
events increases and so does R. The convergence shown in plots of centralized
decision is because nodes, in charge of detecting component events and thus
generating packets, are dying.

---

[2] In PROCON, route discovery overhead of AODV is considerably small since only
event nodes communicate with its next event node.

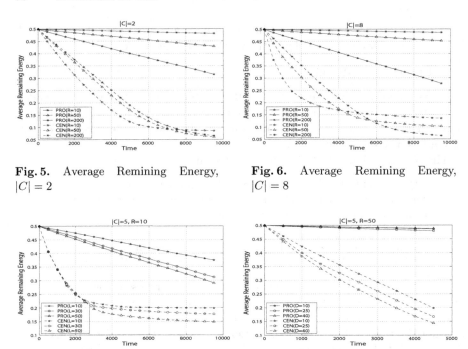

Fig. 5. Average Remining Energy, $|C| = 2$

Fig. 6. Average Remining Energy, $|C| = 8$

Fig. 7. Geographical proximity

Fig. 8. Distance to BS

The effect of geographical proximity P of component events is shown in Fig. 7 with a configuration $R = 10$, $D = 30$, and $|C| = 5$, we conduct simulations while decreasing the proximity P by increasing the edge length of the square L from 10 to 50 by 20. As you notice, overheads of PROCON decrease as component events are closely located since in that case the number of hops delivering ENM to the next event header decreases. The plots of centralized decision show almost equal overheads before converging begins. Since when a node is located near the base station it relays more data, and it is likely for context nodes to be located near the base station as proximity decreases, the plots show different convergence rates for different proximities.

Fig. 8 illustrates the effect of average distance D between component events and a base station. To do this, we conduct simulations with a context configuration of $|C| = 5$ and $R = 50$ while changing D from 10 to 40 increasing by 15. The result shows that, as event headers are located far away from a base station, the overhead of centralized decision increases, while the effect of D to PROCON is negligible.

5.3   Congestion to a Base Station

To show the congestion-free to a BS characteristic of PROCON, we compare snapshots of remaining node energy at a particular time. Fig. 9 and Fig. 10 represent the remaining energy of the 100 nodes containing 8 component events with $R = 30$. Here, the higher the cone, the larger the remaining energy. A base

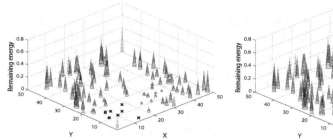

Fig. 9. A pattern of node death location of centralized decision at t=3000, $|C| = 8$

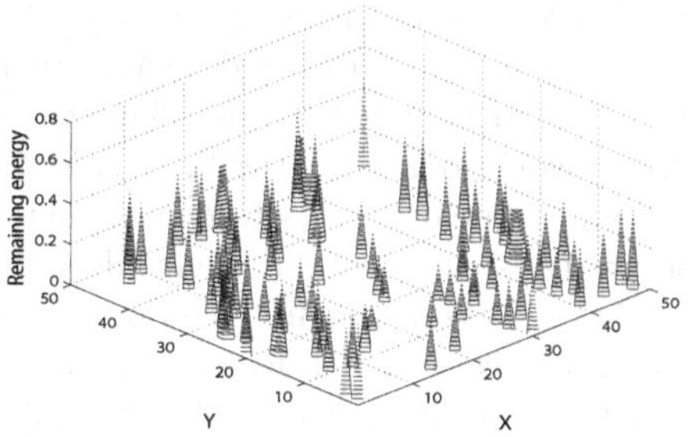

Fig. 10. A pattern of node death location of PROCON at t=18000, $|C| = 8$

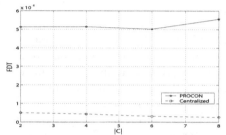

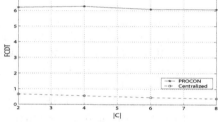

Fig. 11. First node death time

Fig. 12. First component event header death time

station is placed at a coordinate $(0,0)$ and the 8 component events are uniformly and randomly deployed to the entire sensor field. Fig. 9 shows the remaining energy of centralized decision after a 3000 unit time passes. As expected, nodes placed near the base station almost always die first so that the network is separated from the base station. In contrast, as shown in Fig. 10, the remaining energy of nodes of PROCON after an 18000 unit time passes, is almost uniform. In fact, it may consume more energy in the areas where component events are included more than in other areas, but is still sufficiently resistant to the congestion-to-BS problem since the absolute amount of energy consumption is significantly smaller than that of centralized decision.

5.4 Context Service Lifetime

Context service lifetime is demonstrated by comparing 1) the first node death time (FDT); and 2) the first component event header death time (FCDT). Note that in PROCON a context cannot be detected anymore when either 1) one of its component events cannot be detected, or 2) an event notification cannot be delivered (*i.e.*, as isolated from the network) to a proper decision place such as a base station or next event. Fig. 11 shows the FDT while increasing the size of a context from 2 to 8 by 2. As shown, there is a significant difference of FDT between the two decision schemes compared. In PROCON, the first node death occurs almost 10 times later than centralized decision. And the FDT increases as context size becomes larger since λ_{min} decreases as the size increases. Note here that in the centralized decision it is likely for BS-near-nodes to die first as we have already seen above. Thus, the base station is likely to be isolated from the network soon after the first node death occurs. However, in PROCON even if the node death starts to occur, there is no serious congestion at a particular point. Thus, the context service does not end after the first node death.

Fig. 12 shows the first component event header death time. Compared to Fig. 11, in centralized decision the component event header dies soon after the occurrence of the first node death, while in PROCON it occurs around 20% later than that of the first node death. And it is almost independent to the number of component events, but depends on R as shown in Fig. 5 and Fig. 6.

6   Related Works

Query dissemination and response architectures [1][2][4][5] are a mechanism which used to be utilized to collect event data in the centralized context decisions. In directed diffusion [5], a sink node advertises an "interest", which is a list attribute-value pairs, to a sensor network and constructs the "gradients" towards the sink. Then, nodes detecting an event corresponding to the interest sends data to the sink along the gradient. In this process, data sent by several nodes are aggregated and filtered at a intermediate node. This is so-called in-network processing.

TinyDB [1]'s Tag[2] and COUGAR [4] apply the in-network processing concept to sensor database systems. However, while in-network processing for homogeneous type of data, such as obtaining average temperature, is well dealt with, they show limitations in performing in-network processing for heterogeneous types of data. And since the incremental computing of the partial aggregation is performed along a routing tree to the sink, benefits obtained from the in-network processing are significantly limited on where the operator nodes that performs the aggregation are located. In [6], B. J. Bonfils *et al.* presented an adaptive and decentralized algorithm that progressively refines the placement of the operator nodes, and B. Krishnamachari presented analysis on the performance of the data-centric routing utilizing the in-network aggregation in [7]. In [3], S. Nath *et al.* presented a family of techniques, called Synopsis Diffusion, that decouples enabling aggregation algorithms and message routing to be optimized independently. Chia-Hsing Hou *et al.* and F. Michehelles *et al.* studied cases of detecting contexts consisting of several heterogeneous events in [11] and [12], respectively.

7   Conclusion

In this paper we present a new context detection mechanism PROCON for WSN. PROCON detects contexts in a distributed way, by cooperation of sensor nodes, not by cental decision of the base station. This way thus introduces a new WSN architecture that can remove the base station as the data sink and the central decision maker, using distributed detection of context fusion and direct in-network actuation. In addition, from our analytical results and simulations, it turns out that the distributed context decision of PROCON outperforms the centralized one in terms of number of transmissions under the following conditions: 1) when component events are located far away from a central decision point; 2) when component events are closely located to each other; and 3) when the differences of event occurrence rates among component events are large. Moreover, the new BS-free architecture and significant efficiency in energy saving make the context detection service last longer and reliable. In conclusion, this work is a contribution toward WSN which is evolving from simple data transportation networks to functionally rich distributed systems employing actuator nodes as well.

References

1. S. Madden, *et al. TinyDB: An acquisitional query processing system for sensor networks.* In Transactions on Database Systems (TODS), 2005.
2. S. Madden, *et al. TAG: A Tiny AGgregation Service for Ad-Hoc Sensor Networks,* In Proceedings of the 5th Symposium on Operating Systems Design and Implementation (OSDI), 2002.
3. S. Nath, *et al. Synopsis Diffusion for Robust Aggregation in Sensor Networks,* In ACM Sensys, 2004.
4. P. Bonnet, *et al. Towards Sensor Database Systems.* In MDM, 2001.
5. C. Intanagonwiwat, R. Govindan, and D. Estrin. *Directed diffusion: A scalable and robust communication paradigm for sensor networks.* In ACM MOBICOM, 2000.
6. B. J. Bonfils and P. Bonnet. *Adaptive and Decentralized Operator Placement for In-Network Query Processing.* In IPSN, 2003.
7. B. Krishnamachari, D. Estrin, and S. Wicker. *Modelling data-centric routing in wireless sensor networks.* In IEEE INFOCOM, 2002.
8. C. T. Ee and R. Bajcsy. *Congestion Control and Fairness for Many-to-One Routing in Sensor Networks.* In ACM SenSys, 2004.
9. J. Hightower and G. Bordello. *Location systems for ubiquitous computing.* In IEEE Comp., 2001.
10. K. Chintalapudi, *et al. Ad-hoc localization using ranging and sectoring.* In IEEE INFOCOM, 2004.
11. J.S. Hou, H.C. Hsiao, C.T. King, and C.N. Lu, *Context Discovery in Sensor Networks.* In IEEE ITRE, 2005.
12. F. Michahelles, M. Samulowitz, and B. Schiele. *Detecting Context in Distributed Sensor Networks by Using Smart Context-Aware Packets.* In ARCS, 2002.
13. Y. Yu, *et al. Geographical and Energy Aware Routing: a recursive data dissemination protocol for wireless sensor networks.* In UCLA CS Tech. Report, 2001.
14. C. Perkins, E. Belding-Royer, and S. Das. *Ad hoc On-Demand Distance Vector Routing.* In IETF RFC 3561, 2003.

Constraint-Based Distance Estimation in Ad-Hoc Wireless Sensor Networks

Urs Bischoff, Martin Strohbach, Mike Hazas, and Gerd Kortuem

Lancaster University, Lancaster LA1 4YW, UK

Abstract. We propose a lightweight localisation approach for support-ing distance and range queries in ad hoc wireless sensor networks. In con-trast to most previous localisation approaches we use a distance graph as spatial representation where edges between nodes are labelled with distance constraints. This approach has been carefully designed to sat-isfy the requirements of a concrete application scenario with respect to the spatial queries that need to be supported, the required accuracy of location information, and the capabilities of the target hardware. We show that this approach satisfies the accuracy requirements of the ex-ample application using simulations. We describe the implementation of the algorithms on wireless sensor nodes.

1 Introduction

Cooperative localisation algorithms play an important role for wireless sensor networks. In cooperative localisation, nodes work in a peer-to-peer manner to compute a map of the network using only the resources provided by the nodes themselves [1]. This makes cooperative algorithms especially suited for sensor network deployments that require true ad hoc localisation without external infrastructure.

The design of cooperative localisation algorithms requires a careful tradeoff between *fidelity* and *complexity*. Fidelity refers to quality of the computed result and includes precision and accuracy, as well as timeliness. Because measurements used as input to localisation algorithms are to some degree unreliable or inaccu-rate, node locations cannot be determined with absolute certainty. Complexity refers to the amount of resources consumed by an algorithm. In the wireless sensor network literature, complexity is most often considered in the context of energy efficiency and network use, although hardware, memory and time requirements are also important. Complexity is important because typical sensor network com-ponents possess very limited resources for processing and communication.

In this paper, we describe a novel approach to cooperative localisation that focuses on supporting distance and range queries, and trades fidelity against complexity. A *distance query* retrieves the distance between two given nodes, and a *range query* retrieves the IDs of nodes that are within a given distance from a given node. This approach has been carefully designed to satisfy the requirements of a concrete application scenario with respect to the accuracy

K. Römer, H. Karl, and F. Mattern (Eds.): EWSN 2006, LNCS 3868, pp. 54–68, 2006.

of location information, the spatial queries that need to be supported and the capabilities of the target hardware. Our approach can be characterized as in the following ways.

1. In contrast to most previous approaches we use a distance graph as spatial representation where edges between nodes are labelled with distance constraints. Node coordinates (absolute or relative) are not represented.
2. The distance constraint of each edge is represented as an interval [a,b] indicating that the distance between two nodes is at least a and at most b. The distance intervals are used for modelling uncertainty and localisation errors.
3. A constraint propagation algorithm is used to compute an overall consistent distance graph.

The next section discusses the localisation requirements of our application scenario. Following that is a description of the spatial model and the cooperative algorithm. We then evaluate the accuracy of our approach for range and distance queries using simulations, and we describe the resource requirements of an implementation of the algorithm on a specific type of wireless sensor node. Finally, we contrast our approach to some well-known algorithm in wireless sensor networks, and provide a comparative quantification of the computational and memory requirements of our algorithm.

2   Motivating Application Example

The application scenario that motivates this research is taken from the chemical industry work place in which safe handling and storage of chemical containers is of key importance. The goal here is to assist trained staff in detecting hazards of inappropriately stored chemicals. These hazards are defined by safety rules that are defined in terms of the storage conditions of the chemicals. For example, they prescribe that incompatible materials, such as reactive chemicals, must not be stored in immediate proximity. The meaning of "proximity" depends on a number of parameters including the type of involved chemicals.

We have developed a wireless sensor network for detecting possible safety hazards [2,3]. Chemical containers are moved around quite frequently and may end up in a location without global networking capabilities, for example during transport inside the hull of ships or trucks. Moreover, it is generally unrealistic to rely on centralised services in environments that deal with chemical containers. Thus the key design goal was to enable the detection of safety hazards without the involvement of external infrastructure. This required a cooperative approach in which the containers themselves are able to sense their environment and interpret their storage conditions with respect to predefined safety rules. We achieved this goal by embedding perception, safety rules and higher-level reasoning capabilities into sensor nodes attached to chemical containers.

2.1   Peer-to-Peer Position Sensing

The sensor nodes make use of a simplified version of Relate, which is an ultrasonic peer-to-peer positioning system for determining the relative locations of a set of mobile computing devices [4]. The simplified version does not require a connection to a host PC and delivers accurate range information between nodes of a wireless sensor network. Using the Relate technology we can directly measure the distance between co-located nodes and do not have to rely on network measurements such as received radio signal strength. The maximum distance that can be measured by Relate is about two meters. Relate nodes cooperate by broadcasting distance measurements over the network. Thus each node has access to distance measurements between a wide range of nodes and using the algorithm described in this paper can build a spatial model of its network neighbourhood.

2.2   Localisation Requirements

In our application scenario a container A tries to detect whether there are any reactive chemicals in its proximity, whereby proximity is defined as a circular area around A with a domain-specific radius. In this situation A needs to determine which containers are located within the proximity zone and which ones are located outside of it. The cooperative reasoning process described in [2] involves all nodes located within the proximity zone, regardless of their absolute location. Consequently, the spatial model for this application example must be able to support range queries, i.e. queries that return all nodes located in a specified range around a given node.

The required precision of the distance and range information depends in large measures on the physical dimensions of chemical containers. A chemical container as used in our application scenario is barrel-shaped and has a diameter between 60 and 80 cm. We assume that a range measurement precision of about half the diameter of a container is high enough. The Relate system provides measurements with 10 cm granularity or better, but only within the relatively short detection range of its ultrasound transducers (2 m). Thus a localisation algorithm must be able to indirectly compute distances between nodes that are beyond this range.

2.3   Hardware Requirements

The hardware used for instrumenting a chemical container is comparable to that used in other wireless sensor networks nodes such as the Berkeley Motes. The hardware consists of two separate components. The Relate component implements peer-to-peer distance sensing, and the arteFACT component implements the reasoning framework. Both are based on the Particle Smart-its, an embedded wireless sensing platform [5]. Particle Smart-Its incorporate a PIC 18F6720 microcontroller with 128 KB of program flash memory and 4 KB of RAM. Particle Smart-its communicate via a slotted RF protocol and can provide effective data rates of up to 39 kbit/s. In the following we will describe the localisation system we designed for this application scenario.

3   Spatial Model and Algorithm

Our approach is based on the idea of representing localisation information in the form of a constraint network that expresses restrictions on the distance between network nodes. Node coordinates (absolute or relative) are not represented. To represent constraints we use a graph where edges between nodes are labelled with distance intervals. More formally, a *distance graph* is an undirected labelled graph $G = (N, E, C)$ where N is a set of network nodes, E is a set edges and C is a constraint function which assigns to each edge a *distance interval* $[u, v]$ with $u, v \in \mathbb{R}$ and $u \le v$. Distance intervals are used to represent knowledge about the real-world distance between nodes. If the edge between nodes A and B is labelled with the interval $I_{AB} = [u, v]$ and $d(A, B)$ is the real-world distance between A and B, then:

$$u \le d(A, B) \le v. \tag{1}$$

Thus an interval $[u, v]$ indicates that the distance between the two respective network nodes is at least u and at most v. An interval $[u, u]$ indicates that the distance is exactly u. An interval $[0, \infty]$ is the most generic (or empty) constraint since it does not limit the distance between nodes in any meaningful way. An edge labelled with an empty constraint can be omitted from the graph without any loss of information. Figure 1 shows an example of a distance graph.

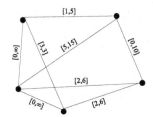

Fig. 1. Example distance graph

The algorithm for computing and updating the distance graph is a modified Floyd-Warshall algorithm for computing all-pairs shortest paths. Instead of adding distances and selecting a minimum distance in each step, it infers and adds distance intervals.

1. Initialize all edges with the empty constraint $[0, \infty]$
2. Receive distance measurements from Relate positioning system.
3. For all edges perform the modified Floyd-Warshall iteration:
   (a) infer new distance interval, and
   (b) combine interval with interval inferred in previous iteration.
4. Go to step 2

Step 2 of this algorithm takes a raw distance measurement d from the Relate system and transforms it into a distance interval $[d - \epsilon, d + \epsilon]$ which accounts for the inaccuracy of the measurement d. ϵ is a constant derived from an error model of the Relate positioning technology. More details on this transformation can be found in Sect. 4. The resulting distance interval $[d - \epsilon, d + \epsilon]$ is added to the graph.

Step 3 of this algorithm traverses the whole graph to infer new or more specific constraints. This is done using a number of transitive inference steps which derive information about I_{AC} from I_{AB} and I_{BC}. Figure 2 illustrates an inference

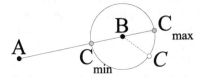

Fig. 2. Two intervals are used to infer a third one

step assuming the position of A and B. For simplicity reasons we assume zero-length (i.e. $u = v$) intervals. The distances $d(A, B)$ and $d(B, C)$ are already known, either because they have been inferred in a previous step or because they represent measurements. $d(A, C)$ must be inferred in this step. We know that C must lie on the circle with radius $d(B, C)$ and centre B. Hence we can represent all possible distances between A and C as $[d(A, C_{\min}), d(A, C_{\max})]$. Equations (2)-(4) illustrate the inference steps for the general case.

$$I_{AB} = [u_1, u_2], \ I_{BC} = [v_1, v_2]$$
$$\Rightarrow \quad I_{AC} = [v_1 - u_2, u_2 + v_2] \quad \text{if} \quad u_2 \leqslant v_1. \tag{2}$$
$$I_{AB} = [u_1, u_2], \ I_{BC} = [v_1, v_2]$$
$$\Rightarrow \quad I_{AC} = [u_1 - v_2, u_2 + v_2] \quad \text{if} \quad v_2 \leqslant u_1. \tag{3}$$
$$I_{AB} = [u_1, u_2], \ I_{BC} = [v_1, v_2]$$
$$\Rightarrow \quad I_{AC} = [0, u_2 + v_2] \quad \text{if} \quad I_{AB} \cap I_{BC} \neq \varnothing. \tag{4}$$

These inference steps for all interval cases are also illustrated in Fig. 3. If the distance intervals I_{AB} between A and B and I_{BC} between B and C do not overlap all nodes have a different position. Hence, $d(A, C) > 0$ and the interval boundaries are calculated according to case (a) (cf. (2)) and (b) (cf. (3)) respectively. Otherwise A and C could have the same position and the minimum distance is chosen to be 0 in the inferred interval (c) (cf. (4)). There could exist several paths between pairs of nodes. In the second iteration step the inferred interval $I_{\inf}$ is therefore compared to the previously inferred interval I_{pre} to obtain the smallest consistent interval I_{new}. Consistency means that there is a position for each node in the graph so that all calculated distances would lie in their respective intervals. Thus, if the graph is consistent before the Floyd-Warshall iteration step, the intervals in step 3b will overlap and the smallest consistent

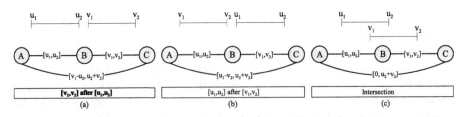

Fig. 3. Three possible inference steps for input intervals $[u_1, u_2]$ and $[v_1, v_2]$

interval is obtained by intersecting them (6). Otherwise, we create a consistent graph by choosing the smallest interval that contains both input intervals (5).

$$I_{\text{pre}} = [u_1, v_1] \quad \text{and} \quad I_{\text{inf}} = [u_2, v_2]$$
$$\text{IF } ((v_1 \leqslant u_2) \text{ OR } (v_2 \leqslant u_1)) \Rightarrow I_{\text{new}} = [\min(u_1, u_2), \ \max(v_1, v_2)] \quad (5)$$
$$\text{ELSE} \Rightarrow I_{\text{new}} = [\max(u_1, u_2), \ \min(v_1, v_2)]. \quad (6)$$

4 Evaluation

In this section we evaluate the feasibility and accuracy of our algorithm and spatial model. Using a simulation environment, we characterise the algorithm results in terms of range query success and in terms of distance accuracy. We also show that our algorithm can be implemented on a resource-constrained wireless sensing platform such as the Particle Smart-Its.

4.1 Accuracy

Accuracy was evaluated in a simulation environment. For the purposes of comparison, our simulation parameters were similar to that described by Shang and Ruml [6].[1] Our test networks consist of two hundred sensor nodes. The nodes are randomly placed, using a uniform distribution, within a $10r \times 10r$ square area. Next, a measurement range is chosen; our standard range is $2r$. Each node can measure the distance to neighbouring nodes that are within the measurement range. These distance measurements build the input to our inference algorithm. A single experiment simulates one hundred random networks each consisting of two hundred nodes.

In early experiments, we used an error model for modelling measurements more realistically. The error model was based on experiments with Relate USB dongles [4] that have similar characteristics as the Relate devices we used. In one experiment it was shown that 90% of the true distances lie in the interval $[\tilde{d} - 2cm, \tilde{d} + 4.5cm]$; $\tilde{d}$ is the measured distance. However, tests showed that the error model does not have a big influence on the final errors. It is the algorithm itself that introduces the biggest errors; so the influence of the initial measurement errors and interval lengths is negligible for the overall end result.

Thus, we decided not to use this error model. This allows us to produce results that are more easily comparable to other algorithms because they are independent of the underlying error model which is based on a specific technology. In the following we present the evaluation results of these experiments.

---

[1] Despite this, the results of our algorithm cannot be *directly* compared to that of Shang and Ruml. Whereas we measure the errors between estimated node-to-node distances and the ground truth distances, Shang and Ruml measure the Euclidean error between estimated locations and ground truth locations. However, it can be shown that for a given spatial configuration of nodes, the distance estimation error (our quantity) roughly corresponds to the location estimation error (computed by Shang and Ruml); this gives some basis for comparison.

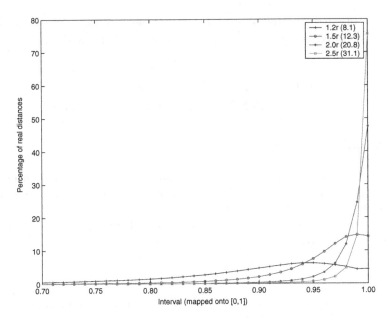

Fig. 4. Distribution of distances within intervals. As shown, this distribution depends on the measurement radius (connectivity).

We first analysed the characteristics of the intervals. As mentioned earlier the algorithm computes intervals; hence, if we want to do range queries, a position within each interval has to be chosen as the represented distance of the interval. We observed that the ground truth distances are not uniformly distributed within the intervals produced by our algorithm. We projected all intervals onto a standard interval [0,1]. These intervals were subdivided into one hundred subintervals. Then, we counted the number of times a real distance falls within the limits of each of the hundred sub-intervals; Fig. 4 shows that most real distances are close to the upper boundary of the interval results.

There are two main reasons for this. It can be shown that the lower boundary decreases faster than the upper boundary increases with each inference step. So, it is more probable that the real distance is not around the centre of the interval but closer to the upper boundary. This effect is intensified if several steps are necessary to infer the distance interval to another node. Because distant nodes are in the majority, we can clearly see this tendency in the overall distribution. There is also a geometric explanation. In Fig. 2, we showed that A sees C as lying on a circle around B. If we assume that the position of C is uniformly distributed on the periphery of the circle, we can see that the distance $\overline{AC}$ is not uniformly distributed between $\overline{AC}_{\min}$ and $\overline{AC}_{\max}$; the probability density is higher toward the boundaries.

By choosing an interval position close to the upper boundary as a representative for the real distance, the total error rate can be minimised. We use values between 0 and 1 to refer to interval positions as a fraction of the interval size. The distance between two nodes A and B can be calculated according to (7).

We have experimented with various interval positions and measurement ranges. An optimal choice of p depends, among other reasons, on the connectivity of the graph. Because we do not know the connectivity in advance, we have to find a good trade-off. We chose the interval position $p = 0.98$ for our next experiments that are based on different sets of simulated networks.

$$I_{AB} = [u, v] \quad \Rightarrow \quad d(A, B) \approx v - p(v - u) \quad \text{with} \quad p \in [0, 1]. \tag{7}$$

Range Query Classification Error. In our range query scenario we are interested in the number of miss classifications. Therefore we distinguish between false positives and false negatives to characterize the accuracy of our algorithm. If a range query classifies a node as being inside the range even though it is outside, it is a false positive. On the other hand, a false negative is a node reported to be outside the query range even though it is inside in reality.

Figure 5 shows the error rate of false negatives, false positives and the total error as percentage of the number of nodes classified as being inside the respective circular query range. The measurement range is chosen to be $2r$. The error rate is displayed with respect to the range specified in the query. Figure 6 depicts the same error but as percentages of the total number of nodes. The maximum false positive error ratio is 1.5% with respect to the number of nodes classified inside the query range. So for a query range of $4r$, 1.5% of the nodes are wrongly classified as being inside the query range. With respect to the total number of nodes we have a maximum of 0.65% false positives, 0.45% of false negatives and a maximum total error of 1.1%.

For small ranges we have direct ultrasound distance measurements. For larger query ranges we depend on inferred distances. In both graphs we can therefore see an increase of the error rate at the beginning. Then, we observe a sharp decrease of the error rate. This is not because distance estimation is more accurate at

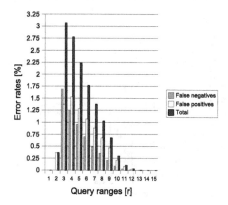

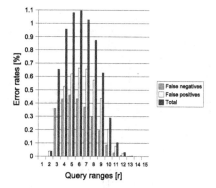

Fig. 5. Error rates in random uniform networks with respect to the number of nodes classified as being inside the range. The measurement range is $2r$.

Fig. 6. Error rates in random uniform networks with respect to the total number of nodes. The measurement range is $2r$.

longer distances, but because we display classification errors as *relative* ones. For example, in Fig. 5 we show the error with respect to the total number of nodes classified inside the respective query range. So if the query range is increased and the absolute error remains the same, the relative error would decrease because of a larger number of nodes inside the query range. Similarly, in Fig. 6, for large query radii, most nodes clearly contain most of the other nodes in their range. Thus the probability of a misclassification is smaller. The maximum possible query radius of around $14r$ affects only a few nodes in the corners of the $10r \times 10r$ square area.

The previous test was based on a uniformly distributed random network. We expect our algorithm to perform worse if the shortest path distance between two nodes is long compared to the Euclidean distance. This is the case for nodes in the two wings of a C-shaped network. These networks consist of 160 nodes randomly positioned in C-shape; they are generated analogously to the random C-shaped placement used in experiments by Shang and Ruml [6].

As expected we observe a higher error rate for the C-shaped network. Figures 7 and 8 show the classification error rates. The error rate is significantly higher. We observe a lot of false negative errors; the discrepancy between the Euclidean distance and the graph distance is the main reason for this. The error rate could be reduced by changing the value of p in (7); the optimal p is topology-dependent. But because we do normally not know the topology in advance, we used the same p as in the experiments with uniform networks.

Distance Error. In order compare with other algorithms, we analysed the distance errors. Again we chose $p = 0.98$ as the distance position inside the intervals. Figure 9 shows a cumulative distribution of all the distance errors in the random uniform networks. In total, almost two million distances were represented in our simulations (100 networks consisting of 200 nodes each). All of these distances were compared with the inferred distances. Figure 9 shows,

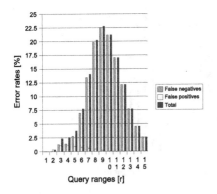

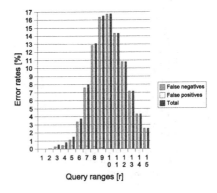

Fig. 7. Error rates in random C-shaped networks with respect to the number of nodes classified as being inside the range. The measurement range is $2r$.

Fig. 8. Error rates in random C-shaped networks with respect to the total number of nodes. The measurement range is $2r$.

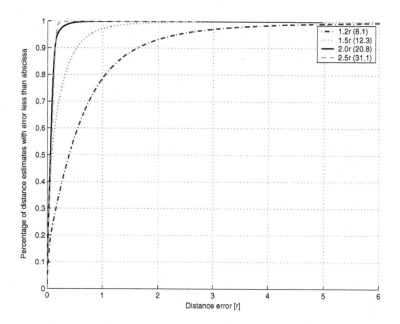

Fig. 9. Cumulative distribution of distance errors for $p = 0.98$ in random uniform topology. The distribution is shown for different measurement ranges (connectivities).

for example, that around 90% of the distances are less than $1.5r$ away from the real distance if we take $1.2r$ as our measurement radius. It is expected that the accuracy is improved if the measurement range (and connectivity) is increased. In the evaluation of the missclassification error, we chose a measurement radius of $2r$. For this radius we expect the distance error of 90% of the nodes to be less then $0.15r$.

Figure 10 shows the cumulative distribution of distance errors in the random C-shaped networks. Although a large portion of the inferred distances are accurate, there is also a significant number of inferred distances that are not. Again the discrepancy between the graph distance and the Euclidean distance explains this observation. However, we have this extreme discrepancy between some pairs of nodes only. Shang and Ruml [6] only report the error medians, rather than their entire error distributions. However, our distance error median is comparable to their position error median.

4.2   Feasibility

The algorithm has been implemented on the Particle Smart-Its. The arteFACT component listens to measurement broadcasts by Relate nodes and maintains its own spatial model. The location model is updated by each node independently whenever a Relate node broadcasts its measurement updates.

Before we update the model, inferred intervals that have not been replaced by new measurements are reset to $[0, \infty]$. In a similar way we reset old measurement

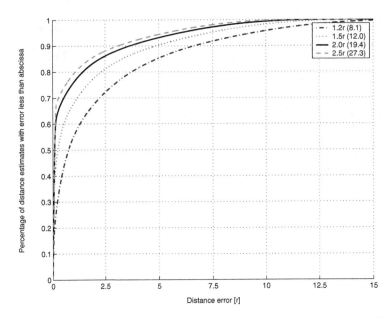

Fig. 10. Cumulative distribution of distance errors for $p = 0.98$ in random C-shaped topology. The distribution is shown for different measurement ranges (connectivities).

intervals to account for the case when devices have moved out of the ultrasound measurement range. This is achieved by timestamping the measurements with the local clock on arrival. In our prototypical implementation we chose a timeout of about 8s. Further experiments will help to choose this parameter according to update requirements. This will also help us to minimize the number of model updates for a given required update rate. Currently we update the model whenever we receive new measurements.

The current implementation supports a network of 10 nodes using 17% of the program memory and 64% of the data memory in the worst case. These are promising results, especially in the light that further optimizations are possible. For example, we use a full $n \times n$ adjacency matrix to represent the graph.

5   Discussion

Our main objective was to find an efficient method for range queries. Thus, false positive and false negative errors are our main concern; distance accuracy is of less importance. Of course, distance accuracy and classification error rate (false negative and false positive errors) are correlated. Using intervals instead of just distances gives us several advantages. First, intervals give us a measure of uncertainty. Second, we can influence the number of false positive errors with respect to the number of false negative errors. Because we have intervals, we know exactly the lower and upper limit of a distance. For example, if we choose $p = 1.0$ in (7), we would not have any false positives but only false negatives; or if we choose $p = 0.0$, we do not have any false negatives, but only false positives (neglecting raw measurement errors). There is an optimal p that minimises the overall error; the goal is to find a good trade-off between false positives and false negatives. However, if the application is very sensitive to only one kind of error, that kind of error could be minimised. We achieved a relatively low error rate for our range queries by exploiting the non-uniform distribution of distances within the intervals.

Irrespective of the number of false positives and false negatives we also showed that the distance errors are small for most of the node pairs. In Sect. 2.2 we stated that the distance accuracy requirements of our application are around 30-40 cm. We showed for a measurement range of $2r$ that the distance error of 90% of the nodes is less than $0.15r$. So if we choose r to be around 1 m (which corresponds to the Relate measurement range of 2 m ($= 2r$)), we expect to satisfy these requirements.

We first evaluated our algorithm on random uniform networks. We assume that these random networks did not represent the worst or best case. The performance of our algorithm is expected to be worse if the Euclidean distance between two nodes is small but a large number of inference steps are necessary to infer the distance interval, i.e. long graph distance between nodes. We modelled this scenario in random C-shaped networks.

For our scenario we have not exploited all the information. We do not directly make use of the fuzzy information that is given by the intervals. The length of the intervals could be an indicator for accuracy; we expect less accurate results if the intervals are longer.

The main advantage of our approach is its low complexity. We showed that it can be implemented on resource constrained embedded sensor nodes. Based on the requirements of our scenario, the algorithm only computes distances. This is in contrast to other location algorithms for wireless sensor networks which generally compute positions (cf. Sect. 6).

6   Related Work

We are not aware of any practical work on range queries in wireless sensor networks. However, there are several research areas that provide theoretical and practical foundations for our work. Hightower and Borriello provide a good overview of positioning systems for ubiquitous computing [7], and there have been a number of surveys describing and classifying positioning algorithms [8–10].

Most important to our work is the Relate project from which we used the sensing hardware. A USB dongle variant was used in [4] to provide relative positioning support for mobile devices. In contrast to our work, Relate dongles rely on host devices such as laptops or PDAs to compute the spatial model.

The Dolphin project developed a 3D peer-to-peer indoor positioning system [11]. They use bidirectional ultrasonic ranging to measure distances between neighbouring nodes. Several anchor nodes have to be manually configured with their position. Then, a distributed iterative multilateration algorithm is used to determine the position of other nodes with respect to the anchor nodes. Compared to other methods the feasibility of their approach was demonstrated by implementing the algorithm on real sensor nodes. However, their technique cannot be directly applied to Cooperative Artefact networks as it relies on anchor nodes which have knowledge of their surveyed locations.

There exist a lot of localisation algorithms for wireless sensor networks. Most algorithms depend on anchor nodes because they compute absolute node positions. Our application cannot depend on anchor nodes. Therefore, we mainly considered relative positioning algorithms: MDS-MAP [12] and the Self-Positioning Algorithm (SPA) [13] are two typical examples, which calculate relative positions using simple connectivity. MDS-MAP uses an all-pairs shortest path algorithm to compute a distance matrix. Then, multi-dimensional scaling (MDS) is applied to find an embedding in the two-dimensional space. In SPA each node forwards distance measurements to neighbouring nodes and calculates node positions using trigonometry in the local neighbourhood. Then, these local coordinate systems are merged into one coordinate system.

MDS-MAP(P) is an improved MDS-MAP algorithm [6]. It is a distributed localisation algorithm which yields median accuracies similar to our algorithm. Table 1 shows the complexity of our algorithm, compared to that of MDS-MAP(P). To compute the complexity of MDS-MAP(P), we used the *Numerical Recipes in C* algorithms for eigenvector decomposition, and Levenberg-Marquardt non-linear regression.[2] The step which merges the local maps, as well as some of the preprocessing steps in the eigenvector decomposition were neglected. In the per node computations which deal only with local maps, it was assumed that distance measurements were available for half the total pairs of neighbours. It was also assumed that the regression takes five iterations to complete.[3]

One of the advantages of the MDS-MAP(P) algorithm is that it is distributed. However, this means that *each* node must first compute its own local map, and then work together with the other nodes to arrive at the global map. Assuming each node has the ten or more neighbours necessary to achieve reasonable accuracy, our interval-based Floyd-Warshall algorithm has lower processing requirements for networks with a total of one hundred nodes or less. It is also important to note that our interval-based Floyd-Warshall algorithm uses only 16-bit integer operations, whereas the MDS-MAP(P) steps mostly rely on floating point operations (such as computing matrix inverses).

---

[2] Because of the nature of location models where distances are related to (x, y) coordinates using the Euclidean relationship, the gradient matrix used by the regression algorithm holds only four non-zero gradients. Using this knowledge, large computational savings ($O(k^3)$ instead of $O(k^4)$) can be made in the Levenberg-Marquardt algorithm. In our computations, we assumed that this optimisation had been made. To compute the complexity of the matrix inverse operations required by the Levenberg-Marquardt method, we used *Numerical Recipes* Gauss-Jordan elimination with full pivoting.

[3] For this type of problem, non-linear regression normally requires between three and ten iterations [6].

Table 1. Resource requirements of MDS-MAP(P) and interval-based Floyd-Warshall. n is the total number of nodes in the network, and k is the number of neighbours to each node.

	Operations	Storage
MDS-MAP(P) per node		
Compute shortest paths	$2k^3 + 6k^2 + 6k + 2$	$k^2 + 2k + 4$
(Floyd-Warshall)		
Multidimensional scaling	$36k^3 + 110k^2 + 114k + 39$	$2k^2 + 7k + 3$
Non-linear regression	$276k^3 - 460k^2 + 756k - 287$	$8k^2 + 35k + 52$
Per node total	$314k^3 - 344k^2 + 876k - 246$	$8k^2 + 35k + 52$
MDS-MAP(P) all nodes	$\approx n(314k^3 - 344k^2)$	$\approx n(8k^2 + 35k)$
Interval-based Floyd-Warshall	$14n^3$	$2n^2 + 5$

Thus, the MDS-MAP(P) algorithm trades off higher computational complexity and storage requirements in order to produce *coordinate location* results. By contrast, our algorithm requires less processing and storage, and instead estimates the node-to-node *distances*.

7 Conclusions

We have presented a lightweight localisation algorithm for ad hoc sensor networks. The algorithm has been designed to satisfy concrete application requirements in terms of the accuracy of location information, spatial queries and the capabilities of the target hardware. In contrast to most previous localisation approaches our algorithm computes constraints on the distance between network nodes in the form of distance intervals. These intervals can be used to represent inaccuracy of distance measurements as well as imprecision as result of inference steps. The length of intervals can be seen as a quality measure for spatial information. In future work we will look at ways to improve the information quality by reducing the interval length. In particular, we are considering combining our approach with Freksa's reasoning method for inferring spatial relations between neighbouring point objects in 2D [14].

References

1. Patwari, N., Ash, J.N., Kyperountas, S., III, A.O.H., Moses, R.L., Correal, N.S.: Locating the nodes: Cooperative localization in wireless sensor networks. IEEE Signal Processing Magazine **22**(4) (2005) 54–69
2. Strohbach, M., Gellersen, H.W., Kortuem, G., Kray, C.: Cooperative artefacts: Assessing real world situations with embedded technology. In: Proceedings of the Sixth International Conference on Ubiquitous Computing (UbiComp). (2004)
3. Strohbach, M., Kortuem, G., Gellersen, H.W., Kray, C.: Using cooperative artefacts as basis for activity recognition. In: Ambient Intelligence: Second European Symposium (EUSAI 2004). (2004)

4. Hazas, M., Kray, C., Gellersen, H., Agbota, H., Kortuem, G., Krohn, A.: A relative positioning system for co-located mobile devices. In: Proceedings of the Third International Conference on Mobile Systems, Applications, and Services (MobiSys). (2005)

5. TecO: Particle webpage. http://particle.teco.edu/devices/index.html (2005)

6. Shang, Y., Ruml, W.: Improved MDS-based localization. In: Proceedings of the 23rd Conference of the IEEE Communications Society (Infocom 2004). (2004)

7. Hightower, J., Borriello, G.: A survey and taxonomy of location systems for ubiquitous computing. Extended paper from Computer 34(8) p57-66 (2001)

8. Langendoen, K., Reijers, N.: Distributed localization in wireless sensor networks: A quantitative comparison. Computer Networks **43**(4) (2003) 499–518

9. Muthukrishnan, K., Lijding, M., Havinga, P.: Towards smart surroundings: Enabling techniques and technologies for localization. In: Proceedings of the First International Workshop on Location– and Context-Awareness (LoCA), Springer-Verlag (2005)

10. Niculescu, D.: Positioning in ad hoc sensor networks. IEEE Network **18**(4) (2004) 24–29

11. Minami, M., Fukuju, Y., Hirasawa, K., Yokoyama, S., Mizumachi, M., Morikawa, H., Aoyama, T.: Dolphin: A practical approach for implementing a fully distributed indoor ultrasonic positioning system. In: Proceedings of the Sixth International Conference on Ubiquitous Computing (UbiComp). (2004)

12. Shang, Y., Ruml, W., Zhang, Y., Fromherz, M.P.J.: Localization from mere connectivity. In: Proceedings of the Fourth ACM International Symposium on Mobile Ad hoc Networking and Computing (MobiHoc), ACM Press (2003) 201–212

13. Capkun, S., Hamdi, M., Hubaux, J.: GPS-free positioning in mobile ad-hoc networks. In: Proceedings of the 34th Annual Hawaii International Conference on System Sciences (HICSS), Washington, DC, USA, IEEE Computer Society (2001)

14. Freksa, C.: Using orientation information for qualitative spatial reasoning. In: Proceedings of the International Conference GIS—From Space to Territory: Theories and Methods of Spatio Temporal Reasoning in Geographic Space, London, UK, Springer-Verlag (1992) 162–178

Sensor Density for Complete Information Coverage in Wireless Sensor Networks

Bang Wang, Kee Chaing Chua, Vikram Srinivasan, and Wei Wang

Department of Electrical and Computer Engineering (ECE),
National University of Singapore (NUS), Singapore
{elewb, eleckc, elevs, g0402587}@nus.edu.sg

Abstract. Coverage is a very important issue in wireless sensor networks. Current literature defines a point to be covered if it is within the sensing radius of at least one sensor. This is a conservative definition of coverage and we have previously proposed a new notion of *information coverage*. Compared with the conventional definition of coverage, a point can still be information covered even if it is not within the sensing disk of any sensor. The density requirements for complete information coverage of a field are analyzed and simulated for a random sensor deployment. Our results show that significant savings in terms of sensor density can be achieved with information coverage.

1   Introduction

Recently, *wireless sensor networks* (WSNs), which consist of a large number of sensors each capable of sensing, processing and transmitting environmental information, have attracted a lot of research attention [1]. A fundamental issue in WSNs is the *coverage problem* [2][3]. In general, coverage is used to determine how well a target region is monitored or tracked by sensors and the coverage concept can be considered as a measure of the quality of service that can be provided by a single sensor or the whole sensor network.

In the literature, the commonest sensor model assumes that a sensor can cover a disk centered at itself with radius equal to the sensing range. A point is said to be covered if its Euclidean distance to a sensor is within the sensing radius of the sensor. We refer to this notion of coverage as *physical coverage* and the point is said to be *physically covered* in this paper. From the viewpoint of parameter estimation, physical coverage assumes that the estimation of a sensed parameter within the sensing disk of a sensor can be performed with a constant confidence level. Furthermore, it is assumed that each sensor makes such an estimation only by itself and does not consider any possible cooperation with nearby sensors. With advances in hardware technologies leading to increased computational capabilities and lower costs, cooperative and distributed processing among a group of nearby sensors is now possible.

This has motivated us to reexamine the notion of coverage in WSNs and to define *information coverage* based on estimation theory [4]. Specifically, if

K. Römer, H. Karl, and F. Mattern (Eds.): EWSN 2006, LNCS 3868, pp. 69–82, 2006.

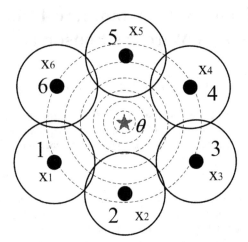

Fig. 1. Illustration of physical and information coverage. The point marked by the star is not physically covered, however, it may be information covered if the estimation error is small enough. To reduce estimation error, more than one sensor can be used for parameter estimation.

any parameter on a point can be reliably estimated, then this point can be claimed to be information covered. Moreover, due to cooperation among sensors for estimation, it is possible that even if a point is not physically covered, it can still be information covered. Fig. 1 illustrates the concepts of physical and information coverage. The physically covered area by the six sensors is the union of their sensing disks. The point marked by the star in the figure is not physically covered. However, this point may be information covered. Let x_k denote the measurement of the parameter θ at the kth sensor. We assume that the measured parameter decays with distance, as illustrated by the dashed co-center circles around the point. We can estimate θ by using more than one measurement to reduce estimation error. If the estimation error is small enough when using, e.g., all the six sensors for estimation, then the point is claimed to be information covered. From this example, we can see that information coverage can extend physical coverage in that a point not physically covered can still be information covered without sacrificing estimation reliability.

Sensor density is defined as the number of sensors per unit area and the minimal sensor density to completely cover an area is an important performance metric for WSNs. For example, it can be used to determine, before actual sensor deployment, how many sensors should be scattered to a field of interest such that all points of the field can be covered. To provide complete physical coverage, all points in a field should be within the sensing range of at least one sensor. However, this normally requires that a large number of sensors be scattered in the field. As will be discussed later, information coverage can be reduced to physical coverage when only one sensor is used to estimate any parameter for each point. Therefore, one application of information coverage is to reduce the number of sensors to completely cover a field.

In this paper, we investigate the sensor density requirements for complete information coverage for a random sensor deployment. We provide an upper bound for the average vacancy, defined as the area not information covered in a sensing field. Extensive simulations are used to illustrate that the sensor density for complete information coverage can be greatly reduced compared to that for complete physical coverage. The rest of the paper is organized as follows. Section 2 briefly reviews the definition of information coverage and its property. The sensor density requirements are analyzed in Section 3 and simulation results are provided in Section 4. Finally, Section 5 concludes the paper.

2   Information Coverage Based on Parameter Estimation

Consider a set of K geographically distributed sensors, each making a measurement on an unknown parameter θ at some location and time. We assume that each sensor knows its own coordinates. An example can be the sensing of an acoustic or seismic signal of amplitude θ. Let $d_k, k = 1, 2, ..., K$ denote the distance between a sensor k and a location with parameter θ. The parameter θ is assumed to decay with distance, and at distance d it is θ/d^α, where $\alpha > 0$ is the decay exponent. The measurement of the parameter, x_k, at a sensor may also be corrupted by an additive noise, n_k. Thus

$$x_k = \frac{\theta}{d_k^\alpha} + n_k, k = 1, 2, ..., K. \tag{1}$$

The objective of a parameter estimator is to estimate θ based on the corrupted measurements. Let $\hat{\theta}$ and $\tilde{\theta} = \hat{\theta} - \theta$ denote the estimate and the estimation error, respectively. A commonly used performance criterion is to minimize the *mean squared error* (MSE) of an estimator, i.e., to minimize $\mathbb{E}[\tilde{\theta}^2]$. When K measurements are available, a well-known *best linear unbiased estimator* (BLUE) [5] can be applied to estimate $\hat{\theta}_K$ and to achieve a minimum mean squared error.

In general, the estimate of a parameter at a point where an event happens (or a target is present) is different from the estimate of the same point without the occurrence of the event (or without the appearance of the target). This is because the signal energy of an event/target (e.g., seismic vibrations caused by a moving target) is larger than the background noise energy. Therefore, if an estimation error is small, not only the event/target can be claimed to be detected but also the event/target parameter can be obtained within a certain confidence level. Note that the estimation error $\tilde{\theta}_K$ is a random variable with zero mean (due to the zero mean uncorrelated noises) and variance $\tilde{\sigma}_K^2$. We can use the probability that the absolute value of the estimation error is less than or equal to a constant A, i.e., $\Pr\{|\tilde{\theta}_K| \leq A\}$, to measure how well a point is monitored. The larger this quantity is, the more reliable the estimate. When it is larger than or equal to a predefined threshold ϵ, i.e., $\Pr\{|\tilde{\theta}_K| \leq A\} \geq \epsilon$, we can define the *information coverage* for K cooperative sensors as follows [4].

Definition 1 *(K-sensor ϵ-error information coverage). A point is said to be (K, ϵ)-covered if there exists K sensors to estimate any parameter at the point* *such that* $\Pr\{|\tilde{\theta}_K| \leq A\} \geq \epsilon$, *where* $0 \leq \epsilon \leq 1$. *A region is said to be completely* (K, ϵ)-*covered if all the points of the region are* (K, ϵ)-*covered.*

A sensor is called *isotropic* if its sensing ability is the same in all directions. For such a sensor, its $(1, \epsilon)$ information coverage is a disk centered at the sensor. This is similar to the physical coverage of a sensor. Accordingly, we can set the disk radius as the maximum distance between a sensor and a point such that the point can be $(1, \epsilon)$-covered. We use D_s to denote such a distance and use it as the sensing range for physical coverage. In this case, $(1, \epsilon)$ coverage is the same as physical coverage. We have the following property of information coverage:

Property 1: If a point is (K, ϵ)-*covered, then it is also* $(K + 1, \epsilon)$-*covered.*

Property 1 is intuitively easy to understand as using one more sensor can surely reduce the estimation error. Based on Property 1, when examining (K, ϵ) information coverage for a point, one can first check $(1, \epsilon)$ coverage for this point. If it is $(1, \epsilon)$-covered, then it is also (K, ϵ)-covered. If it is not $(1, \epsilon)$-covered, one more sensor is added to examine if it is $(2, \epsilon)$ covered and so on. In [4], the most efficient sequence of sensors to estimate a parameter on a point is defined as the one with the minimum variance among all possible sequences. When all sensors have the same noise variance, the most efficient sequence of sensors to information cover a point is to select the sensors closest to the point in the increasing order of their distances to the point. We refer the reader to [4] for more details of the most efficient sensor sequence.

Next we review how to compute the (K, ϵ) coverage in a special case. Consider the case that all noises are Gaussian and independent. The sum of these noises is still Gaussian with zero mean and variance $\tilde{\sigma}_K^2 = \sum_{k=1}^{K} a_k^2 \sigma_k^2$, where $a_k = B_K/d_k^\alpha \sigma_k^2$ and $B_K = \left(\sum_{k=1}^{K} 1/d_k^{2\alpha} \sigma_k^2 \right)^{-1}$. We further assume that all noises have the same variance, i.e., $\sigma_k^2 = \sigma^2$ for all $k = 1, 2....$ Hence we have

$$\Pr\{|\tilde{\theta}_K| \leq A\} = 1 - 2Q\left(\frac{A}{\sigma\sqrt{C_K}} \right), \tag{2}$$

where $C_K = (\sum_{k=1}^{K} d_k^{-2\alpha})^{-1}$ and $Q(x) = \frac{1}{\sqrt{2\pi}} \int_x^\infty \exp(-\frac{t^2}{2})dt$. Define the sensing range of a single sensor, D_s, as the distance where the estimation error performance equals ϵ. Therefore, D_s satisfies $Q(\frac{A}{D_s^\alpha \sigma}) = \frac{1-\epsilon}{2}$. For simplicity, A can be set as $\beta\sigma$, $\beta > 0$. Here, we set $A = \sigma$ and choose a certain ϵ, and compute D_s as the sensing range used to relate physical coverage and information coverage in a single sensor case, i.e., $(1, \epsilon)$ coverage is the same as the physical coverage when the radius of any sensing disk is D_s. Another way is to set $A = \sigma$ and set D_s as the unit for distance, and compute ϵ accordingly. Here, we set $D_s = 1$, and hence $\epsilon = 0.683$.

3   Sensor Density for Complete Information Coverage

In [4], the sensor density requirement for complete information coverage of a field with regular deterministic sensor deployment is studied by using regular polygons to completely tile the whole field. Here, we consider the sensor density requirement for random sensor deployments.

We assume that the process for deploying sensors in a region $\mathcal{R}$ is a stationary Poisson point process with intensity λ. This indicates that (1) the number of sensors in any subregion $\mathcal{R}' \subseteq \mathcal{R}$ is Poisson distributed with mean $\lambda \|\mathcal{R}'\|$, where $\|\mathcal{R}'\|$ is the area of $\mathcal{R}'$; and (2) the numbers of sensors within disjoint subregions are mutually independent random variables (see [6] page 39-40 for more details). This sensor deployment is referred to as *random Poisson deployment*. Let $\chi_K(z)$ denote the indicator function of whether a point z is (K, ϵ)-covered, i.e.,

$$\chi_K(z) = \begin{cases} 1, & \text{if point } z \text{ is not } (K, \epsilon) \text{ covered}; \\ 0, & \text{otherwise.} \end{cases} \tag{3}$$

The vacancy V_K within $\mathcal{R}$ is defined to be the area that is not (K, ϵ) covered:

$$V_K(\mathcal{R}) = V_K \equiv \int_{\mathcal{R}} \chi_K(z) dz. \tag{4}$$

Note that V_K defined above is a random variable and $0 \leq V_K \leq \|\mathcal{R}\|$ for a field with finite area $\|\mathcal{R}\|$. Furthermore, we note that V_1 is the same as the vacancy defined in [6], since $(1, \epsilon)$ coverage is equivalent to physical coverage and the field is to be covered by identical sensing disks. According to Hall (see [6] Theorem 3.3 and its remarks), the event $\{V_1(\mathcal{R}) = 0 \; ; \; \mathcal{R}$ is not completely covered $\}$ has probability 0 for an open and sufficiently regular closed field and finite area (closed or open) shapes with finite mean area to cover the field. That is, $V_1 = 0$ implies that $\mathcal{R}$ is completely physically covered. For a finite K, the area that can be (K, ϵ) covered by any K sensors is finite. Therefore, we argue that $V_K(\mathcal{R}) = 0$ for a finite K also implies $\mathcal{R}$ being completely (K, ϵ) covered. However, since sensors are deployed according to a Poisson point process, it cannot be guaranteed that $V_K = 0$ occurs with probability 1 for a finite density λ, no matter how large λ is. Instead, asymptotic analysis can be used to provide the relationship between λ and the scale factor of a field (e.g., the side length of a square) for fixed sensing range [7] (or the relationship between λ and the sensing range for a field with finite area [8]) for asymptotic complete coverage. For example, for a square with side length L, asymptotic analysis provides the relationship between λ and L to almost surely guarantee $\Pr\{V_1 = 0\} \to 1$ as $L \to +\infty$. In some cases, we are also interested in the problem of finding a sensor density requirement for the average uncovered area within a region with finite area being less than some threshold. For example, we want to know what λ is to guarantee that the average vacancy is less than 0.01. Furthermore, $\mathbb{E}[V_K] = 0$ implies $V_K = 0$ with probability 1. The asymptotic analysis for complete (K, ϵ) coverage is difficult. Instead, we use average vacancy as a measure of sensor density requirements. A field is defined as δ-(K, ϵ) covered if $\mathbb{E}[V_K] = \delta$; and for a given δ, we find the corresponding sensor density requirement. In what follows we provide an upper bound for the average vacancy.

We first provide an upper bound for a single point that is not $(1, \epsilon)$ covered, i.e., to upper bound $\Pr\{\chi_1(z) = 1\}$. To avoid considering boundary effects, we

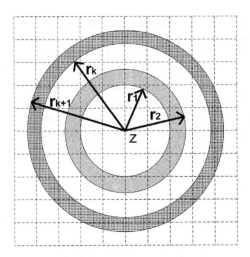

Fig. 2. Illustration of a point z and the related r_k rings and disks for (k, ϵ) coverage

assume torus convention for $(1, \epsilon)$ point coverage, i.e., each disk that protrudes one side of the region $\mathcal{R}$ enters $\mathcal{R}$ again from the opposite side (see [6] page 23). Let the kth-disk denote a disk centered at z with radius r_k and let the $(k+1)$th-ring denote the ring created by the $(k+1)$th-disk minus the kth-disk. We require that the inner circle with radius r_k is not included in the $(k+1)$th-ring. Fig. 2 shows four disks, i.e., 1st-disk, 2nd-disk, kth-disk and $(k+1)$th-disk, and two rings, i.e., 2nd-ring (slashed shade) and the $(k+1)$th-ring (grid shade). Let r_k denote the radius of the disks, given by

$$r_k = \sqrt[2\alpha]{k}, \quad k = 1, 2, \cdots. \tag{5}$$

Before providing an upper bound for (K, ϵ) coverage of point z, we first prove a lemma.

Lemma 1. *A point z is not (K, ϵ)-covered but $(K + 1, \epsilon)$-covered if there is no sensor in the Kth-disk but at least $K + 1$ sensors in the $(K + 1)$th-ring.*

Proof. Without loss of generality, let $d_1 \leq d_2 \leq \dots \leq d_{K+1}$ denote the distances of the first $K + 1$ sensors closest to the point z. Recall that

$$\Pr\{|\tilde{\theta}_K| \leq A\} = 1 - 2Q\left(\frac{A}{\sigma\sqrt{1/(d_1^{-2\alpha} + \cdots + d_K^{-2\alpha})}}\right)$$

and we set $A = \sigma$ and $D_s = 1$. If there is no sensor in the Kth-disk, then $d_1 > r_k$. Hence $\frac{1}{d_1^{2\alpha}} + \cdots + \frac{1}{d_K^{2\alpha}} < 1$ and $\Pr\{|\tilde{\theta}_K| \leq A\} < 1 - 2Q(1) \equiv \epsilon$. On the other hand, if there are at least $K + 1$ sensors in the $(K + 1)$th-ring, then $d_{K+1} \leq r_{K+1}$. And we have $\frac{1}{d_1^{2\alpha}} + \cdots + \frac{1}{d_{K+1}^{2\alpha}} \geq 1$ and $\Pr\{|\tilde{\theta}_{K+1}| \leq A\} \geq \epsilon$. ∎

We note that Lemma 1 only provides a necessary but not a sufficient condition for a point being not (k, ϵ)-covered but $(k + 1, \epsilon)$-covered. This will be further discussed later. Let $Event\_Disk(K)$ denote the event that there is no sensor in the Kth-disk and $Event\_Ring(K+1)$ denote the event that there are at least $K+1$ sensors in the $(K+1)$th-ring. According to the properties of the Poisson point process used for sensor deployment, we have

$$\Pr\{Event\_Ring(K+1) \cap Event\_Disk(K)\} = \Pr\{Event\_Ring(K+1)\} \times \Pr\{Event\_Disk(K)\}.$$

We then present an upper bound of the probability that the point z is not (K, ϵ) covered, $\Pr\{\chi_k(z) = 1\}$, in the following theorem.

Theorem 1. *Assume that for each λ and K, $\lambda\|\mathcal{R}\| \geq K$, we have*

$$\Pr\{\chi_1(z) = 1\} = e^{-\lambda\pi r_1^2}, \quad K = 1, \tag{6}$$

$$\Pr\{\chi_K(z) = 1\} \leq e^{-\lambda\pi r_1^2} - \sum_{k=2}^{K} \Psi(k), \quad K \geq 2 \tag{7}$$

where

$$\Psi(k) = \sum_{i=k}^{\infty} \frac{[\lambda\pi(r_k^2 - r_{k-1}^2)]^i}{i!} e^{-\lambda\pi r_k^2}. \tag{8}$$

and r_k is given by (5).

Proof. The proof proceeds by induction. We first consider the case $K = 1$. In this case, the $(1, \epsilon)$ coverage is the same as the physical coverage of disks with radius $r_1 = D_s \equiv 1$. For any point, the probability that a point is not $(1, \epsilon)$-covered equals that there is no sensor within the disk with radius D_s centered at the point, i.e., $e^{-\lambda\pi r_1^2}$.

Now consider $K = 2$. From the properties of (K, ϵ) information coverage, we have

$$\Pr\{\chi_2(z) = 1\} = \Pr\{\chi_1(z) = 1\} - \Pr\{\chi_2(z) = 0 \cap \chi_1(z) = 1\}.$$

The quantity $\Phi_2 \equiv \Pr\{\chi_2(z) = 0|\chi_1(z) = 1\}$ is the probability that z is not $(1, \epsilon)$ covered but $(2, \epsilon)$ covered. Note that z not $(1, \epsilon)$ covered implies that there is no sensor in the 1st-disk. Furthermore, Φ_2 consists of two parts: (1) there are at least two sensors in the 2nd-ring and no sensor in the 1st-disk; (2) there is exactly one sensor in the 2nd-ring and the distances of the first two sensors closest to z satisfy $\frac{1}{d_1^{2\alpha}} + \frac{1}{d_2^{2\alpha}} < 1$ and there is no sensor in the 1st-disk. We compare Φ_2 with the quantity

$$\phi_2 \equiv \Pr\{Event\_Ring(2) \cap Event\_Disk(1)\}$$

According to Lemma 1, ϕ_2 implies that z is not $(1, \epsilon)$-covered but $(2, \epsilon)$-covered. Since ϕ_2 is only the first part of Φ_2, we have $\Phi_2 \geq \phi_2$. Due to the properties of the Poisson point process, we have

$$\phi_2 = \sum_{i=2}^{\infty} \frac{[\lambda\pi(r_2^2 - r_1^2)]^i}{i!} e^{-\lambda\pi(r_2^2 - r_1^2)} \times e^{-\lambda\pi r_1^2} = \Psi(2)$$

and hence

$$\Pr\{\chi_2(z) = 1\} \le \Pr\{\chi_1(z) = 1\} - \Psi(2)$$

as the desired result for $K = 2$.

Now assume that the theorem holds for K. Again, from the properties of information coverage, we have

$$\Pr\{\chi_{K+1}(z) = 1\} = \Pr\{\chi_K(z) = 1\} - \Pr\{\chi_{K+1}(z) = 0 \cap \chi_K(z) = 1\}$$

The quantity $\Phi_{K+1} \equiv \Pr\{\chi_{K+1}(z) = 0 | \chi_K(z) = 1\}$ is the probability that z is not (K, ϵ)-covered but $(K + 1, \epsilon)$-covered. A closed form of Φ_{K+1} might be very hard, if not impossible, to obtain. However, we can divide it into three parts: (1) there are at least $K + 1$ sensors in the $(K + 1)$th-ring but no sensor in the Kth-disk; (2) there are fewer than $K+1$ sensors in the $(K+1)$th-ring and the distances for the first $K + 1$ sensors closest to z satisfy $\frac{1}{d_1^{2\alpha}} + \cdots + \frac{1}{d_{K+1}^{2\alpha}} < 1$ and there is no sensor in the Kth-disk; (3) others. We give an example of case (3). Suppose that the distances from the first $K + 1$ sensors to z are $d_1 = \cdots = d_{K-1} = \sqrt[2\alpha]{K}$ and $d_K = d_{K+1} = \sqrt[2\alpha]{K + 1}$ for $K \ge 2$. This means that there is no sensor in the $(K - 1)$th-disk, exactly $K - 1$ sensors in the Kth-ring and exactly two sensors in the $(K + 1)$th-ring. It can be shown that $\frac{1}{d_1^{2\alpha}} + \cdots + \frac{1}{d_K^{2\alpha}} < 1$ but $\frac{1}{d_1^{2\alpha}} + \cdots + \frac{1}{d_{K+1}^{2\alpha}} \ge 1$, and hence $\Pr\{|\tilde{\theta}_K| \le A\} < \epsilon$ and $\Pr\{|\tilde{\theta}_{K+1}| \le A\} \ge \epsilon$. Similarly, we compare Φ_{K+1} with the quantity

$$\phi_{K+1} \equiv \Pr\{Event\_Ring(K + 1) \cap Event\_Disk(K)\},$$

which is only the first part of Φ_{k+1}. Similar to the case $K = 2$, we have

$$\phi_{K+1} = \sum_{i=K+1}^{\infty} \frac{[\lambda\pi(r_{K+1}^2 - r_K^2)]^i}{i!} e^{-\lambda\pi(r_{K+1}^2 - r_K^2)} \times e^{-\lambda\pi r_K^2}$$
$$= \Psi(K + 1)$$

and hence

$$\Pr\{\chi_{K+1}(z) = 1\} \le \Pr\{\chi_K(z) = 1\} - \Psi(K + 1)$$

as the desired result for the case of $K + 1$. ∎

Since we approximate the quantity $\Phi(k)$ by a smaller quantity $\phi(k)$, it is expected that the bound becomes looser when K increases. Furthermore, it is easy to show that $\Pr\{\chi_K(z) = 1\} \to 0$ as $\lambda \to +\infty$. To find the expected vacancy we use Fubini's theorem and exchange the order of integral and expectation, i.e.,

$$\mathbb{E}[V_K] = \int_{\mathcal{R}} \mathbb{E}[\chi_K(z)]dz$$
$$= \int_{\mathcal{R}} \Pr\{\chi_K(z) = 1\}dz$$
$$= \|\mathcal{R}\|\Pr\{\chi_K(z) = 1\} \tag{9}$$

where the last equality follows from the fact that $\Pr\{\chi_K(z) = 1\}$ is a constant for all z. We now define $\lambda_K(\delta)$ as the smallest λ that satisfies $\mathbb{E}[V_K] = \delta$, i.e.,

$$\lambda_K(\delta) \equiv \begin{cases} \inf\{\lambda_K : e^{-\lambda_K \pi r_1^2} \leq \delta / \|\mathcal{R}\|\}, & K = 1 \\ \inf\{\lambda_K : e^{-\lambda_K \pi r_1^2} - \sum_{k=2}^{K} \Psi(k) \leq \delta / \|\mathcal{R}\|\}, & K \geq 2 \end{cases} \quad (10)$$

where $\Psi(k)$ is defined in (8).

4   Numerical Examples

In this section, we use simulations to compare the sensor density requirements for physical coverage and information coverage and their implications for random sensor deployment. To reduce any boundary effect, two co-centered square fields with side length 10 and 14 are used. In each simulation run, we randomly scatter a number of sensors according to a Poisson distribution with mean $\lambda \times 14^2$ within the outer square. The density λ is varied from 0.2 to 4.5 in steps of 0.1. Note that the number of sensors deployed in each random Poisson deployment need not be exactly $\lambda \times 14^2$. A grid with 1000×1000 vertices is created for the inner square field. These 10^6 vertices are then examined one by one for their (K, ϵ) coverage by selecting K closest sensors for each vertex. Suppose that in a simulation run, there are m vertices that are not (K, ϵ) covered. Then the vacancy V_K is defined as the area of the inner square times the ratio between the uncovered vertices and all vertices, i.e., $10^2 \times m/10^6$. This process is repeated 100 times to obtain the average vacancy $\mathbb{E}[V_K]$ for each value of λ. The probability of no vacancy, i.e., $\Pr\{V_K = 0\}$, is defined as the ratio between the number of times all vertices are (K, ϵ) covered and the number of simulation times (100). Obviously, $\Pr\{V_K = 0\} = 1$ implies $\mathbb{E}[V_K] = 0$; and vice versa. Therefore, the inner square is considered to be completely covered if $\Pr\{V_K = 0\} = 1$ or $\mathbb{E}[V_K] = 0$.

The theoretical average vacancy for physical coverage is $\|\mathcal{R}\|e^{-\lambda \pi r_1^2}$ as given by (6) and (9); and the theoretical upper bound for the average vacancy of $(K \geq 2, \epsilon)$ information coverage is given by (7) and (9). Fig. 3 plots the bounds and the simulation results of average vacancy for $K = 1, 2$ with respect to different decay exponents. We notice that the simulated average vacancy for physical coverage $(K = 1)$ is not always less than its theoretical value, but fluctuates slightly about the theoretical value. This is a simulation artifact caused by the limited number of simulation runs. However, the simulation results are very close to the theoretical values. This indicates that the theoretical computation of average vacancy can be used to approximate the sensor density requirements for different physical coverage ratios in the finite domain (c.f., the asymptotic analysis of sensor density requirement for complete coverage in [7][8]). It is also observed from the simulation results that the theoretical bounds given by (7) and (9) for information coverage can provide tight bounds of the average vacancy for small values of K, e.g., $K = 2$. We expect that with larger values of K the bound will become looser due to the simplifications in deriving the bound. However, as will be discussed later, when the value of K is large enough, the

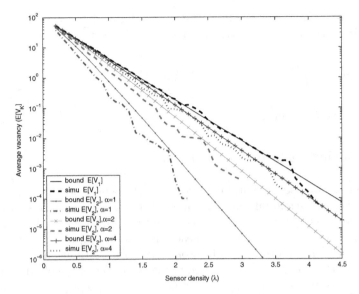

Fig. 3. Comparison of the bounds and simulation results of average vacancy for physical coverage ($(1, \epsilon)$ coverage) and information coverage ($(2, \epsilon)$ coverage)

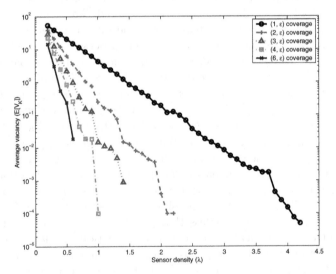

Fig. 4. Average vacancy $\mathbb{E}[V_K]$ vs the sensor density for random deployment ($\alpha = 1.0$, $\epsilon = 0.683$)

sensor density requirement for complete coverage remains constant and no longer decreases. Furthermore, larger values of K may not be used often if another system constraint–complete connectivity–is considered.

Fig. 4 plots the average vacancy $\mathbb{E}[V_K]$ against the sensor density for $\alpha = 1.0$. Not unexpectedly, the average vacancy decreases faster with the increase in the

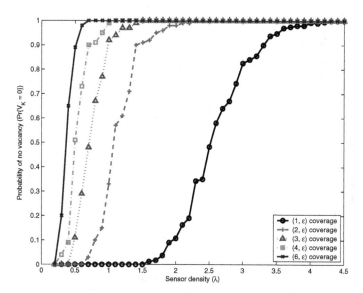

Fig. 5. Probability of no vacancy $\Pr\{V_K = 0\}$ vs the sensor density for random deployment ($\alpha = 1.0$, $\epsilon = 0.683$)

values of K. Fig. 5 plots the probability of zero vacancy (i.e., $\Pr\{V_K = 0\} = 1$) for different sensor densities. It is observed that the sensor density requirements for complete information coverage (i.e., $K > 1$) are significantly reduced compared to that for physical coverage (i.e., $K = 1$). Let λ_K^l denote the largest density such that for any density $\lambda_K \leq \lambda_K^l$ the probability of no vacancy is zero, i.e., $\Pr\{V_K = 0\} = 0$; and let λ_K^h denote the smallest density such that for any $\lambda_K \geq \lambda_K^h$ the probability of no vacancy is one, i.e., $\Pr\{V_K = 0\} = 1$. The gap between the density λ_K^h and the density λ_K^l is often referred to as the *window of phase transition* which is frequently used as an indicator for the coverage convergence rate. It is observed from Fig. 5 that the window of phase transition for information coverage is smaller than that for physical coverage. Furthermore, it is also observed from Fig. 5 that the higher the value of K, the smaller the window and the smaller the sensor density required for complete coverage. When more sensors are used for parameter estimation of a point, the estimation error becomes smaller and hence the likelihood that a point is information covered increases. However, when the value of K is large enough, the sensor density for complete coverage no longer increases and remains constant. This is shown in Fig. 6 which plots the sensor density for complete coverage λ_K^h against the value of K. When more sensors are used for parameter estimation for a point, the estimation error first improves and fewer sensors are required, resulting in a decrease in the sensor density required for complete coverage. However, as the sensor density decreases, sensors are deployed farther apart, which limits their capability to effectively estimate parameter of a point. In this case, further increasing the number of sensors used for parameter estimation, i.e., increasing K, becomes less effective. These results also suggest that it is good enough

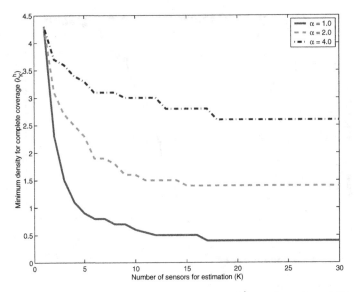

Fig. 6. The density for complete coverage λ_K^h vs the value of K

for each point to use only a few of its nearby sensors, e.g., 6 sensors, for its parameter estimation; while the sensor density gain can still be significant. This further brings additional benefits from reduced communications overheads.

As shown above, using information coverage can greatly reduce the sensor density requirement for complete coverage. However, we need to note that another metric–connectivity–is also very important to WSNs. Two sensors are directly connected if they are within each other's *communication range*; and two sensors can also be connected via multi-hop communications. A *complete connectivity* ensures that the sensed/processed data of any sensor can be transmitted to all other sensors in the sensing field as well as to the fusion center possibly via multi-hop transmissions. The communication unit is implemented by a transceiver and is in general independent of the sensing unit in a sensor [1]. Therefore, when the sensor density decreases, the communication range should increase to maintain complete connectivity. Next, we use simulations to illustrate the relationship between the communication range and the connectivity when complete coverage is achieved. In the simulations, the number of sensors deployed in the field again follows a Poisson distribution with the mean achieving complete coverage. In each simulation run, we calculate the ratio of the number of sensors in the largest connected group to the total number of deployed sensors. The ratio is averaged over 500 simulation runs for each value of communication range (from 0.8 to 3.5 in steps of 0.1). A ratio of one means that all sensors are connected, i.e., complete connectivity. Fig. 7 plots this ratio against the communication range. Since the sensor density is reduced when the value of K increases for a given α, the communication range needs to increase to achieve complete connectivity. If complete connectivity is also a system constraint for WSNs, then the value of K should not be too large as suggested by the simulation results. It is often

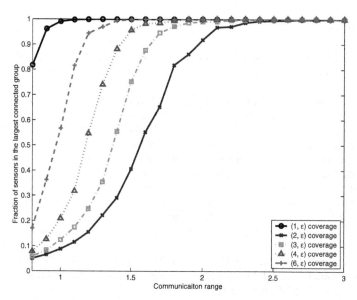

Fig. 7. Fraction of sensors in the largest connected group vs communication range for densities of complete coverage ($\alpha = 1, \epsilon = 0.683$)

assumed that the communication range is equal to or larger than two times the sensing range (for physical coverage) to achieve complete connectivity in a WSN, i.e., $D_c \geq 2D_s$ (see [9][10]). Our simulation results suggest that D_c smaller than the theoretical value of $2D_s$, e.g., $D_c = 1.4D_s$, is enough to achieve complete connectivity for the sensor density that achieves complete physical coverage. If the connectivity constraint is set as $D_c = 2.0$, only small values of K can be used to meet the connectivity constraint. However, it is expected that the density gain is still significant even taking into consideration of the connectivity constraint. For example, from Fig. 6 the sensor density can be reduced from 4.3 when using $K = 1$ (physical coverage) to about 1.5 when using $K = 3$ (information coverage) to achieve complete coverage, i.e., the density gain can be as high as 2.87 (4.3/1.5); while from Fig. 7 the communication range for complete connectivity given such sensor density of 1.5 can still be smaller than the theoretical value of 2 ($2D_s, D_s = 1$) to achieve complete connectivity.

5 Concluding Remarks

In this paper, we have used information coverage based on parameter estimation to study the sensor density requirements for complete coverage of a randomly deployed wireless sensor network. Substantial reductions in the density of sensor deployment can be achieved if the notion of information coverage is used instead of physical coverage. Since the use of information coverage increases spatial reuse in WSNs, it is expected that many new applications can be derived based on the concept and properties of the information coverage.

References

1. Akyildiz, I.F., Su, W., Sankarasubramaniam, Y. and Cayirci, E.: Wireless Sensor Networks: A Survey. *Computer Networks, Elsevier Publishers* (2002) vol. 39, no. 4, 393–422
2. Cardei, M., and Wu, J.: Coverage in Wireless Sensor Networks, *Handbook of Sensor Networks, (Ilyas, M. and Mahgoub, I. Eds) chapter 19, CRC Press* (2004)
3. Huang, C.-F., and Tseng, Y.-C.: A Survey of Solutions to The Coverage Problems in Wireless Sensor Networks, *Journal of Internet Technology*, (2005) vol. 6, no. 1
4. Wang, B., Wang, W., Srinivasan, V., and Chua, K. C.: Information Coverage for Wireless Sensor Networks, *IEEE Communications Letters*, (2005) vol. 9, no. 11, 967–969
5. Mendel, J. M.: *Lessons in Estimation Theory for Signal Processing, Communications and Control*, Prentice Hall, Inc, (1995)
6. Hall, P.: *Introduction to the Theory of Coverage Processes*, John Wiley and Sons, (1988)
7. Zhang, H., and Hou, J., On Deriving the Upper Bound of α-lifetime for Large Sensor Networks, *ACM International Symposium on Mobile Ad Hoc Networking and Computing (MobiHoc)*, (2004)
8. Kumar, S., Lai, T. H., and Balogh, J.: On k-Coverage in A Mostly Sleeping Sensor Network, *ACM International Conference on Mobile Computing and Networking (MobiCom)*, (2004) 114–158
9. Tian, D. and Georganas, N. D.: A Coverage-Preserving Node Scheduling Scheme for Large Wireless Sensor Networks," *ACM International Workshop on Wireless Sensor Networks and Applications (WSNA)*, (2002) 32–41
10. Zhang, H., and Hou, J. C.: Maintaining Sensing Coverage and Connectivity in Large Sensor Networks, Tech. Rep., Technical Report UIUC, UIUCDCS-R-2003-2351, (2003)

Hierarchical Grid-Based Pairwise Key Predistribution Scheme for Wireless Sensor Networks

Abedelaziz Mohaisen and Dae-Hun Nyang*

Information Security Research Laboratory,
Graduate School of IT & Telecommunications - Inha University,
253 YongHyun-dong, Nam-ku, Incheon 402-751, Korea
asm@seclab.inha.ac.kr, nyang@inha.ac.kr
http://seclab.inha.ac.kr

Abstract. Wireless Sensor Network (WSN) consists of huge number of
sensor nodes which are small and inexpensive with very limited resources.
The public key cryptography is undesirable to be used in WSN because
of the limitations of the resources. A key management and predistribution techniques are required to apply the symmetric key cryptography in
such a big network. Many key predistribution techniques and approaches
have been proposed, but few of them considered the real WSN assumptions. In this paper, we propose a security framework that is based on
a hierarchical grid for WSN considering the proper assumptions of the
communication traffic and required connectivity. We apply simple keying material distribution scheme to measure the value of our framework.
Finally, we provide security analysis for possible security threats in WSN.

1   Introduction

Sensors are inexpensive and low-power devices with limited resources[1]. They
are small in size and have limited wireless communication capabilities with short
coverage distance. The typical sensor node contains a power unit, a sensing unit,
a processing unit, a storage unit and a wireless transceiver (T/R). Wireless Sensor Network (WSN) contains a huge number of sensor nodes which have limited
storage and mobility. The concept of micro-sensing and wireless connection of the
sensor nodes promise many new applications into military, environment, health
and many other commercial areas [1]. Due to the different constraints of WSN
resources, the public key cryptography algorithms such like Deffie-Hellman key
agreement [6] or the RSA Signature [17] are undesirable to be used in WSN.
Also using any of those will cost tens of seconds up to few minutes [5] which will
expose a vulnerability to Denial of Service (DoS) attacks [19]. However, many
efforts to modify the current public key cryptography to be used in WSN are
still in progress.

---

* This work was supported by the Korea Research Grant founded by Korean Govern-
ment (R03-2004-000-10023-0). D.-H. Nyang is corresponding author.

K. Römer, H. Karl, and F. Mattern (Eds.): EWSN 2006, LNCS 3868, pp. 83–98, 2006.

For the same reason of constraints, the symmetric key cryptography that uses the same key for encrypting and decrypting the messages is used in the WSN. Due to the nature of the different WSN applications, the main issue in the symmetric key cryptography is how to distribute the secret key or the keying material among different sensor nodes in WSN [8]. Since the sensor nodes are sometimes unreachable and undesirable to be updated after the deployment, many key predistribution schemes - that assign and distribute keying material or secure keys in offline phase - have been proposed. In the following section, we will review some of those schemes attached with our main contribution and with the related work.

1.1 Background Schemes and Related Works

Key Predistribution (KP) mechanisms have been the topic of active research, and many researchers have made their own appearance in the past few years. A detailed survey of such schemes is provided by Camtepe and Yener in [4]. The early scheme of the KP in WSN is Eschenauer-Gligor Scheme [8] (will be referred as **EG**). In this scheme, each node is let to randomly pick up a set of keys S_k (keys ring) out of a big pool of keys P. After the sensors are deployed, the different S_k of the different nodes provides a probabilistic connectivity value p_c, in which two nodes share a secure key (SK). When a key establishment (KE) is required for nodes i, j, the shared key $k : k \in S_{k_i} \bigcap S_{k_j}$ can be used. For those nodes that don't have a shared SK, a path key establishment (PKE) through an intermediate node is performed. To increase the resiliency of EG Scheme, Chan et al[5] proposed their upgrade on EG Scheme, where the keys pool is redesigned and the key rings S_k are drawn from the main pool with *q-composite*. When the secure KE is required, only if there are q-shared keys $k_1, \ldots, k_q \in S_{k_i} \bigcap S_{k_j}$ where S_{k_i} is the ring of the node i, then $hash(k_1||k_2......||k_q)$ is used as the secure key. If n less than q keys are shared, the two nodes perform KPE phase through an intermediate node or more.

Another scheme is Blom[2]. In this scheme, it's allowed for any pair of nodes $(i, j) \in N$ to have their own shared SK using their own keying material. The highest connectivity in a network of size N can be when using different secure keys for each outgoing path from the node itself, and a possible representation of the keys could be within a symmetric matrix of size $N \times N$. In[2], the author proposed a private D and a public G matrices to generate this matrix. A public matrix G of size $(\lambda +1) \times N$ and a private symmetric matrix D of size $(\lambda +1) \times (\lambda +1)$ is defined where D entries are randomly generated. The matrix A is defined as $(DG)^T$ of size $N \times (\lambda+1)$, and each node in the network has its corresponding row in matrix A and column in G. If the secure key is required between two nodes i, j, then the ith row in the matrix A and the jth column in G are selected and multiplied to generate one key value used as a shared SK.

In Du et al. [7] which is mainly based on EG[8] and Blom[2], the data to be stored in each node is the corresponding row and column (A_{R_j} and G_{C_j} respectively). A *multi-space* scheme was proposed considering τ number of private matrices D selected randomly out of ω pre-constructed matrices, and different

A's are created using the different D. τ rows of the different A are selected and loaded for each node. When an SK is required for two nodes(i, j), firstly a *key agreement phase* is performed on the space to be used. If there is any common space $\tau_{i,j} : \tau_{i,j} \in \tau_i, \tau_j$, then the rest of Blom scheme is continued, else, *PKE phase* using an intermediate space is performed. An intermediate node or more are used in this phase. The memory required and the computation to recover the keying material and the communication required for publishing the spaces IDs is much more than any other scheme. The connectivity provided by **EG** scheme is relatively higher than in [7]. However the resiliency in [7] is better than **EG** scheme.

Blundo et. al[3] proposed their scheme to find a method for distributing an SK in a *dynamic conference environment* using *polynomial keying material*. A Symmetric Bivariate Polynomial (SBP) of degree t is used and its shares are distributed among the parties. The polynomial uses some unique seed for each party (e.g. the communicating parties' IDs) for its variables evaluation to generate the different secure keys required to perform a secure connection in the network.

$$f(x, y) = \sum_{i,j=0}^{t} a_{ij} x^i y^j, (a_{ij} = a_{ji}) \tag{1}$$

$$g_{ID}(x) = f(x, ID) \tag{2}$$

In a predeployment stage, each node gets the evaluated SBP $g_{ID}(x)$ in (2), and in the KE pahse, the second party node ID evaluates the second SBP variable to create a shared SK. An efficient way to implement Blundo scheme with reduced computation is in S. Schmidt et al [18].

In Liu-Ning Scheme [12], a two dimensional deployment environment constructing a grid was proposed where different nodes are deployed on different intersection points of the grid. The early discussed Blundo Scheme [3] is applied on each column and row in the grid with different SBP. Since any two nodes belonging to the same row or column have the same SBP, Blundo scheme can be directly performed on those nodes to establish a shared SK. In case there are no direct keys (i.e. $R_i \neq R_j$ and $C_i \neq C_j$), an intermediate node is used in PKE phase. This scheme, even if it seems to be simple, provides a good connectivity providing a high probability to establish a secure direct connection. Even in the case of compromising some nodes, the network still has the ability to survive by establishing an SK using alternative nodes. On the other hand, it is possible to determine if the node can establish an SK with other nodes or not, which reduces the communication overhead. However the computational power required for this scheme is relatively high for computing $t+1$ SBP evaluations. Using an intermediate node for key path is not efficient of computation and communication overhead.

In addition to [8][5][3][12][2][7] which we already discussed. [16], [3] proposed two security architectures. In [16], security architecture was specifically designed for the sensor networks by the name of SPINS. In SPINS, each sensor node in the network shares a secure key with a *Base Station*. Any two nodes that would like to construct a direct path could do that only using the *base station* as *Trusted Third Party* to set up a secret key. In [18], a security architecture is also proposed based on [3].

In this paper we will show the resiliency of our proposal by analyzing attacks against one node, basic zone and the whole network. The structure of this paper is: related works and notations, our scheme details, analysis and conclusion and future works.

1.2   Our Main Contribution

In this paper, we introduce a new scheme using the *Hierarchical Grid* as a deployment framework and Blundo scheme as keying material generator. Through this paper, our main contribution is to:

- Provide a scalable and robust novel framework for the key predistribution giving a perfect connectivity value to establish a pairwise key.
- Optimize the use of the different WSN resources, mainly, communication overhead, memory usage and computational power.
- Analyze and provide a theoretical and mathematical proof of our scheme performance.
- Provide and discuss the alternative against any possible security attack against our scheme.

In our scheme, we use different deployment zones which are more proper to WSN and guarantee a perfect connectivity. In addition, a higher growth in the sensor network requires much smaller keying material to be added to the original network. The network zones are constructed using a hierarchical grid that requires small fraction of information to be represented and keep tracking of the node location. Our scheme is built on Blundo[5] with some modification for generating the key material using different polynomials for the different network zones. We use different polynomials for different sections of the network to take the merit that compromising of $(t+1)$ nodes will only affect the related polynomial zone, and thus, using different polynomials with different t degrees will lead to higher survivability against attacks and to exact amount of computation according to the security level.

1.3   Notations and Definitions

The following definitions and notations will be used throughout the rest of this paper

1. **Definitions**
   - **Network Order** n. Network design parameter that declares the size of the network and the number of SBP used in each sensor node.
   - **Basic Grid or Basic Zone.** The set of sensor nodes in a geographical area that use the same polynomial of degree t_0.
   - **Polynomial Order** O. An integer that decides the scope where the polynomial is used to establish a secure pair-wise key, $O \in \{1, 2, \ldots, n\}$. Each node has some minimum order and maximum order of n.

- **Polynomial Degree** t_0. A security parameter providing the strength of the polynomial and expressing how many distinct nodes carrying shares of this polynomial should be compromised to be able to recover the polynomial itself. The subscription 0 to n expresses the order of the polynomial.

2. **Notations**

 - n: The network order
 - N: Number of sensor nodes in the WSN
 - m: Number of sensor nodes in the Basic Network Zone
 - k: Sensor nodes distribution unit through the network
 - B_z: Basic Zone (Basic Grid)
 - O_x: Order of the xth network grid
 - t_0: Degree of the basic polynomial in the basic grid
 - t_n: Degree of the polynomial for grid of order n
 - i,j: Sensor Nodes
 - ID_i: Identifier of the sensor node i
 - G_n: Number of the Basic Zones in the network

2   Hierarchical Grid-Based Scheme for Pairwise Key Predistribution

Our Scheme uses Blundo[3] as keying material generator to generate an SK for two nodes. The distribution of the keying material is performed on a *Hierarchical Grid* as in Fig. 1. Note that the hierarchical grid has been already used for a robust routing technique in the ad-hoc networks[11]. Our Modification on the grid relies on the growth factor of the network where we use the duplication as the growth factor. In addition, using different SBPs in the same sensor node to establish an SK increases the opportunity to establish a key and communicate with other nodes even if big fraction of nodes is compromised. In the following subsection, we will provide a description of our scheme.

2.1   HGB Scheme Overview

Consider a network consisting of N nodes. The different nodes are allocated as in Fig. 1, and the network is divided into n hierarchical orders of grids. Each order l consists of 2^{l-1} B_z, and the basic zone B_z is bounded by the distribution dimensions $[2k, 2k]$, where k is a uniform distribution unit of the sensor nodes in the WSN. The number of the nodes m in B_z is $(2k)^2$. The highest order O_n contains $G_n=2^{n-1}$ basic grids. The total number of nodes is $N = m \times G_n = (2k)^2 \times 2^{n-1}$. As shown in Fig. 1, B_z is any grid with the dimensions $[G1X, G1Y]$ which has O_1. The dimensions $[G2X, G2Y]$ will be considered for the order 2 grids, and $[G3X, G3Y]$ will be considered for O_3.

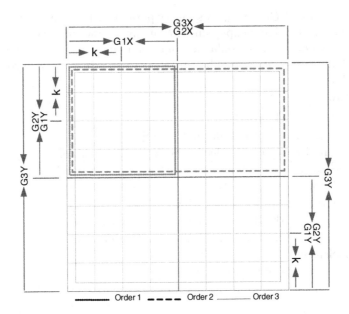

Fig. 1. Sensor nodes deployment in a hierarchical grids network

2.2   Node Identifier

Our scheme uses a smart identification material ID which is unique for each node through the network. The function of this ID is to represent the node location in the grid based network as well as the keying material required to establish an SK between two nodes just by comparing their IDs. The use of the hierarchical grid (HG) with a duplicating growth factor makes it possible to represent the different B_zs as in Fig. 2, where the leaves of the binary tree are the m nodes of the different B_z and the height of the tree is the network order. The allocated value in the end leaf is a sequence number (local ID in a B_z), where $1 \leq ID_{local} \leq m$. The different polynomials are allocated to the internal nodes of the tree. In the tree, left branches have a bit "0", and right branches have "1". The final sensor node ID is the path tracing binary string from the root node which represents the O_n polynomial down to before the leaf which represents the belonging B_z concatenated with the local ID. This structure of ID is shown in Fig. 3, and its length in bit is also shown in (3).

$$|ID| = n + \log_2 m \tag{3}$$

When the network size N is large enough, n can be considered a constant value for a robust design accepting dynamic growth of the network.

How to use this ID to establish an SK using the proper polynomial with the proper t-degree will be shown in the following subsection.

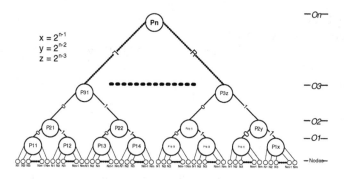

Fig. 2. Node ID Generation Determining the Node Location in the WSN

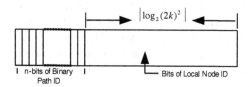

Fig. 3. Sensor Node ID Structure in the Hierarchical Grid Scheme

2.3   Key Material Generation

Using the HGB deployment structure in WSN as in Fig. 1 requires more than one keying material for each order of the network. Basically, SBP of the degree t_0 which is assigned for B_z is used to establish an SK for the pairs of nodes within the same B_z. Using this polynomial will provide a value of $\frac{1}{2n-1}$ direct key establishment opportunity out of the total possible in the network. The other polynomials are used for the connectivity to reach the perfect one. Considering that the highest amount of traffic for the communication is within B_z and other traffic fractions has a much attenuated probabilistic value, we can use polynomial of small degree for small grids, and polynomials of large degree for big order. Algorithm 1 shows the process of generating the different order of polynomials, polynomials evaluation and assignment for each sensor node.

Algorithm 1. Polynomials Generation

```
Input: Network Order n, Path ID for node i (d), Node ID
Output: 2^(n-1) Polynomials sorted in P[n][2^(n-1)],
        n SBP for each node x in Px[n] evaluated in one variable
Loop 1: for i=1 to n
      Loop2:  for j=1 to 2^(i-1)
              p[i][j]= SBP of degree t_0 and belonging to order i
              \\ Generated with coefficients belong to GF(q)
              Next j
```

```
      End Loop2
      Loop 3: For x=1 to N
            Set Px[i]=P[i][d*(1/(2^(i-1)])(ID,y)
            Next x
      End Loop 3
      Next i
End Loop1
```

2.4   Secure Key Establishment

Assume that two nodes i and j would like to establish a pairwise key to communicate with each other. Each node already has its ID in addition to the other node's ID which can be exchanged before the KE phase. Firstly, a polynomial $f^*(x, y)$ is selected out of the shared polynomials in the two nodes. The selected polynomial must be common in both nodes with the minimum *t-degree* on the scope of i, j. To establish the secure key, Algorithm 2 is applied. Note that, this algorithm is applied in both i, j to generate the pairwise key. In addition, the evaluated polynomial of Algorithm 2 is in Equation (2), where x-variable is already evaluated in Algorithm 1.

Algorithm 2. Key Establishment

```
Input: IDi, IDj, Px[n]: array of node's polynomials
Output: kij, kji.
procedure:
      Begin
            Set IDi1 = Path ID of IDi
            Set IDj1 = Path ID of IDj
            Loop 1: for d = n to 1
                  if (IDi1[d] == IDj1[d])
                        Set d = d-1
                        Next d
                  Break
                  Else
                        Break
            End Loop 1
            Use f*(x,y)=Px[d]
            Set Kij=f*(IDi,IDj)
      End
```

2.5   Scheme Variables Assignment

Variables in our scheme are the degree of the polynomial t_0 and the relationship between t_0 and other polynomials degrees. The number of the nodes m in B_z is also variable. The number of the B_z itself is decided by assigning some value for the order n. In [18], the authors assigned t_0 to be 20. However, this assumption doesn't provide correlated dymanic security strength with the change of WSN size. Using the same value of memory as in [9], t_0 can be assigned as $0.6 \times m$ and the other (n-1)-polynomials' degrees $t_1, t_2, \cdots, t_{n-1}$ to follow one of the following approaches: (i) To assign the value of t_0 and the growth of the network order will lead to the same value of the polynomial growth. (ii) To consider the different t degrees independently. In our scheme, we used independent values of t for the different orders and in the analysis we calculated a dependency relations between the different t for a general use.

3 Scheme Analysis

In this part, we will focus on the performance of our scheme on two sides: The overhead analysis and the security analysis. To measure the value of the performance in our scheme, we derived mathematical formulas using the different scheme variables to express the usage of the WSN resources: memory, computation and communication. In the second hand, we follow the security analysis of Blundo[3] in terms of the compromising effect on non-compromised nodes using probablistic attacking model. We study the effect of a selective attack on our scheme compared by [8] and [12]. Node replication attack[15] and the Sybil attack[14] are mentioned. Finally, we conclude the security study by the DoM Attacks [13], DoS Attacks[19].

3.1 Overhead Analysis

Our scheme uses the different resources of the WSN in a reasonable meaning. The reduction in using any resource could affect other correlated resources and down the performance. In this section, we measure the cost of our scheme by analytical and mathematical formulas in terms of the WSN resources. From the details above, the total WSN capacity N is

$$N = 2^{(n-1)} \times (2k)^2 \tag{4}$$

Where n is the largest polynomial order in the network and k is the distribution unit of nodes, the relationship between B_z dimension and distribution unit k and the network order n for different network size is shown in Fig. 4.

Memory Overhead. The amount of memory to represent the ID in equation (3) and the different n-polynomials is required for each node. For any SBP $f(x, y)$ of degree t_0 whose coefficients in $GF(q)$, $(t_0 + 1) \times log(q)$ bits are enough to represent this polynomial. For the memory use, we have two approaches: (i) To make the degree of the polynomials independent from each other and have the same t_0 with some neglected increment in the calculations by assigning the first $t_0 = 0.6 \times m$. (ii) To make the growth of n be the same as that of t. Then, the first order takes t_0 degree and any i^{th} order could have $2^{i-1} \times t_0$. The first case cost is represented in equation (5). The first two terms are for the ID representation and the third term for n-polynomials

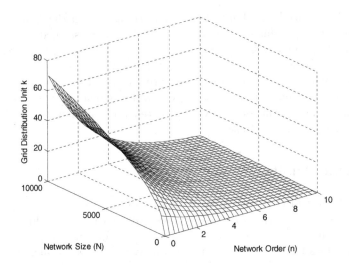

Fig. 4. The relationship between nodes distribution unit k representing the B_z size and n: the network order for different network size (N)

representation. The second case is in (6) where the third term is the summation of the required memory to represent n polynomials of different degree. The memory growth of the first case is shown in Fig. 5.(A) and the second case is in Fig. 5.(B). P_{weight} represents the bits required to represent $f(x, ID)$ of t_0 degree:

$$Memory_1 = n + \lceil log_2 \frac{N}{2^{n-1}} \rceil + n(\frac{0.6N}{2^{n-1}} + 1)log_2(q) \qquad (5)$$

$$Memory_2 = n + \lceil log_2 \frac{N}{2^{n-1}} \rceil + P_{weight} \sum_{i=1}^{n}(2^{i-1})t_0$$

$$= n + \lceil log_2 \frac{N}{2^{n-1}} \rceil + (\frac{0.6 \times N}{2^{n-1}})(2^n - 1)(\frac{0.6N}{2^{n-1}} + 1)log_2(q) \qquad (6)$$

Computation Overhead. In each time an SK is required, one evaluation an SBP $f(x, ID)$ of t-degree is performed. However, the t of $f(x, ID)$ differs depending on O_x. In case of using (5), the required compuatation is one evaluation of $f(x, ID)$. In case of using (6) by assigning different ts with growth, (7) expresses the required computation in terms of the number of multiplications in $GF(q)$, where c is computation power required for two binary strings comparison representing the polynomial path identefier part, p_i is the probability that two nodes reside in different $(i-1)^{th}$ grids and CP_{t_i} is the required power for the ith order SBP evaluation. Fig. 6 shows this growth curve in terms of the number of multiplications in $GF(q)$.

$$CP_{avg} = \sum_{i=1}^{n}(p_i CP_{t_i}) + c \qquad (7)$$

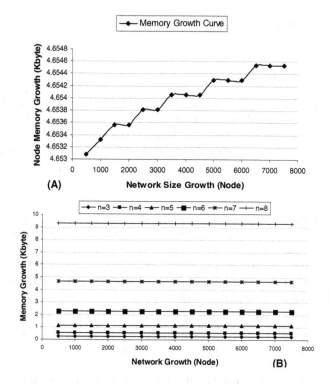

Fig. 5. (a) Network growth versus memory growth when using $n = 7$ and k to be variable. (b) Memory usage growth in the WSN when using different values of n and the same number of nodes per B_z and following the formula 2 of memory usage.

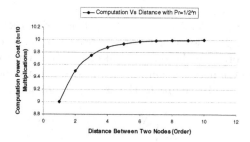

Fig. 6. Computation Overheard growth considering the communication attenuation traffic factor of $1/2^{n-1}$ versus the distance between the nodes in O

Communication Overhead. Our system does not require any extra meaning of communication. Since the different polynomials are distributed for the WSN nodes in predeployment phase, the communication overhead in the network could be in the ID exchange to construct a pairwise key. The data space required to represent the node ID is Equation (3) bits, so the required communication overhead to exchange it is bounded by the $log_2 N$ which is the space for representing N-sized network.

3.2 Security Analysis

Connectivity. Our scheme is divided hierarchically to provide a connectivity using more than one SBP for different B_z. The total provided connectivity C among the whole network is about 1. The polynomial for B_z provides connectivity of only $\frac{m}{m \times 2^{n-1}} = \frac{1}{2^{n-1}}$. Also, the polynomial for the ith order grid provides connectivity of $\frac{m \times 2^{i-1}}{m \times 2^{n-1}} = \frac{1}{2^{n-i}}$. Thus, a node can establish a shared key with any node always with connectivity 1.

Blocked Communication Traffic Fraction. Basically, this paper presents a new framework for the key management in WSN. When we applied Blundo's scheme [3], we obtained that even though the ith order SBP where $1 < i \leq n$ is compromised, this will not affect the other network any more than the amount of traffic (links) within the ith order grid. Assume the ith order SBP is compromised. Then, the fraction of the blocked traffic will be $\frac{m \times 2^{i-1}}{m \times 2^{n-1}} \times p_i = \frac{1}{2^{n-i}} \times p_i$ where p_i is the fraction of traffic between nodes resides in different the $(i-1)^{th}$ order grids. Using the current $p_i = \frac{1}{2^{i-1}}$ distribution will guarantee that the blocked communication is always constant value regardless to i value.

Compromising effects and resiliency strength. The attacking scenarios against the network can be one or more of the following:

- **An attack against N_c Nodes:** In case of compromising a set of nodes whose size is N_c that is less than t_0, the fraction of the affected nodes by those compromised ones is 0, even if all of the nodes belong to the same B_z even assuming a selective attack [9].
- **An attack against B_z:** Assume that a set of nodes s where $t_0 < |s| \leq m$ are compromised. If at least $t_0 + 1$ nodes from s belongs to one B_z, then it will lead to compromise the polynomial of the B_z. However, this seems to be so hard since the network contains 2^{n-1} polynomials and the probability p_r for t_0 nodes to be belonging to the same polynomial shares is:

$$p_r = 1 - \sum_{i=0}^{t_0-1} \binom{N_c}{i} \left(\frac{m}{N}\right)^i \left(\frac{N-m}{N}\right)^{N_c-i} \tag{8}$$

- **An attack against the whole network:** The attack against the whole network can't be in synchronized way. However, in the worst case, it's possible to compromise the whole network by compromising all of $f(x, y)$ of t_0 one by one. To compromise B_z requires t_0 nodes to be compromised. Since the network consist of G_n different B_z, it requires to compromise $G_n \times t_0$ which is a big fraction (i. e more than 60% of the network size). Without this value of compromised nodes, the fraction of affected nodes is still less than 50% of the sensor nodes.

- **Selective Versus Random Node Attack**[9]: Even if the nodes are deployed in a random environment, the knowledge of the nodes deployment and the assigned polynomials for each group and the ability to distinguish the different nodes based on their B_z will lead to a selective attack. Fig. 6(B) shows the effect of this attack on WSN. In the second hand, the ranodm node attack follows probabilistic model as in (8) and differs in that m varies on intervals of $t_0, t_1 \ldots t_{(n-1)}$ to be $m_1, m_2 \ldots N$.

- **Sybil and Node Replication Attacks**[14][15]: There are two problems belonging to the dynamic growth of WSN. Sybil attack is done illegally by using more than one ID for the same node j. Node replication attack is performed using the same ID more than one time in the network. Our framework resists in front of those threats because it requires a structured ID that has uniform and unique structure over the entire network. When an attacker fabricates a structured ID, it should follow limited structure of our own and to be depolyed in specific area to communicate with the same B_z.

- **DoM and DoS attacks:** Denial of Messages[13] is the ability of some nodes (the attacker nodes) to deprive others of receiving some broadcast messages. Our framework doesn't require node of any broadcast capability. If any, it'll be mainly used in the same grid and thus, this attack will only affect a small fraction of the whole network. An example of the Denial of Service[19] is "attempts to prevent a particular individual from accessing a service" and this mainly happens owing to heavy communication or computation because of the keying material or any outside reason like attacker messages flooding. However, for the first case it's hard to apply DoS on our system since all the computation and communication operations are small, and take short time. In the second case, to perform a DoS, node replication attack is required.

Recovery from Compromising. When $t + 1$ nodes are compromised, an alternative secure SBP will be used. In the case that an SBP of the cth order grid is compromised, the SBP for the $(c + 1)^{th}$ order grid is used till the system recovery and assigning another polynomial to the affected grid. Even when the highest order polynomial is compromised, the amount of traffic compromised will be only $\frac{1}{2}p_{(i=n)}$, where p_i is the fraction of the traffic between nodes that resides in different $(n - 1)^{th}$ order grids. If we assume that the fraction is decreased by half whenever the order of grid increases by 1, for p_n will be $\frac{1}{2^{n-1}}$. However, the internal network connectivity will not be affected, and more than that, the majority of the secure traffic in the network will not be broken since the deployment framework guarantees that most of the traffic is in B_z.

4   Comparison with Other Schemes

We selected GBS[12], Multi-space[7], EG[8], Q-Composite and RPS [5] for the comparison with our scheme. The compared features are communication, computation and memory. The comparison for security is also shown, which is the

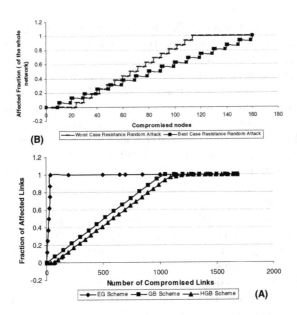

Fig. 7. (A) Worst Case Vs Best Case Selective Attack on the HGBS. (B) HGBS Selective Attack comparison with EG [8] and GBS[12] - $N = 1680$ Nodes, $t_0 = 0.6m$ for EG scheme $d = 40$.

fraction of affected non-compromised links between compromised node to the number of the compromised nodes. Table 1 shows the first part of the comparison. In our scheme, both computation and memory are shown in Equations 5, 6, and 7.

To evaluate the degree of security of our scheme and compare it with others, we used a network of 1680 nodes and mainly compared the security with GBS[12]. Parameters used in the analysis are: $N = 1680$ nodes, $n = 8$ orders, $m = 14$ nodes, $|ID| = 12$ bits that provides 7% dynamic extension of the real size ($\lceil log_2 m \rceil = 4 \mapsto m_u = 16$, dynamic extension is $\frac{(m_u - m) \times G_n}{N} \times 100\%$), $G_n = 128B_z$. For the fair comparison of GBS[12], we used the same network

Table 1. Comparison between our HGB Scheme and other Schemes: GBS of Liu Ning, EG, RPS for Chan et al. q-composite of Chan et al. and Muli-space of Du et al.

	Communication	Computation	memory
GBS[12]	Constant	SBP Evaluation	ID+2 SBP
EG[8]	$ClogS_k$	$\frac{(2C+p-p_k)}{2}logC$	S_k keys
RPS[5]	Constant	c	S_k keys
Q-Composite[5]	$ClogS_k$	$ClogC$ Comparison	S_k keys
Multi-space[7]	$Clog(n \times \tau)$	2 Vectors Multiplication of size λ	$\tau + 1$ of size λ Vectors
HGBS*	Constant	SBP Evaluation	ID+n SBP

size and $m = 41$. We applied the test of the fraction of affect non-compromised nodes between compromised nodes using a selective attack. Fig. 7 (A) shows this comparison. Fig. 7 (B) shows two cases of attacking against our scheme: *Selective attacking* with the worst case consideration and *Selective attacking* with the best case consideration. The whole compromising growth in our scheme and the GBS is the same, but our scheme is right-shifted by $n \times t_0$.

Remark: The constant value of communication in GBS depends on whether it's possible to construct a direct key or not. In case of using an intermediate node, the communication cost of the intermediate should be considered. The amount of communication traffic in our scheme is always constant because of its nature.

5   Conclusion and Further Work

In this paper, we proposed a novel proper framework for the secure key management and predistribution in the WSN. We proposed hierarchical grid for the sensor nodes deployment that bounds the heavily communicated nodes in one basic grid that has strong secure keying material.

We also designed an ID structure which is unique for the node and expresses the location as well as the keying material to be used. To measure the performance of our framework, we used Blundo[3] as a keying material generator block. Mathematical analysis of the computation, communication and memory was provided. The different possible attacks were lightly touched. The performance shown comparison expressed the value of our framework.

The next works will be an enhancement for the keying material assignment on the framework, in addition to deeper security analysis and more rigorous mathematical model derivation on security. We will provide a detailed key establishment algorithm that considers the framework connectivity, communication traffic, security and design parameters.

References

1. Akyildiz, I.F., Su, W., Sankarasubramaniam, Y., Cayirci, E.: *Wireless Sensor Networks: A Survey*, Computer Networks (Elsevier) Journal, Vol. 38, No. 4, pp. 393-422, March 2002.
2. Blom, R.: *An optimal class of symmetric key generation systems*, Advances in Cryptography, Proceedings EUROCRYPT 84 , LNCS , Springer-Verlag, 209, pp. 335-338, 1985.
3. Blundo, C., DE Santis, A., Herzberg, A., Kutten, S., Vaccaro, U., and Yung, M.: *Perfectly secure key distribution for dynamic conferences*, In Advances in Cryptology - CRYPTO '92, LNCS 740, pp. 471-486, 1993.
4. Camtepe, S. A. Yener, B.: *Key Distribution Mechanisms for Wireless Sensor Networks: a Survey*, Rensselaer Polytechnic Institute RPI, Technical Report TR-05-07, (March 23, 2005).
5. Chan, H., Perrig, A., Song, D.: *Random key predistribution schemes for sensor networks*, IEEE Symposium on Security and Privacy, pp. 197-213, May 2003.

6. Diffie, W., Hellman, M. E.: *New directions in cryptography*, IEEE Trans. Inform. Theory, IT-22, pp. 644-654, November 1976.
7. Du, W., Deng, J., Han, Y. S., and Varshney, P.: *A pairwise key pre-distribution scheme for wireless sensor networks*, In Proceedings of 10th ACM Conf. on Computer and Communications Security (CCS'03), pp. 42-51, 2003.
8. Eschenauer, L., Gligor, V. D.: *A key management scheme for distributed sensor networks*, In Proceeding of the 9th ACM Conf. on Computer and Communications Security, pp. 41-47, 2002
9. Huang, D. , Mehta, M., Mehdi, D, Harm, L.: *Location-aware Key Management Scheme for Wireless Sensor Networks*, Proc. of 2004 ACM Workshop on Security of Ad Hoc and Sensor Networks (SASN'04), pp. 29-42, October 2004.
10. Hwang, J. M., Kim, Y. D.: *Revisiting random key pre-distribution schemes for wireless sensor networks*, Workshop on Security of ad hoc and Sensor Networks archive, Proceedings of the 2nd ACM workshop on Security of ad hoc and sensor networks, pp. 43 - 52, 2004.
11. Li, J., Janotti, J., DeCouto, D. S. J. , Karger, D. R., Morris, R.: *A Scalable Location Service for Geographic Ad Hoc Routing*, The Sixth Annual International Conf. on Mobile Computing and Networking, pp. 120-130, August 2000.
12. Liu, D., Ning, P.: *Establishing Pairwise keys in distributed sensor networks*, In Proceedings of 10th ACM Conf. on Computer and Communications Security (CCS'03), pp. 52-61, 2003.
13. McCune, J., Shi, E., Perrig, A., Reiter, M.: *Detection of Denial-of-Message Attacks on Sensor Network Broadcasts*, In Proceedings of the IEEE Symposium on Security and Privacy, May 2005.
14. Newsome, J., Shi, E., Song D., Perrig A.: *The Sybil Attack in Sensor Networks: Analysis and Defense.*, In Proceedings of Information Processing in Sensor Networks (IPSN), April 2004.
15. Parno, B., Perrig, A., and Gligor V.: *Distributed Detection of Node Replication Attacks in Sensor Networks*, Proceedings of the 2005 IEEE Symposium on Security and Privacy, May 2005.
16. Perrig, A., Szewczyk, R., Wen, V., Culler, D. E., Tygar, J. D.: *SPINS: security protocols for sensor networks*, MOBICOM, pp. 189-199, 2001.
17. Rivest, R. L., Shamir, A., Adleman, L. M.: *A method for obtaining digital signatures and public-key cryptosystems*, Communications of the ACM, 21(2): pp. 120-126, 1978.
18. Schmidt, JS. , Krahn, H., Fischer, S., Watjen, D.: *A Security Architecture for Mobile Wireless Sensor Networks*, Security in Ad-hoc and Sensor Networks, LNCS 3313, pp 166-177, Springer-Verlag Berlin Heidelberg 2005
19. Wood, A.,Stankovic, J. A.: *Denial of Service in Sensor Networks*, IEEE Computer, 35(10): pp. 54-62, October 2002.

Generic Routing Metric and Policies for WSNs

Olga Saukh, Pedro José Marrón, Andreas Lachenmann, Matthias Gauger,
Daniel Minder, and Kurt Rothermel

IPVS, Universität Stuttgart, Universitätsstr. 38,
D-70569 Stuttgart, Germany
{saukh, marron, lachenmann, gauger, minder,
rothermel}@informatik.uni-stuttgart.de

Abstract. Energy-aware algorithms have proven to be a crucial part
of sensor network applications, especially if they are required to operate for extended periods of time. Among these, efficient routing algorithms are of utter importance since their effect can be experienced by
all other layers. Thus, the optimization and accurate prediction of the
lifetime of the system can only be performed in the presence of accurate execution models that take energy consumption into account. In
this paper, we propose a generic routing metric and associated policies
that encompass most other existing metrics in the literature and use this
model for the optimal construction of a routing tree to the sink. We also
provide experimental results that show the benefits of using our novel
metric.

1 Introduction

Sensor networks are getting more and more popular, especially in the area of
intelligent monitoring, where the deployment of standard sensing equipment is
too expensive or even impossible. Application domains such as habitat monitoring, environmental observation or intelligent building monitoring usually need
a cheap, easily deployable and self-organized system that is able to operate for
years on a single set of batteries. Such applications pose strict energy-awareness
requirements to the hardware and software used.

Many classic algorithms have been analysed and optimized to make them
energy-aware. A number of new algorithms have been proposed specifically for
sensor networks which try to minimize energy consumption while still providing
the desired QoS level. However, energy is usually not included in the model as
a parameter, and when included, it is mostly in the form of a constraint rather
than a real optimization parameter.

The basis of any working network, particularly a sensor network, is an efficient
routing protocol. Since wireless communication is the most energy-consuming
task, the routing module needs to be carefully tailored towards saving energy as
much as possible. Of great interest is not the routing protocol itself, which usually
gives a constant overhead for each transmitted packet, but rather the underlying
routing tree topology defined by a metric, which is directly responsible for the

K. Römer, H. Karl, and F. Mattern (Eds.): EWSN 2006, LNCS 3868, pp. 99–114, 2006.

quality, stability and energy-awareness of the routing tree. Existing solutions usually concentrate on selecting best quality paths by means of end-to-end packet reception rate. In many cases energy-awareness is defined in terms of the number of retransmissions, which definitely influences energy consumption albeit only in an indirect way.

The challenge is, therefore, to find an optimal routing tree structure, which selects the best paths using QoS parameters, like reliability of a given path, and/or its energy demands. Although the compromise between these two parameters might not fit the requirements of different applications to the routing module, we expect such a generic solution to be parameterized and tunable. There might be applications that require reliable packet delivery at any price, or those that might tolerate losses but should be optimized to operate for several years. Finally, we are interested in examining the characteristics of the resulting routing tree topology defined by our metric.

The rest of the paper is organized as follows. Section 2 gives an overview of related work. In section 3 we present an example that shows the limitations of existing approaches and motivates our work. Section 4 lists our assumptions and provides a detailed description of the generic metric as well as the policies used in our model. Section 5 presents the results obtained through experimental evaluation of our model on real hardware. Finally, section 6 concludes the paper and describes future work.

2   Related Work

Relevant papers available in the literature that relate to our model can be grouped in three topic areas: routing metric definition and analysis, transmission power level tuning approaches and energy consumption modeling.

Routing Metric Definition and Analysis. Most papers in this area have been developed for traditional computer networks and for ad-hoc networks, and sometimes they also apply to sensor network research. Let us discuss three representative examples. The Shortest Path First metric (SPF) discussed in [3, 6] selects the route based only on path length information. It has been shown to be not suitable for sensor networks, since it selects the neighbor further away with the lowest link quality to route packets. An optimized version of it, called $SPF(t)$, applies a blacklisting procedure to filter the links with quality less than t before using the SPF algorithm on the resulting topology. Clearly, $SPF(t)$ shows better behavior than SPF, but it might lead to a disconnected routing tree, as shown in [6]. The Success Rate (SR) metric tries to find the paths with the highest end-to-end success rate as a product of link qualities p_{ij} along the path *Path*: $\prod_{(i,j)\in Path} p_{ij}$ [5]. However, it usually underestimates the path quality, since it does not take into account the possibility of packet retransmission. It might also lead to cycles in the routing graph. Finally, the ETX metric was originally developed for ad-hoc networks, but is used in sensor networks as well. Its goal is to minimize the sum of the expected number of transmissions over each link $(i, j) \in Path$: $\sum_{(i,j)\in Path} 1/p_{ij}$. Compared to the other two, this metric has been shown to behave best, especially in the presence of low mobility [1]. Other metrics based on latency, like the ones presented in [2], have shown poor behavior when used in sensor network scenarios.

Transmission Power Level Tuning. In [4], the authors have investigated means of influencing the packet reception rate of a link by tuning the transmission power level in single-hop scenarios. In [7], the dependence between the received signal strength and the packet reception rate is investigated on the physical and MAC layers. Finally, the authors of [8] used the transmission power level to regulate the number of available neighbors, and therefore, mitigate the number of collisions in dense networks.

Energy Consumption Modeling. Energy has been modeled at different levels in a number of papers. [9] presents an analytical model to predict energy consumption in saturated IEEE 802.11 single-hop ad-hoc networks under ideal channel conditions. In [10] the energy spent to send and receive a message is accurately modeled and a power aware routing protocol is proposed that adapts routes to the available power. For the approach proposed in this paper, we can use any of the low level models available in the literature, since our goal is the optimization of the routing paths themselves. [11] tries to find the optimal traffic scheduling in energy contrained networks to optimize the lifetime of the network. In [12] the authors have shown, that always using lowest energy paths may not be optimal from the point of view of network lifetime and long-term connectivity. They propose a scheme that occasionally uses sub-optimal paths to provide sustainable gains.

However, to the best of our knowledge, our work is the first to combine transmission power control, number of transmissions, energy consumption and success rate in one routing metric. In the next section we present an example which motivates the need for proper modeling and direct inclusion of energy consumption into the routing metric.

3   Motivation

Fig. 1 shows an example of a network with four nodes, where node 3 tries to send some data to the sink (node 0). There are two possible routes to reach the sink, either via node 1 or via node 2. The links $(3,1)$, $(2,0)$ and $(1,0)$, $(3,2)$ have link qualities 1.0 and 0.1 respectively. In this example, we assume that all

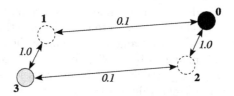

Fig. 1. Motivating example

nodes spend an equal amount of energy for each attempt to transmit a packet over any available link and that no retransmission of lost packets is in place.

The three metrics mentioned in the related work consider both paths to be equivalent. The SPF metric assigns a value of 2 to both paths because there are two hops to the sink. The SR metric guesses the end-to-end success rate to be the same $(0.1 \cdot 1.0 = 0.1)$. Finally, the ETX metric estimates the number of transmissions to be $\dfrac{1}{0.1} + \dfrac{1}{1.0} = 11$ for both paths.

However, the expected energy spent by the sensor network if the first route is selected is nearly twice as much as the energy spent in the case of the second route. The reason for this is that node 2 forwards packets from 3 only in 10% of the cases. If we assume that transmitting all packets generated by 3 costs 1 energy unit, then node 2 spends 0.1 energy units for forwarding. This way, the energy costs of the routes via node 1 are 2 energy units and via node 2 are 1.1 energy units.

Moreover, if we assume that all nodes operate at different send power levels and have different numbers of retransmission possibilities, the resulting energy demands of using either path might change considerably. Therefore, in the next section, we analyse the general case and build a model which takes these facts into account: path quality and energy consumption of the path. Based on this model, we propose a new routing metric and discuss its properties and ways to tune it by means of application-specific policies.

4 Formal Model

The goal of our approach is to determine a routing tree structure that provides the highest end-to-end packet success rate while taking the amount of consumed energy into account. For the success rate, it suffices to independently determine its value at any given point in time. All metrics in the related work section work using this method. However, including the consumed energy in the model requires the consideration of past history, since the amount of available energy depends on the history of previous system performance.

For this reason, our model contains two optimization metrics: end-to-end packet success rate, which depends mostly on the topology of the network and the environmental characteristics; and energy consumption, which, as stated above, depends on past system performance. Our approach involves the optimization of the ratio of these two metrics taking into account the following two assumptions: First, we only consider two independent parameters, transmission count and transmission power level that allow us to tune the direction of optimization. Second, we only allow these two parameters to change their values over time, and assume that they are managed by application-specific policies.

Using these values, at each point in time the metric selects the best possible route based only on the current values and not taking into account previous history. Changes to these parameters over time will be considered later when we deal with application-specific policies.

4.1   The Metric

Terminology. Let $G = (N, E)$ be a fully connected undirected graph, where N is a set of nodes numbered $[0..n]$ and node 0 is called the *sink*. $\forall i, j \in N$ each *link* $(i, j) \in E$ has a pair of characteristics: $(p, e) \in (Pr, En)$.

For any two nodes $i, j \in N$, we define the *link quality* $p_{ij} \in Pr$ to be the product of the probabilities indicating that a packet sent by node i is received correctly by node j and vice versa. If no blacklisting is used, $Pr = [0, 1]$. Two nodes $i, j \in N$ are defined to be *neighbors*, if $p_{ij} \neq 0$. This implies that implicit acknowledgements can be used in our model, since neighbors can always hear each other.

The sequence of links $(i, k_1), (k_1, k_2) \ldots (k_f, 0)$ is a *path* $Path_i$ from node i to the sink 0, if each link $(i, k_1), (k_1, k_2) \ldots (k_f, 0)$ connects two neighbors. Without loss of generality we assume that all paths end at the sink. The metric defines a partial order over all paths. We consider only paths from the same node to the sink to be comparable. If node j is chosen to be a parent of node i along the path, then we define the notation $p_i = p_{ij}$.

Additionally, $e_i(l) \in En$ is a discrete function which represents the dependency between the transmission power level l and energy e_i needed for one transmission of a packet using this power level. En is the domain of such discrete functions that might be different for each radio type.

Each node $i \in N$ initially possesses the amount of energy Ξ_i. If possible, it might manage the transmission power level l_i of the radio and change the number of possible packet transmissions r_i. The number of possible retransmissions in the case of send failures is then $(r_i - 1)$. Both techniques have an effect on the amount of energy spent to send the packet and may influence p_{ij}. We consider l_i and r_i to be the input parameters of our model and to be tunable by application-specific policies.

Our model tries to describe and analyse the *end-to-end packet reception rate* or *path quality* referred to as $Gain_{path_i}$ and the *total energy* spent by all nodes along this path denoted as $Energy_{path_i}$. If we consider any possible path, the notation $Gain$ and $Energy$ is used.

Mathematical Description. Transmitting a packet over a link can be modeled as a Bernoulli trial. However, transmitting a packet over a path is not a Bernoulli process, because if the packet is lost on one of the links, it is not forwarded any further. This fact is the basis of our model which considers *expected energy consumption* $Exp(Energy)$ and *expected path quality* $Exp(Gain)$ from the point of view of the influence of transmission power control and the available number of retransmissions.

Tuning the transmission power and applying a retransmission mechanism might look like different techniques, but both leave their print on the energy consumption of the link and its quality. By performing one retransmission, we spend twice as much energy, even though the packet might still be lost. By increasing the transmission power level we expect to increase the signal to noise ratio and hope for better link quality. However, as explained in [7], this is not

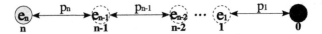

Fig. 2. Path evaluation: general case

guaranteed. These facts make retransmissions and transmission power control similar instruments in our model.

Let us now assume that a packet is originated at node n and should be forwarded to the sink 0 using some $Path_n$ (see Fig. 2). The link qualities along the path are $p_n, p_{n-1}, \ldots p_1$ and the energy spent by each node to transmit a packet via a link in the absence of retransmissions is $e_n(l_n), e_{n-1}(l_{n-1}), \ldots e_1(l_1)$. The possibility to retransmit a packet directly influences both parameters and moreover, separates the model into several cases dependent on the maximum number of times r the packet is allowed to be transmitted. Commonly, there are between 1 and 3 transmission attempts available.

First, we consider the case, where nodes do not have the possibility to perform retransmissions. Later, the model is extended by removing this limitation. Finally, we discuss the case when the number of transmissions is unlimited on each link.

Case 1: No retransmissions ($r_i = 1$). This is the simplest case, when the retransmission mechanism is not used and the packet is allowed to be sent only once ($r_i = 1$). We are interested in the evaluation of the path characteristics ($Energy_{path}$ and $Gain_{path}$) given the qualities p_i and power consumptions $e_i(l_i) = e_i$ of each link dependent on the current transmission power levels l_i. The mathematical expectation of each characteristic is:

$$Exp(Gain_{path})_{r_i=1} = p_n(p_{n-1}(\ldots p_2(p_1)\ldots)) \tag{1}$$

$$Exp(Energy_{path})_{r_i=1} = e_n + p_n(e_{n-1} + p_{n-1}(\cdots + p_2(e_1)\ldots)) \tag{2}$$

As can be found from the expressions, there is no need for global knowledge to calculate the values at each node. It is enough if each node propagates its accumulated values through the routing tree.

Case 2: Limited number of transmissions ($r_i = x_i \ll \infty$). Let us assume, that in this case all the nodes in the network may perform a maximum of x_i transmissions, that is, ($x_i - 1$) retransmissions on the link ($i, i-1$) if the packet is lost. Then the probability that the packet sent by node i is received by node ($i-1$) is:

$$a_i = \sum_{k=1}^{x_i} p_i(1 - p_i)^{k-1}$$

and node i is expected to perform

$$b_i = \sum_{k=1}^{x_i} k p_i(1 - p_i)^{k-1} + x_i(1 - p_i)^{x_i}$$

attempts to send a packet given $r_i = x_i$ possible transmissions. The aforementioned formula needs some explanation. After the first attempt to send a packet, it is successfully received by the node $(i-1)$ with probability p_i. However, with probability $(1-p_i)$ the packet needs to be retransmitted. In other words, with probability $(1-p_i)$ we need to perform at least two attempts to send a packet. But during the second try, only $(1-p_i)p_i$ packets are expected to be successfully delivered. Therefore, with probability $p_i(1-p_i)^{k-1}$ a packet is transmitted via link i after k transmission attempts. If we are limited to x_i transmissions, with probability $(1-p_i)^{x_i}$ we are still not able to send a packet successfully and are expected to give up. In this case we have made x_i unsuccessful attempts.

If each send attempt costs e_i energy units, node i spends $b_i e_i$ energy units to send a packet given $r_i = x_i$ transmissions.

So, the expectation values of both metrics are:

$$Exp(Gain_{path})_{r_i=x_i} = \prod_{i=1}^{n} a_i \tag{3}$$

$$Exp(Energy_{path})_{r_i=x_i} = b_n e_n + a_n(b_{n-1}e_{n-1} + a_{n-1}(\cdots + a_2(e_1)\dots)) \tag{4}$$

Case 3: Infinite number of transmissions ($r_i = \infty$). If we have an infinite number of transmissions and $p_i \neq 0$, sooner or later the packet will be transmitted via any link $(i, i-1)$ with probability 1:

$$a_i = lim_{n\to\infty} \sum_{k=1}^{n} p_i(1-p_i)^{k-1} = 1$$

If $p_i = 0$, the link does not connect any neighboring nodes, so it cannot be selected to transmit packets. The expected number of attempts for delivery over a link is then:

$$b_i = lim_{n\to\infty} \sum_{k=1}^{n} kp_i(1-p_i)^{k-1} + n(1-p_i)^n = lim_{n\to\infty} \frac{p_i}{1-p_i} \cdot \sum_{k=1}^{n+1} k(1-p_i)^k = \frac{1}{p_i}$$

Therefore, in the case of an infinite number of transmissions, we have:

$$Exp(Gain_{path})_{r_i=\infty} = 1 \tag{5}$$

and if each send attempt at node i costs e_i energy units, we have:

$$Exp(Energy_{path})_{r_i=\infty} = \sum_{i=1}^{n} \frac{e_i}{p_i} \tag{6}$$

Discussion. Analyzing already existing metrics like ETX, SR and SPF from the perspective of the model we just described, we can see, that they cover only partial cases and none takes either the possibility to control the transmission power level or to set the maximum number of transmissions into consideration.

The ETX metric corresponds to equation (6) when $e_n = e_{n-1} = \cdots = e_1 = 1$ and accounts for an infinite number of transmissions, which simplifies the model but does not fit reality. The SR metric coincides with equation (1). The SPF accounts for neither energy consumption nor the path quality and in the general case is expected to behave unpredictably over both characteristics.

Therefore, the SR and ETX metrics are just two special cases of our model.

GEM. Let us now use the model we have just defined to create a metric that can be optimized to find better routes. A metric is a rule which builds the routing tree and lays the foundation for its efficiency. Therefore, there are some features we would like our metric to reflect. It should be based on the model used and should be able to find a compromise between path quality (and, therefore, gain) and energy consumption. We define our metric to be:

$$\text{GEM} = \frac{Exp(Gain)}{Exp(Energy)} \qquad (7)$$

GEM stands for **G**ain per **E**nergy **M**etric and, as we will see in the experimental section, behaves better in practice than other existing routing metrics. From a more theoretical point of view, GEM has some nice features:

GEM finds the best throughput paths taking energy into account. Both expected end-to-end success rate ($Exp(Gain)$) and expected resource demands ($Exp(Energy)$) are directly included into the target function and, therefore, changes to any of these parameters influence the GEM path estimation value. Moreover, GEM is tunable by changing the values of the number of transmissions r_i and transmission power levels $e_i = e_i(l_i)$ at each node, which allows for the definition of application-specific policies very easily.

The evaluation of a path as done by GEM is based on the realistic assumption that the link layer always has a limited number of retransmissions available. However, the application itself might decide to retransmit a packet as many times as needed. In this case, $1/Exp(Gain)$ reflects the expected number of transmissions needed over a path (not a link) to transmit a packet successfully at the application layer.

In order to calculate the value of GEM, there is no need to have global knowledge about the system. GEM makes the route selection based on the accumulated values for the expected end-to-end success rate and energy consumption propagated by each node starting from the sink. Additionally, it obviates the necessity of blacklisting, and, therefore, accounts for a wide range of link loss ratios and even the existence of asymmetric links.

Finally, GEM leads to the formation of a naturally structured routing tree in the sense that it decreases the probability of a decomposition of the tree into a forest. This feature comes from including energy demands directly into the metric. The nodes that are far away from the sink have a tendency to select the furthest nodes first for data forwarding. The rational behind it is that if a packet gets lost, it is better to lose it as soon as possible, as shown in the motivating example. On the other hand, the closer the node is to the sink, the more reliable and better quality paths are selected by our metric. This natural tree structure contributes to routing tree stability and, as a result, makes GEM a perfect candidate for defining hierarchical structures.

4.2   Energy-Aware Policies

Although GEM accounts for both energy consumption of a path and end-to-end path quality, it is simply a ratio that needs to be optimized. In many applications it is important to stress which of these two parameters is more important and in which way. Simple parametrization is not much of a help, since it is usually impossible for the application to define the exact relative importance between energy and gain.

Therefore, we propose the use of policies, a more complex, but application spe-cific type of parametrization. Each policy is aimed at optimizing either the energy or the end-to-end success rate characteristic of a path and might be applicable to a certain type of applications. Therefore, a policy is responsible for setting the right values for the transmission power level and retransmission count over time, that is, taking the history of the system into account. In general, a policy should know how often the application has requested to send a packet, which signal strength it used and what number of retransmissions was needed to forward the packet to the next node along the path. This information together with data about the environment obtained through the observation of link quality changes over time and the goals of the application serve as input parameters for the policy.

Below we present some examples of policies that perform different optimiza-tions and can be modeled using our approach. All of them are based on tuning either the transmission power level or setting an appropriate maximum trans-mission count for each node in the network.

Policy Examples. In [8] the authors examined the *Neighborhood Based Policy* (NB), a policy that decreases the transmission power level if the number of neighbors exceeds a predefined value and vice versa. This might be useful for adaptation of routing algorithms to sparse and dense networks and is supported by our model by setting r_i to a fixed value.

In [10] the authors describe a model of the node lifetime based on the node power function ξ_i, which describes the node energy demands at each point in time. $\Psi_i(t) = \Xi_i - \int_{t_0}^{t} \xi_i(t)dt$ shows the energy left on the node at a certain point in time t[1]. The policy called *Lifetime Based Policy* (LTB) is then able to keep track of $\Psi_i(t)$, predict the lifetime of the system, and modify its characteristics by adjusting both transmission power level and transmission count.

Some policies might be based on tuning the maximum transmission count as well as the transmission power level. For example, it is possible to differentiate packet content and distinguish more or less important information, but still keep track of the energy spent to send packets to a sink. More important packets might be sent using a higher transmission power level or be allowed to be retransmitted more times in case of send failures (*Packet Type Based Policy* (PTB)).

---

[1] Recall that Ξ_i is the initial amount of energy on node i.

Both tuning parameters can also be set individually by each node to make link qualities in the routing tree be equal. Then the goal is to select the lowest energy paths without affecting the end-to-end packet success rate (*Equal Gain Based Policy* (EGB)). In this case, GEM is expected to perform close to ETX with the only difference that the maximum transmission count is always limited, even if to a large value and, therefore, gains in energy consumption along the path will be measured. This would be the case especially in sparse and poorly structured networks.

The transmission power level as well as the number of transmissions might be used to optimize the packet reception rate of the link with the current parent (*Link Quality Based Policy* (LQB)). According to [7], increasing the transmission power level does not guarantee a better link quality. However, if LQB is based on this parameter, it should help making the links from the transitional region be more stable and, therefore, in many cases, should still increase the link quality as shown by the experiments in [4].

Obviously, these are just examples and a more exhaustive classification of policies and an analysis of their characteristics must be performed and is left for future work. However, in order to show their potential effects, we present some results of GEM combined with LQB and compare it to only using GEM.

5   Experimental Results

For the experiments presented in this paper we used 10 Tmote Sky motes based on the TI MSP430 microcontroller with a CC2420 radio module located in an office environment. The nodes were distributed in a room of 4.8×2.4 meters and the initial transmission power levels were set to one of the lowest possible values in oder to organize them into a multihop network.

There are some routing module settings that need to be mentioned. We have used a moving average to estimate the link quality with a window size of 10 (see [3]). The acceptable number of missed packets is equal to 5, after which the entry is deleted from the routing table. The routing table size was set to 10, so that all the nodes had equal chances to be selected as parents for packet forwarding. Initially, all nodes communicate at power level $l_i = 2$ (range is $[1..31]$).

We have tested the three metrics from related work and compared them in the first set of experiments with GEM without using any policy (GEM-off). In the second set of experiments we investigated the effect of the LQB policy (GEM-lqb) and compared it to GEM-off.

5.1   GEM Without Policies

In this set of experiments we evaluated the ETX, GEM-off, SPF and SR metrics for the case of 1, 2 and 3 maximum available transmissions and equally fixed transmission power levels. In our setting, the experiment lasted 100 seconds and was repeated a total number of five times. The graphs present the average of these five experiments.

As evaluation criteria we have included the end-to-end packet success rate, which shows the percentage of successfully received packets from each node in the network; energy consumption of the selected path from each node; hop distribution along the path from each node to the sink; route stability, that is, the average number of parent changes during one experiment; and route maintenance overhead, that is, how much information needs to be sent accross links to maintain the routing tree.

End-to-End Success Rate. The three graphs on the left-hand side of Fig. 3 show the percentage of packets which were successufully delivered to the sink node by each one of the nodes. The SPF metric has the worst behavior because it selects the minimal-hop paths and, therefore, the longest low quality links

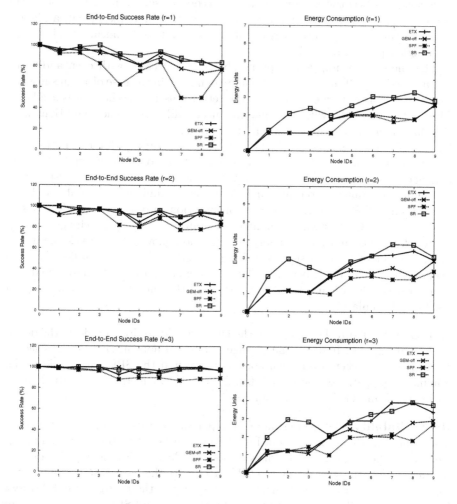

Fig. 3. End-to-End success rate and energy consumption distribution in case of 1 to 3 transmissions

to route packets to the sink. GEM is not influenced by any policy and reflects energy consumption and gain as a simple ratio. However, it shows nearly the same level of packet success rate as ETX. The reason for this is that the links from the transitional region are unstable, and, therefore, usually not considered for routing packets. This does not happen as a result of blacklisting but rather because the packets are received accidentally via such links. The SR metric shows a good packet success rate, since it is targeted at maximizing this parameter characteristic.

Energy Consumption. The three graphs on the right-hand side of Fig. 3 display the energy demands of using the selected path from each node. In all our examples we calculate the energy consumption of a path in energy units. One energy unit is the amount of energy needed to send a packet at the lowest possible transmission power level ($l = 1$). Using the Tmote Sky specification it is easy to estimate how many energy units are spent if communication takes place with higher power levels.

The energy consumption of paths obviously increases with each additional retransmission. SPF has the lowest energy demands in the case of 1 transmission. However, this is not true anymore if the retransmission mechanism is available. This is because links with low qualities need additional send operations and, therefore, increase energy consumption of paths.

The SR metric shows the highest energy consumption for the paths from nearly every node. This makes sense since it is the only metric that does not take energy consumption into account. ETX does this indirectly by estimating the number of transmissions and SPF does it by minimizing the number of hops.

ETX and GEM both take energy consumption into account (ETX is just a special case of GEM with the number of transmissions approaching infinity). However, the distribution of energy consumption shows that considering an infinite number of transmissions still leads to energy losses (according to these experiments up to 30%), because ETX considers all paths to be undirected (see formula (6)), which is not the case considering the energy demands of the path itself (see formula (4)).

Hop Distribution. The graph on the left-hand side of Fig. 4 reflects the depth of the routing tree. It shows the average number of hops needed by the selected path to route packets from each node. As expected the SPF metric selects the minimal hops paths to route packets whereas the SR metric selects the longest paths. ETX and GEM behave similarly.

Route Stability. The average number of parent changes during one experiment is presented in the right graph of Fig. 4 and reflects the stability of the routing tree. As can be seen, the results show a good correlation with the hop distribution metrics. The paths selected by the SPF metric are the most stable, whereas SR shows the least stability and might lead to cycles in the routing tree. ETX and GEM behave similarly and have values between SR and SPF.

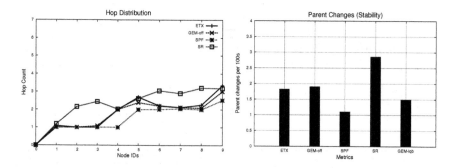

Fig. 4. Hop distribution and routing tree stability

Route Maintenance Overhead. For all metrics, the amount of data required for route maintenance is relatively low. SPF simply forwards a hop count to the sink. Analogously, SR propagates the product of the link qualities to the sink, whereas ETX sends the expected number of transmissions. GEM requires the two values $Exp(Gain_{path})$ and $Exp(Energy_{path})$ to make its decision.

In general, without any policy, GEM shows a slightly worse end-to-end success rate than SR and ETX but considerable gains in energy that allow it to influence the success rate if needed by the application using helper techniques like retransmissions and transmission power level tuning. Theoretically, since GEM-off tries to maximize the ratio of expected end-to-end packet success rate and energy consumption, the losses in end-to-end success rate are expected to be proportional to the gains in energy. However, in practice, link qualities are not uniformly distributed. Links from the transitional region show high variations in link quality and, therefore, the link quality estimator degrades their value as candidates to be part of the selected route in stable scenarios. This makes GEM select good quality paths even for the case where retransmissions are not available, and show comparatively high energy savings.

5.2   GEM Combined with LQB

In this set of experiments we use GEM in combination with the LQB policy. The initial power level was chosen to be the same as in previous experiments $l_i = 2$. We have implemented the LQB policy to increment the transmission power level l_i by one, if at some moment p_i appears to be less than 50% and decrement l_i if the link quality is over 95%, which are some intuitive values for our scenario. We compare the GEM-lqb with GEM-off results and analyse the policy behavior in case of no retransmissions. We have used the same evaluation criteria as for the previous section, but have added convergence, which is a policy-specific criteria that indicates whether or not changes to the power level eventually stabilize.

End-to-End Success Rate. GEM-lqb shows an about 15% better success rate than GEM-off (Fig. 5, top left graph). The reason for this is the influence of the policy, which has increased the transmission power levels where needed to make individual nodes communicate with better quality.

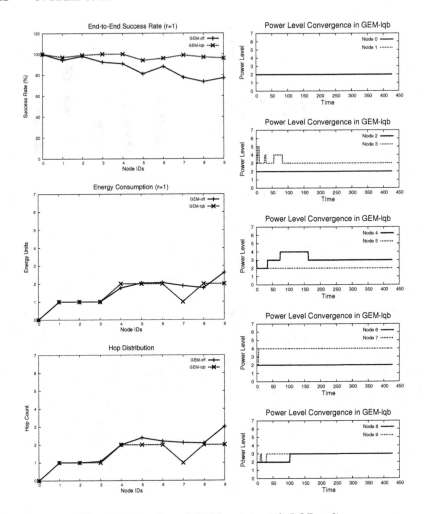

Fig. 5. Evaluation of GEM-metric with LQB policy

Energy Consumption. In many cases the overall evergy consumption along the path from each node to the sink is minimized even if communication now needs more energy units for one send operation (Fig. 5, left center graph). Increasing the transmission power level by one makes a send operation only up to 10% more expensive (the dependency is nonlinear on the Tmote hardware). However, it might lead to the selection of a parent node which is closer to the sink but still provides good gains. For nodes 7-9 the number of hops to the sink was minimized by increasing the transmission power range and, therefore, the energy demands were heavily reduced.

Hop Distribution. Small changes in transmission power levels have minimized the depth of the routing tree to be two hops instead of three as in the previous set of experiments (Fig. 5, bottom left graph), leading to a shorter tree.

Route Stability. Since the overall number of hops decreased and the selected routes were of a better quality, the average number of parent changes for GEM-lbq is lower than that of GEM-off (1.5 instead of 2, as shown in Fig. 4).

Route Maintenance Overhead. The LQB policy does not generate any overhead by means of additional packets or packet fields. Its decision is solely based on local information.

Convergence. In the graphs on the right-hand side of Fig. 5, we show the transmission power level of nodes 1 – 10 during the first 450 seconds of the experiment. We can observe that GEM-lbq does not perform any further changes after about 160 s. However, in general convergence is not guaranteed. It might be interesting to study the conditions under which convergence can be guaranteed, but for now, we assume that it is the responsibility of the policy to ensure that this is the case.

A more detailed analysis of policy types and their specific characteristics like convergence, applicability to certain scenarios, the extents of influence on end-to-end packet success rate and energy consumption, etc. still need further research.

6   Conclusion and Future Work

In this paper we have shown that the choice of a metric for the construction of routing structures needs to explicitely take energy into account. This is especially true for long-running monitoring applications. We have proposed a new routing metric GEM and presented its mathematical foundation together with some application-specific policy examples that make it able to adapt to application needs and specifics of the environment. Our mathematical model covers most routing metrics found in the literature and present them as special cases of it. The evaluation results show that the application of GEM alone provides considerable energy savings with equivalent end-to-end packet success rate when compared to other metrics. Moreover, the resulting routing tree is naturally structured and, therefore, has good stability. GEM is parameterizable and benefits from a combination with additional application-specific policies. However, there is still a number of interesting questions that we would like to address in the future, such as a more systematic classification of policies, their convergence characteristics, connectivity, general applicability, etc. All these topics together with more thorough testing in simulation and real-life experiments are left for future work.

References

1. D. Couto, D. Aguayo, J. Bicket, R. Morris, A High-Throughput Path Metric for Multi-Hop Wireless Routing, M.I.T. Computer Science and Artificial Intelligence Laboratory, September 2003.
2. R. Draves, J. Padhye, B. Zill, Comparison of Routing Metrics for Static Multi-Hop Wireless Networks, Microsoft Research, 2004.

3. A. Woo , T. Tong , D. Culler, Taming the underlying challenges of reliable multihop routing in sensor networks, Proc. of the 1st intl. conf. on Embedded networked sensor systems, November 05-07, 2003, Los Angeles, California, USA.

4. D. Son, B. Krishnamachari, J. Heidemann, Experimental study of the effects of Transmission Power Control and Blacklisting in Wireless Sensor Networks, In Proc. of SECON (2004), Santa Clara, California, USA, October 4-7, 2004.

5. O. Gnawali, M. Yarvis, J. Heidemann, R. Govindan, Interaction of Retransmission, Blacklisting, and Routing Metrics for Reliability in Sensor Network Routing, In Proc. of SECON (2004), October 2004.

6. D. D. Couto, D. Aguayo, B. Chambers, and R. Morris. Performance of multihop wireless. First Workshop on Hot Topics in Networks (HotNets-I), October 2002.

7. J. Zhao, R. Govindan, Understanding Packet Delivery Performance in Dense Wireless Sensor Networks, In Proc. of SenSys'03, Los Angeles, California, USA, 2003.

8. M. Kubisch, H. Karl, A. Wolisz, L.C. Zhong, and J. Rabaey, Distributed Algorithms for Transmission Power Control in Wireless Sensor Networks, Wireless Communications and Networking (WCNC'03), March 2003.

9. M. Carvalho, C. Margi, K. Obraczka, J. Gracia-Luna-Aceves, Modeling Energy Consumption in Single-Hop IEEE 802.11 Ad Hoc Networks, University of California Santa Cruz, 2004.

10. A. Salhieh, J. Weinmann, M. Kochhal, and L. Schwiebert, Power Efficient Topologies for Wireless Sensor Networks, ICPP 2001, September 2001.

11. C. Shurgers and M.B. Srivastava, Energy Efficient Routing in Wireless Sensor Networks, MILCOM'01, September 2001.

12. R.C. Shah and J.M. Rabaey, Energy Aware Routing for Low Energy Ad Hoc Sensor Networks, WCNC2002, March 2002.

On the Scalability of Routing Integrated Time Synchronization

János Sallai[1], Branislav Kusý[1], Ákos Lédeczi[1], and Prabal Dutta[2]

[1] Institute for Software Integrated Systems, Vanderbilt University,
2015 Terrace Place, Nashville, TN 37203, USA
{sallai, kusy, akos}@isis.vanderbilt.edu
[2] Computer Science Division, University of California,
Berkeley, CA 94720, USA
prabal@cs.berkeley.edu

Abstract. Reactive time synchronization is becoming increasingly popular in the realm of wireless sensor networks. Unlike proactive protocols, traditionally implemented as a standalone middleware service that provides a virtual global time to the application layer, reactive techniques establish a common reference time base *post facto*, i.e. after an event of interest has occurred. In this paper, we present the formal error analysis of a representative reactive technique, the Routing Integrated Time Synchronization protocol (RITS). We show that in the general case, the presence of clock skews cause RITS to scale poorly with the size of the network. Then we identify a special class of sensor network applications that are resilient to this scalability limit. For applications outside this class, we propose an in-network skew compensation strategy that makes RITS scale well with both network size and node density. We provide experimental results using a 45-node network of Berkeley MICA2 motes.

1 Introduction

In a large class of sensor network (*sensornet*) applications, such as environmental monitoring [1], [2], target tracking [3], or countersniper systems [4], [5], sensor nodes are deployed in the environment to detect certain physical phenomena, or *events*. Typically, the sensed data is tagged with the location of the sensor node and the time of event detection. The location and time of event allow the sensornet to combine data from multiple sensors into high level information, that is, to perform *data fusion*, independently from the time when the data is received at a data fusion node. However, the data fusion can be only achieved if the time tags of events have a common time base across multiple sensors, or in other words, the sensors are *time-synchronized*.

The most common way to achieve time synchronization (*timesync*) is to use one of the many *proactive* timesync protocols [6], [7]. The term *proactive* is used because these protocols establish a virtual global time base in advance, namely, before the sensornet application starts registering events from

K. Römer, H. Karl, and F. Mattern (Eds.): EWSN 2006, LNCS 3868, pp. 115–131, 2006.
© Springer-Verlag Berlin Heidelberg 2006

the environment. Commonly, proactive protocols use periodic message broadcasting to compensate for different sources of error (e.g. clock drifts, clock frequency noise, and clock glitches). The need for periodic message exchange, however, conflicts with the power constraints and lifetime requirements of sensornet applications.

The observation that the global virtual time of an event is *not* used at the node registering the event, but only at the data fusion node, together with the fact that proactive protocols suffer from severe messaging overhead, lead to the development of power-aware *reactive* timesync protocols [8], [7], [9]. The general idea of reactive approaches is *not* to synchronize the local clocks, but instead to timestamp the events using unsynchronized local clocks. Synchronization takes place *after* the event had been detected; henceforth, this approach is often called *post-facto* synchronization.

We concentrate on the analysis of the Routing Integrated Time Synchronization protocol (RITS) [8] that integrates post-facto timesync into a routing service. RITS, as well as reactive techniques in general, is superior to many proactive timesync protocols with respect to communication overhead. However, by decreasing the number of synchronization messages, we trade precision for power saving. While with a proactive protocol a node can frequently update its knowledge of the virtual global time, RITS is limited to using routing messages for synchronization.

In this paper, we show that the timesync error of RITS can significantly grow in the presence of clock skews and communication delays in message routing. We provide a formal analysis to explain the effects of error in such cases. The analysis of the components of RITS error shows that RITS is well-suited, without any enhancements, for applications where the sensor fusion algorithm works on time difference of arrival (TDOA) of events that are collocated in space and time. For the general case, we propose an in-network skew compensation strategy that can be adopted to improve the timesync error of RITS in particular, and reactive timesync protocols in general.

Based on the observation that information on clock skews of neighboring nodes is implicitly present in the timestamped messages they exchange, nodes can maintain a neighbor table storing skew information without any communication overhead. RITS converts the event timestamps from the local time of the sender node to the local time of the receiver node as the message is being passed from hop to hop along the routing path. We propose that the conversion of the timestamp includes compensation for the clock skew between the sender and the receiver at every hop.

It is imperative that sensornet applications be scalable not only with network size, but also with node density. In a dense network, however, it is not possible to store skew information for all neighbors. Our skew compensation approach addresses this requirement with a space efficient skew table maintenance strategy that operates with predefined table size. We store skew information only for a small selected subset of the neighbors. Unknown skews are estimated based on the locally available skew information.

Our experimental results, acquired from a 10-hop network of 45 MICA2 motes with artificially introduced routing delays, show that employing skew compensation reduces the timesync error of RITS from $29\mu s$ to $5.3\mu s$ on average.

We organize the paper as follows: Section 2 provides a detailed description of the leading reactive timesync protocols found in the literature. We formally analyze the timesync errors of RITS and discuss the implications on the general applicability of RITS in Section 4. To support sensornet applications in the general case, Section 5 presents an in-network skew compensation technique that improves the scalability of RITS with network size, communication delays, and node density. Finally, we offer our conclusions in Section 6.

2   Reactive Time Synchronization Protocols

Traditional *proactive* timesync protocols require the clocks of sensor nodes to be synchronized before an event happens. Because the clock rates of the nodes drift and vary in random and unpredictable ways, depending on the required timesync accuracy of sensornet applications, a non-trivial amount of system resources needs to be spent to keep the clock rate information accurate and actual. *Post-facto* (or *reactive*) timesync protocols propose to start the synchronization process after the event is detected to avoid performing timesync when it is not needed. This way nodes can be kept in a low-power sleep mode, conserving energy during periods of inactivity.

Post-facto synchronization was first suggested in [10] and later extended in [11]. The authors propose two forms of post-facto synchronization: *single-pulse synchronization* which requires advance calibration to be accurate, but reconstructs the global timescale quickly, and *post-facto synchronization with RBS* which takes longer to converge but does not require any a priori knowledge. The approach described in [9] transforms timestamps exchanged between nodes to the local time of the receiver, rather than adjusting the clocks to the global time base. The low message overhead of this method renders the protocol suitable for sensornets. Finally, the approach advocated in [8] claims to provide accurate and instantaneous timesync using no extra radio messages and requiring no a priori information. We delve into the details of these synchronization schemes in the remainder of this section.

Single-Pulse Synchronization. Single-pulse synchronization [11] requires a third party node, *a beacon*, to broadcast a synchronization pulse right after an event of interest was detected in the network. Nodes that receive the pulse use it as an instantaneous time reference and normalize their timestamps of the event detection to the synchronization pulse. This scheme works well for short distances (i.e. within the broadcast range of a single node) provided the stimulus timestamps are recorded close in time to the synchronization pulse. The three main error sources of this scheme were characterized as the receiver clock skew, variable delays in receivers, and propagation delay of the synchronization pulse. The clock skew error is the most significant source of error, therefore single-pulse scheme works the best, if a priori calibration of clock frequencies is performed and clock skew estimates are used to correct the stimulus timestamps.

Post-facto Synchronization with Reference Broadcast. The second scheme proposed in [7] resolves the drawbacks of single-pulse synchronization scheme: it achieves timesync over large distances, and synchronizes nodes that have no mutually shared information. After a stimulus event is detected in the network, an algorithm estimating the clock skews between the nodes is executed and the resulting clock skew estimates are used to correct the stimulus event timestamps in the past. This scheme resolves the problems of the single-pulse, but also brings in some disadvantages: the RBS estimator needs multiple synchronization pulses to obtain clock skew estimates, so the timesync is not achieved instantaneously. If a long time passes between the stimulus event and skew estimator conversion, the clock skew estimates may significantly differ from the clock skews at the event detection introducing additional errors.

Time Synchronization with Timestamp Conversion. This protocol [9] proposes not to synchronize the local clocks of the devices, but instead to generate timestamps using unsynchronized local clocks. When the locally generated timestamps are passed from a node to node in the network, they are converted to the local time of the receiving device. Due to the limited precision of the timestamp conversion used, the algorithm uses time intervals as a lower and upper bound for the exact value. Comparison of timestamps relies on a special interval arithmetic, hence there are cases when the temporal ordering of timestamps cannot be determined. One distinctive feature of this approach is that the timestamp transformation has the following correctness property: the partial ordering of event timestamps in the local time of a give node reported by the algorithm is a subset of the total ordering of the times of the event in real time. This approach explicitly targets communication of timestamps over long distances, making it particularly suitable for multi-hop ad hoc networks.

3   The Routing Integrated Time Synchronization Protocol

RITS [8] is a reactive timesync protocol, which can be used to obtain times of event detections at multiple observers in the local time of the sink node(s). We provide a more detailed description of the protocol later when formally analyze the timesync errors it introduces.

From the application's point of view, RITS is an extension of the routing service with a well-defined interface. The interface defines commands to send and timestamp a data packet, a callback function to signal the reception of a packet, and a command to query the timestamp of a received packet. On detecting an event, the application on the sensor node generates a data packet containing the event information, and timestamps it with the value of the local time of detection. It forwards the packet with the timestamp to the routing service, which delivers it to the sink. RITS places no assumptions on the network topology or routing algorithm beyond those that are required by the application. Rather than performing explicit timesync after the event of interest is detected, RITS performs inter-node time translation along the routing path from an observer node to the sink: as the data packet travels from node to node in the network, RITS converts the corresponding timestamp from the local time of the sender to that of the recipient. When the packet arrives at the sink, the routing service signals an event to the application layer that a packet has been received. The application can then query the routing layer for the timestamp of the received packet, which is returned in the local time of the sink.

The prototype implementation of RITS builds on the Directed Flood Routing Framework (DFRF) [12]. DFRF is a generic routing framework that supports rapid prototyping and implementation of large class of application specific routing protocols that are based on directed flooding. Integrating reactive timesync with the routing service has several benefits over a standalone timesync service:

- **Coupling of event data and event timestamps.** There is a tight logical coupling between event information and the corresponding timestamps. RITS retains this coupling: in a data packet, event data and timestamps are physically collocated. RITS thus implements *implicit* timesync, that is, the flow of time information is embedded in the flow of data. There are no pure timesync messages, hence RITS has virtually no communication overhead.
- **Network-transparent event timestamps.** As data packets propagate in the network, RITS converts the corresponding time stamp hop by hop to the local time of the recipient node. As a result, all data packets received by a given node contain event timestamps in the recipient node's local time, independently from where in the network the events originated.
- **Packet aggregation.** Packet aggregation helps decrease the number of message transmissions. In fact, not only does the number of radio messages decrease, but also the overall payload size. This is because in an aggregated radio message, n data packets (containing event information and event timestamp) share only one transmit timestamp.
- **Packet filtering.** Through packet filtering support, it is possible to discard outdated messages at intermediate nodes *enroute* to the destination, thus decreasing the message load.
- **Orthogonality to the routing policy.** DFRF allows for the customization of routing behavior via routing policies. RITS is orthogonal to the policies, that is, the same time conversion is used with different routing behaviors.

4   Analysis of the Error of RITS

The RITS protocol claims to achieve highly accurate instantaneous post-facto timesync without using extra radio messages [8]. RITS provides these properties only for a relatively small subset of sensornet applications, for which a particular set of assumptions is fulfilled. We formally express the error of RITS and derive the set of properties that RITS requires from sensornet applications.

As noted in both [11] and [8], reactive protocols are susceptible to multiple sources of error. The two most egregious ones are the error caused by different clock rates of the nodes on the routing path, and the error in timestamping the radio message arrival.

We use the following notation: we have a set of N nodes that can be receivers r_i and/or senders s_i, $i \in \{1, \ldots, N\}$. Each node has its own local clock that measures the local time t_i. We denote a fictious universal time with u. The offset of the local time from the universal time can change over time because the clock rate of a node can differ from the rate of universal time, we express the relation of the local and universal time as

$$t_i = \alpha_i u + \beta_i. \tag{1}$$

The clock skews α_i are assumed to be constant in the time interval a packet spends at node i. This assumption is justifiable for a reasonably fast routing service, nevertheless the crystal clock rates, though slowly, do change in the real hardware. Furthermore, we assume that the clock skews α_i are independent random variables from a symmetric distribution with mean one (that is, the *universal time rate*). We impose no assumptions on the initial clock offsets β_i.

We express the synchronization mechanism of RITS as follows: receiver r_k synchronizes with the sender s_j by receiving a synchronization message m_i. We denote the sender timestamp of message transmission by y^s_{ij} and the receiver timestamp of message arrival by y^r_{ik}. Both y^s_{ij} and y^r_{ik} are known to the receiver. If e^s_{ij} and e^r_{ik} are timestamping errors of sender and receiver, respectively, and u_i is the universal time when the message was transmitted, then

$$y^s_{ij} = \alpha_j u_i + \beta_j + e^s_{ij} \tag{2}$$
$$y^r_{ik} = \alpha_k u_i + \beta_k + e^r_{ik}. \tag{3}$$

Similarly, if the i-th node records the local time of an event E, we denote this timestamp as y_{Ei}.

According to [6] it is assumed that both e^r_{ik}, and e^s_{ij} are independent identically distributed random variables with zero mean. Since low-power transceivers have limited communication range, we can further assume that the propagation delay between the sender and receiver is negligible, therefore the universal time of sending and receiving message m_i are the same (i.e. u_i).

If the receiver (r_k) wishes to transform a time of stimulus event E from the sender's (s_j) timeline to its own timeline, provided a radio message m_i has been sent, the receiver performs the following calculation:

$$y_{Ek} = y_{Ej} + y^r_{ik} - y^s_{ij}. \tag{4}$$

It is important to note that the timestamp conversion of RITS does not consider the clock skews. Henceforth, we expect that skew related errors will accumulate.

4.1   Error Along a Routing Path

Now let us apply the transformation iteratively as a message is being passed along routing path to get the following general result. Timestamps converted to the local times of the second, the third node and the n-th node ($y_{01}^r = y_{E1}$) are:

$$y_{E2} = y_{E1} + y_{12}^r - y_{11}^s$$
$$y_{E3} = y_{23}^r - (y_{22}^s - y_{12}^r) - (y_{11}^s - y_{E1})$$
$$y_{En} = y_{E(n-1)} + y_{(n-1)n}^r - y_{(n-1)(n-1)}^s = y_{(n-1)n}^r - \sum_{i=1}^{n-1}(y_{ii}^s - y_{(i-1)i}^r).$$

We denote the timestamping error introduced by the i-th node with e_i and define it as $e_1 = e_{11}^s$ and $e_i = e_{ii}^s - e_{(i-1)i}^r$ for $i > 1$ and use e_i along with Equations 2 and 3 to further rewrite y_{En}:

$$y_{En} = y_{(n-1)n}^r - \sum_{i=1}^{n-1}\alpha_i(u_i - u_{i-1}) - \sum_{i=1}^{n-1}e_i.$$

Furthermore, for the sake of simplicity, let us assume that for all i, $u_i - u_{i-1}$ is constant, that is, the message spends equal amount of time at each node along the routing path. Let us denote this constant with τ. This way we can separate the first summation into skew-independent and skew-dependent components:

$$y_{En} = y_{(n-1)n}^r - \tau(n - 1) - \tau\sum_{i=1}^{n-1}(\alpha_i - 1) - \sum_{i=1}^{n-1}e_i, \qquad (5)$$

where the first term is the time when the message arrives at the last node, the second term is the age of the packet, the third and fourth terms are errors introduced by the clock skews and the message timestamping, respectively.

4.2   RITS and TDOA Measurements

In an important class of monitoring applications, sensor fusion works with time differences of arrival (TDOA) of events. Let us assume that the event E was detected at time u_E by two nodes r_1 and r_1', and the two time tags arrived to the data fusion node along two different paths P and P', such that $P = r_1, \ldots, r_n$ and $P' = r_1', \ldots, r_m'$. We further know that the final node of both P and P' is the same (the data fusion node), so $\alpha_n = \alpha_m' = \alpha_{df}$. Without loss of generality we can assume that $n < m$. Consequently, we express the error that RITS introduces to the TDOA data when routing the timestamps to the data fusion node:

$$y_{Em}' - y_{En} = \tau\sum_{i=1}^{n-1}(\alpha_i - \alpha_i') + \tau\sum_{i=n}^{m-1}(\alpha_{df} - \alpha_i') + \sum_{i=1}^{n-1}e_i - \sum_{i=1}^{m-1}e_i'. \qquad (6)$$

Due to the assumptions on the distribution of the skews and the message time-stamping errors, the expected values of the first, third and fourth terms are zero. Interestingly, the expected value of the second term is $\tau(m - n - 1)\alpha_{df}$. This means that the clock skew of the data fusion node introduces an error proportional to the clock skew of the data fusion node and the difference of delivery times of the messages.

The variance of the two skew related terms sum up to $\tau[(n-1)+(m-1)]V(\alpha)$, meaning that the variance is proportional to the time the messages spend at a given hop and to the sum of the lengths of the paths. The message timestamping related error has a variance of $[(n-1)+(m-1)]V(e_i)$, which grows with the sum of the path lengths.

An important special case is when the two paths overlap. Without loss of generality, we assume that $P' = r_1,\ldots,r_j,\ldots,r'_{j+1},\ldots,r'_m$. Using partially overlapping paths, the TDOA calculated by RITS changes as follows:

$$y'_{Em} - y_{En} = \tau \sum_{i=j+1}^{n-1} (\alpha_i - \alpha'_i) + \tau \sum_{i=n}^{m-1} (\alpha_{df} - \alpha'_i) + \sum_{i=1}^{n-1} e_i - \sum_{i=1}^{m-1} e'_i. \quad (7)$$

Since the skew related errors introduced by the nodes that are on both paths cancel out, the variance of the skew related error decreases to $\tau[(n-1)+(m-1)-j]V(\alpha)$. That is, the variance of the skew related errors is proportional to the time the packet spend at the nodes and to the length of the disjoint regions of the routing paths. Another factor is that the event times need to be close to each other. Otherwise, the clock skew of the sender node introduces a large error. In particular, the events should be kept on a node for as short period of time as possible.

4.3   Implications of Theoretical Results

We provide typical expected timestamping errors and clock skews for the most common sensornet platforms to match the formal results of the previous section to real world hardware in Table 1. We further concentrate on the applicability of the RITS protocol and show an experimental test case, where the timesync error of RITS does not scale well with the number of hops. Consequently, we provide a set of properties that RITS requires from the sensornet applications. Finally, we use the error analysis results and suggest two improvements of RITS.

Applicability of RITS. The design of RITS was heavily influenced by the requirements of a specific sensornet application, acoustic event localization [4]:

- only time differences of arrivals are required to localize an acoustic event,
- fast routing to the sink is required, because the event source is mobile,

Table 1. Survey of timesync errors expected from timestamping and clock skews for common sensornet platforms [13], [14]

Platform	Timestamping error	Clock skew error
Mica2 external crystal (32 kHz, CC1000 radio)	30.5 μs (= 1 clock tick)	50ppm typically 30.5 μs per second
Mica2 internal oscillator (7MHz, CC1000 radio)	1.4 μs	50ppm typically $\leq 20\mu s$ per second
Telos internal oscillator (8MHz, CC2420 radio)	0.125 μs	50ppm

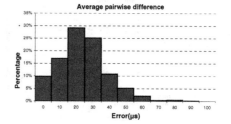

Fig. 1. Large scale network detects an event, the timestamps are then routed along a spanning tree to the sink node

Fig. 2. The histogram of average errors for the experiment with simulated transmission delays of 5 seconds at each node

- preservation of temporal ordering of events is not a requirement, and
- detected events are close to each other in space and time.

These properties are important because they place bounds on the terms in Formula 6 that contribute to the error of RITS. Maximum RITS error of $80\mu s$ and the average error of $8\mu s$ were reported in [8] using Mica2 platform and 7MHz internal clock in a 10 hop network. However, only a small class of applications can achieve similar results, the main problem being the error introduced by the (uncompensated) clock skews. Table 1 shows that this error can become significant even over moderate time intervals.

We experimentally verified the poor scalability of RITS if the routing time to the sink node increases. We carried out an experiment similar to the one described in [8]: we used 45 Mica2 motes arranged in a grid forming a 10-hop network. Events that triggered nodes within a certain radius were periodically simulated at random points in the network. Each event was simultaneously detected at all triggered nodes, and the timestamps of these detections were sent to the data fusion node (sink), as shown in Figure 1. We introduced an artificial delay of five seconds between receiving and forwarding the message, thus inflating the time intervals it takes to route the event detection times. The maximum and average synchronization errors are computed as the maximum and average pairwise difference of all timestamps received by the sink that correspond to the same event detection. Compared to the non-delayed case [8], the measured maximum and average synchronization errors across 700 simulated events grew significantly from $80\mu s$ to $265\mu s$, and from $8\mu s$ to $29\mu s$, respectively. The histogram of average errors can be seen in Figure 2.

Mitigating the Error of RITS: Routing Strategies. Formula 6 shows that if we fix a routing path P, then the variance of the term $\tau \sum(\alpha_i - 1)$ grows with the increased routing time to the sink. This causes a large timesync error along the path P. The important observation is that this error is consistent, i.e. has a relatively small variance, as it is caused by the timestamping errors alone, since the skew related errors cancel out.

We verified this experimentally by deploying 50 Mica2 nodes logically arranged on a line, forming a 50-hop network. The first node, the coordinator, broadcasts a RITS packet with its current time. Other nodes retransmit the

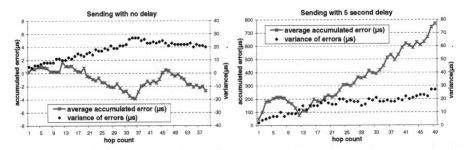

Fig. 3. 50 nodes arranged on a line experiment: errors of the RITS calculated time compared to a single-node time for the no-delay and 5 seconds delay strategies are shown. The accumulated errors are averaged over multiple runs and we plot the variance of these errors.

packet upon receiving it, until the packet reaches the last node. The coordinator overhears all retransmissions, uses RITS to convert the timestamp in the packet to its local time and records the error of the timestamp after each hop. This allowed us to study the error of RITS across multiple hops. Figure 3 shows the accumulated error after each hop, averaged over multiple rounds. To make the clock skew errors prevail over timestamping errors we introduced a delayed strategy for the RITS packet retransmission: a node waits 5 seconds after receiving the packet and only then retransmits it.

The promising fact is that the variance of the accumulated error is the same in both experiments, which means that the motes introduce significant, but consistent error. Consequently, we specify the applications requirements and propose improvements to the RITS protocol to make it scale for large networks:

- The original RITS protocol did not discuss the implications of using different routing strategies. We observe the advantage of overlapping routes, and suggest using spanning tree routing which ensures this property. In contrast, gossip or epidemic protocols which can result in dynamic routing paths, will not support scalability of RITS.
- The sink node introduces large error if the time between receiving two different events is long. This error is caused by the clock skew error of the sink and can be mitigated by synchronizing the sink with a high precision external clock source.

With these improvements, RITS scales well with the number of hops and communication delays, provided an application has the following properties:

- Applications need to be TDOA based; we know that a routing path introduces large error which is unknown to the sink node, therefore, relating this time to any global time scale is not possible,
- the stimulus event detections must be located within a small neighborhood, as shown in Figure 1, so that the significant portions of the spanning tree paths overlap.

5   Skew Compensation

The main features of RITS were that it does not require any a priori information, does not need to know or maintain the skews of the nodes, and uses no
additional timesync messages to achieve synchronization. The improvements to
RITS discussed in the previous paragraph did not need to sacrifice any of these
features. Supporting a general class of applications, however, drives us to drop
one of these properties. We show that it is possible to estimate the clock skews
without using additional timesync messages, provided that there exists a lower
bound on the frequency of the stimulus events in the deployment area.

5.1   RITS with Clock Skew Compensation

Compensating for the skews between the clocks of the nodes along the routing
path can significantly decrease the variance of the timesync error. Recall that
RITS converts the event timestamps from the local time of the sender node to
that of the receiver node as the message is being passed from hop to hop. Without skew compensation, this conversion is achieved by adding the offset of the
clocks of the sender and the receiver nodes to the event timestamp in the local
time of the sender to yield the event timestamp in the local time of the receiver.

When skew compensation is employed, the conversion is more involved. We
do not assume that a node knows its clock skew from the nominal clock rate
(referred to as the *absolute skew*), however, it is assumed that it knows the
skews of their neighbors relative to its local clock rate (referred to as the *relative
skew*). This means that there is no global clock rate to which the elapsed time
at each hop could be converted.

The absolute skew of node i is defined as its skew relative to the nominal
clock rate f_{nom}, that is, $\alpha_i = \frac{f_i}{f_{nom}}$. Relative skew of node i with respect to node
j is defined as $\alpha_{i,j} = \frac{f_i}{f_j}$.

5.2   The Approach

The proposed skew compensation approach is the following. When receiving a
packet – which includes event description and event timestamp in the sender's
local time – the receiver node calculates the *age of the packet* in the sender's time:

$$age^s = y_m^s - y_E^s,$$

where y_m^s is the transmit timestamp of the message and y_E^s is the event timestamp, both in the sender's local time. Because a clock skew is present, the age
of the packet needs to be converted from the sender's clock rate to the receiver's
clock rate, which is achieved simply by dividing it with the relative skew.

$$age^r = \frac{age^s}{\alpha_{s,r}}$$

Subtracting the converted packet age from the receive timestamp of the message
yields the event timestamp in the receiver's local time.

$$y_E^r = y_m^r - age^r$$

Expressing the conversion in one formula gives

$$y_E^r = y_m^r - \frac{y_m^s - y_E^s}{\alpha_{s,r}}.$$

Eventually, when the packet reaches the sink node, the event timestamp is converted to the sink node's local time. In contrast with RITS without skew compensation, the conversion takes into account differences of *both offsets and skews* between the sink node and nodes registering the events.

5.3   Measuring the Relative Skew

Relative skew of a neighbor w.r.t. a given node is computed as the fraction of the number of ticks of the neighbor's clock and the number of ticks of the local clock during a reference time interval.

While determining the clock offset of neighboring nodes requires only one common reference point in time, acquiring their relative skew necessitates having two of them. The estimation of relative skews is based on a neighbor skew table, which contains records with the transmit and receive timestamps of the most recent message from the neighbor, as well as the most up-to-date relative skew to the neighbor, if known.

Maintenance of the skew table is carried out as follows. When a message is received, we locate the sender's record in the skew table. The record contains the transmit and receive timestamps of the previous message from the sender. The difference of the actual and the previous transmit timestamps (in Figure 4 denoted by y_{21}^s and y_{11}^s, respectively) gives the time elapsed between the two messages in the sender's clock. Similarly, the difference of the actual and the previous receive timestamps, $y_{22}^r - y_{12}^r$, gives the time elapsed between the two messages in the receiver's clock. The relative skew is the fraction of the two differences, which is exponentially averaged with the previously calculated skew value, and stored in the skew table.

Our approach employs an implicit skew measurement technique. All radio messages are timestamped by the sender and the receiver, regardless of message content. Since the relative skew information is implicitly carried in the message timestamps, measuring the skews requires no dedicated communication. This solution, however, has its caveat: since the clock frequencies of the devices are not

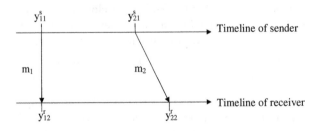

Fig. 4. Skew measurement

stable, relative skews become outdated if nodes communicate rarely. The problem can be solved by periodically generating dummy messages, though RITS leaves this to the application layer. A method to find the optimal beaconing period has already been proposed by Ganeriwal et al. in [15] and [16].

5.4   The Challenge of Memory Constraints

Networked sensor nodes are severely constrained devices, where RAM is a precious resource. It is not unusual that the operating system, the middleware services (multi-hop routing, timesync, etc.) and the application layer have to share no more than 4kB of RAM. The neighbor table that augments skew measurements and stores the relative skew values contains records in the following structure.

```
typedef struct {
    uint16_t nodeID;          // ID of the neighbor
    float    skew;            // relative skew w.r.t the neighbor
    uint32_t lastTxTimeStamp; // Tx timestamp of last recvd message
    uint32_t lastRxTimeStamp; // Rx timestamp of last recvd message
} neighborRec;
```

The size of this record is 14 bytes, which might seem negligibly small, however, sacrificing a few hundred bytes for a neighbor table of one of the many middleware components might not always be a viable option.

We face two conflicting constraints here: small memory footprint versus scalability with node density. If the size of the skew table is too small, skew compensation will fail in dense networks, whereas a large neighbor table is not affordable because of the memory constraints.

5.5   Maintaining a Bounded Skew Table

Clearly, the need for scalability with network density necessitates limiting the size of the skew table. Furthermore, we may want to control which neighbors' relative skews we store, and we need to decide how to compensate for the skews of those neighbors for which no skew information is available. Our approach is that a node stores the relative skews only for a subset of its neighbors. Using the stored values, the node estimates its relative skew to the rest of the neighbors.

The most important property of this strategy is that the absolute skew of the node itself does not influence which neighbors are stored in the skew table: this decision is made purely on the observed relative skew values of the neighbors. This way the skew compensation will work well even if the node itself has a significant absolute skew.

5.6   Estimation of Unknown Skews

An appealing strategy is to keep the skew information of neighbors having the *worst* absolute skews in the skew table, and not storing the relative skew information of the remaining *well-behaved* neighbors. When a packet is received from

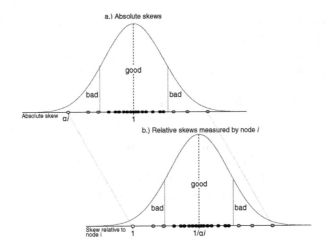

Fig. 5. Distribution of absolute and relative skews measured by an arbitrary node i. The white dot denotes node i, the grey and the black dots denote the *bad* and the *well-behaved* neighbors, respectively.

a *bad* neighbor, which would normally introduce a considerable skew related timesync error, the stored value is used for skew compensation. This way the worst timesync errors will be compensated for. When receiving a packet from a *good* neighbor, which has only minor contribution to the timesync error, we compensate with an estimate of the mean of the relative skews of the neighbors.

Since the absolute skews cannot be measured directly, the categorization of good and bad neighbors has to rely on the information carried in the relative skew measurements. The neighbor's relative skew values, as perceived by a node, are normally distributed with the same variance as the distribution of the absolute skews w.r.t. the nominal skew, but the values are centered around the reciprocal of the node's own absolute skew, not around 1. We can observe that the relative skews of the *good* neighbors fall close to the median of the measured values, while those of the *bad* neighbors are far from it.

If the bounded skew table is maintained such that the categorization of good and bad skews is based on their distance from the median of the measured skew values, the skew table will store the left and right tails of a random sample representing the relative skews of the neighbors (even if the clock rate of the local node significantly differs from the nominal rate). The values that are not stored must fall between the maximum skew of the left tail and the minimum skew of the right tail; from here, we estimate the unknown skews with the average of the two.

The corresponding table maintenance strategy is implemented as follows. The size of the skew table, denoted by n, is set to an even number. The skew records are sorted by the skew values. When the skew table is full, and a new skew measurement is completed, the new value is compared with the skews of the two records in the middle (at positions $\frac{n}{2}$ and $\frac{n}{2}+1$). If it is between the two values, it is discarded. If it is below (above) the two values, the record at position $\frac{n}{2}$

(at position $\frac{n}{2}+1$) is evicted, and the new measurement is inserted in the skew table. In a steady state, the two middle values give a lower and an upper bound on the skews of the neighbors that are not stored.

5.7   Experimental Results

We repeated the experiment described in Section 4.3 using RITS augmented with clock skew compensation. The 45 Mica2 motes were arranged in a grid forming a 10-hop network, using a sufficiently large neighbor table. As in the previous experiment, we introduced an artificial routing delay of five seconds at every hop, to allow skew related errors to manifest.

To test the performance of our skew compensation algorithm, we set the size of the skew table large enough to hold the skew information of all neighbors. As Figure 6 shows, employing in-network skew compensation drastically reduced the timesync error of RITS. Compared to the previous results (see Figure 2), the average synchronization errors decreased from $29\mu s$ to $2.8\mu s$. Not considering the bootup period of the skew compensation algorithm when the skew table is not populated, the maximum error decreased from $265\mu s$ to $44\mu s$.

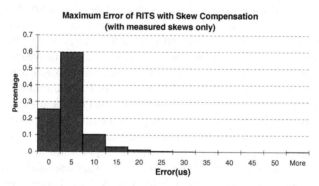

Fig. 6. The histogram of maximum errors for the experiment with a large skew table holding the skew values of all neighbors

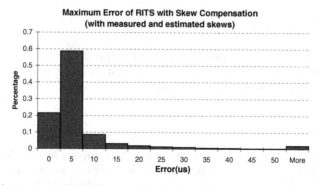

Fig. 7. The histogram of maximum errors for the experiment with a limited skew table holding the skew values of 6 neighbors

In the next experiment, we limited the size of the skew table to hold only six records. As expected, the measured timesync errors increased compared to the fully compensated case. Although the maximum error we experienced was $258\mu s$, which is comparable to the non-compensated case, only 1% of the errors were above $100\mu s$. This can be attributed to the drastically small neighbor table. However, as Figure 7 shows, skew compensation with partial skew information is still a significant improvement over the non-compensated case, as the average synchronization error was only $5.3\mu s$.

6   Conclusions and Future Work

The Routing Integrated Time Synchronization protocol was specifically designed with a single application in mind [4]. Although it was successfully tested in a number of medium-scale deployments, our analysis found that its scalability with network size and communication delay limits its general applicability.

In this paper we investigated the reasons for the scalability problems and presented an error analysis of RITS. We showed that the variance in clock rates is responsible for the largest time synchronization errors. We found that the clock skew related errors do not manifest in a special class of sensornet applications, where only the time difference of arrival of the registered events are of concern, and where event detections are close to each other in space and time. We presented an in-network skew compensation technique that improves the scalability of RITS, making it suitable for a wide range of sensornet applications.

We further plan to investigate scalability limits of RITS augmented with skew compensation. Since the skew measurement errors and the skew estimation errors are expected to propagate in a multiplicative fashion, the precision of the skew measurements and a probabilistic upper bound on the estimation error have to be controlled. This can be achieved by setting a proper lower and upper limit on the time difference of reception of the two messages that are used to measure the skew and by choosing the size of the neighbor table large enough, such that the skews of the *good* neighbors are bounded by a relatively small interval. Finding the proper values of these constants demands further research.

Acknowledgments

The DARPA/IXO NEST program has partially supported the research described in this paper. We also wish to thank Miklós Maróti and anonymous reviewers for their valuable comments on our work.

References

1. Xu, N., Rangwala, S., Chintalapudi, K.K., Ganesan, D., Broad, A., Govindan, R., Estrin, D.: A wireless sensor network for structural monitoring. SenSys '04: Proceedings of the 2nd international conference on Embedded networked sensor systems (2004) 13–24

2. West, B.W., Flikkema, P.G., Sisk, T., Koch, G.W.: Wireless sensor networks for dense spatio-temporal monitoring of the environment: A case for integrated circuit, system, and network design. 2001 IEEE CAS Workshop on Wireless Communications and Networking (2001)

3. Wang, H., Elson, J., Girod, L., Estrin, D., Yao, K.: Target classification and localization in a habitat monitoring application. Proc of IEEE ICASSP (2003)

4. Simon, G., Maróti, M., Lédeczi, A., Balogh, G., Kusý, B., Nádas, A., Pap, G., Sallai, J., Frampton, K.: Sensor network-based countersniper system. SenSys '04: Proceedings of the 2nd international conference on Embedded networked sensor systems (2004) 1–12

5. Lédeczi, A., Nádas, A., Völgyesi, P., Balogh, G., Kusý, B., Sallai, J., Pap, G., Dóra, S., Molnár, K., Maróti, M., Simon, G.: Countersniper system for urban warfare. ACM Transactions on Sensor Networks 1 (2005) 153–177

6. Maróti, M., Kusý, B., Simon, G., Lédeczi, A.: The flooding time synchronization protocol. SenSys '04: Proceedings of the 2nd international conference on Embedded networked sensor systems (2004) 39–49

7. Elson, J., Girod, L., Estrin, D.: Fine-grained network time synchronization using reference broadcasts. SIGOPS Oper. Syst. Rev. 36 (2002) 147–163

8. Kusy, B., Dutta, P., Levis, P., Maroti, M., Ledeczi, A., Culler, D.: Elapsed time on arrival: A simple and versatile primitive for canonical time synchronization services. International Journal of Ad Hoc and Ubiquitous Computing 2 (2006)

9. Römer, K.: Time synchronization in ad hoc networks. Proceedings of MobiHoc 2001 (2001)

10. Elson, J., Estrin, D.: Time synchronization for wireless sensor networks. Proceedings of the 15th International Parallel and Distributed Processing Symposium (IPDPS-01) (2001)

11. Elson, J.: Time synchronization in wireless sensor networks. Ph.D. Thesis (2003)

12. Maróti, M.: Directed flood-routing framework for wireless sensor networks. Proceedings of the 5th ACM/IFIP/USENIX international conference on Middleware (2004) 99–114

13. Hill, J., Culler, D.: Mica: A wireless platform for deeply embedded networks. IEEE Micro 22 (2002) 12–24

14. Polastre, J., Szewczyk, R., Culler, D.: Telos: Enabling ultra-low power wireless research. Proceedings of the 4th Int. Conf. on Information Processing in Sensor Networks: Special track on Platform Tools and Design Methods for Network Embedded Sensors (IPSN/SPOTS) (2005)

15. Ganeriwal, S., Ganesan, D., Hansen, M., Srivastava, M.B., Estrin, D.: Rate-adaptive time synchronization for long lived sensor networks. Proceedings of the ACM international conference on Measurement and modeling of computer systems. (SIGMETRICS 2005) (Short Paper) (2005)

16. Ganeriwal, S., Ganesan, D., Sim, H., Tsiatsis, V., Srivastava, M.B.: Estimating clock uncertainty for efficient duty cycling in sensor networks. SenSys '05: Third ACM Conference on Embedded Networked Sensor Systems (2005)

Distributed Dynamic Shared Tree for Minimum Energy Data Aggregation of Multiple Mobile Sinks in Wireless Sensor Networks

Kwang-il Hwang, JeongSik In, and Doo-seop Eom

Department of Electronics and Computer Engineering, Korea University,
5-1ga, Anam-dong, Sungbuk-gu, Seoul, Korea
brightday@final.korea.ac.kr

Abstract. Sink mobility creates new challenges for several sensor network applications. In mobile sink environments, each sink must propagate its current location continuously, through a sensor field, in order to keep all sensor nodes updated with the direction of data forwarding. This method consumes large amounts of energy. Although several protocols, such as DD, TTDD, and SEAD, have been proposed, in order to solve mobile sink problems, no existing approaches provide both a low delay and energy-efficient solution to this mobile sink problem. In this paper, a distributed dynamic shared tree for minimum energy data aggregation with low delay in highly mobile sink environments, is proposed. In the proposed protocol, the tree is shared with the other slave sinks. Through simulations it is shown that the DST is an extremely energy-efficient, robust protocol with relatively low delay, when compared to DD, TTDD, and SEAD.

1 Introduction

Advances in MEMS, and microprocessor and wireless communication technologies have enabled the development of various applications through the deployment of sensor networks, composed of hundreds or thousands of tiny, low cost nodes.

It is important to note that power is one of the most expensive resources in sensor networks. Due to the difficulty in recharging of thousands of devices in remote or hostile environments, maximizing battery lifetime by conserving power is a matter of paramount importance.

These distributed sensors enable remote monitoring and event detection in a geographically significant region or an inhospitable area. For example, as shown in Fig. 1, explosion area rescuers or robots equipped with handheld devices can obtain dynamic information from sensor nodes thrown over the area. In this paper multiple mobile sinks environments are considered, while sensors are stationary. In the above example, the rescuers or robots may change location, but must be able to aggregate data continuously.

K. Römer, H. Karl, and F. Mattern (Eds.): EWSN 2006, LNCS 3868, pp. 132–147, 2006.

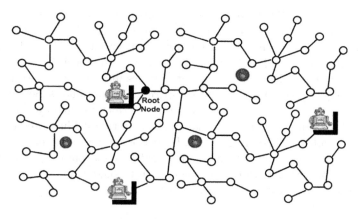

Fig. 1. An example of mobile sink application in sensor networks

Sink mobility formulates attractive challenges for several sensor network applications. Several data aggregation protocols have been developed for sensor networks, such as SPIN [5], Direct Diffusion [2] and GRAB [8]. These protocols can efficiently aggregate data with low delay by constructing one or more aggregation paths on the basis of sink. In-network processing [6] from sources on the paths is also enabled. Nevertheless, these protocols must propagate the sink location continuously through a sensor field in order to keep all sensor nodes updated with the direction of data forwarding.

In order to reduce flooding effect caused by sink mobility, SAFE [3], which uses geographically limited flooding, is proposed. However, in case of highly mobile sinks, local flooding to retrieve the gate connecting itself to the tree increases proportional to the number of sinks in the area.

While the above sink-oriented protocols require continuous reporting of all nodes or paths as sinks move, source-oriented dissemination protocols, such as TTDD [1] and SEAD [4], use mobile sinks' access method to dissemination paths, constructed from each source. Each data source in TTDD proactively builds a grid structure, which enables mobile sinks to continuously receive data regarding the move, by flooding queries within a local cell only. SEAD creates a near-optimal dissemination tree by considering the distance and the packet traffic rate among nodes. Each agent node continuously tracks sink movement. Evidently, these source-oriented protocols perform energy-efficient data dissemination. However, the path per source makes in-network processing impossible. In addition, due to the sinks' access time, more delay is required to aggregate data. No existing approaches provide both a low delay and energy-efficient solution to mobile sink problems.

In this paper, an energy-efficient data aggregation protocol with low delay in highly mobile sink environments is proposed. In order for an aggregation tree to continuously pursue a dynamic sink, *forward sink advertisement* and *distributed fast recovery* is exploited. In the proposed protocol, the shape of the tree is dynamically transformed according to master sink movement, and the tree is shared with the other slave sinks. Therefore, this is called, the Dynamic Shared Tree

(DST) protocol. The DST conserves a considerable amount of energy, despite maintaining robust connection from all sources to sinks, since tree maintenance of the DST is accomplished by distributed local exchanges. In addition, since this represents a kind of sink-oriented tree approach, the DST can aggregate data with low delay along the tree and facilitates in-network processing.

The subsequent sections of this paper are organized as follows. Section 2 introduces the proposed DST protocol. Section 3 describes the maintenance method of the DST to minimize energy consumption. Section 4 illustrates the shared approach of multiple sinks in the DST. In section 5, the energy efficiency of the DST is analyzed in terms of total communication cost compared with DD and TTDD. A comparative performance evaluation through simulation is presented in Section 6. Section 7 concludes this paper.

2   Distributed Dynamic Shared Tree

In this section the basic model of the DST, which is designed to cope well with the highly mobile sink environment, is presented. Then, the DST operation is described in details. The network model for the DST makes the following basic assumptions:

- Homogeneous sensor nodes are densely deployed.
- Sensor nodes communicate with each other through short-range radios. Long distance data delivery is accomplished by forwarding data across multiple hops.
- Each sensor node is aware of its own location (for example through receiving GPS signals or through localization techniques such as [9]).
- Sensor nodes remain stationary at their initial location.
- Sink nodes possess much more energy than that of general sensor nodes, since the battery of a sink node can be recharged and replaced by users.

2.1   Basic Design Concept

The main design goal of the DST protocol is for a tree to continuously pursue a dynamic sink. That means the shape of the tree is dynamically transformed according to the sink's trajectory to maintain a sink-oriented tree as presented in Fig 2.

In the DST protocol, a sink node appoints a Root node. The Root node as an agent of sink becomes an actual root of entire tree, and has an upstream connection to a sink node on behalf of the tree as shown in (a) of Fig. 2. In the distributed DST protocol, the Root node is dynamically changed according to the sink's location, and then nodes in its local area are forced to change their current parent direction to the newly appointed Root node. This DST operation is accomplished by the *forward sink advertisement* and *distributed fast recovery protocol*. For the *forward sink advertisement*, the DST employs a periodic Update Request, which is a periodic local broadcast message. In addition, for *distributed fast recovery*, Root node uses a Sink Lost timer. If a Root node does

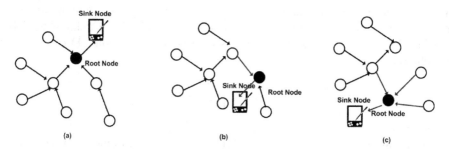

Fig. 2. Description of basic DST operation

not listen to the periodic Update Request message in a given update interval as the sink moves, the Root node's Sink Lost timer expires and the Root node notifies neighbors that the current Root node is disconnected from the sink. If the periodic Update Request interval and time-out value of Sink Lost timer are given by the following Equations (1) and (2), which are related to radio range and maximum sink speed, the current sink's location is discovered by at least one node within two hops of the old Root node, which lost the sink's Update message. Therefore, the nodes, which listen to both the current Update message of the sink and Sink Lost message of the old root, notify its sink that the node itself can become a new root. As soon as the sink receives the notification, it appoints one of them as a new Root (The selection criteria of a new root is arrival time of Root request message). After completing choice of a new root, Root id field in periodic Update message of sink node is changed into new root id. By the changed information, other nodes within sink radio range update parent direction to new root node.

Eventually, according to sink's movement, the original shape (a) of the tree is transformed as shown in (b) and then (c) of Fig. 2. This distributed DST protocol is simple but maintains a robust connectivity to sink. In addition, this distributed approach solves the problems with the excessive energy drain and increased collisions in the traditional sink location update message-based protocols, such as flooding or Directed Diffusion, which require more frequent sink's location update throughout the sensor field. Compared with such sink oriented protocols, the proposed DST save considerable energy more since sink's periodic update message requires the link reversal [7] of only the nodes in the new Root's local area, not entire sensor nodes in the sensor field.

In addition, since the update rates are used with Equation (1), which is proportional to the radio range and inversely proportional to sink speed, the DST can cope well with highly mobile sink environments, and energy waste caused by an excessive update rate can be minimized.

$$Interval = \frac{D}{V_{s-\max}} - (T_p + \alpha) \tag{1}$$

$$Timeout = 1.1 \times Interval \tag{2}$$

$V_{s-\max}$ denotes the maximum sink node speed (m/s), D is a maximum radio range, T_p is a propagation time delay, and α is an additional delay caused by the MAC layer and processing. For realistic interval calculation, (1) is rewritten as follows:

$$Interval = \frac{D}{V_{s-\max}} \times K \tag{3}$$

where $K < 1$.

Note that the K factor is an important performance parameter for the DST. The optimal K factor is retrieved heuristically by experiment, including the MAC and propagation delay. We choose $K = 0.3$ as a heuristically optimal value in Section 6.

2.2   Overview of DST Protocol

For distributed operation of the DST in all sensor nodes, each node, except for sink nodes, can have one of four states: Member, Root candidate, Old root, and Root node as shown in Fig. 3.

All the nodes start with a member node state. If a member node listens to the Update Request message with the any specific node's address from a sink, the node's state is changed to the Root candidate state. Each candidate Root maintains a candidate timer during the time receiving the Update request with other node's address. If the sink node moves far from the range of a candidate, the candidate timer expire and the candidate nodes turn to a member state, again. However, if one of them receives the Update Request with its own address, it changes to the Root node state and becomes a new Root node.

A Root node also maintains the Sink Lost timer during receiving the update request with its own address. If the sink moves far from the range of Root node, the Root node cannot hear the next Update request, and therefore the timer expires. As soon as the timer expires, the node changes to the Old root

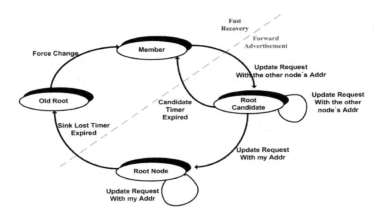

Fig. 3. State transition diagram in each sensor node for distributed DST operation

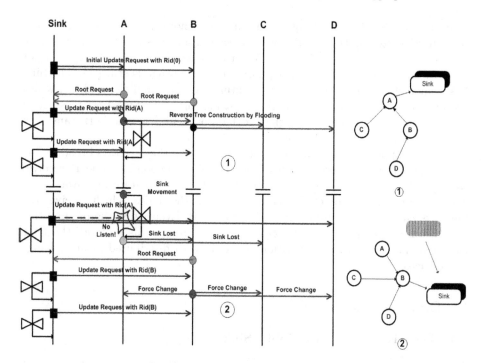

Fig. 4. Message flow in DST operation

state and broadcasts the Sink lost message. The current Root candidate nodes simultaneously transmit the Root Request message to the sink nodes and the only one of candidate nodes is chosen as a new Root node. The newly appointed Root node forces its neighbors to change their parent direction into the new Root node by broadcasting a Force change message. The Old Root node, which hears a Force change message, simultaneously becomes a member node again.

Figure 4 illustrates the message flow for dynamic operation of the distributed DST. Suppose that sensor nodes are initially deployed as in (1) of the Fig. Initially, sink node enters the sensor field, with broadcasting the Update request message periodically. Note that the initial Update request message from the sink is broadcasted with Rood id (0). The nodes, which receive the Update request message from sink, become a Root candidate node and transmit a Root request message to the corresponding sink node as soon as each node receives the Update request with Root id (0). In Fig. 4, the sink node selects node A as a root node and broadcasts the Update request with Root id (A). The node A checks whether the parent already exists and then if it has no parent, which means there is currently no existing tree in the sensor field, it starts flooding. As a result of flooding, a reverse tree as in (1) of the Figure is constructed. While the sink remains within range of the current root, node A, the tree remains stationary without any transforming.

Now, as the sink moves, the DST shows its ability to deal with the mobile sink in earnest. Due to sink's movement, the current Root node, node A, cannot listen to the next Update Request message any more. Instead, node B and D come to listen to the Update Request message from the sink. That means node B and D became Root candidates. Note that since there is no change of Root node by sink, the Root id in an Update request message is still (A). The Sink Lost timer of current root, node A, eventually expires and the node A, which becomes an Old root, broadcasts Sink Lost message. The Sink Lost message of node A can hear only node B so that of the root candidates, node B transmit a Root Request message to the sink.

The sink appoints node B as a new Root node and then restarts broadcasting the Update Request message with Root id (B). As soon as node B receives the new Update message with its own id, it changes the state into Root node and then broadcasts Force Change message. All the nodes, which receives the message, change their parent direction to node B. Eventually, the original tree is transformed, as presented in (2) of Fig. 4. Through this method, the DST can maintain a dynamic aggregation tree only with distributed local exchange of messages.

3   DST Maintenance

3.1   Data Forwarding to Mobile Sink

The DST is intentionally designed to cope well with the mobile sink, so that data forwarding from each source to mobile sink can be easily accomplished along the aggregation tree. The distributed DST protocol can provide seamless data aggregation without concern about the sink's movement, as if the sink had been stationary at the location. The DST outwardly follows a tree-based data aggregation approach so that the data forwarding cost from the source node to sink along the tree is available with $O(\sqrt{N})$. The DST also makes it possible to perform data aggregation combined with In-network processing [6].

3.2   Self-recovery from Partitioned Tree

There are two kinds of situation that cause a partition of a tree.

Failure of fast recovery: This happens when the old Root misses the sink. In this case, the old Root cannot hear the Force Change message of the new root so that the loss of new Root node creates a partitioned tree in which the old Root becomes a root.

Link Failure: All sensor nodes always overhear their own parent's upstream data delivery, except for Root node. When a node, which has upstream data to its parent, cannot overhear its parent node's upstream data forwarding, the node identifies that its sub-tree is partitioned from its parent's tree.

Both of these partitioned trees can be recovered by the *self-recovery process* as follows. Figure 5 demonstrates the self-recovery process of the DST. If the tree is partitioned by some failure factors as presented in (a) of Fig. 5, as soon as a node identifies a failure, the node broadcasts the a Find Root message in the local area as presented in (b) of Fig. 5. Nodes hearing the Find Root message, propagate the message to its upstream along the tree as presented in (c) of Fig. 5. Since the root of a partitioned tree is the sender, itself (problem detection node), the direction of Find Root message propagation is inclined only toward active tree, which is connected to sink as presented in (c) of Fig. 5. In this propagation of Find Root message, each parent avoids transmission of duplicate messages from different children nodes by using a *join request cache*. The reason that the root partitioned tree retrieves only the current Root of active tree, not the other members, is because information from current root is considered as the most reliable.

Eventually, the message reaches the current Root node and the current root node unicasts the PERMIT JOIN message to the root of partitioned tree, through route information obtained from Find Root message as presented in (d) of Fig. 5. Therefore, the Root node of partitioned tree, which received the PERMIT JOIN message, reconfigures its parent's direction to the originator of the message, the current Root node. Finally, as presented in (f) of Fig. 5, the partitioned tree completes the successful joining of the active tree.

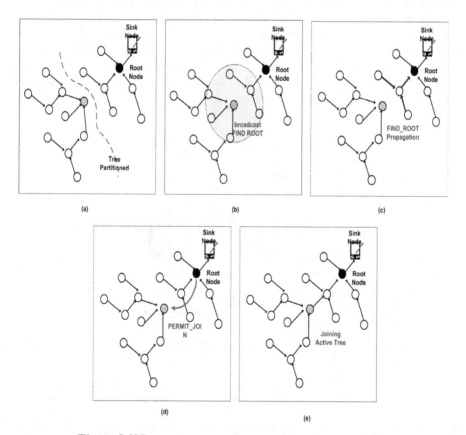

Fig. 5. Self-Recovery process from partitioned tree in DST

4   Multiple Sinks' Share of DST

One of the outstanding features of the DST is the ability to accommodate multiple mobile sinks simultaneously on the same tree. As presented in Fig. 6, multiple mobile sinks share a dynamic tree, which is already constructed by a master sink. Two types of sink are defined in the DST: Master sink and Slave sink. The former is a sink, which is first attended in the sensor filed and directed by root node of the tree. The latter are slave sinks, which join the tree already constructed by a master sink. The master sink must be the only one in a sensor field.

As presented in Fig. 6, slave sinks operate as a leaf node. However, it is different from general member nodes in that the information is transmitted upstream by periodically broadcasting the Periodic Reporting. For the delivery of slave sinks' Periodic Reporting, each node stores multiple sinks' information using a *Sink info cache* table and each parent checks the freshness of Reporting. Each node, which receives the Periodic Reporting message from its child, stores a pair of child id and Slave sink id as well as its sequence number into the Sink info cache. If an identical message is received, the parent ignores the packet. However, if the identical sink id and sequence number received, but from different node, the parent node changes its child id to id of the node of later received message. This is to maintain the freshest routing information in each node. The child ids are used as routing information for downstream data delivery from master to corresponding slave, later. Eventually, the Periodic Reporting message from a slave reaches the master sink node. The master sink transmits the aggregated

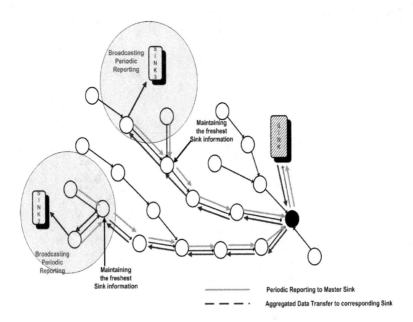

Fig. 6. DST allows data dissemination from each source to multiple mobile sinks on the same tree

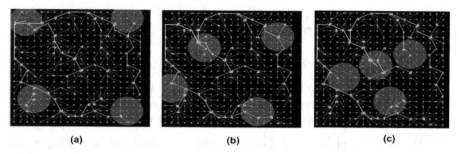

Fig. 7. Dynamic operation of the distributed DST as four sinks move: the operation of the DST conducted on a SHOW_ROUTE program based on the result of NS-simulator

data result to each slave sink through the freshest routing information in the each node's Sink info cache as presented in Fig. 6.

This shared-tree approach of the DST for multiple mobile sinks has advantages described below. The first is to conserve considerable energy. This is because all slave sinks are processed as dynamic leaf nodes on the tree, without requiring additional flooding or each sink's private agents. In addition, by virtue of each parent's route maintenance refresh, each sink's movement is not affected to entire network, but locally processed. The second is that the DST creates a logical star topology between master and slave sinks. Each sink can communicate through a master. In other words, the DST provides a completely two-tiered network structure: the first is sink-oriented tree structure for sensor nodes and the second is a star structure for sink nodes. This structure can facilitate operations of a group of military units on the battlefield.

5   Efficiency Analysis

In this section the energy efficiency of the DST is analyzed. A specific metric is measured: *total communication cost* for data aggregation of the DST, DD and TTDD, respectively.

It is assumed that a square sensor field of area A in which N sensor nodes are uniformly distributed, so that on each side there are approximately $\sqrt{N}$ sensor nodes. There are m event sources and n sink nodes. For grid structure analysis, it is assumed that sensor fields are divided into cells; each cell has α sensor nodes. N_X is defined as the number of cells on the X-axis, and N_Y is the number of cells on the Y-axis.

Directed Diffusion. For event forwarding, Directed diffusion requires four steps: Interest flooding, Exploratory data forwarding, Reinforcement, and Data forwarding. Since Interest forwarding by sink node uses flooding, its cost, in the worst-case, is expressed as mN. The cost for the exploratory data forwarding process to setup multi-paths from source to sink can be approximately given by $\sqrt{N} \times \sqrt{N} = N$. The cost for reinforcement to select single path among the multi-path by exploratory forwarding is also $\sqrt{N}$. Eventually, cost data forwarding along the path is simply given by $n\sqrt{N}$. Accordingly, total communication cost C_{DD} for DD is given by

$$C_{DD} = (m+1)N + (n+1)\sqrt{N} \tag{4}$$

Therefore, in a sink mobile environment, total communication cost is represented as $O(mN)$, including all cost required to construct and maintain a dissemination path and data forwarding with respect to sink movement.

TTDD. TTDD exploits local flooding within the local cell of a grid, which sources build proactively. Each source disseminates data along the nodes on the grid line to the sinks. The TTDD can be divided into three independent steps: Geographical forwarding for grid construction, Query forwarding by sinks, and Data forwarding from sources. Initially, only nodes on the grid line take part in the forwarding process during geographical forwarding. In addition, since the grid is independently constructed by each source, the cost for geographical forwarding is expressed as $n \times N_x \times N_Y \times \sqrt{\alpha}$.

Next, the query is flooded using a sink within a cell and then forwarded along the grid line. Therefore, the cost for query forwarding becomes $\alpha m + m(\sqrt{2N})$. Finally, data forwarding from each source to sink is expressed by $n\left(\sqrt{2N} + \frac{\sqrt{2\alpha}}{2}\right)$. This is because the worst-case sink will be found at the edge cell of diagonal line from source. Eventually, the total communication cost for TTDD is given by

$$C_{TTDD} = n\left(N^*\sqrt{\alpha} + \frac{\sqrt{2\alpha}}{2} + \sqrt{2N}\right) + m(\sqrt{2N} + \alpha) \quad , Where N^* = N_x \times N_y \tag{5}$$

Therefore, the total cost is $O(m\sqrt{N})$ or $O(n\sqrt{N})$ where $N^* << N$, however, TTDD' cost largely depends on the cell size. In addition, in case of many sources, the cost rapidly increases.

DST. Similar to DD, the DST begins with flooding. However, the DST does not require additional flooding with regard to increasing the sinks. Since the tree constructed by flooding, is shared with other sinks, the tree construction cost is only $N + m\sqrt{N}$. In addition, the cost to maintain the tree is negligible, since the DST maintains the tree with some messages exchanged locally when the sink moves. Data is forwarded upstream along the tree and then forward to each slave sink along the tree, so the data forwarding cost is expressed by $(m+n)\sqrt{N}$. Eventually, the total communication cost for the DST is given by

$$C_{DST} = N + (2m+n)\sqrt{N} \tag{6}$$

However, in spite of sink's continuous movement, since flooding is required only in initial tree construction phase, the actual communication cost becomes $O(n\sqrt{N})$, where m_in.

In summary, the DST is similar to the sink oriented data aggregation approaches in shape, however, the DST does not generate any additional flooding or create sizeable communication overhead. Therefore, the energy efficiency for the DST is as good as the TTDD. However, the realistic TTDD' cost largely depends on the cell size as well as the number of sources. More realistic measures are presented with a simulation in Section 6.

6   Performance Evaluation

In this section, the performance of the DST is evaluated through simulations. Simulation metrics and methodology are described in Section 6.1. The main goal in simulating the DST is to evaluate how well it actually conserves energy, maintaining the robust DST connection and low delay in highly mobile environments. The parameters affecting the robustness of DST, are first studied. Then, the performance of the DST is compared to DD, TTDD, and SEAD.

6.1   Metrics and Methodology

The DST is implemented as an independent routing agent module in ns-2.27. In the basic simulation setting, the same energy model is used, which is two-ray ground model and omni-directional antenna, as adopted in Directed Diffusion, and TTDD implementation in ns. A 802.11 DCF is used as the underlying MAC protocol. A sensor node's transmitting, receiving, and idle power consumption rates are set to 0.66W, 0.395W and0.035W, respectively. The network in the simulation consists of 400 sensor nodes randomly or uniformly distributed in a 1000m x 1000m. Each simulation run lasts for 500 seconds. Each query packet is 36 bytes and each data packet is 64 bytes in length, in order to facilitate comparisons with other protocols.

Three metrics are used to evaluate the performance of the DST.

Success rate is the ratio of the number of successfully received data at a sink from source. This metric demonstrates the robustness of the aggregation path.

Average end-to-end delay is measured by averaging delay from source to sinks. This metric indicates the freshness of data packets.

Energy consumption per node is defined as the total communication energy the node consumes. The communication energy includes tree construction, data dissemination, and sink mobility management.

6.2   Robustness of DST

We first study on a parameter affecting the performance of DST. In Section 2, we already emphasized the impact of k-value which is a parameter determinig period of Update Request of sink for continuous connection of the dynamic tree according to sink's mobility.

Figure 8 (a) demonstrates the success rate at different sink speeds. Note that the success rate with k-val more than 0.4 is drastically deteriorates around a sink speed of 15 m/s. This is because the breaking probability of the tree is increased

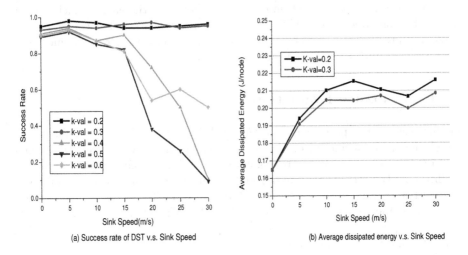

(a) Success rate of DST v.s. Sink Speed   (b) Average dissipated energy v.s. Sink Speed

Fig. 8. Robustness of the DST

with a large k value. However, it can be shown that the DST maintains a success rate more than 0.9 with a k value of 0.2 and 0.3 in spite of the high mobility of sink. Prior to choosing the best k value by the heuristic result of this experiment in (a), another observation related to the k value is made presented in (b) of Fig. 8. This represents the energy consumption of each k value, 0.2 and 0.3. Intuitively, we know that the larger k value, the more energy increases. The result in Fig. 8 (b) proves this fact. Consequently the two observations provide the most efficient value for k, 0.3, for both robustness and energy conservation.

6.3 Impact of Sink's Mobility

In this subsection the impact of sink mobility on the performance of the DST, is evaluated. In the simulation setting, 8 mobile sinks and 30 randomly chosen sources, in the sensor field, were used. Energy consumption and average end-to-end delay according to varying the maximum speed of a sink, are measured from 0 to 30 m/s.

Figure 9 (a) presents the average dissipated energy as the sinks' speed is varied. In this Fig, the DST presents superior energy consumption over the other protocols. This is because the DST can maintain the aggregation tree dynamically as the sinks migrate. In addition, the DST does not require additional flooding or location notification to access nodes or agents. In DD, the entire topology is changed so the new location of the mobile sink is propagated throughout the sensor filed in order for all nodes to obtain the sink's location. The TTDD is designed for mobile sinks, but cannot avoid rebuilding a new multi-hop path between the sink and the grid to track the sink's location. Although SEAD based on the source-oriented steiner tree shows smooth energy increase, SEAD has the overhead that each sink must recognize their specific location to continuously access nodes or to change access nodes.

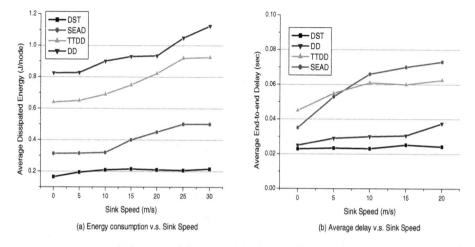

Fig. 9. Impact of sink's mobility

Since the DST only uses local interactions on the basis of the sink to maintain dynamic tree, the increase of energy consumption in terms of the entire sensor network is considerably moderate, as presented in (a) of Fig. 9.

Figure 9 (b) presents the average end-to-end delay as the sinks' speed is varied. This Figure demonstrates that DD and DST maintain relatively lower delay than TTDD and SEAD. TTDD and SEAD are source-oriented data dissemination protocols so that they require finding a valid path from source to each sink, whenever a source generates an event. Finding the valid path adds extra delay to the protocols. Conversely, the DST and DD, which are sink-oriented approaches, do not require such additional delay, since all sensor nodes already know the path to each sink. Nevertheless, as a sink's speed increases, DD demonstrates gradual increase in delay. This is because of the flooding effect according to sink mobility. However, the DST which maintains a dynamically dissemination tree oriented to sink, shows an almost constant delay variation as presented in (b) of Fig. 9.

6.4   Impact of the Number of Sinks

In this subsection, the impact of the number of sinks on the performance of the DST, is evaluated. In this simulation, the sinks' speed is set at 10 m/s and energy consumption is measured as the number of sinks increases to 8.

Figure 10 presents the energy consumption as the number of sinks is varied. This Fig demonstrates that in case of a single sink TTDD and SEAD outperform the sink-oriented protocols, the DST and DD. This is because the DST requires basic energy consumption to maintain the tree using the periodic Update message. However, as the number of sinks increases, energy consumption in the DST only slightly increases, in contrast to the other protocols. This is because the dynamic tree is shared with the other multiple sinks. As a result, there is little additional energy per sink, in contrast to the other protocols, such as DD, TTDD, and SEAD.

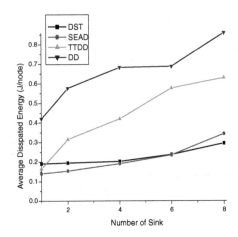

Fig. 10. Energy consumption v.s. number of sinks

7   Conclusions and Future Work

In this paper, an energy-efficient data aggregation protocol with low delay in highly mobile sink environments in sensor networks, is proposed. In order to continuously maintain aggregation tree, a *forward sink advertisement* and *distributed fast recovery,* was utilized. In the proposed protocol, the tree is shared with the other slave nodes so that it is called the Dynamic Shared Tree (DST) protocol. Through simulations, we showed that the DST is a considerably energy-efficient, robust protocol with low delay, compared to Directed Diffusion, TTDD, and SEAD, in highly mobile sink environments.

The DST is currently being investigated on a large-scale sensor network test-bed.

References

1. Haiyun Luo, Fan Ye, Jerry Cheng, Songwu Lu, Lixia Zhang, "TTDD: Two-tier Data Dissemination in Large-scale Wireless Sensor Networks," *ACM/Kluwer Mobile Networks and Applications, Special Issue on ACM MOBICOM,*2002.
2. C. Intanagonwiwat, R. Govindan, and D. Estrin "Directed diffusion for Wireless Sensor Networking," *IEEE/ACM Transaction on Networking*, Vol. 11, 2003.
3. Sooyeon Kim, Sang H. Son, John A. Stankovic, Shuoqi Li, Yanghee Choi, "SAFE: A Data Dissemination Protocol for Periodic Updates in Sensor Networks," In *Proceedings of the 23 rd International Conference on Distributed Computing Systems Workshops (ICDCSW'03),*2003.
4. Hyung Seok Kim, Tarek F. Abdelzaher, Wook Hyun Kwon "Minimum-energy asynchronous dissemination to mobile sinks in wireless sensor networks," In *Proceeding of Embedded Networked Sensor Systems (SenSys03)*, Los Angeles, California, USA, 2003.

5. W. Heinzelman, J. Kulik, and H. Balakrishnan, "Adaptive Protocols for Information Dissemination in Wireless Sensor Networks," *ACM International Conference on Mobile Computing and Networking (MOBICOM'99)*, 1999.
6. B. Krishnamachari, D. Estrin, and S. Wicker, "The Impact of Data Dissemination in Wireless Sensor Networks," In *Proceedings of the 22nd International Conference on Distributed Computing Systems Workshops*, 2002.
7. C. Busch, S. Surapaneni, and S. Tirthapura. "Analysis of Link Reversal Routing Protocols for Mobile Ad Hoc Networks," *SPAA 2003*, pp. 210-219, San Diego, California, June 2003.
8. F. Ye, S. Lu, and L. Zhang. GRAdient Broadcast: A Robust, Long-lived Large Sensor Network.
9. K. Langendoen and N. Reijers, "Distributed Localization in Wireless Sensor Networks," Computer Networks (Elsevier), special issue on Wireless Sensor Networks, August, 2003.

Constrained Tracking on a Road Network*

Michał Piórkowski and Matthias Grossglauser

School of Computer and Communication Sciences,
Ecole Polytechnique Fédérale de Lausanne (EPFL),
CH-1015 Lausanne, Switzerland
`firstname.lastname@epfl.ch`

Abstract. Many applications of wireless ad hoc sensor and actuator networks (WSANs) rely on the knowledge of node locations. These are challenging to obtain when nodes are mobile and are not equipped with any specific positioning hardware. In this paper, we are interested in scenarios where there are constraints on the movement of nodes, such as with cars on a road network.

We develop and analyse a tracking algorithm called MOONwalk that explicitly takes such constraints into account in order to improve the tracking precision. Furthermore, MOONwalk does not require global knowledge of the network, and therefore lends itself well to large-scale and high-mobility applications.

We evaluate the accuracy of MOONwalk by comparing it to the optimal maximum likelihood estimator, under different radio conditions and deployment scenarios. We find that MOONwalk performs well despite its localized operation.

1 Introduction

Numerous applications of sensor and sensor-actuator networks need to track mobile objects, such as people, animals, cars, planes, etc. We are interested in scenarios where the tracked object is equipped with a communication device, but not with a positioning device, such as GPS. Such a situation may arise because of energy, cost, or radio constraints, or because the tracking system has to be operational indoors. In this case, an estimate of the location of the tracked object can be computed from channel measurements between the tracked object and a set of fixed devices. Several papers have considered this tracking problem, where the estimated position of the tracked object is unconstrained, i.e., can lie anywhere in Euclidean space [1–8].

In this paper, we study a related problem, but where the space of possible locations is constrained to a graph. More specifically, the vertices of this graph each correspond to a point in space, and each edge corresponds to a line segment

---

* The work presented in this paper was supported (in part) by the National Competence Center in Research on Mobile Information and Communication Systems (NCCR-MICS), a center supported by the Swiss National Science Foundation under grant number 5005-67322. (`http://www.mics.org`)

K. Römer, H. Karl, and F. Mattern (Eds.): EWSN 2006, LNCS 3868, pp. 148–163, 2006.

connecting its adjacent vertices. The tracked object's position always lies on this graph. This formulation of the tracking problem is inspired by the tracking of cars on the road network, where vertices model intersections and interpolation points of curved roads.

Our main application for this problem is a fully distributed system called SmartPark, which assists drivers in locating free parking spots and guides them to these spots with turn-by-turn instructions [9]. The key idea is that every parking spot is equipped with an embedded sensor, and a car is equipped with a simple guidance device. For related projects, see [10, 11].

Although it would be possible to solve this problem by relying on an unconstrained tracking algorithm and projecting the location estimate onto the road network, this may give rise to suboptimal precision and efficiency. In this paper, we therefore develop constrained tracking algorithms from first principles, i.e., where the constraint is explicitly taken into account from the outset.

We first formulate this constrained tracking problem in a maximum-likelihood (ML) framework, where the uncertainty stems from fading effects in the radio channel between the car and the sensors. Although the resulting algorithm is optimal, it is computationally demanding and requires knowledge of the full road network graph, as well as knowledge of all the sensors and their geographic positions, and it assumes a specific radio channel model.

In a system such as SmartPark, however, requiring every sensor and car to have full knowledge of the road network and of all the sensors in parking spots would be impractical. Moreover, none of the existing radio channel models fully captures the real characteristics of radio propagation in an urban environment. A realistic algorithm therefore has to be robust to channel uncertainties and has to be able to compute the car's location on the road network with only very limited local information configured in the sensors, and no knowledge in the car. This is because the set of sensors may be large (hundreds of thousands in a large city), and may change over time (e.g., because of node outages). Furthermore, it may be undesirable to configure sensors with their precise geographic position.

In this paper, we describe an algorithm called MOONwalk that relies on considerably weaker assumptions than the ML algorithm. A key feature of this algorithm is that the car's guidance device does not need any a-priori knowledge about the road network graph and about the set of sensors present in its vicinity. This is challenging, because it implies that the guidance device loses valuable information when a particular sensor is not able to communicate with the guidance device, because it is not a-priori aware of the existence of this sensor. In the ML formulation, this information is explicitly taken into account. MOONwalk relies on some very limited state information in sensors to get around this problem, which is particularly important in cases where sensor distributions are very heterogeneous in space.

Another important feature of MOONwalk concerns the a-priori knowledge in sensors, which typically has to be configured by hand or inferred through some other process. ML requires the precise geographical position of each sensor but MOONwalk only requires a set of *potential* positions on the road network (rather than in Euclidean space). This simplifies configuration and makes the tracking process more robust to small configuration errors.

This paper is organized as follows. In Section 2, we describe the models and assumptions. The ML formulation is introduced in Section 3, and the MOON-walk algorithm in Section 4. We report simulation results in Section 5, and show that MOONwalk performs well compared to the optimal ML algorithm, despite the complications cited above. In Section 6, we give a more detailed description of related work. In Section 7, we conclude the paper and describe future research.

2   System Model

2.1   The Road Network Model

A vehicle is constrained to move on the road network. In the case of vehicle tracking this fact becomes an opportunity, because one has to look for the vehicle only within a road network. To model the road network we define the graph $G(V, E)$, where the set V of vertexes represents *intersections* and the set E of directed edges represents *line segments* connecting the intersections [12, 13]. The proposed model can abstract any curved road as a set of straight roads connecting virtual intersections. For the sake of simplicity we assume that G is strongly connected and E contains one-way line segments only, i.e., any two adjacent vertexes are directly connected only by one directed edge. We intend to relax this assumption in the future. Since parking sensors are deployed usually along the roads they can abstract the road topology as a G. At each sensor the information about the line segment $e = (v, w)$ and a distance from v and/or w to its geographical location can be stored. Thus we distinguish between two different types of locations of a sensor i, i.e., the *geographical location* in $\mathbb{R}^2$: X_i, and the *road network location* on G represented by so-called *location-tuple*: L_i. The location-tuple is defined by two functions $L_i = (e(X_i), \beta(X_i))$ that characterise the line segment and the distance between the actual location of a sensor X_i and the location of the preceding (or the following) intersection X_v. In order to simplify the notation we write the following $L_i = (e_i, \beta_i)$, where i represents the sensor, $e_i = (v_i, w_i) \in E$ specifies the line segment on which i is located, and $\beta_i \in [0, 1]$ specifies i's location on e_i. The β_i might be expressed as $\beta_i = \frac{||X_i - X_v||}{||X_v - X_w||}$, where $||X_i - X_v||$ is the Euclidean distance between a sensor and the preceding intersection and $||X_v - X_w||$ represents the length of e_i. However, one can use some other metrics for the β_i, e.g. a time needed to get from the preceding intersection to the actual location X_i. Without loss of generality, as a metric for the β_i we use the ratio between the Euclidean distances. In the case of the vehicle tracking on a road network one can rely on the parking sensors as they can abstract the road network topology. We believe that this approach is appropriate, since the navigation is performed based on the abstracted road topology, i.e. the driver obtains the turn-by-turn instructions in the following format: *"Drive straight until the nearest intersection, then turn right. Your parking spot is the fifth on the right side."*

2.2   The Radio Model

All sensors and wireless guidance devices use omnidirectional antennas and narrowband radio signals for communication. We investigate the probability of signal reception at a given distance from a vehicle and at a certain time, thus we use the *path loss* radio communication combined with *multipath propagation* model. The path loss attenuation between transceivers is given by $d^{-\alpha}$ [14], where α is the path loss exponent, which varies from 2 (free space) up to 6 (harsh environment), and d is the Euclidean distance between transceivers. The received power level shows rapid and deep fluctuations about the local mean with the movement of a mobile node and presence of obstacles. These fluctuations are caused by multipath propagation. They are approximated by the Rayleigh distribution [15]. In our radio model we use the Rayleigh fading model, because it is particularly appropriate when there is no direct line-of-sight between the transmitters, which is often the case in a very harsh outdoor environment. The value of the received power is in fact a random variable that depends on the actual radio propagation characteristics and the distance to the transmitter. We have verified, by means of simulations, that the proposed radio propagation model is consistent with the experimental results achieved in [16]. We do not show these results for the lack of space. Assuming that the transmitted power is 1 mW the received power at the receiver is:

$$P_i(t, d, \alpha, \gamma) = \gamma(t)^\theta d^{-\alpha} \tag{1}$$

where $\gamma(t)$ is the random number drawn according to the Rayleigh p.d.f.:

$$p(r) = \begin{cases} \frac{r}{\sigma^2} exp(-\frac{r^2}{2\sigma^2}) & \text{for } r \geq 0 \\ 0 & \text{otherwise,} \end{cases} \tag{2}$$

where r is the envelope amplitude of received signal and σ^2 is its variance. The random variable γ is chosen in such a way that its expected value is equal to one. In that case the expected value of P_i is equal to $d^{-\alpha}$ [14]. The exponent θ represents the intensity of the fading, for example, when the multipath effect decreases the level of received signal by 20 dB, then the θ is equal to 2.

3   Maximum Likelihood Approach

In this section we consider the case where the vehicle's location estimate is obtained without any restrictions on used hardware, decentralized implementation or energy budget. We are looking for a scheme that will be optimal in terms of accuracy. We expect that it will also give us an insight into how to develop and implement an algorithm for more realistic scenarios.

We consider the following setting: the vehicle is equipped with a wireless guidance device and it moves on the road network with a constant speed. It broadcasts periodically a *hello* message. All sensors i that are in the vehicle's radio communication range are able to receive this message.

We introduce a random variable $Z_i(t)$ that describes the reception of a message by a parking sensor. A message is received when the received power level exceeds some predefined power reception threshold P_{th}:

$$Z_i(t) = \begin{cases} 1 \text{ if } P_i \geq P_{th} \\ 0 \text{ otherwise} \end{cases} \qquad (3)$$

In this method we assume that the following information is available for the vehicle explicitly at any time t:

a) road network topology: $G(V, E)$,
b) geographical locations of all sensors: X_i,
c) instantaneous radio communication conditions: α, distribution of γ; and all sensor's reception power threshold: P_{th},
d) all instantaneous sensor's message reception events: $Z_i(t)$.

Based on the aforementioned information, the vehicle executes the proposed algorithm in order to determine its location on a road network. The random variable $Z_i(t)$ is characterized by the conditional probability $p(z_i(t)|X_i)$. Knowing the power reception threshold and the radio communication conditions we can express this conditional probability as follows: $p(z_i(t)|X_i) = \mathcal{P}(P_R > P_{th}) = \exp(-\frac{d^{2\alpha/\theta}P_{th}^{2/\theta}}{2\sigma^2})$. For the purpose of the ML algorithm we define a vector $\bar{z}$ of N sensor's reception events: $\bar{z}(t) = (z_1(t), z_2(t), ..., z_N(t))$, that represents values of $Z_1(t), Z_2(t), ..., Z_N(t)$. We define a likelihood function corresponding to the vehicle's location on the road network as:

$$\mathcal{J}(e, \beta) = p(\bar{z}(t)|X) \qquad (4)$$

Due to the multipath propagation, when a transmitter sends a radio message, its reception by spatially distributed sensors within an urban area is independent. This implies that $Z_1(t), Z_2(t), ..., Z_N(t)$ are independent, hence the $p(\bar{z}(t)|e_i, \beta_i)$ is the product of the marginals:

$$p(\bar{z}(t)|X_i) = \prod_{i=1}^{N} p(z_i(t)|X_i) \qquad (5)$$

Applying the radio model from section 2.2, we obtain:

$$\mathcal{J}(e, \beta) = \prod_{i=1}^{N} \begin{cases} \exp(-\frac{d^{2\alpha/\theta}P_{th}^{2/\theta}}{2\sigma^2}) & \text{if } z_i(t) = 1 \\ 1 - \exp(-\frac{d^{2\alpha/\theta}P_{th}^{2/\theta}}{2\sigma^2}) & \text{if } z_i(t) = 0, \end{cases} \qquad (6)$$

where $d = ||X_{car} - X_i||$ is the distance between a sensor $i = 1...N$ and a hypothetic vehicle location X_{car}. The maximization is done on two sets - one discrete: E and one continuous: $\beta \in [0, 1]$. This allows us to find a value of β that maximizes (6) for all given $e \in E$ separately. Afterwards we simply select the line segment e for which the (6) takes the maximum value. Therefore we obtain the

ML estimates for both, the line segment e and the β parameter that define the location estimate of the vehicle on the road network $\hat{L}_{car}$.

The ML tracking method is optimal in terms of accuracy and is robust to node outages. We use this method to examine the best achievable accuracy of the constrained tracking. Note that it depends on the instantaneous radio propagation conditions that are different for each transceiver in the network. Even if we knew explicitly the multipath characteristics, it would be hard to know the current path loss exponent for each transmitter. The path loss exponent depends on the specific spatial distribution of the obstacles within the area where SmartPark operates. As such, it is very difficult or even impossible to characterize the path loss exponent statistically [14].

4   MOONwalk Algorithm

4.1   From ML Towards a Realistic Scenario

In this section we develop an algorithm that, in contrast to the ML algorithm, does not require to know:

a) the whole road network topology,
b) the precise geographical location of all deployed parking sensors,
c) specific radio channel assumptions,
d) sensors that got the *hello* message and those that did not.

We assume that right after the deployment, during the so-called *warm-up* phase, all parking sensors have to discover where they are located on a road network. They can infer their location-tuples $L_i = (e, \beta)$, from a set of the vehicle's movement observations, i.e. they might obtain information about the time needed to get from a certain intersection to a given position on a certain line segment. How these location-tuples are derived, is out of scope of this paper. However, we assume that they might be imprecise, especially in the case of sensors that are close to intersections. Because of this, we allow each sensor to have more than one location tuple, so we define a *set of location-tuples* as: $\mathcal{L}_i = \{(e_i^k, \beta_i^k), ..., (e_i^l, \beta_i^l)\}$ that represents the set of possible candidates for the real location of a sensor i. We also assume that the vehicle, while estimating its road network location L_{car}, can only rely on sensors' road network locations: L_i and the *received signal strength* measurements of each received message: P_i. We consider the following scenario: the vehicle moves on the road network and broadcasts periodically a *hello* message. All sensors that can hear this message respond to the vehicle with a *reply* message. Due to the multipath effects some of the sensors will not be able to receive messages as shown in Figure 1.

The ML algorithm uses the geographical locations of all sensors to estimate the road network location of the vehicle. We seek an algorithm that will not use any information about the sensor's geographical location nor any distance measurement techniques. However, we can rely on distances between sensors and the vehicle, while estimating the location, by using the relationship between

Fig. 1. An example of the interaction between vehicle and parking sensors

distance and P_i. In a certain propagation direction the expected P_i is monotonically decreasing [16, 17], thus we assume that the expected P_i should be higher for sensors that are closer to the vehicle. Note that we do not make any assumptions about the correlation between absolute distance and the expected P_i. Relying only on instantaneous P_i measurements is not sufficient to design a robust method for location estimation because of the multipath effects.

There might be different densities of sensors on different line segments; if a vehicle can know these densities, such knowledge can help it to decide on which line segment it is at the moment. This kind of information is very useful, e.g. in cases when a vehicle is close to an intersection and it can communicate with sensors that belong to different line segments as shown in Figure 1. Knowing sensors that did and did not receive a *hello* message, helps to infer their densities on line segments. In the ML algorithm the vehicle knows all the sensors that did not receive its *hello* message. A naive approach, where one could take into account only the sensors that respond to the *hello* message, would bias the results of location estimation in favour of high sensor densities, thus it is hard to design a robust real-life algorithm that may know about non-responding sensors. However, even without direct sensor-to-sensor communication, sensors can learn about all neighbouring sensors. For this purpose one could use vehicles that would propagate information about sensors they were able to communicate with recently. Based on such information, each sensor could learn over time about its neighbourhood. The reason we want to rely only on sensor-to-vehicle communication is that the radio channel between sensors might be very obstructed, as they are deployed in the ground. Moreover, the vehicle has an almost infinite resource of energy thus we can easily extend the lifetime of the whole system if we preserve sensors from direct communication between each other. The long-term sensor's observation of its neighbourhood could be sent to the passing by vehicles. Thus a vehicle would be able to find out which sensors were able or not to receive its *hello* message. Note that the accuracy of such information depends on the number of vehicles that pass by and the radio propagation conditions. The more vehicles and the better radio propagation conditions, the better approximation of the sensor's real surrounding.

4.2   How to MOONwalk

The vehicle and parking sensors perform a *three-way communication* that is needed to estimate the vehicle's road network location as shown in Figure 1.

The *hello* message contains a location query. The *reply* message contains the sensor's ID: i, the set of location-tuples: $\mathcal{L}_i$ and its *neighbour table*: N_i. The neighbour table N_i represents a sensor's knowledge of its neighbourhood. Each entry of this table: n_{ij} represents the number of occurrences of a sensor j in the neighbourhood of sensor i: $N_i = \{(j, n_{ij})\}$. Each sensor has an entry for itself in this table. Note that the N_i does not represent a *direct* observation of i's neighbourhood, since there is no sensor-to-sensor communication. After collecting all *reply* messages the vehicle finds two sets - the *reply* message set: $R = \{(i, N_i, \mathcal{L}_i)\}$ and the so-called *one-hop neighbourhood set*: K_{car}. The definition of a neighbour is the following: if a sensor i can communicate directly with the vehicle, after receiving a *hello* message, then i is called a vehicle's neighbour, thus $K_{car} = \{i : i \in R\}$. The K_{car} relies on bi-directional connectivity - if there is only a uni-directional link between two transceivers, they are not considered as neighbours. The K_{car} represents only a snapshot of vehicle's instantaneous neighbourhood at a given time. Once the K_{car} is found, the vehicle broadcasts it to all the sensors in the vicinity, so that they can update their N_i tables. Note that the n_{ii} element in N_i table corresponds to the total number of such messages. We assume that both the set of location-tuples $\mathcal{L}_i$ and the neighbour table N_i of each sensor are given, i.e., all sensors have observed their surrounding long enough.

Since the position of a node on the road network is specified by a location-tuple, we can split the algorithm into two phases. During the first phase the algorithm will identify the proper line segment on which a given vehicle is located. In the second phase the algorithm will find the position on the line segment found in the first phase.

In order to find the proper line segment we need to specify a statistic that represents the certainty of the vehicle's presence on the corresponding line segment. This statistic is a function of the vehicle's observation (K_{car}), local density of sensors that belong to the same line segments (N_is) and the P_i measurements. The proper line segment is found by comparing the statistics. Below we present the MOONwalk algorithm in more details.

Phase I. After performing the three-way communication, a vehicle creates a matrix n_{ij}^{car} using all the N_i tables it has collected:

$$n_{ij}^{car} = \begin{cases} n_{ij} & \text{if } n_{ij} \in R \\ 0 & \text{otherwise} \end{cases} \tag{7}$$

The size of this n_{ij}^{car} matrix is the number of all the sensors that are in the K_{car} and the sensors that are neighbours of the sensors from K_{car}. Each element of this matrix takes a value from a corresponding N_i table as shown in Table 1. All the elements of the n_{ij}^{car} matrix represent the number of times a sensor j appeared in the sensor i's neighbourhood. If neighbourhoods of two sensors overlap, they should *see* each other equally often, i.e. if the distance between two sensors i and j is short enough, then it is more likely that they can receive the same *hello* message from a vehicle. This shows how strong two sensors are correlated with respect to their neighbourhoods. For this reason we apply a correlation technique called Pearson's correlation, which in general shows how strong is the association between two variables:

$$\phi_{ij} = \frac{\sum_k (n_{ik} - \bar{n}_{i\cdot})(n_{jk} - \bar{n}_{j\cdot})}{\sqrt{\sum_k (n_{ik} - \bar{n}_{i\cdot})^2}\sqrt{\sum_k (n_{jk} - \bar{n}_{j\cdot})^2}} \tag{8}$$

Thus for all non-zero elements of the n_{ij}^{car} matrix the vehicle finds the Pearson's correlation coefficients matrix ϕ_{ij}^{car}.

Table 1. N_i tables for sensors A,B, and C respectively (left) and a corresponding n_{ij}^{car} matrix (right)

Sensor ID	# occur.
A	13
B	10
C	13
D	2

Sensor ID	# occur.
A	8
B	11
C	11

Sensor ID	# occur.
A	10
B	9
C	12
D	4

$\Longrightarrow$

...	A	B	C	D
A	13	8	10	0
B	10	11	9	0
C	13	11	12	0
D	2	0	4	0

After finding all correlation coefficients, for each line segment e, taken from all the received position-tuples from R, the vehicle finds corresponding S_e set that contains all the sensors from K_{car}, which belong to this line segment e: $S_e = \{i : e \in \mathcal{L}_i\} \subset K_{car}$. Note that $K_{car} = \cup_e S_e$. For each such set S_e the vehicle obtains a submatrix of coefficients from the ϕ_{ij}^{car} matrix. The size of such a submatrix is $q \times q$, where $q = |S_e|$. In such a submatrix both rows and columns correspond to the sensors that belong to the same line segment. Suppose that the vehicle has to decide whether it is on a line segment $e = 1$ or $e = 2$ as shown in Figure 1. By inspecting the position-tuples, the vehicle knows that $S_1 = B, C$ and $S_2 = A, B, C$ as shown in Table 2.

Table 2. An example of the two submatrices of the ϕ_{ij}^{car} that contain pairwise correlation coefficients of the sensors that belong to S_1 (left) and S_2 (right)

...	B	C
B	1.0000	0.9142
C	0.9142	1.0000

...	A	B	C
A	1.0000	0.8889	0.9707
B	0.8889	1.0000	0.9142
C	0.9707	0.9142	1.0000

After finding these submatrices, the vehicle calculates the average correlation for each candidate line segment: $\Phi_e^i = \frac{1}{q}\sum_{j=1}^q \phi_{iS_e[j]}$, which approximates the sensor's belief about its line segment membership. Thus for different line segments we have different coefficients for the same sensors. We use the Φ_e^i coefficients as weights to determine the relative importance of the information about a certain location provided by a sensor. At this point we also use the vehicle's set of P_i measurements and the size of each sensor's neighborhood to define a statistic T used to find the proper line segment. By doing so we counterbalance the effect of received responses of nodes which neighbours did not respond. The T statistic takes a maximum value for a line segment for which the certainty of the vehicle's presence is highest.

Phase II. Once the estimated line segment: $\widehat{e}$ is found, the vehicle can search for the estimate $\widehat{\beta}$ of the position on $\widehat{e}$. Here the P_i measurements can be used again. We are only considering the P_i measurements of the sensors that belong to the same line segment $\widehat{e}$, found in the first phase of the algorithm. Usually the parking spots are placed along roads, so the expected P_i of each message, sent by the sensors from the parking spots, should monotonically decrease with the distance between the vehicle and a sensor. Thus we can expect that the sensor for which P_i is the maximum is the closest to the vehicle. We simply take the β parameter of such a sensor as the vehicle's estimate of its position on a certain line segment: $\widehat{\beta}$.

5   Evaluation

5.1   Methodology

In this paragraph we define the performance metric that will measure the accuracy of the proposed methods. The proposed metric is in fact a cost function that shows how much effort a driver would have to devote to get from the estimated location to the real one. Our motivation comes from the following observation: it is easier to move between the real location and the estimated one if both are on the same line segment, even if a driver would have to use the reverse gear. Whereas it is much more difficult to get from the estimated location to the real one through an intersection. Since the tracking subsystem will provide other SmartPark subsystems (e.g. navigation and reservation subsystems) with an actual vehicle's location information, we need to define a performance metric that will express the driver's effort needed to recover from misleading instructions received from SmartPark. Therefore we specify the cost function in the following way. If a driver has to move on the same line segment to get to the estimated location, she does not have to spend more than C effort. When she has to cross an intersection, she has to devote at least C effort. In our approach we express the cost function as a *road graph distance error* Δd_G as follows:

$$\Delta d_G = \begin{cases} |\beta - \widehat{\beta}| & \text{if } \widehat{e} = e \\ 2 - |\beta - \widehat{\beta}| & \text{if } \widehat{e} \neq e \end{cases} \tag{9}$$

One can notice that a driver will have to devote at most $C = 1$ effort in the first case, whereas in the second case the minimal cost will be at least $C = 1$. Therefore we expect from the proposed algorithms that their accuracy in terms of proposed error metric should be at least below 1 and close to 0 as much as possible.

We compare the performance of the two proposed methods under different conditions. The four differrent evaluation areas are illustrated in Figure 2. The

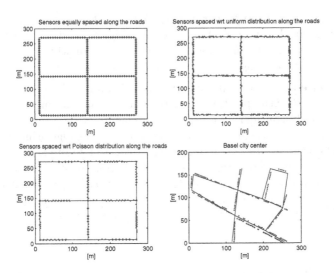

Fig. 2. Four different simulation areas used in tests

first three differ only in terms of sensors' distribution along the line segments. The fourth one is a part of a city centre that contains 220 sensors that are placed along the line segments - all parking spot coordinates and the road network characteristics were taken from the map of Basel city centre.

First we check how the performace depends on the radio conditions for four different deployments of sensors along the line segments. Next, we check the accuracy of the two algorithms with respect to different sensor densities, within three different simulation areas. For this case, we generate five different sets of sensors for each deployment scheme on the grid road network topology.

Because of the MOONwalk algorithm requirements related to the warm-up phase, we had to perform a special pre-computation that defines the road network mapping and the N_i tables for each parking sensor. For this purpose we have projected the road topology onto the parking sensors in the following way. Since all sensors are deployed along the streets, we define an area A that is a rectangle, whose symmetry axis is the given line segment e. If a sensor node is inside this rectangle A, it means that it belongs to the line segment e. It may happen that one parking sensor will be inside more than one such rectangle, which is usually the case if it is close to an intersection; then this parking sensor has more than one location-tuple that forms the set of location-tuples: $\mathcal{L}_i$. The projection technique is shown in Figure 3.

In case of the N_i tables, we specified five different intervals of occurrences i.e $< 25, 20 >$, $< 20, 15 >$, $< 15, 10 >$, $< 10, 5 >$ $< 5, 0 >$ and five corresponding radii $R_1 < R_2 < R_3 < R_4 < R_5$. The technique we used to construct the N_i for each sensor was the following - if the distance between sensors i and j was smaller than R_k then the number of occurrences of j in i's neighbourhood was uniformly chosen from the kth interval.

In our simulations we use one vehicle that is placed at a random intersection and moves randomly with the constant speed, according to pre-defined road

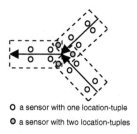

○ a sensor with one location-tuple
◉ a sensor with two location-tuples

Fig. 3. The projection of the road network topology onto the fixed part of SmartPark

rules. We develop our own simulator written in MATLAB. Because the exact distribution of Δd_G is unknown, we evaluate the performance based on the lower quartile, the median and the upper quartile of Δd_G.

5.2 Comparison of the Algorithms

Using the same pre-defined path and radio communication conditions, we evaluate the performance of the proposed algorithms through the cumulative distribution of Δd_G, shown in Figure 4. The ML method outperforms the MOONwalk algorithm in all the cases. However the Δd_G is significantly lower than 1 for at least 80% of cases for both algorithms.

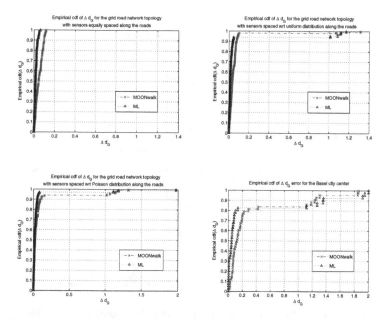

Fig. 4. Comparison of the ML and MOONwalk algorithms based of the empirical cdf of the Δd_G; simulation setup - pathloss exponent: 4, multipath fading: 20 dB, size of each journey: 9 line segments, vehicle's speed: 40 km/h

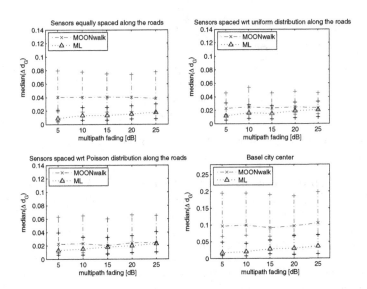

Fig. 5. Performance evaluation of ML and MOONwalk algorithms for different intensities of multipath fading on different simulation areas; simulation setup - pathloss exponent: 4, size of each journey: 70 line segments (approximately 350 Δd_Gs), vehicle's speed: 40 km/h

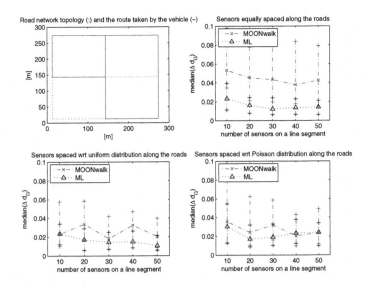

Fig. 6. Performance evaluation of ML and MOONwalk algorithms for a different number of sensors per line segment on different simulation areas; simulation setup - pathloss exponent: 4, multipath fading: 20 dB, size of each journey: 9 line segments, vehicle's speed: 40 km/h

During the second test, we let the vehicle travel through 70 line segments. We calculate the lower quartile, the median and the upper quartile of the Δd_G. We do this for different intensities of Rayleigh fading. The median value of Δd_G grows with multipath intensity for the ML algorithm, which is not the case for the MOONwalk method, as shown in Figure 5. The results of the third test are shown in Figure 6. Here we check how the number of active sensors affect the algorithms performance. The median value of Δd_G decreases with the number of sensors for both algorithms. The improvement is, however, not significant. This is a good sign because the performance of both algorithms does not suffer from sensor outages - if 80% of the sensors from a line segment cannot communicate with a vehicle at a given time, the Δd_G decreases at most of 0.0128 and 0.0123 for ML and MOONwalk algorithms, respectively.

The MOONwalk algorithm depends mostly on the proper projection of the road network topology onto the fixed part of SmartPark. However, its strong advantage is that it does not require as much input data as ML in order to achieve comparable accuracy. Moreover, its accuracy does not decrease in the case of significant multipath fading and it is much easier to implement in a real-life scenario than ML. This shows us that MOONwalk is a good candidate for the tracking subsystem of SmartPark.

6   Related Work

Extensive research has been done on localization and tracking for wireless sensor networks. A general survey on localization is found in [18]. Systems focused on the locating problem on a large geographic scale use, for example, GPS. In the past decade, there have been many different types of location-based projects that work outdoors, where the radio signal is highly disturbed by the presence of obstacles and moving objects. These systems are usually supported by networks of small spatially distributed wireless devices. Here, we focus only on localization techniques suitable for sensor networks that use only the Radio Frequency (RF) based approach.

In [7] Gupta and Das have developed a simple detection and tracking algorithm that involves only simple computation and local communication only to the nodes in the vicinity of the target. They focus only on the unconstrained tracking approach, where the target is unknown to the system and its appearance alerts all sensors along the projected path of the target. In this approach all sensors are capable of estimating the distance of the target to be tracked from the sensor readings. This requires additional effort to map the sensor readings to the distance. In order to track the target they use the triangulation method.

In [17] Youssef et. all present a method for inferring the location of a device based on FM radio signal strengths. The proposed method is robust to measurement differences between devices by basing the inferences on rankings of radio stations rather than on their absolute received signal strength. The method does not require any manual survey of received signal strength as a function of location. However, it requires the usage of the simulated radio maps designed for a given area, validation of simulated received signal strength maps and an additional pre-processing needed to reduce the number of rank vectors that correspond to given locations.

Our approach also uses a RF-based method needed to perform the localization of a mobile node within a wireless sensor network. However, in contrast to the above-mentioned systems where the tracking is unconstrained, our work focuses on the problem of how to build the mobile node's movement constraints into the tracking algorithm in order to meet the application needs. Given the fact that we use a decentralized architecture of small devices that are relatively inexpensive, our constrained tracking approach, especially MOONwalk with the option where no extra hardware is needed, represents an attractive and powerful solution to the vehicle tracking on a road network problem.

7   Conclusion and Future Work

The MOONwalk algorithm is a good candidate for the tracking subsystem of SmartPark mainly because it does not require any additional range-measurement hardware. Its accuracy is comparable with that achieved by the optimal approach specified by ML algorithm. We believe there is still place for improvement. If we introduce more vehicles we can rely not only on the sensor-to-vehicle, but also on the vehicle-to-vehicle communication. We currently are investigating this approach called *collaborative tracking* in more detail. Another possible improvement is to let the vehicle send a *hello* message with the maximum RF power and to let the parking sensor send back several *reply* messages, using different RF power levels. One could combine this approach with the collaborative tracking. By this it might be possible to achieve a sufficient trade-off between communication overhead and accuracy. We are also working on the dynamic version of both methods where we are using the dead reckoning techniques. In order to improve the accuracy of the location estimation, we apply the past location estimates of a vehicle. Preliminary results show that the improvement is significant. We are also investigating the problem of the road network topology projection onto the fixed wireless network of parking sensors. We are currently evaluating the MOONwalk algorithm on a test-bed in a real-life scenario.

References

1. J. Heidemann N. Bulusu and D. Estrin. GPS-less Low-Cost Outdoor Localization for Very Small Devices. *IEEE Personal Communications*, 7:28–34, October 2000.
2. D. Niculescu and B. Nath. DV Based Positioning in Ad Hoc Networks. *Telecommunication Systems*, pages 267–280, January-April 2003.
3. H.T. Kung and D. Vlah. Efficient Location Tracking Using Sensor Networks. In *IEEE Wireless Communications and Networking WCNC2003*, volume 3, pages 1954–1961, March 2003.
4. T. He, C. Huang, B.M. Blum, J.A. Stankovic, and T. Abdelzaher. Range-free Localization Schemes for Large Scale Sensor Networks. In *The 9th Annual International Conference on Mobile Computing and Networking*, pages 81–95, September 2003.

5. D. Estrin N. Bulusu, V. Bychkovskiy and J. Heidemann. Scalable, Ad Hoc Deployable RF-based Localization. In *The Grace Hopper Celebration of Women in Computing Conference*, October 2002.

6. A. Smith, H. Balakrishnan, M. Goraczko, and N. Priyantha. Tracking Moving Devices with the Cricket Location System. In *MobiSYS '04: Proceedings of the 2nd international conference on Mobile systems, applications, and services*, pages 190–202, New York, NY, USA, 2004. ACM Press.

7. R. Gupta and S.R. Das. Tracking Moving Targets in a Smart Sensor Network. In *IEEE Vehicular Technology Conference VTC2003-Fall*, volume 5, pages 3035–3039, October 2003.

8. L. Hu and D. Evans. Localization for Mobile Sensor Networks. In *MobiCom '04: Proceedings of the 10th annual international conference on Mobile computing and networking*, pages 45–57. ACM Press, 2004.

9. SmartPark project website. http://smartpark.epfl.ch.

10. Vehicle Information and Communication System. http://www.vics.or.jp/english/index.html.

11. www.roadtraffic-technology.com : The web site for the road traffic industry. http://www.roadtraffic-technology.com/contractors/parking/.

12. J. Tian, L. Han, K. Rothermel, and C. Cseh. Spatially aware packet routing for mobile ad hoc inter-vehicle radio networks. In *Proceedings of the IEEE 6th International Conference on Intelligent Transportation Systems (ITSC '03)*, October 2003.

13. A. Leonhardi, Ch. Nicu, and K. Rothermel. A Map-Based Dead-Reckoning Protocol for Updating Location Information. In *IPDPS '02: Proceedings of the 16th International Parallel and Distributed Processing Symposium*, page 15, Washington, DC, USA, 2002. IEEE Computer Society.

14. W.C. Jakes. *Microwave Mobile Communications*. Wiley-IEEE Press, May 1994.

15. B. Sklar. Rayleigh Fading Channels in Mobile Digital Communication Systems .I. Characterization. *IEEE Communications Magazine*, 35:90–100, July 1997.

16. D. Ganesan, B. Krishnamachari, A. Woo, D. Culler, D. Estrin, and S. Wicker. Complex Behavior at Scale: An Experimental Study of Low-Power Wireless Sensor Networks, February 2002.

17. A. Youssef, J. Krumm, E. Miller, G. Cermak, and E. Horvitz. Computing Location from Ambient FM Radio Signals. In *IEEE Wireless Communications and Networking Conference (WCNC 2005)*, March 2005.

18. J. Hightower and G. Borriello. Location Systems for Ubiquitous Computing. In *IEEE Computer*, volume 34, pages 57 – 66, August 2001.

Range-Based Localization in Mobile Sensor Networks

Bram Dil[1], Stefan Dulman[2], and Paul Havinga[1,2]

[1] Embedded Systems, University of Twente, The Netherlands
[2] Ambient Systems, The Netherlands
b.j.dil@student.utwente.nl, havinga@cs.utwente.nl,
dulman@ambient-systems.net

Abstract. Localization schemes for wireless sensor networks can be classified as range-based or range-free. They differ in the information used for localization. Range-based methods use range measurements, while range-free techniques only use the content of the messages. None of the existing algorithms evaluate both types of information. Most of the localization schemes do not consider mobility. In this paper, a Sequential Monte Carlo Localization Method is introduced that uses both types of information as well as mobility to obtain accurate position estimations, even when high range measurement errors are present in the network and unpredictable movements of the nodes occur. We test our algorithm in various environmental settings and compare it to other known localization algorithms. The simulations show that our algorithm outperforms these known range-oriented and range-free algorithms for both static and dynamic networks. Localization improvements range from 12% to 49% in a wide range of conditions.

1 Introduction

A wireless sensor network is a network where small sensors with limited hardware capabilities communicate wirelessly with each other. First all nodes are placed in a random matter (like dropping them from an airplane). "When the nodes are dropped", they are capable of communicating with each other within a certain communication radius. The network can be considered as an undirected graph using its connectivity and range measurement information. When certain information is propagated through the network, nodes can be located by using that information.

Wireless sensor networks hold the promise of many new applications in the area of monitoring and control. Examples include target tracking, intrusion detection, wildlife habitat monitoring, climate control, and disaster management ([3]). Localization of the nodes is one of the main issues in a wireless sensor network. While many algorithms have been proposed to estimate the position of the nodes, there is still no algorithm that performs best in all networks.

As range measurements between nodes contain some error, the nodes' locations can only be estimated. This is called "the range error" problem ([2]). Node

K. Römer, H. Karl, and F. Mattern (Eds.): EWSN 2006, LNCS 3868, pp. 164–179, 2006.

localization algorithms dependent on range measurements are sensitive to range errors. While range-free algorithms overcome this problem, they perform badly in irregular networks ([3], [4]). Several studies have been performed to minimize the impact of these range measurement errors. These studies estimate a node's position by giving a certain weight to each measurement or estimated node's location. These weights are then used to compute a least square solution by using an Iterative Weighted Least Square Method (IWLSM) ([2], [7], [19]).

In general, localization algorithms follow the following scheme ([3]): anchor-unknown distance determination, deriving a node's position given the anchor distances, and then refinement of the position estimates. Because mobile sensor networks are changing fast as time progresses, not much effort has been invested in researching the refinement phase. However, this phase can be successfully applied to static networks ([1], [2]).

Most of the current proposed localization algorithms apply an Iterative Weighted Least Square Method ([1], [2], [6], [7], [18], [19]). They differ in determination of the anchor-unknown distances and in weights used in the IWLSM.

Improved MDS-MAP ([5]) uses a different technique: Multi-Dimensional Scaling (MDS). This method uses all available local information around a node and computes a local map for each node. By merging these local maps and known anchor positions, a global map can be computed. With this global map available, the nodes can estimate their position. This centralized localization technique uses a lot of communication and is therefore not applicable in mobile sensor networks. In this study, we compare our algorithm with an IWLSM, using the same weights as our localization scheme. These weights are based on standard and available knowledge of the accuracy of the range measurement hardware.

In addition, we compare our algorithm with the following range-free algorithms: DV-hop ([18]) and an SMCL method ([13]). With increasing range measurement error, the positioning error increases of the range-based algorithms. We made a comparison with range-free algorithms when high range measurement errors are present in the network.

Our algorithm adapts a Monte Carlo Localization (MCL) method, which has been successfully implemented in robotics localization ([11], [12]) and range-free localization in a mobile wireless sensor networks ([13]). Our Monte Carlo Localization algorithm combines range-free and range-based information to improve its performance. It uses the range-free information to increase its robustness even when high range measurement errors are present in the network. In addition, it improves the localization accuracy and lowers the computational costs by using the range measurements. In addition, we use the mobility in the network to increase accuracy.

This paper is organized as follows: After the problem formulation in Section 2, Section 3 describes a known Sequential Monte Carlo Localization solution in a range-free mobile wireless sensor network. In section 4, we introduce our new algorithm that uses all of the range-free information described in Section 3. Section 5 presents the simulation reports and comparisons with other localization algorithms. In Section 6, we analyze the results of our algorithm and compare them with the results of other localization algorithms. Section 7 summarizes the conclusions.

2   Problem Formulation

In a mobile sensor network, we assume that the time is divided into fixed constant time units. In a time unit, the node moves away from its previous location to its current location. When a time unit has elapsed, the localization algorithm has to locate the unknowns with the information available. Our algorithm is interested in estimating the filtering distribution of a node when range measurements are available in the network. The Sequential Monte Carlo approach provides simulation based solutions to estimate the posterior distribution of nonlinear discrete time dynamic models ([9]).

We formulate the mobile localization problem in a state space form as follows: Let t be the discrete time given in time units; l_t is the position distribution of a node given at time t; o_t represents the observations of a node received from the anchors between time $t - 1$ and t. We are interested in estimating recursively in time the so-called filtering distribution: $P(l_t|o_{0:t})$. The filtering distribution is represented by N weighted samples which are updated every time unit, using an importance function. The performance of the Sequential Monte Carlo Localization algorithm is highly dependent on this latter distribution function. In the ideal case samples are drawn from the posterior distribution: $P(l_{0:t}|o_{0:t})$, but most of the time it is impossible to sample directly from the posterior distribution. The general Sequential Monte Carlo method looks like ([15]):

$$P(l_{0:t}|o_{0:t}) = P(l_0|o_0) \prod_{k=1}^{t} P(l_k|l_{0:(k-1)}, o_{0:k}) \qquad (1)$$

Different importance functions have been proposed through the years, which are most of the time special cases of this general algorithm ([15]). An overview of Sequential Monte Carlo methods can be found in ([15]).

3   Known SMCL Solution

A Sequential Monte Carlo Localization algorithm for mobile wireless networks is described in [13]. In this article no range measurements are present so the observations of the node (o_t) only consists of anchor positions. Connectivity constraints are constructed from these anchor positions. They use a prior importance function ([17]), which implies that the importance function draws samples without any knowledge of the observations. They use the following recursive function:

$$P(l_t|o_{0:t}) = P(l_0) \prod_{k=1}^{t} P(l_k|l_{k-1}) \qquad (2)$$

$$\widetilde{w}_t^{(i)} = \widetilde{w}_{t-1}^{(i)} P(o_t|l_t^{(i)}) \qquad (3)$$

Their algorithm is divided into three phases which are described in the next three subparagraphs. In the last subparagraph we discuss the observations and extensions.

3.1   Prediction Phase

In the prediction phase the samples are drawn from the previous predictions: $P(l_t|l_{t-1})$. The algorithm assumes that nodes know their maximum speed V_{max}. Given a previous position l_{t-1} and speed constraint V_{max}, possible predicted positions by l_{t-1} are within a circular region with origin l_{t-1} and radius V_{max}. This gives the following constraint:

$$P(l_t|l_{t-1}) = \begin{cases} \frac{1}{\pi V_{max}^2} & \text{if } d(l_t, l_{t-1}) \le V_{max}, \\ 0 & \text{otherwise.} \end{cases} \tag{4}$$

Here $d(l_t, l_{t-1})$ is the distance between the current prediction l_t and the previous prediction l_{t-1}. Our algorithm also uses this speed constraint (Section 4.2).

3.2   Filtering Phase

In the filtering phase the predictions that do not lie within the connectivity constraints are filtered (Equation 3: $P(o_t|l_i)$). Because the transmission range is modelled as a perfect circle and only two-hop away information is available, the following condition holds:

$$\text{filter}(p) = \forall a \in S, d(p, a) \le tr \cap \forall b \in T, tr \le d(p, b) \le 2tr \tag{5}$$

Here is p the prediction; S is the set of one-hop away anchors, T is the set of two-hop away anchors; tr is the transmission range and $d(p, a)$ is the distance between prediction p and anchor a. Because $P(o_t|l_i)$ (Equation 3) can only be 1 or 0, the weights associated with the predictions are also 1 (valid) or 0 (invalid). Our algorithm uses an extended version of this filtering condition (Section 4.2).

3.3   Re-sampling

After one prediction and filtering step, the number of valid predictions is of variable size. To keep the number of valid predictions of constant size, the process of predicting and filtering is repeated until N valid samples are drawn. The simulations proved that $N = 50$ was sufficient ([13]). The final position estimate is the mean of the predictions.

3.4   Observations and Extensions

In the first time unit, no previous predictions are available ($P(l_0)$). In [13], these previous predictions are placed randomly in the possible area. Placing the previous predictions randomly gives poor results in the first few time units.

We propose that if no previous predictions are available, the algorithm makes predictions based upon the first connectivity constraint received: $P(l_1|o_1^{(1)})$. This proposal, shortly mentioned in [13], not only improves the results in the first few time units but also decreases the "initialization phase" time. We then use the following recursive function:

$$P(l_t|o_{0:t}) = P(l_1|o_1^{(1)}) \prod_{k=2}^{t} P(l_k|l_{k-1}) \tag{6}$$

The importance function draws predictions based only on previous predictions. This means that if the constraints based upon connectivity and previous predictions are tight, many predictions have to be made to come to N valid predictions. It is even possible that this algorithm cannot make any valid predictions. That is why we use a looping limit that limits the number of times the process of predicting and filtering is done. When the looping limit is reached and no valid predictions are made, the algorithm makes predictions as if it had no previous predictions.

4   SMCL and Range Measurements

In this section, we discuss the case when range measurements are present in the network. When we include the range measurements into the recursive Sequential Monte Carlo computation, we obtain the following filtering distribution:

$$P(l_t|o_{cc,0:t}, o_{rm,0:t}) \tag{7}$$

Here $o_{cc,0:t}$ are the connectivity constraints and $o_{rm,0:t}$ are the range measurements.

We made an approximation of the optimal solution ([10]) by dividing the optimal solution into several suboptimal solutions as the optimal solution cannot be evaluated directly. We propose the following new recursive computation:

$$P(l_t|o_{cc,0:t}, o_{rm,0:t}) \approx \sum_{o_{rm,1}^{(i)} \in o_{rm,1}} P(l_1|o_{cc,1}, o_{rm,1}^{(i)})$$

$$\prod_{k=2}^{t} \sum_{o_{rm,k}^{(i)} \in o_{rm,k}} P(l_k|l_{k-1}, o_{cc,k}, o_{rm,k}^{(i)}) \tag{8}$$

Figure 1 shows an overview in pseudocode of the algorithm. The nodes locally use this algorithm to estimate their positions with the received information of the anchors. The different phases of the algorithm are discussed in the following subsections.

```
FOR EVERY "time unit" DO
    saved predictions become saved previous predictions      (section 4.2)
    receive, save and forward anchor-unknown distances       (section 4.1)
    FOR ALL "received range measurements" DO
        Compute Nlocal                                        (section 4.3)
        Predict and save Nlocal predictions                  (section 4.2)
    END FOR;
    Compute weight for each saved prediction                  (section 4.4)
    Compute final position                                    (section 4.4)
END FOR;
```

Fig. 1. Pseudocode of the range-based SMCL algorithm

4.1   Anchor-Unknown Distances

In this phase, the nodes determine their distance to one or multiple anchors by using different range measurements. This information is needed by our algorithm to localize the nodes. Our algorithm uses sum-dist to determine this distance, nameless in [1] and later named in [3]:

First, anchors start flooding the network with their position, a hop distance and path length set to zero. Each receiving node adds the measured range to the path length and increases the hop distance by one. Only the shortest hop distance and path length is forwarded for each anchor. At the end of this phase, every node has stored the anchor positions, minimum hop distances, and minimum path lengths to several anchors.

4.2   Prediction Phase

In the prediction phase, samples are drawn from the previous predictions, connectivity constraints and one range measurement:

$$P(l_k|l_{k-1}, o_{cc,k}, o_{rm,k}^{(i)}) \tag{9}$$

Our algorithm assumes that the nodes know their maximum speed V_{max} (Section 3.1, Equation 4), and the filtering condition that represent the connectivity constraints (Section 3.2, Equation 5) is updated to support n-hop away anchors:

$$\text{filter}(p) = \forall a \in S, d(p,a) \leq tr \cap \forall b \in T, tr \leq d(p,b) \leq n \cdot tr \tag{10}$$

Here is T the set of n-hop away anchors, where $n \geq 2$. We also assume that the transmission range is a perfect circle.

The algorithm needs to evaluate one extra observation compared to the other SMCL scheme: the range measurement. By using standard geometry, we can easily evaluate Equation 9. We must do this for all range measurements. We use this construction because the optimal solution cannot be evaluated directly. An approximation is made by dividing the optimal solution into several suboptimal solutions:

$$P(l_t|l_{t-1}, o_{cc,t}, o_{rm,t}) \approx \sum_{o_{rm,t}^{(i)} \in o_{rm,t}} P(l_t|l_{t-1}, o_{cc,t}, o_{rm,t}^{(i)}) \tag{11}$$

In this case, every range measurement can be seen as a sampling function, not considering the other range measurements. Given range measurement rm to anchor position a, the predictions according to the range measurement are somewhere located at the edge of the circle with origin a and radius rm. This gives the following constraint:

$$P(l_t|o_{rm}) = \begin{cases} 1 & \text{if } d(l_t, a) = rm, \\ 0 & \text{otherwise.} \end{cases} \tag{12}$$

Note that after the prediction phase we only have valid predictions, so we do not need a filtering phase.

4.3   Weights and Sample Size

Our algorithm uses a constant number of predictions: N. This is done to keep the computational costs at a low and constant level. In the prediction phase, the sampling of the predictions is divided into several sampling functions by the range measurements. So every sampling function samples a portion of N predictions: N_{local}. The size of N_{local} depends on the precision of the range measurement, formulated as: $\frac{1}{\sigma_{rm}^2}$. σ_{rm}^2 stands for the variance of the range measurement. This variance is based on the hop distance associated with the range measurement. Every range measurement consists of "hop count" independent range measurements. We use an approximation made in [19]:

$$\sigma_{rm,i}^2 \approx i \cdot \sigma_{rm,1}^2 \tag{13}$$

Here i stands for the number of hops. Our algorithm uses this approximation to compute the ratio between the precisions of the various range measurements. This ratio is used to compute the size of N_{local}, and is later used to compute the final position estimation. Note that this ratio can be calculated only using the "hop count" because we assume that the nodes have the same distance measurement hardware ($\sigma_{rm,1}^2$ is a constant).

4.4   Computing the Final Position Estimation

In this phase, the algorithm uses the predictions, made in the prediction phase, to compute its position estimation. With the available range measurements and associated weights (Equation 13), a weight is estimated for each prediction. Let $p_1 \ldots p_i$ be all predictions with locations $x_1, y_1 \ldots x_i, y_i$. Let $A_1 \ldots A_j$ be all known anchor positions with associated range measurements $R_1 \ldots R_j$ to the specific node. The weights of the predictions are computed by the summed squared error multiplied by the appropriate range measurement weights:

$$\sigma_{p_i}^2 = \sum_{k=1}^{j} \frac{1}{\sigma_{rm,k}^2} \left(d(p_i, A_k) - R_k \right)^2 \tag{14}$$

$\frac{1}{\sigma_{rm,k}^2}$ stands for the precision estimate of range measurement R_k. We take the summed square error as an estimate of the variance of prediction p_i: $\sigma_{p_i}^2$. Using this estimate, the precision of prediction p_i is $\frac{1}{\sigma_{p_i}^2}$. If we have N predictions then the optimal position (x, y) is where: $\sum_{i=1}^{N} \frac{1}{\sigma_{p_i}^2}\left((x_i-x)^2+(y_i-y)^2\right)$ is minimized. This weighted least square solution can be computed with an iterative weighted least square method. It can also be computed with a weighted mean method. The weighted mean method uses less computation power and is therefore a good replacement:

$$
x = \frac{1}{\sum_{i=1}^{N} \sigma_{p_i}^{-2}} \cdot \sum_{i=1}^{N} \sigma_{p_i}^{-2} \cdot x_i
$$

$$
y = \frac{1}{\sum_{i=1}^{N} \sigma_{p_i}^{-2}} \cdot \sum_{i=1}^{N} \sigma_{p_i}^{-2} \cdot y_i
$$

(15)

This algorithm uses the ratio between the weights to compute the weighted least square solution.

4.5 Observations

It is possible that no valid predictions can be made. In this case, the algorithm makes predictions as if it had no previous predictions. When the range measurements are really bad, it is even possible that our algorithm cannot make any valid predictions with no speed constraints. In that case, the recursive function proposed in Section 3.4 is used (Equation 6).

A range measurement that does not satisfy its own connectivity constraint changes its value to the nearest number that satisfies this constraint. This increases the performance of the algorithm in several ways:

- More predictions can be made, giving a better representation of the position distribution.
- Peaks in the range measurements have less influence on the final position estimation.

5   Simulations

In this section, we analyze our algorithm by running several simulations using MatLab. In these simulations, we test our algorithm with different values for algorithm-specific parameters and under various environmental settings. In addition, we compare our results to other localization techniques: these are the IWLSM, the range-free MCL scheme ([13]) and DV-HOP ([18]). We analyze the results of the localization schemes by looking at the mean error versus the communication costs.

5.1   General Simulation Set-Up

Except when stated otherwise, we use the same general set-up for all simulations. The sensor nodes are uniformly placed within a $1x1$ units^2 area and a transmission range tr of 0.125 units is used. For simplicity, the transmission range is simulated as a perfect circle and messages are always received correctly.

The parameters we vary are:

- The number of predictions drawn by the sampling function. In general, we use a number of 50 samples.
- The number of nodes placed within the area. In general, we use a number of 180 nodes. The node density (average number of 1-hop away nodes) is determined by simulation. The general set-up has a node density of: 13.9.
- The number of anchors placed within the area. In general, we use a number of 20 anchors. The anchor density (average number of 1-hop away anchors) is determined by simulation. The general set-up has an anchor density of: 1.3.
- The speed of the nodes, which we choose randomly from $[0, Vmax]$. The nodes' speed is given as a ratio of the transmission range. In general, we use a speed of $[0, 1]$.
- The Time-To-Live (TTL) of the messages. This value indicates the number of times a message is forwarded. We keep the communication costs per algorithm the same with this parameter, so the performance of the different algorithms are determined by the localization error. DV-Hop isn't affected by the TTL and has different communication costs than the other algorithms. In general, we use a TTL of 4 for every algorithm.
- The range measurement errors, which we simulate by a Gaussian distribution with the real distance as the mean. The standard deviation of the error is represented as a ratio of the real range. In general, we use a standard deviation of 0.2 ([7]). This value is based on the picoradio ([8]) that uses Received Signal Strength Indication (RSSI) for range measurements.
- We tested each simulation setup for 50 runs, each consisting of 50 time units.

We adopt a modified ([13]) random waypoint mobility model ([16]) for the nodes. With this model, a node randomly chooses its destination. After arriving at its destination, the node chooses a new destination. Furthermore, the speed of the nodes are changed and randomly chosen from $[0, Vmax]$ after each time unit and when the nodes arrive at their destinations. We use this model to maintain an average speed. Before localization, we run the modified random waypoint mobility model for several time units to maintain the distribution created by this mobility model.

We use the following settings for the other localization schemes:

- The extensions proposed in this article (Section 3.4 and Equation 6) are used for the range-free SMCL scheme ([13]). We also need another update to support different values of TTL (Section 4.2, Equation 10). We use a looping limit of 10 and a sample size of 50, which should be enough according to [13].
- The IWLSM uses the same weights and range measurement values as our algorithm.
- We use the DV-hop localization scheme as proposed in ([18]).

5.2 Accuracy

In this section, we analyze the performance of the various algorithms in case of the general settings, described in section 5.1. Figure 2 shows the mean error as a

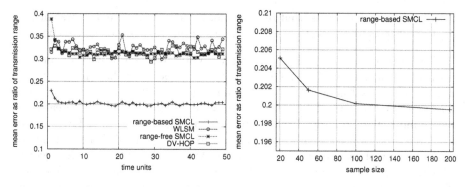

Fig. 2. Mean error per time unit   **Fig. 3.** Mean error per sample size

ratio of the transmission range for all the nodes that received information from three or more anchors. For both of the SMCL schemes, the localization process can be divided into the initialization phase and the stable phase ([13]). In the initialization phase, the positioning error decreases rapidly as new observations are evaluated. The region of the position distribution becomes smaller until a stable phase is reached. In the stable phase, the impact of the mobility and connectivity constraints on the position distribution remain in equilibrium, and the mean error fluctuates around some mean value. From the first to the last time unit our SMCL scheme outperforms the other algorithms in terms of the mean error. All the algorithms have the same communication costs (TTL), except for DV-hop that has a higher communication cost.

The localization error in the first time unit gives an indication of the mean error in a static network. The simulations show an improvement of the mean error in the dynamic case of 36% and in the static case of 27%.

5.3 Sample Size

The predictions and associated weights are a representation of the probability distribution. When more predictions are made, a better approximation of the probability distribution is made. While maintaining more samples improves accuracy, it also increases the computational and memory costs for the node. In this section we try to find a balance between the benefits and losses.

Figure 3 shows that increasing the sample size beyond 20 has a minimal effect on the positioning error with these specific simulation settings. Choosing the right sample size mainly depends on the quality and quantity of the received observations per node. This quality and/or quantity is directly influenced by the TTL of a message, seed density and precision of the range measurements. So more samples are needed when the accuracy of the received observations increases.

5.4 Message TTL

The increase of the number of times a message is forwarded is equivalent to an increase of the average amount of information received by a node. Using this amount, we distinguished two types of nodes:

- Good connected nodes, that receive information from three or more anchors.
- Bad connected nodes, that receive information from two or less anchors.

These two types of nodes are not only divided by connectivity to anchors, but also by localization error. Therefore, the ratio between the number of good and bad connected nodes mainly determines the overall mean error. This ratio is affected by the TTL. Figure 5 shows that increasing the TTL, decreases the overall mean error rapidly. The drawback is that increasing the TTL, increases the communication costs. Figure 6 shows what affect the TTL has on the average number of messages sent by a node. After each TTL wave the received information is combined and forwarded in one message, so this average number of messages represents the minimum. "Other algorithms" in Figure 6 and 7 represent the range-based, range-free and IWLSM localization algorithms, because the communication costs for these algorithms are equal. The communication costs of the DV-hop algorithm cannot be changed by the TTL, because it consists of two predefined phases. Figure 6 shows that the communication costs for the DV-Hop algorithm are more than twice as big as for the other algorithms.

Hence, every time a message is forwarded, the range measurements become less precise and the connectivity constraints become less tight. This is illustrated

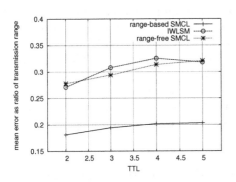

Fig. 4. Mean error per TTL, good connected nodes

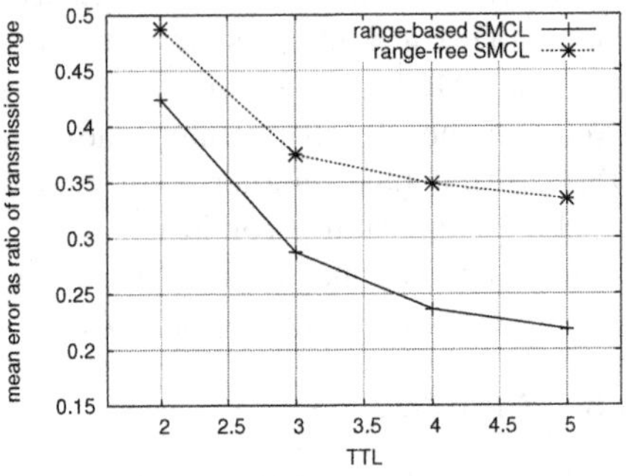

Fig. 5. Mean error per TTL, good and bad connected nodes

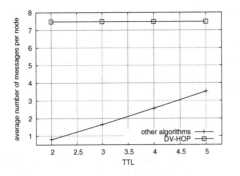

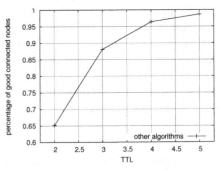

Fig. 6. Number of messages per TTL

Fig. 7. Good connected nodes per TTL

by Figure 4, which shows a decrease of accuracy of good connected nodes with increasing TTL. Figure 4 also shows that this decrease of accuracy with increasing TTL is minimal.

The bad connected nodes have a dramatically high mean error compared to the good connected nodes. So including the position estimates of the bad connected nodes is questionable. When these position estimates are not included, the chosen TTL for a mobile wireless sensor network mainly depends on the desired localization coverage. Figure 7 shows the increase of good connected nodes when the TTL increases.

Therefor, in this paper we use the good connected nodes for the determination of the mean error.

5.5   Anchor Density

Increasing the number of anchors in the network increases the average number of observations per node. The localization accuracy depends on this number. The drawback is that deploying more anchors increases the network and deployment costs. Figure 8 shows the effect of anchor density on the mean error. The number of 10, 20 and 30 anchors represent the following anchor densities: 0.65, 1.3 and 1.9. Our algorithm performs in terms of mean error 31% better with low anchor density and 33% with high anchor density than the best other algorithm.

5.6   Node Density

Figure 9 shows the effect of the node density on the localization accuracy. The number of 100, 150, 200, 250 and 300 nodes represent the following node densities: 7.4, 10.6, 13.9, 17.0 and 20.1.

We only need the hop-distance to several anchors for the range-free SMCL scheme to work. That is why this algorithm only requires a low node density to run properly ([13]). Increasing the node density slowly increases the number of observations per node, so the mean error of the range-free SMCL scheme remains practically stable while the node density is changed. We know that range-based algorithms, especially the performance of sum-dist, are affected by the node

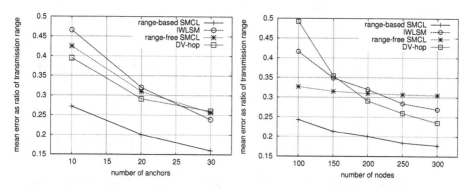

Fig. 8. Mean error per anchor density   **Fig. 9.** Mean error per node density

density ([3]). Increasing the node density leads to straighter paths between the nodes and anchors, so that the shortest path becomes a better approximation of the real distance. When the real distances are better approximated, the range-based algorithms perform better.

Figure 9 shows an improvement of the mean error of 25% with low node density and 25% with high node density than the best other algorithm compared with our algorithm.

5.7 Node Speed

The frequency of the localization announcements influences the traveled distances of the nodes per time unit. Therefore, if localization announcements are more frequent, the speed of the node per time unit decreases. Updating the position estimate more frequently improves localization accuracy at the cost of communication.

Increasing the speed, increases the size of the prediction surface, which is constructed by the speed and connectivity constraints. This size affects the localization error, because it limits the position distribution.

In this simulation set-up, we only compare our algorithm with its range-free counterpart because the node speed is only used by the SMCL schemes. Figure 10 shows that our algorithm performs in terms of mean error 36% better with a low speed and 49% with a high speed than the range-free MCL scheme.

5.8 Range Measurement Error

The precision of the range measurements has a significant influence on the accuracy of the range-based localization schemes.

Figure 11 shows that our algorithm performs 40% better with a low range measurement error and 41% with a high range measurement error than the IWLSM. Even with a range measurement error of 0.4 our algorithm has a 12% lower mean error than the best range-free algorithm.

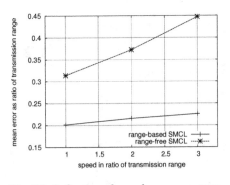

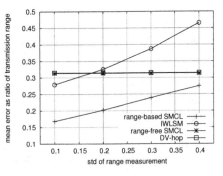

Fig. 10. Influence of speed on mean error

Fig. 11. Influence of range measurement error on mean error

6   Analysis

In this section, we analyze our algorithm and compare it with other known algorithms. Our algorithm is interested in the filtering condition (Equation 7). We made an approximation of the optimal solution by using several suboptimal solutions (Equation 11) as the optimal solution cannot be evaluated directly. In our case, we use the range measurements to characterize these suboptimal solutions. We use the same range measurements in the final position estimation. This construction has several benefits:

- Bad range measurements filtered by the connectivity and/or speed constraints do not have any influence on the position distribution.
- Every range measurement gives an indication of the real position of the node, so that all measurements are evaluated in the final position estimation.
- The performance of our algorithm is less dependent on the range measurement errors (Figure 11).

The range-free MCL scheme([13]) uses a prior sampling function. This means that this MCL scheme makes predictions based upon its previous predictions and filters bad predictions with the connectivity constraints. This iterative two-step construction is needed because the posterior distribution cannot be evaluated directly. Our range-based algorithm uses a non-iterative MCL scheme and evaluates as much information as possible in the sampling function. This has several benefits over its range-free counterpart:

- Every previous prediction has a more equal chance to make a prediction.
- The computational costs are more constant and less situation dependent.
- Our algorithm is less dependent on the speed of the node (Figure 10).
- Using the range measurements, our algorithm decreases localization error by 12% to 49% (Figure 11).

Many of the known range-based and range-free localization algorithms use an Iterative Weighted Least Square Method to estimate positions. The IWLSM starts from an initial estimation and improves the position until the improvement is smaller than a certain value. The position estimate is the global or local minimum of the summed weighted squared error, using the range measurements and associated weights. In most situations, especially when the range error increases, there are more local minima. Dependent on the starting position the IWLSM chooses one of these local minima. Our approach uses the fact that these local minima are located near the range measurements. Our algorithm tries to make predictions near these local minima to evaluate the entire surface, while not picking one of these local minima.

As an example, consider the case when the positions of the anchors are collinear and the range measurements contain no error. In the perfect case, the IWLSM chooses one of the local minima, while our algorithm chooses the mean of the two local minima. If we also evaluate the previous position distribution, the mobility and connectivity constraints the collinearity problem [1] is often solved.

In this paper, the communication costs for the different algorithms are equal, except for the DV-hop algorithm that uses much more communication (Figure 6).

7   Conclusions

In this paper, we proposed a non-iterative MCL scheme that uses all information to improve localization accuracy and robustness. This information consists of range measurements, connectivity constraints, and mobility information. Simulations show that our algorithm decreases the localization error by 12% to 49% in static and dynamic networks under a wide range of conditions, even when the node and network resources are limited. Future work aims at testing our algorithm in other mobility models and real life settings.

References

1. A. Savvides, H. Park and M. Srivastava: The Bits and Flops of the N-Hop Multi-lateration Primitive for Node Localization Problems. In First ACM International Workshop on Wireless Sensor Networks and Application, Atlanta, GA, September 2002.
2. C. Savarese, J. Rabay and K. Langendoen: Robust Positioning Algorithms for Distributed Ad-Hoc Wireless Sensor Networks. USENIX Technical Annual Conference, Monterey, CA, June 2002.
3. Koen Langendoen and Niels Reijers: Distributed localization in wireless sensor networks: A quantitative comparison. In Computer Networks (Elsevier), special issue on Wireless Sensor Networks, 2003.
4. Y. Shang, W. Ruml, Y. Zhang and M. Fromherz: Localization From Mere Connectivity. MobiHoc'03, Annapolis, Maryland, June 2003.
5. Yi Shang and Wheeler Ruml: Improved MDS-based localization. In Infocom 2004
6. L.Evers,W.Bach, D.Dam,M.Jonker, H.Scholten, and P.Havinga: An iterative quality based localization algorithm for adhoc networks. In Department of Computer Science, University of Twente, 2002.
7. L.Evers, S.Dulman, P.Havinga: A distributed precision based localization algorithm for ad-hoc networks. Proceedings of Pervasive Computing (PERVASIVE 2004).
8. Jan Beutel: Geolocation in a picoradio environment. In MS Thesis, ETH Zurich, Electronics Lab, 1999.
9. J.E.Handschin: Monte Carlo Techniques for Prediction and Filtering of Non-Linear Stochastic Processes. Automatica 6. pp. 555-563. 1970.
10. V.S.Zaritskii, V.S.Svetnik, L.I.Shimelevich: Monte Carlo technique in problems of optimal data processing. Automation and Remote Control 12: 95-103. 1974.
11. F.Dellaert, D.Fox, W.Burgard, S.Thrun: Monte Carlo Localization for Mobile Robots. IEEE International Conference on Robotics and Automation (ICRA). May 1999.
12. S.Thrun, D.Fox, W.Burgard, F.Dellaert: Robust Monte Carlo Localization for Mobile Robots. Artificial Intelligence Journal. 2001.
13. L.Hu, D.Evans: Localization for Mobile Sensor Networks. Tenth Annual International Conference on Mobile Computing and Networking (MobiCom 2004), USA. 2004.

14. A.Kong, J.S.Liu, W.H.Wong: Sequential Imputations and Bayesian Missing Data Problems. Journal of the American Statistical Association. Volume 89, pp. 278-288. 1994.
15. A.Doucet, S.Godsill, C.Andrieu: On Sequential Monte Carlo Sampling Methods for Bayesian Filtering. Statistics and Computing. Volum 10, pp. 197-208. 2000.
16. T.Camp, J.Boleng, V.Davies: A survey of Mobility Models for Ad Hoc Networks Research. Wireless Communications and Mobile Computing. Volume 2, Number 5. 2002.
17. H.Tanizaki, R.S.Mariano: Nonlinear and non-Gaussian statespace modeling with Monte-Carlo simulations. Journal of Econometrics 83: 263-290. 1998.
18. D.Niculescu, B.Nath: Ad hoc positioning systems. In: IEEE Globecom 2001, San Antonio. 2001.
19. S.Dulman, P.Havinga: Statistically enhanced localization schemes for randomly deployed wireless sensor networks. DEST International Workshop on Signal Processing for Sensor Networks, Australia. 2004.

Hierarchical Localization Algorithm Based on Inverse Delaunay Tessellation

Masayuki Saeki[1], Junya Inoue[2], Kok-How Khor[3], Tomohiro Kousaka[1], Hiroaki Honda[3], Kenji Oguni[3], and Muneo Hori[3]

[1] Tokyo University of Science, 2641 Yamazaki, Noda-shi, Chiba 278-8510, Japan
saeki@rs.noda.tus.ac.jp
[2] The University of Tokyo, 7-3-1 Hongo, Bunkyo, Tokyo 113-0033, Japan
inoue@material.t.u-tokyo.ac.jp
[3] Earthquake Research Institute, The University of Tokyo,
1-1-1 Yayoi, Bunkyo, Tokyo 113-0032, Japan
oguni@eri.u-tokyo.ac.jp

Abstract. This paper presents the hierarchical sensor network system for robust localization. This system consists of parent nodes with a low priced L1 GPS receiver and child nodes equipped with an acoustic ranging device. Relative positions between child nodes are estimated based on acoustic ranging through the inverse Delaunay algorithm. This algorithm localizes all the nodes simultaneously, thus, the accumulation of the error in the localization is suppressed. Relatively localized child sensor nodes are given global coordinates with the help of GPS on parent nodes. Field experiment was conducted with three GPS parent nodes and twenty-one child nodes (MOTE).

1 Introduction

This paper presents the concept and the implementation of the hierarchical sensor network system for robust localization. The physical implementation of this system consists of child nodes with acoustic ranging device, parent nodes with low cost L1 GPS and the central CPU (called as GPS server). Localization of the sensor nodes in this system is achieved by a distributed algorithm called "Inverse Delaunay Algorithm." One of the final targets to apply this system is civil infrastructures. High resolution sensing and on-site simulation using dense sensor network on civil infrastructures can be regarded as a typical example of sensor embedded society.

The sensor network applied to civil infrastructures should cover wide area with high spatial resolution. This results in the requirement for numerous sensor nodes with low cost. This cost consists of cost for sensor itself and the installation cost. Especially to reduce the installation cost, automatic localization of the sensor nodes is needed. Although the required accuracy of localization depends on the application, we aim at the accuracy of less than 10cm for all the sensor nodes distributed over the space of the size of a whole city. Installation of GPS receivers on all the sensor nodes is not a realistic option because of the cost

K. Römer, H. Karl, and F. Mattern (Eds.): EWSN 2006, LNCS 3868, pp. 180–195, 2006.

of available GPS receivers with the accuracy under consideration. Therefore, hierarchical sensor network with parent nodes equipped with GPS (to provide reference coordinates) and child nodes with low cost devices (to determine relative positions) is the option we came up with.

Localization of the sensor nodes presented in this paper uses relative distance between neighboring nodes measured by the acoustic ranging as input data. Direct application of the techniques in surveying (i.e., starting from reference nodes, localization is done on the nodes consecutively through the triangulation) does not work in this case because of the noisy measurement on the relative distance and the accumulation of the error. It seems that the distributed algorithm consisting of i) construction of local cluster of nodes with relative positions identified in the local coordinates for the cluster and ii) inter-cluster patching algorithm, works better for localization based on noisy measurement on the relative distance between nodes. Existing work based on this approach is summarized in Moore *et al.* [1] as attempts for graph realization problem. In this problem, reduction of the flexibility of the local cluster of the nodes (e.g., flip ambiguity, discontinuous flex ambiguity) is the major concern[2]. The inverse Delaunay algorithm presented in this paper is categorized in the attempts for graph realization problem.

This paper presents the hierarchical localization algorithm and its physical implementation as follows: In the second section, the overview of the system is presented. A distributed algorithm, inverse Delaunay algorithm, for robust localization of the sensor nodes is presented in the third section. The ingredients for physical implementation of the system, the parent node with low cost L1 GPS is presented in the fourth section, then the acoustic ranging devices and the algorithm implemented with the child node (Mote) are presented in the fifth section. Discussion on GPS in the fourth section is mainly focused on the improvement of the accuracy of the low cost L1 GPS up to a few cm order. This improvement solves the dilemma between the cost and the accuracy, and makes the pervasive use of the proposed system on the civil infrastructures possible. Acoustic ranging discussed in the fifth section uses off-the-shelf acoustic actuator (sounder) and acoustic sensor (microphone) on the Mica2. Unlike tone detection often used in the ranging with ultrasonic wave, our method depends on the digital data processing on the observed acoustic wave. This feature increases the tolerance against the noise. By data stacking, accuracy of the ranging can be improved. (Theoretically speaking, numerous stacking improves the accuracy upto the resolution of ADC.) Finally, the results from field experiment showing the performance of the system are presented in the sixth section.

2   Hierarchical Sensor Network

2.1   Hardware

The hierarchical sensor network system is composed of parent sensor nodes and child sensor nodes. Both of the nodes are built upon the widely used Mica mote platform developed by UC Berkeley [3]. Specifically, the second generation

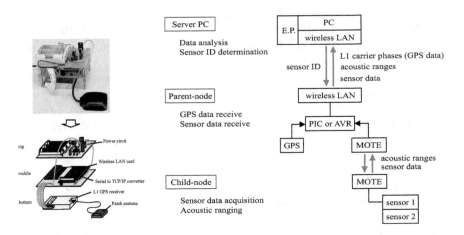

Fig. 1. Parent node   **Fig. 2.** Hierarchical functions of the unit at each rank

Mica2, featuring a 7.3 MHz 8-bit Atmel ATmega 128L low power microcontroller, a 315MHz Chipcon CC1000 multi-channel transceiver with 38.4kbps transfer rate and a 4kB RAM and 128kB flash memory, is used. Each sensor node is connected to an aoustic sensor board with a 4kHz sounder and a microphone for local measurement of distance between nodes using acoustic ranging technique. The parent node is equipped with an additional communication board with a 4MHz 8-bit Microchip PIC microcontroller, a L1 GPS receiver, and a Wireless LAN adopter (IEEE 802.11b). Figure 1 shows the schematic view of the parent node. GT-8032 GPS receiver (FURUNO CO., Ltd) is adopted in the present research. The receiver has 16 channels to search for the C/A codes and capability to track 12 satellites simultaneously. Data in the extended NMEA format, which stores navigation data, ephemeris, and L1 carrier phases, accompanied by some other useful information, is generated every one second from a serial port. 1 PPS signal synchronized to UTC (Coordinated Universal Time) is also available in the data. A patch antenna is connected to the L1 GPS receiver. This type of antenna has its advantage in the cost at the expense of the measurement accuracy. Since the measurement of the L1 carrier phase cycles is significantly affected by the multipath noise, espcially in the case where the low cost L1 GPS receiver is utilized with a patch antenna, a new algorithm is developed to compensate the disadvantage. A communication board is designed to convert data format between serial data for Mica mote platform and TCP/IP for Wireless LAN adopter. For this purpose, EZL-80C (Sollae Systems Co., Ltd) is installed in the communication board. A greater communication capability compared to the 38.4kbps transfer rate of a Chipcon CC1000 is achieved by the use of Wireless LAN adopters.

2.2 System Overview

The overview of the hierarchical sensor network system can be summarised as in the Figure. 2.

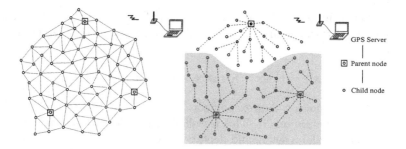

Fig. 3. Schematic veiw of the hierarchical sensor network (left) and the routing path (right)

The typical hierarchical sensor network system deployment will consist of one GPS server, several parent nodes, and several tens of child nodes placed at different locations in a large area of a study field as shown in Figure.3. The communications between child nodes and parent nodes utilizes an ad hoc wireless sensor network built on the Mica mote platform, and those between parent nodes and a GPS server is based on a conventional ad hoc wireless LAN network.

After deployment, the child nodes start to find the closest route to one of the parent nodes, based on the gradient convergecast policy[4], thus separate the whole area of study into several subregions in which one parent node becomes the only sink for the data acquired by corresponding child nodes as shown in Figure.3. Since there will be no direct communication between a GPS server and a child node, the resulting structure of the data transfer paths is in a tree topology. Consequently, the total data transfer rate of the whole system can be easily controlled by the number of parent nodes in the system. Once the routes are established, measured distances between each sensor nodes will be delivered to the GPS server.

The L1 GPS receiver on a parent node collects continuous data sets which contains cycles of the L1 carrier phase as well as the C/A code. The L1 carrier phase will be analysed by the method developed in the current study to obtain a receiver absolute position which will be an anchor point for determining the absolute localizations of sensor nodes through the inverse Delaunay algorithm, as discussed later. Since the receiver also outputs an accurate time stamp that is synchronized to the UTC, combined with the well-known RBS[5] and TPSN[6] approach, one can implement a time synchronization module on TinyOS for better time synchronization in data acquisition system. However, this feature has not been implemented in the present research.

3   Inverse Delaunay Algorithm for Relative Localization

Before discussing the details of the inverse Delaunay algorithm, mathematical definition and the characteristic of the Delaunay diagram [7] are given below.

For a set of finite number of points $X = \{\mathbf{x}^1, \mathbf{x}^2, \cdots, \mathbf{x}^n\}$ on 2-dimensional real space ($\Re^2$) with a definition of Euclid distance $d(\mathbf{x}, \mathbf{y})$ between points $\mathbf{x}$ and $\mathbf{y}$, define

$$V(\mathbf{x}^i) = \left\{\mathbf{x} \mid \mathbf{x} \in \Re^2, \ d(\mathbf{x}, \mathbf{x}^i) < d(\mathbf{x}, \mathbf{x}^j), \ j \neq i\right\}. \tag{1}$$

Then, $V(\mathbf{x}^i)$ becomes a convex polygon and a set $\left\{V(\mathbf{x}^1), V(\mathbf{x}^2), \cdots, V(\mathbf{x}^n)\right\}$ provides a tessellation on $\Re^2$. This tessellation is called Voronoi tessellation (or Voronoi diagram) for a set X and denoted as $V(X)$. Points in a set X are called mother points of $V(X)$, and $V(\mathbf{x}^i)$ is called a Voronoi region for a mother point $\mathbf{x}^i$. When $V(\mathbf{x}^i)$ and $V(\mathbf{x}^j)$ share the Voronoi edge (i.e., edges of the Voronoi polygon), conjugate geometry to Voronoi diagram can be obtained by connecting $\mathbf{x}^i$ and $\mathbf{x}^j$. This diagram is called Delaunay diagram and the tessellation using Delaunay diagram is called Delaunay tessellation. The vertices and the circum-centers of the Delaunay polygon correspond to the mother points in Voronoi tessellation and vertices of the Voronoi polygons, respectively. **Polygons in the Delaunay diagram on 2-dimensional real space are the triangles with no mother point in their circumscribed circle.** We use this characteristic of the Delaunay diagram for the construction of local clusters.

The inverse Delaunay algorithm consists of two steps discussed in the following subsections. For the sake of simplicity, description of the algorithm is given for 2-dimensional problem setting.

3.1   Construction of Local Cluster – Delaunay Cluster

Figure 4 shows a typical example of the local cluster. In this local cluster, the center node is surrounded by the Delaunay triangles and all the nodes are localized in the local Euclidean coordinate system with the center node set as the origin. Also, the nodes surrounding the center node (satellite nodes) are numbered counter-clockwise in the local coordinate system. This numbering determines the direction of the face of the local cluster. This Delaunay cluster is identified for each node in the network.

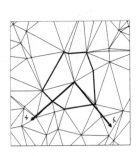

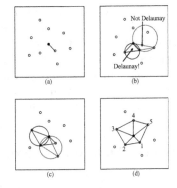

Fig. 4. Typical example of the local cluster   **Fig. 5.** Delaunay cluster construction

The local cluster is constructed in the manner as shown in Figure 5.

1. A node is picked up as a center node (filled circle in the figure) and the closest neighboring node is identified based on the measurement of the relative distance. (Figure 5 (a))
2. Triangles are formed and checked whether it is Delaunay or not. Triangle with dotted line in the Figure 5 (b) is not Delaunay since other node is located in the circumscribed circle.
3. Delaunay check is continued using the edge of the constructed Delaunay triangle as a starting edge of the next Delaunay triangle (Figure 5 (c)).
4. After surrounding the center node by Delaunay triangles, the satellite nodes are numbered. The Delaunay cluster shown in Figure 5 (d) has the clockwise numbering. This means the local coordinate for this Delaunay cluster is flipped with respect to the global coordinate (which can be identified after the global localization is done).

3.2   Cluster Merging Procedure

Once the local Delaunay clusters are constructed for all the nodes, the remaining task is to merge those clusters together. Figure 6 shows this cluster merging procedure.

1. Clusters are divided into two groups, i.e., the atomic clusters and the bridging clusters. The atomic clusters are those with satellite nodes not being occupied by other clusters (i.e., polygons depicted by the edges with thick lines in Figure 6). The bridging clusters are others. This categorization is done by first-come-first-serve basis in the current version of our source code. However, the categorization based on the reliability or the shape of the Delaunay cluster can be implemented.
2. Connect the atomic clusters (or groups) by the bridging clusters. If the order of numbering of the corresponding satellite nodes of both clusters (or groups) coincides, direction of the faces of these clusters (or groups) are different. Either one of them should be flipped. In Figure 6, corresponding nodes in the atomic and the bridging patch are numbered as $1 \rightarrow 2$ and $2 \rightarrow 3$, respectively, i.e., both have the ascending order. Therefore, the bridging cluster is flipped.

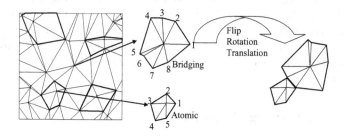

Fig. 6. Cluster merging procedure

3. Apply the necessary flip, rotation and translation to the cluster or group to be consolidated.
4. Continue the second and the third process until all the clusters are merged into a group.

Note that the computational complexity of the construction of the Delaunay clusters and this merging process are $O(n)$, where n is the number of the nodes.

3.3   Discussion on the Inverse Delaunay Algorithm

As shown in the previous subsections, the proposed localization algorithm gives the relative location of the nodes using local clusters consisting of the Delaunay triangles. Thus, the algorithm is named as the inverse Delaunay algorithm. Although the description of the algorithm in this paper is given in 2-dimensional setting, it can be applied to 3-dimensional space by extending the space under consideration to $\Re^3$. In this case, Delaunay polygons become tetrahedrons, the construction of the Delaunay cluster and cluster merging takes more time than 2-dimensional case. However, the computational complexity remains $O(n)$.

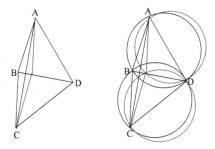

Fig. 7. Left: the quadrilateral is not robust because of the measurement noise in the length BD, right: regardless of the position of node B, inverse Delaunay algorithm works

The major advantage of the inverse Delaunay algorithm is the robustness against the measurement error in ranging. To close the discussion on this algorithm, consider the situation shown in Figure 7 as a typical example. In this situation, most of the localization algorithms based on robust quadrilaterals regard this quadrilateral as a potential source of the flip ambiguity and discards this quadrilateral. As a result, failure in localization of some nodes in the network is often observed. On the other hand, as shown in Figure 7, this situation does not cause any problem to the inverse Dealunay algorithm. This is due to the bigger margin allowed in checking the Delaunay condition than that for robustness of the quadrilateral.

4   GPS Positioning Algorithm

This section is related to the determination of the absolute position of sensor nodes based on low cost L1 GPS receivers.

A L1 GPS receiver is the receiver that is able to collect and output cycles of the L1 carrier phase as well as the C/A code. The receiver position can be determined by the accuracy of a few centimeters or less than a centimeter using the relative positioning approach. This type of receiver was so expensive that it was difficult to distribute such receivers in dense. However, in the last few years, the price of some kind of L1 GPS receivers became drastically cheaper, e.g., Novatel Superstar II and Furuno GT-8032. Therefore, it is now possible to equip such L1 GPS receiver into the sensor nodes.

These low cost L1 GPS receivers are recently equipped in the deformation measurement system for volcano monitoring [9]. They develop the deformation monitoring system and assess its performance. They also conduct field experiments and detect the deformation of the volcano. The difference between their and our application is the noise environment. In our application, the noises due to the troposphere and ionosphere are negligibly small. On the other hand, the cycle slip frequently occurs.

The detection of the cycle slip and its repair is the important problem. Therefore, a lot of approaches are developed. For example, Lee *et al* [10] detect and repair the cycle slip using the help of the INS (Inertial Navigation System) device. In the most techniques, the external information is used as well as the L1 carrier phases. However, if the two receivers are very close to each other and the positions are fixed, it is not difficult to detect and repair the cycle slip using only the information of the L1 carrier phases.

In this section, first, the basic formulation for estimating the position and integer ambiguities is summarized. Second, the simple cycle slip detection and repair technique are presented. It uses only the information of the L1 carrier phases but uses the feature of the sensor network.

4.1 Basic Formulation

There are many algorithm of the relative positioning [8]. The basic formulation employed in this algorithm is summarized below.

Suppose that the position of the reference receiver is known and a receiver whose position is unknown is fixed at a position. In the relative positioning, the corrected carrier phases $\Phi(t)$ are modeled as the eq.(2)

$$\Phi(t) = A(t)\mathbf{x} \tag{2}$$

where $\mathbf{x}$ is the unknown vector that includes the coordinates of the small perturbation around the approximate position and the integer ambiguities N_{ij}^{kl}. $A(t)$ is the coefficient matrix of the unknown vector $\mathbf{x}$ which depends only on the geometry of the satellites and the receiver. The components of the corrected carrier phases $\hat{\phi}_{ij}^{kl}(t)$ are given as eq.(3).

$$\hat{\phi}_{ij}^{kl}(t) = \phi_{ij}^{kl}(t) - \hat{\rho}_{ij}^{kl}(t) \tag{3}$$

where $\phi_{ij}^{kl}(t)$ is the double difference of the observed L1 carrier phases, $\hat{\rho}_{ij}^{kl}(t)$ is the double difference of the distance between the approximate position and the satellites.

When n_s satellites are tracked on both of i and j receivers, the number of unknown variables is $n_s + 2$ that is the sum of 3 for the components of the small perturbation and $n_s - 1$ for N_{ij}^{kl}. On the other hand, the number of the independent equations is $(n_s - 1)n_t$, where n_t is the number of sampling data. Eq.(2) is solved using maximum likelihood method. As the result, the unknown vector $\mathbf{x}$ is given as

$$\mathbf{x} = \left[\sum_t A(t)^T R(t)^{-1} A(t) \right]^{-1} \sum_t A(t) R(t)^{-1} \Phi(t) \tag{4}$$

where $R(t)$ is the variance-covariance matrix at time t. This solution $\mathbf{x}$ is called the float solution.

The obtained N_{ij}^{kl} are the float values. In order to estimate the accurate position, it is needed to find out the correct integer values that are called the fixed solution. The integers are searched to minimize the following objective function.

$$J = \left(\hat{N}_{ij}^{kl} - N_{ij}^{kl} \right) R_N^{-1} \left(\hat{N}_{ij}^{kl} - N_{ij}^{kl} \right)^T \tag{5}$$

where $\hat{N}_{ij}^{kl}$ is the fixed solution of the integer ambiguity, R_N is the variance-covariance matrix of the estimated N_{ij}^{kl}. The accurate position is estimated by solving the eq.(2) with the estimated $\hat{N}_{ij}^{kl}$.

4.2   Cycle Slip Correction Based on the Kalman Filtering

When an obstacle passes through the straight line between the receiver and the satellite, the carrier phase is unlocked and jumps by an integer value. This phenomenon is called cycle slip. The cycle slip also occurs when people or a car pass by the receiver. In order to estimate the accurate position of the sensor nodes, it is needed to correct the observed carrier phases.

If the positions of the two receivers are known, the double difference of the integer ambiguities are accurately estimated using the equation

$$\hat{N}_{ij}^{kl}(t) = \hat{\phi}_{ij}^{kl}(t)/\lambda. \tag{6}$$

where λ is the wavelength of the L1 carrier wave. In the general case in which the position is unknown, the value $\hat{N}_{ij}^{kl}(t)$ gradually varies with time. And when the cycle slip occurs, $\hat{N}_{ij}^{kl}(t)$ jumps by an integer value at the time. Figure 8 shows an example of the temporal variation of the $\hat{N}_{ij}^{kl}(t)$ that is calculated from the data observed in the field experiment discussed in the later section. The vertical and the horizontal axes correspond to the estimated $\hat{N}_{ij}^{kl}(t)$ and the time [min] from the start of the observation, respectively. The legends show the satellite numbers used in the calculation. The data are plotted at every 5 seconds. In this data, the cycle slip occurs 15 times in 10 minutes.

Here, we consider the behavior of the observation error. In the hierarchical sensor network, the distance between the neighboring parent nodes is at most

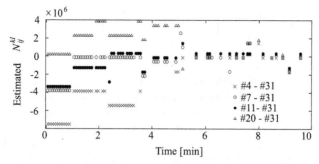

Fig. 8. Temporal variation of the estimated N_{ij}^{kl}

several hundreds meters. In this case, the noises due to the ionosphere and the troposphere are negligibly small. The dominant noise is caused by the multipath effect. The maximum change in $\hat{N}_{ij}^{kl}(t)$ due to the multipath noise is less than 1/4. Therefore, if the $\hat{N}_{ij}^{kl}(t)$ is estimated by the accuracy of 1/4, $\hat{N}_{ij}^{kl}(t)$ can be easily corrected by subtracting the integer value from $\hat{N}_{ij}^{kl}(t)$ to minimize the difference between the original and the corrected $\hat{N}_{ij}^{kl}(t)$. The estimation of $\hat{N}_{ij}^{kl}(t)$ is carried out using the Kalman filter.

Since the $\hat{N}_{ij}^{kl}(t)$ is almost linear in a short period of time, the value at the next step $\hat{N}_{ij}^{kl}(t + \Delta t)$ can be modeled as

$$\hat{N}_{ij}^{kl}(t + \Delta t) = a\Delta t + b + \epsilon \tag{7}$$

where a and b are constants. The observation equation can be defined as

$$y_k = Hx_k + \epsilon_k, \tag{8}$$

where y_k is the observation vector and x_k is the state vector.

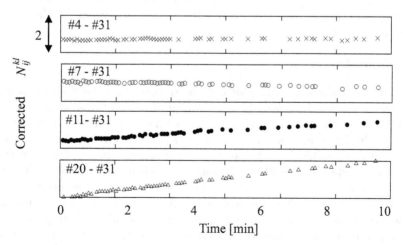

Fig. 9. The temporal variation of the corrected $\hat{N}_{ij}^{kl}(t)$

$$y_k = \begin{bmatrix} \hat{N}_{ij}^{kl}(t + \Delta t) \\ \hat{N}_{ij}^{kl}(t) \end{bmatrix}, \qquad H = \begin{bmatrix} \Delta t & 1 \\ 0 & 1 \end{bmatrix}, \qquad x_k = \begin{bmatrix} a \\ b \end{bmatrix}$$

The state vector x_{k+1} at the step of $k + 1$ is estimated using the conventional Kalman filter with the observation equation (8).

Figure 9 shows an example of the temporal variation of the corrected $\hat{N}_{ij}^{kl}(t)$. The original data is shown in Figure 8. The vertical and horizontal axes correspond to the temporal variation of the corrected $\hat{N}_{ij}^{kl}(t)$ and the time [min] from the start of the observation, respectively. The hight of the vertical axis of each graph is set to be 2. The frequent cycle slips shown in Figure 8 are totally suppressed.

5   Acoustic Ranging

The concept of acoustic ranging is based on measuring the time of flight of the sound signal between the signal source and the acoustic receiver. The range estimate can be calculated from the time measurement, assuming the speed of sound is known. Note that the constant value of the speed of sound is greatly dependent on the temperature. To accurately measure the time of flight (TOF), synchronization mechanism needs to be performed. Since the sound propagates much slower in air (approximately 10^6 times) than RF signals, TOF can be precisely estimated from the time difference of arrival (TDOA) of simultaneously emitted acoustic and radio signals. This can be achieved by having actuator notify the receiver via a radio message at the same time when the acoustic signal is emitted. The difference of the arrival times of the sound and radio signals is a good indicator for the estimation of TOF.

The acoustic ranging can be done as following: Acoustic signals from acoustic actuator are sampled by acoustic sensor using ADC. Lower and upper bounds for the frequencies are 4.0 and 4.5kHz, respectively (same as the Mica2 sensor board sounder specification); the sensors are, thus, tuned to search for the acoustic signals in that frequency range.

5.1   Noise Reduction

To locate the beginning of the chirp, we need to increase the SNR ratio of the samples. Since disturbances such as ambient noise are of Gaussian nature, they are independent for each chirp, whereas the useful signal content will be identical. The acoustic signal used in this research consists of a series of chirps, all of the same length, with difference in intervals of silence in between. Delays between consecutive chirps are varied to avoid a situation when multiple samples have the same noise pattern at the same offset, which is a common phenomenon caused by acoustic multi-path effects such as echoes from a wall in indoor environment. The length of intervals and the actual emission time of each chirp are preset in sensor and actuator. Once the sensor has received the radio message from actuator, it controls the sampling timing based on the preset timing described above. The chirps are sampled one by one, then added together and processed as a single sampled signal. Adding together the series of samples improves the SNR by $10\log(N)$dB, where N is the number of chirps used. Specifically, in our implementation, by using 64 consecutive chirps in an acoustic ranging signal, the SNR is improved by 18dB.

5.2   Bandpass Filter

For finding integer coefficients of the band pass filter employed in this acoustic ranging application, the real acoustic signal samples containing both chirps and silence obtained by Mica2 is used as input for Rectangular window functions. Rectangular window function is used in order to gain the equal weight for 4.0kHz~4.5kHz frequency range of the sounder. By using the rectangular window function, tap number is varied and the SNR ratio which serves as the highest factor in effectively detect the first peak is used. The SNR ratio can easily be calculated since the positions of the chirps and the silence are known. Since 64 series of samples are stacked to form a single sample, there is no big difference in SNR ratio by varying the tap number from 21 to 41 for the samples generated by ADC with the sampling rate of 28.6kHz in the present study. Knowing the Mica2 hardware limitation, 21-tap FIR filter with integer coefficients in the [-7, 7] interval was chosen.

5.3   Time of Flight Detection Algorithm

In order to effectively locate the time of arrival, the following algorithm is proposed.

1. Locate all the peaks for the filtered signals.
2. Pick up the maximum amplitude A_{max} from the first 40 samples of the located peaks. For the frequency range between 4.0kHz and 4.5kHz, the 40th sample of the located peaks corresponds to about 100cm distance in the real space. Since the spacing between child nodes are more than 100cm in our application, the maximum amplitude A_{max} is the maximum ambient noise level.
3. Using A_{max} as a reference point, compare the following peaks with it. Locate position T_s where the following peaks are all bigger than A_{max}. This is based on the fact that, when acoustic signal arrives at the sensor, its amplitude is much bigger than the ambient noise after the filtering. Using A_{max} also speeds up the process of detecting the general position of time of arrival.
4. Perform adverse look-back to find the exact position of time of flight T_{TOF}. The exact position of time of flight is defined as a point in which the initial rising slope intersects the average output level of ADC, as shown in Figure.10. Assuming the rising slope linear, a simple Kalman filter is adopted for extrapolating the initial rising slope.

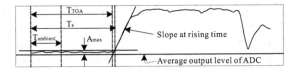

Fig. 10. TOF detect algorithm. A thin solid line shows the original signal, dashed vertical lines are the event positions, and the thick solid lines represent the lines estimated from the original signal.

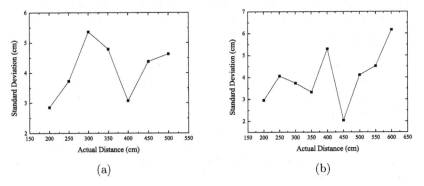

Fig. 11. Measurement error as a function of the distance: (a) Indoor environment with severe echo (b) Urban noise environment

5.4 Performance Evaluation

The performance of the acoustic localization method is evaluated in the indoor environment where we observe severe echoes as well as the moderate urban noise environment. Figure.11(a) and (b) show the measurement errors for the indoor and the outdoor environments, respectively. It is clearly visible that the precision of the measurement in the urban noise is better, especially around 300cm. This is because of the fact that we have conducted the indoor experiment in 6m×6m×8m room surrounded by hard walls which reflect acoustic wave so that the effect of the echo is severe. However, it can be concluded that the accuracy of the present acoustic localization method is within 6cm even in the indoor environment.

6 Field Experiment

Field experiment was conducted to evaluate the performance of the whole system for localization of sensor nodes spread on the plane (i.e., 2-dimensional arrangement). Three parent nodes were deployed as shown in Figure 12 (left). The GPS data were continuously received for 2 hours. The collected data were transmitted to the GPS server using wireless LAN. The GPS positioning analysis was carried out after the measurement. In the experiment, we intentionally walked around the antenna (which caused frequent cycle slip) to give a hard time on the GPS receivers and show the robustness of the parent nodes.

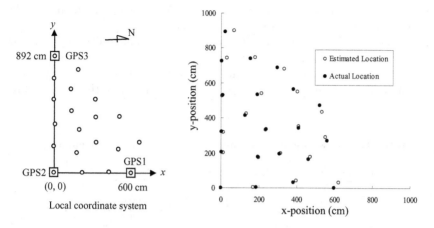

Fig. 12. Schematic view of the deployment of sensor nodes (left) and a comparison of the global positions of the nodes localized by our system with the actual positions of the nodes (right)

Together with the parent nodes, twenty-one child nodes (Mote) were pseudo-randomly spread on the site except three child nodes set on the foot of parent nodes. These three nodes worked as the reference for global coordinates. Child nodes measured the distances of the neighboring nodes by the acoustic ranging method mentioned in the previous section.

6.1 Inverse Delaunay Localization

Figure 12 (right) shows the estimated global coordinates of the child nodes. Child nodes were relatively localized by the Inverse Delaunay algorithm, then given the reference of the global coordinates by the parent nodes. The details of the GPS positioning of the parent nodes are mentioned in the section below.

The measurement error in the acoustic ranging in this experiment was ±3.8cm in average (maximum of 16.8cm) against average distance between nodes of 321.6cm. In spite of this noisy measurement of the relative distance, no node was missed in the localization and the error in the estimation was suppressed in the reasonable range. The error in the estimation of the location of the boundary nodes are relatively large. However, it should be noted that no attempt to redistribute the error throughout the domain, such as Laplacian smoothing or spring relaxation, was not applied in this estimation. No sign of the flip ambiguity, accumulation of the error can be observed. Although more detailed validation such as numerical simulation on the arrangement of thousands of nodes with noise in the ranging as a controlling parameter is required, this experimental result implies the robustness of the system.

6.2 GPS Positioning

In the analysis, a small data segment is cut from the measurements and analyzed using the developed GPS positioning algorithm. This operation is applied to the various segments. The lengths of the segments are 5, 10 and 15 minutes. The start time of the segment is shifted every 5 seconds.

The success rate of determining the correct integer ambiguities is shown in Table 1. The success rate increases with the data length. The main cause of the failures in the case of GPS1→3 is the data blank due to the failure of the wireless LAN communication. In every case, the cycle slips are correctly detected and repaired.

Table 1. Success rate of determining the correct integer ambiguities

Data length [min]	GPS1→3 rate [%]	GPS2→3 rate [%]
5	94.0	94.5
10	98.9	99.9
15	98.9	100.0

7   Conclusion

In this paper, a hierarchical sensor network system for robust localization is presented. This system consists of parent nodes with a low priced L1 GPS receiver and child nodes equipped with an acoustic ranging device. The GPS positioning algorithm discussed in this paper employs cycle slip correction based on Karman filtering. This enables a low priced L1 GPS receiver to determine its position within the accuracy of a few centimeters. Relative position of the child nodes is determined by the inverse Delaunay algorithm. The major advantage of the inverse Delaunay algorithm is its robustness against the error in the ranging. Compared with the localization algorithms based on so-called "robust quadrilaterals", the inverse Delaunay algorithm is tougher against the flip ambiguity caused by the erroneous measurement in the distance between nodes.

The proposed GPS positioning algorithm and the inverse Delaunay algorithm are implemented with noise tolerant acoustic ranging algorithm to localize a sensor network consisting of three parent nodes and twenty-one child nodes. This field experiment shows robustness of the hierarchical sensor network system presented in this paper.

References

1. Moore, D., Leonard, J., Rus, D. & Teller, S. (2004), Robust Distributed Network Localization with Noisy Range Measurements, *Proc. Second ACM SenSys.*
2. Eren, T., Goldenberg, D., Whiteley, W., Yang, Y. R., Morse, A. S., Anderson, B. D. O. & Belhumeur, P. N. (2004), Rigidity, computation, and randomization in network localization, *Proc. IEEE INFOCOM.*
3. Hill, J. & Culler, D. (2002), Mica: A Wireless Platform for Deeply Embedded Networks, *IEEE Micro*, 22(6), pp.12–24.
4. Maroti, M. (2004), The Directed Flood Routing Framework, *Proc of ACM/IFIP/USENIX 5th International Middleware Conference.*

5. Elson, J., Girod, L. & Estrin, D. (2002), Fine-grained network time synchronization using reference broadcasts, *ACM SIGOPS Operating Systems Review*, issue SI, 36.
6. Ganeriwal, S., Kumar, R. & Srivastava, M.B. (2003), Timing-sync protocol for sensor networks, *Proc. First ACM SenSys*.
7. de Berg, M., van Kreveld, M., Overmars, M. & Schwarzkopf, O. (1997), *Computational Geometry, Algorithms and Applications*, Springer-Verlag Berlin Heidelberg.
8. Hofmann, B., Wellenhof, H. Lichtenegger & J. Collins (2001), *GPS, Theory and Practice*, Springer Wien NewYork.
9. Seynat, C., Hooper, G., Roberts, C. & Rizos, C. (2004), Low-cost deformation measurement system for volcano monitoring, *Proceedings of The 2004 International Symposium on GNSS/GPS*.
10. Lee, H.K., J. Wang, C. Rizos, B. Li, & W.P. Park (2003), Effective cycle slip detection and identification for high accuracy integrated GPS/INS positioning, *6th Int. Symp. on Satellite Navigation Technology Including Mobile Positioning & Location Services*, Meibourne, Australia, 22-55 July, 2003, CD-ROM proc., paper 43.

Power Management for Bluetooth Sensor Networks

Luca Negri[1] and Lothar Thiele[2]

[1] Politecnico di Milano, Dept. of Electrical Eng. and Comp. Science (DEI)
[2] ETH Zurich, Computer Eng. and Networks Lab (TIK)

Abstract. Low power is a primary concern in the field of wireless sensor networks. Bluetooth has often been labeled as an inappropriate technology in this field due to its high power consumption. However, most Bluetooth studies employ rather over–simplified, fully theoretical, or inadequate power models. We present a power model of Bluetooth including scatternet configurations and low–power sniff mode and validate it experimentally on a real Bluetooth module. Based on this model, we introduce a power optimization framework employing MILP (Mixed–Integer Linear Programming) techniques, and devise optimal power management policies in the presence of end–to–end delay constraints. Our optimizations, if backed by power–aggressive hardware implementations, can make Bluetooth viable for a wider range of sensor networks.

1 Introduction

Low power consumption has always been a primary goal in the design of wireless sensor networks. Moreover, communication accounts for a relevant power contribution on sensor nodes, fact that is true even for more complex mobile systems [1]. Communication among sensors can be implemented with custom solutions or standardized radio interfaces. If on one hand custom solutions carry the greatest power optimization potential, the choice of widespread wireless communication standards guarantees interoperability as well as ease of connection with existing commercial devices.

Communication protocols are often endowed with power/performance tradeoffs, which can be used to match application requirements with power consumption; such protocols are known as *power–aware protocols* [2]. Power–aware is a broad term and may denote a protocol that (i) manages power/performance tradeoffs offered by lower layer protocols, (ii) exposes further tradeoffs to the layers above or (iii) both. Examples of power/performance tradeoffs are modulation scaling [3] and power control [4] at the physical layer, Bluetooth's low–power modes (hold, sniff, park) and WiFi's Power Save Protocol (PSP) at the MAC layer. In order to exploit these features an abstraction describing power behavior on tradeoff curves is required: such abstraction is called a *power model*.

Bluetooth (BT) is a leading standard for short–range ad–hoc connectivity in the Personal Area Networks (PAN) field. Although initially designed for simple point–to–multipoint cable replacement applications, Bluetooth has proved

K. Römer, H. Karl, and F. Mattern (Eds.): EWSN 2006, LNCS 3868, pp. 196–211, 2006.
© Springer-Verlag Berlin Heidelberg 2006

very appealing also to build multi–hop ad–hoc networks (called *scatternets*) [5] and even for high bandwidth sensor networks [6]. BT provides low–power modes (hold, sniff, park) which trade throughput and latency for power. We believe these features, if backed by a power–aggressive hardware implementation, can make the protocol fit for a wider range of sensor networks, allowing for an appropriate tuning of communication performance (and power) on the application requirements. Nevertheless, to achieve this, a power model describing all possible states (number of links, low–power mode of each link etc.) is necessary.

There is indeed a lack of such a model in the literature to date. Many Bluetooth power–optimization proposals, such as [7] and [8], are based on over–simplified power models, not considering number and role (master vs. slave) of links. Also, such models are normally not based on experimental measurements, but rather on theoretical assumptions. Other BT–related studies employ rather old and inadequate power models that were derived for other wireless systems [9]. Finally, the few power measurements for Bluetooth in the literature (see [10] and [6]) do not cover low–power modes and scatternet configurations.

In this paper we describe a full power model of Bluetooth in a complex *scatternet scenario* where each link can be in active or low–power *sniff* mode. The model is experimentally characterized and validated (RMS error below 4%) for the *BTnode*, a BT–based ad–hoc network prototyping platform developed at ETH Zurich [11]. We employ then the power model to build a flexible power optimization framework based on Mixed–Integer Linear Programming (MILP), which can be used to solve a number of power vs. Quality of Service (QoS) problems. In particular, in this paper we focus on the *power/delay* tradeoff offered by BT's *sniff mode* and determine the best network configuration that grants the lowest power consumption while meeting given end–to–end delay requirements. Such a *power management* policy can be either centrally determined and distributed to all nodes when needed or pre–computed for different requirements sets and stored in the nodes themselves.

After Section 2 briefly introduces Bluetooth and describes the BTnode platform, the main contributions of this work are presented: the power model of BT in Section 3, the power/delay problem in Section 4 and its solution for selected topologies in Section 5. Section 6 concludes the paper, outlining further possible usages of the optimization framework and its re–application to different protocols and scenarios.

2   Bluetooth and the BTnode Platform

The Bluetooth standard is based on 79 independent channels working at 1 Mbit/s ($1\mu s$ symbols) selected thorough a *frequency hopping* algorithm. The MAC layer is based on a TDMA (Time Division Multiple Access) scheme using slots of $625\mu s$ each, and supports up to 8 devices within the same *piconet* (set of nodes sharing the same hopping sequence), one of them being the *master* of the piconet and polling the other *slave* devices. Master/slave communication is handled in a TDD (Time Division Duplexing) fashion, where the master uses even slots and

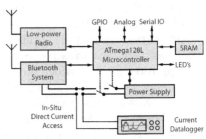

Fig. 2. Experimental setup with current datalogger connected for Bluetooth power consumption measurements

Fig. 1. The BTnode rev3 node

the polled slaves respond in the odd ones. Nodes are allowed to participate in more than one piconet in a time–sharing fashion, to form a *scatternet*.

During normal piconet operation (*active* mode), a master regularly polls its attached slaves every T_{poll} slots. However, slaves are completely unaware of the polling algorithm and are required to listen to the channel at the beginning of each master slot, to find out whether a packet is sent to them. *Sniff* mode allows for a lower duty cycle on both sides, with a master polling its slaves at regularly spaced beacon instants. Since beacon spacing can be in the range of seconds, rather than tens of slots (as for T_{poll}), this mode allows for power savings. More precisely, sniff mode is regulated by three parameters called Sniff Interval (SI), Sniff Attempt (SA) and Sniff Timeout (ST), which are specified in number of slot pairs[1]. SI is the time between beacons. At each beacon the slave listens to its master for SA slot pairs, during which it is allowed to send data if polled. The slave continues then listening for an extra ST slot pairs after the last packet received from the master.

The BTnode (see Figure 1) is a versatile, lightweight, autonomous platform based on a Bluetooth radio, a second independent low-power radio and a microcontroller [12]. The device is designed for fast prototyping [11] of ad-hoc and wireless sensor network applications and is well suited to investigate different protocols, operation parameter tradeoffs and radio alternatives. The Bluetooth radio is a Bluetooth 1.2 compliant device (Zeevo ZV4002) with radio circuits, baseband, MAC and link controller and an ARM7 core integrated on a single system-on-chip. The Atmel ATmega128l microcontroller serves as Bluetooth host controller and interfaces to the Host Controller Interface of the ZV4002 via UART. Embedded applications are integrated into BTnut, a custom C-based threaded operating system that offers drivers for the peripherals as well as communication protocol stacks for the radios. Benefits of this platform are a small form factor of 5x3 cm and comfortable programmability while maintaining interoperability through its standardized wireless interface. Simple sensors and actuators can be attached and powered through generic interfaces. Three direct

---

[1] However they are often specified in second in this document.

current access points are available where *in-situ* measurements of the power consumption of the radios and the microcontroller core can be performed (see Figure 2). This allows for very fine grained and subsystem-specific power consumption measurements in the live system under standard operating conditions as opposed to an artificial lab setup with developer boards only.

3   Power Model of Bluetooth

3.1   Experimental Phase

The TDMA, connection–oriented nature of Bluetooth makes it substantially different from other systems employing contention–based MAC protocols (e.g. 802.11). This reflects in a different power model, where power contributions also exist to merely keep links alive, even with no data transfer. In [13] and [14] we presented a complete power model of BT for the *point–to–point* case, i.e. limited to a device being master or slave of a single link. Such a model highlights three major contributions: (i) a *standby* power consumption P_{stby}, always present, (ii) a *Link Controller* (LC) power consumption varying if the device is master (P_{master}) or slave (P_{slave}) of the link and (iii) an additional *data* level consumption for transmission (P_{tx}) and/or reception (P_{rx}) of data over the link. In this model 'stby', 'master', 'slave', 'tx' and 'rx' are called *logical activities*, and the model is said to be *characterized* for a specific BT implementation once a value has been assigned to the correspondent P_{stby}, P_{master}, etc.

The work in [13] shows that the modeling abstraction of summing up power related to useful data transmissions and to link maintenance activities holds well for the point–to–point case when validating the model for a real BT device. We have run some tests in the presence of multiple links, and verified that the same property also holds for a multipoint scenario[2]. Therefore, we concentrate here on the Link Controller layer model and *extend* it to the *piconet* and *scatternet* cases, allowing for an arbitrary number of master/slave, active/sniff connections (within the limits of BT specifications).

In order to extend the model we have followed the same methodology outlined in [13] and [14]. We have run a set of roughly 100 experiments on BTnodes, tracing in each experiment the current draw of the Zeevo BT chip on the BTnode (see Section 2) for 20 seconds via a bench multimeter. The voltage, which we assumed constant during the experiments, was previously measured at 3.3 V and the multimeter was set to operate at 50 samples/s (integration time 20 ms). The following parameters have been varied among the experiments: (i) *number* of nodes connected to the device under test and *role* of these connections (maximum 7 slaves and 3 masters supported by the Zeevo chip) (ii) *mode* of these connections (active vs. sniff). In sniff mode, Sniff Interval (SI), Sniff Attempt (SA) and Sniff Timeout (ST) were also varied.

Figure 3 and Figure 4 compare the current consumption curve in active and sniff mode, for a master and slave role connection, respectively. We denote with

---

[2] In particular, this is true for low duty cycle or bursty traffic patterns.

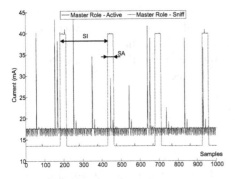
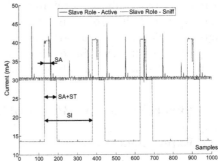

Fig. 3. Current in active and sniff mode on a master (SI=5.12 s, SA=ST=0.64 s)

Fig. 4. Current in active and sniff mode on a slave (SI=5.12 s, SA=ST=0.64 s)

master role connection a connection to a slave (since the device is master of the link) and with *slave role connection* a connection to a master. The active–mode slave role curve (around 30 mA) is significantly *higher* than the master one (just above 15 mA); we believe this is due to the continuous listening activity a slave is required to perform.

Figure 3 and Figure 4 also highlight the bursty behavior of sniff mode, with periodic peaks every SI slot pairs. The baseline value is lower than the active master and active slave ones, and is equal to the *standby* current, which had been previously measured at 13.51 mA. Conversely, the height of the peaks surpasses both active master and slave values, reaching 40 mA; this can be justified with the increased frequency of POLL packets sent by the master during the SA (Sniff Attempt), which also causes higher power consumption on the slave receiving them. According to BT specs, the slave continues then listening for an extra ST slot pairs, and this justifies the wider peaks in Figure 4.

Figure 5 concentrates on the effects of multiple active–mode connections on the total power consumption. The left cluster of bars represents the *average* current in *piconet* mode, with an increasing number of connections to slaves (0 to 6), but no master attached. These values exhibit the interesting property that each additional slave after the first one brings a nearly *constant* power penalty.

The right cluster of bars in Figure 5 is the average current when an increasing number of slaves are attached (0 to 6, as before) but when the device also has a *master*; in this situation the BTnode is in *scatternet* mode. The values are higher than in piconet mode, and all lie in the neighborhood of 30 mA, which is the *active slave role* consumption as discussed for Figure 4. This can be explained as follows: with no data transfers, the only duty of the node in its piconet (as a master) is to poll its slaves, which accounts for a small time fraction; hence, the node spends far more time in slave mode, listening in the second piconet, and its current consumption is then much closer to the slave than to the master one. A second interesting property emerges: the total power is only slightly affected by the number of active slaves attached if an active master is present. In one word, the slave role *dominates* the master one.

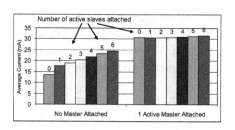

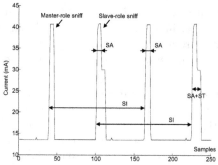

Fig. 5. Average current with sole active–mode links. Left cluster: 0 to 6 slaves attached (piconet mode); right cluster: 0 to 6 slaves plus one master (scatternet mode).

Fig. 6. Current with mixed master (one) and slave (one) sniff–mode links (SI=2.56 s, SA=ST=0.16 s)

Figure 6 refers to scatternet mode, but where all links are in *sniff mode*; more specifically, one master and one slave role links are present here. The exhibited behavior is a simple extension of that with a single link in sniff mode (as in Figure 3 and Figure 4), with the BT module scheduling each sniff attempt as far away as possible from the others.

Figure 7 shows the current plots in the case of multiple coexisting links in active and sniff mode; all links are here towards slaves (master roles) and the device is not in scatternet mode. The graph represents a single period of the 20 seconds experiments, whose waveforms are periodic with SI, namely 2.56 seconds or 128 samples. The first curve (dashed) represents the case of 3 active slaves, and shows no major peaks. The second curve (solid, 2 active and 1 sniff slaves) has a lower baseline average value but exhibits one peak of width SA. The third curve (solid with dots, 1 active and 2 sniff slaves) presents an even lower baseline value but features two peaks of width SA, according to what said for Figure 6. Finally, the fourth curve (solid with squares) has a baseline value

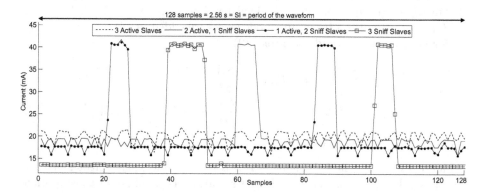

Fig. 7. Current with active and sniff master roles: 3 slaves attached, switched from active to sniff mode one after the other in a sequence (SI=2.56 s, SA=ST=0.16 s)

equal to *standby* but contains three sniff attempts, two of which are clustered together in a peak of width $2 \cdot SA$; this behavior is in line with the fact that all links are now in sniff mode. The rules emerging from Figure 7 are the following: (i) outside sniff attempt peaks power consumption is determined by the number of active–mode links; (ii) the height of the sniffing peaks is not influenced by the number of active links.

A set of experiments similar to that of Figure 7 has been performed on coexisting slave–role active and sniff–mode links (not shown here). The behavior in this case is slightly different: although there are still a baseline value and regular peaks due to sniff, the baseline value shows only *marginal fluctuations* around the value of active slave power consumption (circa 30 mA), regardless of the number of active slave roles (1, 2 or 3). The same holds true if active master roles (connections to slaves) are added, and this confirms the rule of the slave role dominance introduced earlier when discussing Figure 5.

3.2   Model Characterization and Validation

We extend here the set of LC *logical activities* of the point–to–point model (P_{master}, P_{slave}) to handle multiple connections and sniff mode. We seek a compact set of activities A_i, each with power consumption P_i, whose *linear combination* approximates with a reasonable error the actual consumption of the device in all cases. Our choice is driven by the knowledge gained in the experimental phase, which can be summarized in the following rules:

1. Power consumption is the sum of three terms: (i) a *standby* term (P_{stby}) always present, (ii) a *baseline* power value on top of standby due to active connections and (iii) periodic *peaks* due to sniff links.
2. When an *active slave role* connection exists, this fixes the baseline value at P_{slave}, regardless of additional active masters and/or slaves attached. l
3. When *no active slave role* connection exists, baseline value is determined by the number of active master roles, with the first contributing P_{master} and each additional one contributing P_{add_slv} (with $P_{add\_slv} < P_{master}$).
4. On top of the previously determined baseline value, which shall be called P_{BAS}, contributions from sniff–mode peaks are added as follows, respectively for master roles (1) and slave roles (2):

$$P_{M,SN} = (P_{sniff} - P_{BAS}) \cdot \left(\frac{SA}{SI}\right) \tag{1}$$

$$P_{S,SN} = (P_{sniff} - P_{BAS}) \cdot \left(\frac{SA}{SI}\right) + (P_{slave} - P_{BAS})\left(\frac{ST}{SI}\right) \tag{2}$$

where P_{sniff} is the peak value during sniff attempts.

Figure 8 shows a generic BTnode having K masters and J slaves attached, that is K slave roles and J master roles. In this situation the total power consumption as predicted by the model is:

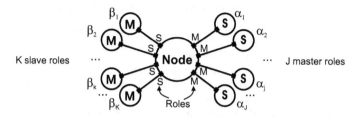

Fig. 8. The four main degrees of freedom of Link Controller state including multiple master/slave and active/sniff links

$$P = \overbrace{P_{stby} + \sum_{j=1}^{J}\left[(1-\alpha_j)P_{M,SN}\right]}^{\text{Sniff Master Roles}} + \overbrace{\sum_{k=1}^{K}\left[(1-\beta_k)P_{S,SN}\right]}^{\text{Sniff Slave Roles}} + \tag{3}$$

$$\underbrace{\beta_0 P_{slave}}_{\text{Active Slave Roles}} \underbrace{+ (1-\beta_0)\alpha_0(P_{master} - P_{add\_slv}) + (1-\beta_0)\sum_{j=1}^{J}\left[\alpha_j P_{add\_slv}\right]}_{\text{Active Master Roles}}$$

where:

$$\alpha_j = 1 \Leftrightarrow \text{link to j--th slave is active } (1 \le j \le J)$$
$$\beta_k = 1 \Leftrightarrow \text{link to k--th master is active } (1 \le k \le K)$$
$$\alpha_0 = 1 \Leftrightarrow \exists \text{ one active link to a slave } (\alpha_0 = \alpha_1 \vee \alpha_2 \ldots \vee \alpha_J)$$
$$\beta_0 = 1 \Leftrightarrow \exists \text{ one active link to a master } (\beta_0 = \beta_1 \vee \beta_2 \ldots \vee \beta_K)$$

The extended set of logical activities that make up the model are hence P_{stby}, P_{master}, P_{add_slv}, P_{slave}, P_{sniff}. To characterize the model for the BTnode means to assign numeric values to these quantities, following the methodology fully described in [13]. For each experiment, the *average power* measured during the experiment is equaled to the prediction of the model according to (4). For a single experiment j, all α_j and β_k coefficients are fixed, and thus (4) becomes a linear combination the activity power consumptions:

$$V \cdot \overline{I}_j = \sum_{i=0}^{N} P_i t_{ji} \tag{4}$$

where $P_1 = P_{stby}$, $P_2 = P_{master}$, etc. are to be determined, $\overline{I}_j$ is the average current during the experiment, t_{ji} are coefficients determined by the values of the α_js and β_ks, and V is the operating voltage of 3.3 V.

Since the number of experiments is significantly higher than the number of unknowns, the equations (4) for all experiments, if taken together, form a strongly over--constrained linear system, which can be solved reliably with the Least Squares method. Doing so yields the values that best fit the experimental data, shown in Table 1.

Table 1. Numerical power model for the BTnode

Activity	Description	Value
P_{stby}	Always present	44.58 mW
P_{master}	Being master of 1 slave	12.97 mW
P_{add_slv}	Having additional slaves	4.55 mW
P_{slave}	Being slave	56.63 mW
P_{sniff}	Peak value in sniff mode	86.96 mW

We have validated our linear model using the LOO (Leave One Out) technique [15] as described in [13]. This implies solving the model repeatedly, excluding each time a different test, and using that test to calculate a residual (difference between measure and prediction). The RMS value of such residuals (actually, percentile residuals) is the *validation error* and amounts to 3.7%, whereas the maximum residual among all experiments is around 10%. Although the numbers in Table 1 might seem very specific to the BTnode, our experience and further measurements on other Bluetooth modules confirm that the power model and some of the trends highlighted by Table 1, such as $P_{sniff} > P_{slave} > P_{master} > P_{add\_slv}$, are common to most BT implementations [14].

4   The Power/Delay Problem in Bluetooth Scatternets

The presented power model, while guaranteeing an accuracy below 4%, is analytically simple enough to be used in solving a number of power management problems. We define a generic *power management problem* as the seek of a network configuration that minimizes some power figure (total power of the network, maximum power of a node, standard deviation of power over all nodes etc.) whilst satisfying some QoS requirements.

In particular, in this work we focus on the power/delay problem, which can be stated as follows: *given* a scatternet topology, a power model for each node and a set of end–to–end maximum delay requirements between a root node and all other nodes in the network, *determine* the best configuration (whether each link should be in active or sniff mode, and the value of SI, SA, ST in the second case) that *minimizes* the total power in the network, or alternatively optimizes some other objective functions. We approximate the delay introduced by a single link as equal to SI in sniff mode, or 0 if active. We limit our study here to tree topologies, which eliminates routing issues. Figure 9 visualizes the problem in graphical notation: the same delay requirement D_{max} is applied here to all leaves (which implies to all nodes) of the tree considering node 1 as the root, topology and master–slave orientations are given.

This kind of optimization problem suits well all situations in which the main limiting requirement is delay and not throughput, which maps to all applications that use Bluetooth but would not strictly require its whole bandwidth of 1 Mbit/s. This includes all sensor networks handling time–critical data with relatively low packet sizes, such as security, health and environmental monitoring

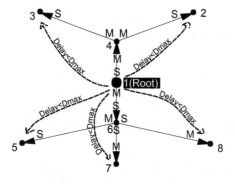

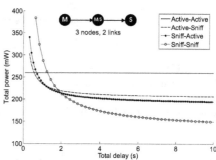

Fig. 9. The power/delay problem in a tree of BTnodes; links are oriented away from root, delay requirements are from node 1 (root) to all leaves, M and S indicate Master and Slave roles on links

Fig. 10. Power vs. delay Pareto curves for a chain of three nodes (two links) varying SI with fixed SA,ST. Depending on the target delay, active or sniff mode are more convenient.

systems. The framework can be as well applied to throughput–constrained scenarios; this is discussed as ongoing work in Section 6.

Figures 3 and 4 in Section 3 suggest a power *tradeoff* between active and sniff mode as the Sniff Interval (SI) is varied. This is confirmed by Figure 10, which plots the power consumption of three nodes connected in a chain (two links) according to (4) as the mode of the links is switched between active and sniff, and as SI is varied (SA, ST fixed).

When the number of links in the network grows, it is inefficient to evaluate all possible combinations of link mode and sniff interval. Hence, we have chosen *MILP* (Mixed–Integer Linear Programming) as an optimization tool to solve the problem for bigger networks. The problem must be slightly modified before it can be handled by a MILP optimizer; in fact, the model is *linear* w.r.t. the power consumption of the logical activities P_{stby}, P_{master}, P_{slave}, P_{add_slv}, P_{sniff} but *not* linear w.r.t. other parameters, such as the link mode binary variables α_j and β_k and the Sniff Intervals SI. However, these issues can be tackled with standard techniques as adding additional variables and constraints, as well as approximating nonlinear functions (such as $P \propto 1/SI$).

An initial complexity study on our power/delay linear programs (using Cplex on a Unix workstation) exhibits a quadratic behavior with the number of nodes for medium–size networks (up to 300 nodes) and an exponential growth thereafter, when the MILP optimizer starts employing different algorithms.

5   Selected Case Studies

5.1   Total Power in a Chain of Nodes

Figure 11 shows a chain of 10 BTnodes, where each node has different master/slave roles (M-M,M-S,S-M,S-S). In this case all sniff parameters are fixed at SI=2s, SA=ST=.01s, and only the mode (active vs. sniff) of each link is treated

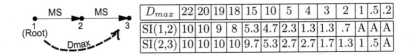

Fig. 11. Chain of 10 nodes, each link can be in active mode or sniff mode with SI=2s, SA=ST=.01s, objective is sum of power over all nodes. As delay requirement from root to other nodes is decreased from 18 s to 10 s links start switching from sniff to active mode; the order in which this happens is indicated by the letters (A, then B, etc.).

D_{max}	22	20	19	18	15	10	5	4	3	2	1	.5	.2
SI(1,2)	10	10	9	8	5.3	4.7	2.3	1.3	1.3	.7	A	A	A
SI(2,3)	10	10	10	10	9.7	5.3	2.7	2.7	1.7	1.3	1	.5	A

Fig. 12. Chain of 3 nodes, each link can be in active mode or sniff mode with SA=ST=.01s and variable SI between 0.1 s and 10 s, objective is sum of power over all nodes. Table shows best configuration for decreasing values of D_{max}. A stands for Active, numbers are SIs.

as an optimization variable. The objective function is here the sum of power over all nodes. In Figure 11, the optimization is run repeatedly as the end–to–end delay requirement D_{max} from node 1 (root) to all other nodes is gradually lowered from 18 s to 10 s. Initially, all links are in sniff mode; as D_{max} decreases, links start switching to active mode; the order in which this happens is indicated in figure by capital letters (A first, then B, etc.). The lessons learned with this simple experiment are:

– As delay requirement is decreased links switch from sniff to active mode.
– Active links stick together. This is convenient power–wise, as experiments have proved that additional active roles cost less than the first one.
– Active links appear first on S-S nodes, then on M-S and finally on M-M nodes. This can again be justified with the rules described in Section 3.2.

Figure 12 still refers to a chain of nodes (three in this case), but where the Sniff Interval is also an optimization variable, in the range $0.1s \leq$ SI $\leq 10s$. The objective function is still the total power consumption in the network, and the end–to–end delay requirement is decreased from 20 s to 0.2 s. The table in Figure 12 shows the best combination of link mode and SI for both links. Further considerations are:

– The best combination of Sniff Intervals on a chain of links is the one in which all intervals are equal to $D_{max}/$(number of links)^3.
– The switch from sniff to active happens earlier for higher values of SA/ST.

---

[3] This can be proved analytically. We have verified that the deviation from this 'symmetric' behavior exhibited by the values in Figure 12 is due to linearization.

5.2   Total Power in a Tree of Nodes

In Figure 13 a fixed–SI optimization (SI=2) is applied repeatedly to a tree topology. Again, for sufficiently high values of the maximum delay requirement D_{max}, all links are in sniff mode. Conversely, as D_{max} is decreased, links start switching to active mode, in the order indicated by the capital letters in Figure 13 (A first, then B, etc.). The observed behavior can be summarized as follows:

- The first candidates to become active are the links (thus the nodes) that serve a higher number of downstream nodes at the same time. They are followed by minor branches and, at last, by leaves. The tree in Figure 13 has a sort of *backbone* (main branch) along nodes 1, 18, 15, 14, 5, 11, then branches from node 11, and finally numerous leaves along the backbone and branches: the above rule is clearly obeyed.
- In addition, the same rules found for the simple chain of nodes apply: S-S nodes are the best candidates, followed by M-S and M-M.

Figure 14 refers to the same tree shown in Figure 13, but now the Sniff Intervals are used as optimization variables ($0.1 \leq$ SI ≤ 10 s). The table is divided into three parts:

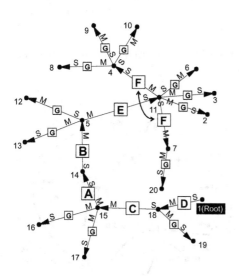

Fig. 13. Random tree, each link can be active or sniffing with SI=2s, SA=ST=.1s, objective is total power. D_{max} from root to other nodes is decreased from 15 s to 0 s; letters indicate order in which links switch from sniff to active (A first, then B, etc.).

		D_{max}		
Link	15	10	5	2.5
1,18	1.3	1.3	0.6	A
18,15	1.3	1.3	1	A
15,14	1.3	A	A	A
14,5	1.3	A	A	A
5,11	3	1.3	A	A
11,4	3.3	2.6	1.3	1.1
11,7	3.3	3.3	A	A
18,19	10	8.6	4.3	2.5
15,16	10	7.3	3.3	2.5
15,17	10	7.3	3.3	2.5
5,12	9.6	7.3	3.3	2.5
5,13	9.6	7.3	3.3	2.5
11,2	6.6	6	3.3	2.5
11,3	6.6	6	3.3	2.5
11,6	6.6	6	3.3	2.5
4,8	3.3	3.3	2	1.3
4,9	3.3	3.3	2	1.3
4,10	3.3	3.3	2	1.3
7,20	3.3	2.6	3.3	2.5

Fig. 14. Random tree (see Fig. 13), optimizing total power with variable SI, SA=ST=.1s; optimal SI (or A=Active) for different values of D_{max}

- The first five links are those of the backbone, and first switch to active.
- The second block contains links (11,4) and (11,7), which represent branches from node 11, each with its own leaves. Interestingly, for $D_{max} = 5s$, (11,7) is *active* but (11,4) is not, forcing two active slave roles on node 11; at the same time, (15,18) and (1,18) on the main backbone are *not* active. This suggests that a tradeoff exists between the previously devised rules concerning size of branches and node roles (S-S, M-S, M-M), and that the order of application of these rules is not fixed.
- The third and last block groups all "leaf links", whose sniff interval decreases with D_{max} as well as with the distance from the root (e.g. $SI(18, 19) < SI(11, 2) < SI(4, 8)$). However, in certain cases, some values can increase for lower D_{max}, as other links closer to the root switch to active (see link (7,20) for instance).

5.3   Coping with Real World Constraints

The solutions we have presented so far do not take into account an important limitation of the BTnode's BT subsystem: if *multiple sniff links* are activated on a node they must have *equal SI*. This constraint, which simplifies link scheduling for the BT hardware, definitely changes the structure of the problem. Figure 15 and Figure 16 depict the optimal solutions for the same scenario of Figure 13 with this additional constraint, for $D_{max} = 15s$ and $D_{max} = 10s$ respectively. It is worth noting that:

- Applying the SI equality constraint implies that the *whole network* must use the same SI *unless* some active links exist.

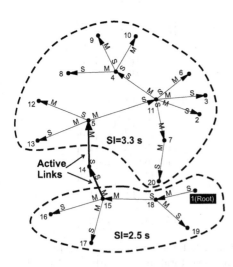
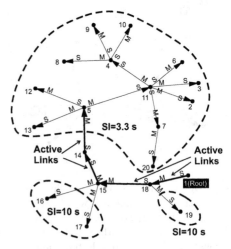

Fig. 15. Total power optimization with variable SI, but fixed SI for each node. $D_{max} = 15s$.

Fig. 16. Total power optimization with variable SI, but fixed SI for each node. $D_{max} = 10s$.

- If *active* links exist, they act as separators among *iso–SI clusters* of nodes.
- These two rules cause the best solution already for $D_{max} = 15$ (Figure 15) to contain two active links, as compared to all sniff links in Figure 14.

5.4   Total Power vs. Maximum Power Optimization

Table 2 compares the optimal solution for different values of D_{max} as different combinations of objective functions and constraints are employed:

- Columns *a* refer to the results already presented, taking the *total power* in the network (sum over all nodes) as objective to be minimized. This is equivalent to minimizing the average power consumption of a node, but with no check on the standard deviation. This causes the optimum to be quite unfair among the nodes, e.g. links (15,14) and (14,5) are switched early (as D_{max} decreases) to active mode as it is best for the whole network, however this quickly drains the battery of node 14.
- To overcome this limitation, columns *b* use a different objective function, namely the *maximum power* consumption of a *single node*[4]. The results for

Table 2. With reference Fig. 13, SA=ST=.1s, optimal mode and SI for each link with different objective functions and constraints: a) minimizing total power; b) minimizing maximum power of a single node; c) as in b but with equal SI on all links on each node

Link	$D_{max} = 15$ a	b	c	$D_{max} = 10$ a	b	c	$D_{max} = 5$ a	b	c	$D_{max} = 2.5$ a	b	c
1,18	1.3	1.3	2.14	1.3	0.6	1.42	0.6	0.6	ACT	ACT	ACT	ACT
18,15	1.3	1.3	2.14	1.3	1.1	1.42	1	0.6	ACT	ACT	0.6	1.25
15,14	1.3	1.3	2.14	ACT	1	1.42	ACT	ACT	ACT	ACT	ACT	ACT
14,5	1.3	2.5	2.14	ACT	1.3	1.42	ACT	ACT	ACT	ACT	ACT	ACT
5,11	3	2.5	2.14	1.3	1.3	1.42	ACT	0.6	1.6	ACT	ACT	ACT
11,4	3.3	2.6	2.14	2.6	2.4	1.42	1.3	1.3	1.6	1.1	ACT	ACT
11,7	3.3	4.7	2.14	3.3	3.1	1.42	ACT	1.6	1.6	ACT	ACT	ACT
18,19	10	10	2.14	8.6	9.3	1.42	4.3	4.3	ACT	2.5	2.5	1.25
15,16	10	10	2.14	7.3	8.2	1.42	3.3	3.6	5	2.5	1.8	1.25
15,17	10	10	2.14	7.3	8.2	1.42	3.3	3.6	5	2.5	1.8	1.25
5,12	9.6	8.5	2.14	7.3	5.8	1.42	3.3	3.6	1.6	2.5	1.8	1.25
5,13	9.6	8.5	2.14	7.3	5.8	1.42	3.3	3.6	1.6	2.5	1.8	1.25
11,2	6.6	6	2.14	6	4.5	1.42	3.3	3	1.6	2.5	ACT	ACT
11,3	6.6	6	2.14	6	4.5	1.42	3.3	3	1.6	2.5	ACT	ACT
11,6	6.6	6	2.14	6	4.5	1.42	3.3	3	1.6	2.5	ACT	ACT
4,8	3.3	3.3	2.14	3.3	2	1.42	2	1.6	1.6	1.3	ACT	ACT
4,9	3.3	3.3	2.14	3.3	2	1.42	2	1.6	1.6	1.3	ACT	ACT
4,10	3.3	3.3	2.14	3.3	2	1.42	2	1.6	1.6	1.3	ACT	ACT
7,20	3.3	1.3	2.14	2.6	1.3	1.42	3.3	1.3	1.6	2.5	1.8	1.25

---

[4] The actual objective is a linear combination of the maximum power of a single node and of the total power, where the latter has a lower weight.

$D_{max} = 10$ show lower sniff intervals and no active links, as compared to strategy a, meaning that power consumption, even though higher, is more evenly distributed among nodes. This trend is confirmed by the cases of $D_{max} = 5$ and $D_{max} = 2.5$, where sniff–mode links have low SIs, leveling their power consumption with that of active links.

- Finally, columns c have the same objective as b, but with the additional constraint introduced in Section 5.3, which imposes the same SI on all links on each node. Comparing the results with those of Figure 15 and Figure 16 it is apparent that iso–SI clusters begin forming for lower values of D_{max}. In fact, for $D_{max} = 10$, all links are here in sniff mode with SI=1.42 s, whereas in Figure 16 (still $D_{max} = 10$, but minimizing total power) 4 active links and 3 clusters exist.

6 Conclusions and Extensions of the Framework

We have presented a real–world power model of a Bluetooth device in a scatter-net scenario, where links can be in active or low–power sniff mode. The model has been validated experimentally with an average validation error below 4%. Based on our model, we have described a framework which employs Mixed–Integer Linear Programming to solve power/delay optimization problems. Results have been shown for selected topologies ranging from chains to trees of nodes.

The results provide useful rules to determine the best network configuration power–wise given certain requirements. These rules constitute a power management policy for the network, which can be implemented in different ways. The policy can be centrally computed in the root and distributed to all nodes every time the requirements change; alternatively, the solution for the most used requirements sets (e.g. high responsiveness, low responsiveness, idle) for the network can be pre–computed and stored in the nodes as look–up table.

Building on top of this work, we are currently exploring a number of extensions, including mesh topologies (which implies routing), park and hold modes, mixed delay and throughput requirements as well as a traffic matrix on top of open connections. Additionally, heterogeneous networks (e.g. different power budgets in the nodes) and battery models could be taken into account.

Although the BTnode employed in this study presents a standby consumption which is too high to implement long–life sensor networks, the methodology we have followed could be easily re–applied in the future to more power–aggressive implementations of Bluetooth as well as to other protocols (e.g. Zigbee) that promise a better power/performance ratio. In this direction we are investigating the possibility of completely switching off and on the BT radio of the BTnode using the microcontroller to obtain a low–power mode that performs better than sniff for extremely low duty cycles.

References

1. Raghunathan, V., Pering, T., Want, R., Nguyen, A., Jensen, P.: Experience with a low power wireless mobile computing platform. In: Proc. ISLPED-04, ACM Press (2004) 363–368
2. Jones, C.E., Sivalingam, K.M., Agrawal, P., Chen, J.C.: A survey of energy efficient network protocols for wireless networks. Wireless Networks (7) 343–358
3. Schurgers, C., Aberthorne, O., Srivastava, M.: Modulation scaling for energy aware communication systems. In: Proc. ISLPED 2001, (ACM Press) 96–99
4. Rulnick, J.M., Bambos, N.: Mobile power management for wireless communication networks. Wirel. Netw. 3 (1997) 3–14
5. Kazantzidis, M., Gerla, M., Johansson, P., Kapoor, R.: Personal area networks: Bluetooth or ieee 802.11? Intl. Journal of Wireless Information Networks, Special Issue MANETs Standards, Research, Applications (2002)
6. Leopold, M., Dydensborg, M.B., Bonnet, P.: Bluetooth and sensor networks: a reality check. In: SenSys '03: Proc. 1st international conference on Embedded networked sensor systems, New York, NY, USA, ACM Press (2003) 103–113
7. Chakraborty, I., Kashyap, A., Rastogi, A., Saran, H., Shorey, R., Kumar, A.: Policies for increasing throughput and decreasing power consumption in bluetooth mac. (In: Proc. 2000 IEEE intl. conf. on Personal Wireless Comm.) 90–94
8. Zhu, H., Cao, G., Kesidis, G., Das, C.: An adaptive power-conserving service discipline for bluetooth. In: 2002 IEEE intl. conf. on Communication. Volume 1. (2002) 303–307
9. Ashok, R.L., Duggirala, R., Agrawal, D.P.: Energy efficient bridge management policies for inter-piconet communication in bluetooth scatternets. In: Proc. Vehicular Tech. Conf. (2003)
10. Meier, L., Ferrari, P., Thiele, L.: Energy-efficient bluetooth networks. Technical Report 204, Comp. Eng. and Networks Laboratory (TIK), ETH Zurich (2005)
11. Beutel, J., Kasten, O., Mattern, F., Römer, K., Siegemund, F., Thiele, L.: Prototyping wireless sensor network applications with BTnodes. In: Proc. 1st European Workshop on Sensor Networks (EWSN 2004). Volume 2920 of Lecture Notes in Computer Science., Springer, Berlin (2004) 323–338
12. Beutel, J., Dyer, M., Hinz, M., Meier, L., Ringwald, M.: Next-generation prototyping of sensor networks. In: Proc. 2nd ACM Conf. Embedded Networked Sensor Systems (SenSys 2004), ACM Press, New York (2004) 291–292
13. Negri, L., Sami, M., Macii, D., Terranegra, A.: Fsm–based power modeling of wireless protocols: the case of bluetooth. In: Proceedings of the 2004 international symposium on Low power electronics and design, ACM Press (2004) 369–374
14. Negri, L., Zanetti, D., Tran, Q.D., Sami, M.: Flexible power modeling for wireless systems: Power modeling and optimization of two bluetooth implementations. In: Proc. WoWMoM 05 - IEEE Intl. Symp. on World of Wireless, Mobile and Multimedia Networks. (2005) 408–416
15. Hassoun, M.: Fundamentals of Artificial Neural Networks. MIT Press (1995)

FlexCup: A Flexible and Efficient Code Update Mechanism for Sensor Networks

Pedro José Marrón, Matthias Gauger, Andreas Lachenmann, Daniel Minder,
Olga Saukh, and Kurt Rothermel

IPVS, Universität Stuttgart, Universitätsstr. 38,
D-70569 Stuttgart, Germany
{marron, gauger, lachenmann, minder, saukh,
rothermel}@informatik.uni-stuttgart.de

Abstract. The ability to update the program code installed on wireless sensor nodes plays an import role in the highly dynamic environments sensor networks are often deployed in. Such code update mechanisms should support flexible reconfiguration and adaptation of the sensor nodes but should also operate in an energy and time efficient manner. In this paper, we present FlexCup, a flexible code update mechanism that minimizes the energy consumed on each sensor node for the installation of arbitrary code changes. We describe two different versions of FlexCup and show, using a precise hardware emulator, that our mechanism is able to perform updates up to 8 times faster than related code update algorithms found in the literature, while consuming only an eighth of the energy.

1 Introduction

The continuous miniaturization process of computing devices combined with the proliferation of sensor technology has led to an increase in the number and the variety of devices that are able to sense their environment, gather and process data and communicate their results either to a base station or to other neighboring devices. Such wireless sensor networks are usually characterized by the limited resources available at each individual device, and the fact that each sensor node cooperates with its peers in a distributed fashion to accomplish a common task.

The ability to update the program code installed on wireless sensor nodes is an important feature in such systems, necessary not only for correcting errors but also for being able to adapt the running software to changed environmental conditions or modified application requirements. In particular, we expect a growing demand for adaptive system software support in sensor networks due to the increasing complexity of applications and the inherent dynamics of typical sensor network environments.

Current system software implementations do not provide the flexibility needed to dynamically adapt the software running on sensor nodes. This motivates the work of the TinyCubus project in our research group [1], which aims at developing a generic and reconfigurable system software for sensor networks based

K. Römer, H. Karl, and F. Mattern (Eds.): EWSN 2006, LNCS 3868, pp. 212–227, 2006.

on TinyOS. Two important building blocks of TinyCubus are support for structured cross-layer optimizations provided by the Tiny Cross-Layer Framework and adaptation capabilities for system and application components provided by the Tiny Data Management Framework.

In this paper, we present FlexCup ("FLEXible Code UPdates"), a code update mechanism that enables on the fly reinstallation of software components in TinyOS-based sensor nodes in an efficient way. FlexCup has been developed as part of TinyCubus to provide code update capabilities for the adaptation of components in the Tiny Data Management Framework, but it can also be used independently as a general code update mechanism for sensor networks.

A code update mechanism for sensor networks needs to take into account that sensor networks usually consist of small devices with extreme resource limitations. The optimization of resource usage and energy considerations are therefore crucial challenges that needed to be addressed in the development of FlexCup.

The mode of operation of FlexCup is divided in two phases: the code generation phase, where relevant information is generated at compile time; and the linking phase, where the modified components are combined with other components at runtime.

The remainder of this paper is structured as follows. Section 2 starts by giving information about existing approaches and their shortcomings. Section 3 deals with the details of our code update approach and its compile time and runtime algorithms. Section 4 gives experimental results on the complexity and efficiency of FlexCup by comparing it to other approaches. Finally, section 5 concludes this paper and gives some insight regarding future work.

2   Related Work

TinyOS [2] is probably the most widely-used operating system for sensor networks and is the target system for FlexCup. It has been ported to several hardware platforms including the MICA2 motes from Crossbow Technologies. Thanks to the wiring and event abstractions available in nesC, the component-based programming abstraction for TinyOS [3], this operating system is well suited for the requirements of sensor network applications. However, TinyOS does not allow components to be replaced at runtime. Instead, the entire program image containing both system and application components has to be exchanged if any one of the components needs to be replaced.

Another operating system developed for sensor networks and other resource constrained devices is Contiki [4]. In contrast to TinyOS, Contiki does provide support for dynamic loading of applications and system services as a core functionality of the system. However, this flexibility requires additional levels of indirection for calls to these dynamic services which adds some runtime overhead.

Maté [5] executes application code using a virtual machine. Since the actual application is only stored in RAM, this system can easily deal with code updates, but the overhead of running a virtual machine on each sensor node is considerable. The advantage of virtual machine approaches is that the size of their bytecode can be smaller than native code, which reduces the energy consumed for code transfers. However, for long-running applications the energy overhead generated by code interpreted at runtime outweighs this advantage [5].

There are several middleware solutions for sensor networks that provide some functionality related to our work. For example, Impala [6] adds abstractions that allow for dynamic updates of modules and adaptation. Modules which are already linked and which are reused in a new software version do not have to be re-linked. However, both the update and the adaption mechanism have not been implemented in the actual system yet. MiLAN [7] monitors the network situation and manages the quality needs of applications by adapting its behavior and optimizing the network topology. While MiLAN is in that way able to change its operation at runtime, it does not include support for dynamic code updates.

Several approaches try to efficiently disseminate code updates in a sensor network using multi-hop communication [8,1,5,9,6]. However, the efficient distribution of code is an issue orthogonal to our approach, which aims at reducing the size of such updates and adding the flexibility needed for adaptation. With little effort, FlexCup can be combined with any of these approaches.

Many current algorithms dealing with code updates always transmit the complete code image (including the system software), which usually amounts to several kilobytes of data. One example of this approach is Deluge [8]. Deluge is included in recent TinyOS releases and provides functionality to disseminate code updates in multi-hop networks while keeping the number of network packets low.

A more advanced approach found in the literature to reduce the number of packets to be transmitted for each code update is to compare the new code with the previously installed software version and transmit only the differences. Reijers and Langendoen [10] use a diff-like approach to compute a diff script that transforms the installed code image into a new one. Likewise, the incremental network programming protocol presented by Jeong and Culler [11] uses the Rsync algorithm [12] to find variable-sized blocks that exist in both code images and then only transmits the differences. However, both of these approaches just compare the code image using very limited knowledge about the application structure, if at all.

Koshy and Pandey [13] describe a scheme that uses incremental linking (on a PC) to reduce the number of changes in the code and transmit the code update with a diff-like algorithm. They leave most parts of the previous program image unchanged and modify only those functions that actually change. In order to avoid address shifts when the size of a function changes they add empty space behind each function. However, this approach does not provide the flexibility offered by FlexCup since the linking process is still performed at the base station. Koshy and Pandey even argue that linking on the sensor nodes – the very approach of FlexCup presented in this paper – cannot be done in practice due to high costs for transmission and storage of object files.

Most approaches assume that code updates will be distributed to all nodes in the network. However, the complexity of applications and the need for reconfiguration indicate that it might be desirable to install the required components only on those nodes that need it and maybe store other components in a free part of flash memory for later adaptation, since flash memory is typically less limited than program memory. Therefore, our solution uses knowledge about the application structure by grouping the components forming the application and the operating system. It offers more flexibility than just replacing arbitrary pieces of code because it makes it possible to dynamically change the current set of installed components through adaptation. That way, the sensor nodes can store several instances of a component at a time even though they only need one of them to fulfill their current task. When the task changes or other factors make it necessary, the node can easily replace the currently used component with a more efficient one.

3   FlexCup

FlexCup implements an efficient code update algorithm that allows exchanging only the components of a program that have actually changed. This helps saving deployment time as well as energy on the sensor nodes.

To perform its tasks, FlexCup needs to be involved in the process of compiling the components on the base station, and installing the code update on the sensor nodes: During the code generation process, FlexCup generates meta-data that describes the compiled components. FlexCup then uses this meta-data during a code update to place the new component inside the running application, relink function calls to the appropriate locations and perform address binding of data objects, as we will see in the next sections.

Using this method, FlexCup is able to reconfigure, exchange or reinstall parts of an application running on sensor nodes without having to retransmit the whole program image. Furthermore, since there is no real distinction between system and application components in current sensor network devices, FlexCup can be used for updating parts of TinyOS or TinyCubus just as it can be used for exchanging application components.

We have implemented and tested FlexCup using the MICA2 sensor platform available from Crossbow Technologies. Although developed as part of TinyCubus, the implementation of FlexCup is independent of any operating system or system software. This has two advantages: First, since FlexCup is written in ANSI C and does not have dependencies to specific system libraries, it can be easily ported to other frameworks. Second, FlexCup only runs during the process of installing code updates and does not impose further restrictions on the RAM available for application components.

3.1   Component and Meta-data Generation

Component Generation. TinyOS applications developed using the nesC programming language consist of a set of system and application components that are "wired" to generate a running program. The nesC compiler produces a single C file combining the source code of all these components, thereby generating a tightly interwoven application. This approach has the advantage that the compiler can perform optimizations like function inlining on the entire program. However, there is no simple way of replacing only a part of the compiled program like exchanging a component or a function inside a component.

This potential limitation is to some extent addressed by a new concept introduced in a recently released version of the nesC compiler (nesC 1.2). The new concept allows compiling a set of nesC components into a separate object file, a so called *binary component*. Such binary components can be wired like traditional nesC components and are then combined by the linker to create the complete application code. However, this linking is still done on the base station prior to the deployment in the sensor network.

FlexCup uses the concept of binary components and extends it by performing the linking process on the sensor node itself.

The use of binary components still allows the compiler to perform code optimizations inside of the individual binary components. Global optimizations are no longer possible. However, if the application developer segments the application based on the semantic relation of the components, we expect an application using binary components to perform similarly to a globally optimized version.

Our experience with FlexCup indicates that a reasonable segmentation of an application into binary components can be easily identified by examining the semantics of the components and their use in the system. We used several heuristics including the degree of interaction with other components and the expected likelihood of components being exchanged together. Typical examples of components combined into individual binary components are the ones implementing radio communication, the sensor access and the application components.

The segmentation of components into binary components is a design decision to be made by the system and application developers. In the long run, we expect most system components of TinyOS to be available segmented into binary components, so that the application developer will only have to consider his own components implementing application-specific functionality.

Meta-data Generation. FlexCup requires meta-data to be able to integrate new components into the existing program code on a sensor node. On the sensor nodes, this meta-data is stored in external flash memory and consists of the following three parts: generic *program information*, a program-wide *symbol table*, and a *relocation table* for each binary component in the program. The generic program information lists the number and relative offsets of all binary components, as well as the addresses of the symbol and relocation tables. The symbol table contains information about the global data and function symbols used in all components, sorted by their identifiers in ascending order. The relocation tables list the references from inside the component code to data or function symbols specified in the symbol table. Fig. 1 shows a pictorial representation of a sample program consisting of three binary components and its representation in the external flash memory after being loaded onto a sensor node.

As can be seen in Fig. 1, FlexCup stores a copy of the program code in the external flash right after the meta-data. This copy is used for constructing the

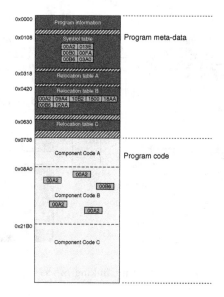

Fig. 1. Sample code and meta-data

new program code during a code update. Our implementation leaves free spaces (hatched blocks in Fig. 1) between the symbol table, each relocation table and the program code to allow for size changes of this data without having to pay the penalty of moving large pieces of data or even the whole program code.

Optimizations. The transmission and storage of the meta-data required for the dynamic linking of the components incurs an overhead on the sensor nodes. We have implemented several optimizations to minimize these effects: First, symbols in the symbol and relocation tables are identified by a two-byte id instead of a human-readable string. Second, we compress the size of the relocation tables by combining entries with the same id. For example, if there are several relocation entries referencing the same symbol, all entries are grouped together so that the identifier is needed only once. These simple optimizations incur savings in space of over 40% with respect to our original implementation.

3.2 Runtime Linking

Fig. 2 outlines the sequence of operations performed by `FlexCup` on a sensor node during the update of a binary component. The operation of the algorithm can be split up into five steps: (1) Storage of code and meta-data; (2) symbol table merge; (3) relocation table replacement; (4) reference patching; (5) installation and reboot.

(1) Storage of Code and Meta-Data. The first step in the runtime linking process involves receiving the update data, including code and the meta-data of the component, and storing it into flash memory. The external flash memory

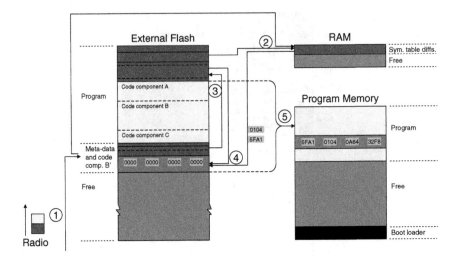

Fig. 2. Runtime linking process

of the MICA2 sensor nodes has a capacity of 512 kBytes and is normally used to store sensor readings and measurement results. For the purposes of FlexCup, flash memory is used as an external memory component where code updates and program meta-data can be stored for processing.

Even though accesses to the flash memory are very costly, using the flash memory for storing the received data is necessary for two reasons: First, the size of a code image is usually much larger than the 4 kBytes of RAM available on the nodes, so that the code image cannot be prepared completely in RAM. Second, the program code can only be written to program memory from a special bootloader section and writes are only possible on a page by page basis, so that the code image must be prepared externally before writing it to program memory. However, the degree of use of the external flash memory directly influences the amount of energy consumed by the algorithm.

Regarding the actual transmission of the modified binary component and meta-data, FlexCup allows two different modes of operation. The first one, called FlexCup Basic, transfers the whole binary component and its meta-data without considering the data already stored on the sensor node. This algorithm can be inefficient, especially if the binary component is relatively large and the number of changes is small. For this reason, FlexCup also supports a diff-based approach, called FlexCup Diff, that only transfers the incremental changes between the new binary component and the one already stored on the sensor node. FlexCup Diff can operate more efficiently than pure diff-based solutions as the processed binary code does not yet contain references to specific addresses in memory (only default values). For this reason, address shifts, which are one of the main reasons for change entries in pure diff-based approaches, do not increase the size of the data transmitted. However, just like in all diff-based approaches, the base station needs to have knowledge about the exact configuration of the sensor nodes in order to be able to prepare the diff script.

(2) Symbol Table Merge. The second step of the linking process involves combining the existing program symbol table with the newly received symbol data. Since both tables are sorted by symbol id in ascending order, an algorithm similar to merge sort is used to create the new symbol table.

Merging is performed with the help of 3 kBytes of temporary buffer in RAM used by `FlexCup` to store all changed symbol information. This buffer space is guaranteed to be available since `FlexCup` does not run in parallel to the application[1]. The advantage of this buffering is that accessing RAM is much faster and much more energy efficient than using the external flash for all operations. At the end of this step, the new symbol table is written back to the external flash at once.

A challenging task for `FlexCup` is the management of the application's data variables. Each component uses a set of variables, initializing some of them with predefined values. `FlexCup` has to cope with possible size changes, changed initialization data and the addition and the removal of such variables. It needs to calculate an adequate layout for the storage of the variables in data memory and needs to set the symbol addresses accordingly. `FlexCup` also has to prepare the initial values that are then loaded during the startup of the system.

(3) Relocation Table Replacement. This step deals with the replacement of the relocation table. This task is much simpler than the previous step, because each binary component contains an individual relocation table sent as part of the component update. Correspondingly, this step only involves copying the new relocation table to the appropriate location and, if necessary, shifting the following tables backward by the right amount of bytes.

(4) Reference Patching. The fourth step involves going through the entries of the relocation tables of all components, and checking whether any of the references needs to be updated. An update is required for all references coming from the new component code and for all references to symbols that changed their destination address during the update. If an update is required, `FlexCup` jumps to the address specified in the relocation table and writes the new destination address value. This procedure strongly benefits from the fact that the change set of entries in the symbol table is already buffered in RAM and does not need to be searched for again in flash memory. At the end of the reference patching step, all references of the components point to the right location in program or data memory and the code image is ready to be copied to program memory.

(5) Installation and Reboot. The last step takes care of copying the program code from external flash to program memory and reboots the sensor node afterwards. This is done using a custom bootloader installed in the bootloader section of the processor's program memory.

One important reason for rebooting the sensor nodes are potential layout changes of the application. Without a reboot, pointer variables might point to

---

[1] It is not possible to use all 4 kBytes of RAM for the symbol table because `FlexCup` itself needs 724 bytes of RAM for its operation.

locations in memory that are no longer valid. If the sensor network application needs to preserve state despite a reboot, it is necessary to use an external mechanism that saves the application state to non-volatile memory.

4   Experimental Evaluation

To evaluate the performance of FlexCup in terms of time and energy consumed for the update of sensor network applications, we compare FlexCup Basic and FlexCup Diff with two related approaches found in the literature: Deluge [8] and a diff-based update mechanism (from now on "MOAP-Diff") available as part of the MOAP project [9,14]. Deluge transmits the whole program image as a monolithic block of code, whereas MOAP-Diff implements a modified version of Reijers and Langendoen's original diff algorithm.

4.1   Experimental Setup

For the performance measurements detailed below, we have used a modified version of the MICA2 emulator atemu [15] which we calibrated using measurements on real sensor hardware. The modified version of the emulator includes an implementation of the external flash memory component found on the MICA2 sensor nodes and allows precise measurements of the energy consumption and the time needed to run the algorithms under test. The experimental results have been obtained by calculating the average results over 20 runs.

Selected Applications. For our performance comparisons we have selected three typical applications that can be downloaded from the TinyOS CVS repository:[2] OscilloscopeRF, Surge and AcousticLocalization. OscilloscopeRF is a simple application that periodically reads a sensor value and transmits it via radio to a base station located within transmission range. Surge is similar to OscilloscopeRF, but includes a multi-hop routing protocol that dynamically builds a routing tree along which sensor readings are forwarded to the base station. Finally, AcousticLocalization is able to determine the distance of neighboring sensor nodes by taking advantage of the difference in speed of radio waves and sound. Table 1 gives details about the complexity of the three applications showing the respective code size, the number of nesC components and the number of binary components.

Code Modifications. Using the described applications as test cases for the code update algorithms, we examine three different classes of changes to the code, ranging from small updates or bug fixes through internal updates affecting only a single binary component to external changes that imply the modification and update of several binary components at the same time.

Table 2 gives an overview of the changes we have performed for the experiments below, as well as the class they belong to. The three modifications to the

---

[2] http://cvs.sourceforge.net/viewcvs.py/tinyos/

Table 1. Complexity of sample applications

Applications	Size (bytes)	Number of nesC components	Number of binary components
OscilloscopeRF	11784	39	6
Surge	17096	53	10
AcousticLocalization	24272	69	15

Table 2. Changes performed on the applications

Application	Class	Code Update
OscilloscopeRF	small	global constant
OscilloscopeRF	small	additional call
OscilloscopeRF	small	sensor reading
Surge	internal	function exchange
Surge	internal	wiring configuration
AcousticLocalization	external	component exchange

OscilloscopeRF application are relatively simple. They involve changes to the port data is sent to (global constant), the addition of a call to an initialization function (additional call), and a modification of the value returned by the sensor (sensor reading).

The two internal modifications to Surge involve, in the first case, the replacement of the shortest-path-first routing algorithm with MintRoute, another routing algorithm providing the same interface that considers the quality of links for route selection. The second change involves the removal of the LED interface used for visual feedback which causes changes to the wiring configuration of the application. Finally, our last and only external modification changes the routing algorithm in the AcousticLocalization application to disallow the forwarding of messages – changing the modified nodes to behave as leaf nodes.

4.2   Size of Components and Meta-data

The first characteristic that distinguishes one code update algorithm from another is the amount of code and meta-data involved in the process of a code update installation. We consider two different metrics: (1) the size of the code update algorithm itself, and (2) the amount of data transmitted over radio for each update. For the evaluation of the second metric, we assume that both the original application and the code update algorithm have already been installed in program memory. Therefore, the sensor node is able to receive the code update and, depending on the algorithm, process the code image (Deluge), interpret the diff script (MOAP-Diff), or perform the linking process (FlexCup Basic and FlexCup Diff).

Table 3 shows the average size of the three code update algorithms we evaluate in this paper as they are installed in program memory. MOAP-Diff is about 55% larger than Deluge, and FlexCup is in turn about 60% larger than MOAP-Diff. For all three algorithms, the exact sizes differ between applications because they

Table 3. Average size of code update algorithms

Application	Program Code Size (bytes)		
	Deluge	MOAP-Diff	FlexCup
OscilloscopeRF	10868	16742	26715
Surge	11326	17213	27466
AcousticLocalization	10650	16728	26692

Table 4. Size of components and meta-data (in bytes)

	Transmitted Data Size								Flash Memory Data Size			
		MOAP-	FlexCup Basic			FlexCup Diff				MOAP-	FlexCup	
Code Update	Deluge	Diff	Meta	Code	Total	Meta	Code	Total	Deluge	Diff	Basic	Diff
global const.	23142	11	799	1198	1997	530	15	545	23142	28538	37337	35885
additional call	23142	1230	801	1202	2003	760	5	765	23142	28542	37343	36105
sensor reading	23142	2835	537	886	1423	523	114	637	23142	28608	36743	35977
function exch.	28652	7684	1056	3258	4314	1110	1587	2697	28652	33440	43561	41944
wiring config.	28652	375	1355	2142	3497	1290	8	1298	28652	34272	42744	40545
comp. exch.	34162	7802	2565	4773	7338	2611	532	3143	34162	40156	58014	53736

have to be compiled together with the application code. The resulting size differences are due to differences in the set of system components already included by the applications and to different optimizations performed by the nesC compiler. In the case of FlexCup, however, there is a fixed part of 16212 bytes that is compiled and executed independently of the application and is, therefore, not subject to these effects. As program memory size does not seem to be a limiting factor for most current sensor network applications, we do not expect these differences in code size to inhibit the use of FlexCup.

Apart from the size of the code update algorithms and the one-time penalty that sensor nodes have to pay for their installation, a more relevant metric is the amount of data to be transmitted when an application is modified. The left-hand side of Table 4 shows the number of bytes transmitted by Deluge, MOAP-Diff, FlexCup Basic and FlexCup Diff for performing the six code updates introduced in the previous section. For example, for the modification of the OscilloscopeRF application so that it returns a different sensor reading (third code update in Table 4), Deluge has to transmit 23142 bytes, whereas MOAP-Diff only requires transmitting 2835 bytes. As detailed in section 3, both FlexCup Basic and FlexCup Diff need to transmit meta-data, i.e., the symbol and relocation tables, as well as the code of the component that changes. In total, FlexCup Basic transmits 1423 bytes and FlexCup Diff only 637 bytes. This implies more than 90% savings in the number of packets comparing FlexCup Basic to Deluge and more than 75% if we compare FlexCup Diff to MOAP-Diff.

Only in cases where the actual change is very small, like for the change of a global constant in OscilloscopeRF or the update of the wiring configuration in Surge, does MOAP-Diff perform much better than any other algorithm under test. For FlexCup Diff, much of the overhead comes from the transmission of the new meta-data information. Looking at the pure code size, FlexCup Diff would easily outperform MOAP-Diff in most cases. In general, FlexCup Basic only requires between 6% and 21% of the number of transmissions of Deluge. FlexCup Diff saves more than 75% in the best case compared to MOAP-Diff and requires less transmission volume than MOAP-Diff in four out of six cases.

However, there is another relevant factor. The right part of Table 4 shows the size of the information that needs to be stored in flash memory for performing a given update. In the case of Deluge, this is just the data received over the radio link, but for MOAP-Diff and FlexCup this also includes the code of already installed components and meta-data. For that reason, Deluge is in all cases more efficient than the three other approaches in terms of space complexity. This might be an important factor in scenarios where the application stores large amounts of data locally on the sensor nodes before uploading it to a base station. Although the size of the flash memory on the MICA2 nodes amounts to 512 kBytes and should be sufficient for most applications, long-running applications might still benefit from the extra space. In general, MOAP-Diff requires between 16 and 25% more space than Deluge. FlexCup Diff needs about 50% more space and the space requirements of FlexCup Basic are 50 to 70% higher than the requirements of Deluge depending on the specific code update. Most of the overhead of the last two approaches comes from the storage of the symbol and relocation tables.

4.3 Efficiency of the Code Update Algorithms

Let us now look at the performance characteristics of the four code update algorithms. For the purpose of the experiments below, we measure the efficiency of the algorithms based on two metrics: execution time and energy consumption.

In general, it is clear that both metrics are not independent from each other and that a longer execution time usually also implies a higher energy consumption. However, the diverse energy characteristics of the hardware components, especially the external flash memory and the radio interface, indicate that considering the execution time alone is not sufficient for determining which algorithm is more energy-efficient.

In the experiments, we consider execution time and energy consumption throughout the three phases "Transmission", "Processing" and "Installation". To guarantee a fair comparison between the algorithms, we assume perfect conditions during the transmission phase, ignoring possible collisions, errors and the specific protocol overhead. To simplify the evaluation, we also assume that each node receives the code update data exactly once and then forwards it to its neighbor nodes.

Execution Time. Fig. 3 shows the duration of the three phases of the four code update mechanisms for all six code updates. As one can see, the time required for installation is dominated by the transmission time in the case of Deluge and by the processing time for MOAP-Diff, whereas in the case of FlexCup Basic and FlexCup Diff, transmission and processing times are of similar magnitude.

FlexCup Basic and FlexCup Diff are about 4 times faster than MOAP-Diff and have on average almost 8 times better execution times than those of Deluge.

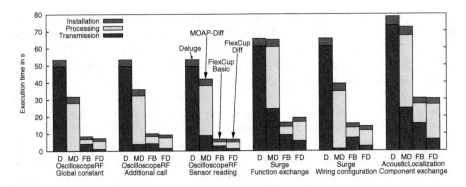

Fig. 3. Execution times of the code updates

FlexCup Diff is marginally faster than **FlexCup Basic** by saving a significant part of the transmission time while requiring some additional time for processing the diff script.

In general, **MOAP-Diff** is faster than **Deluge**, although large parts of its savings in transmission time are spent for processing the diff script in the processing phase. An extreme example can be seen in the 'function exchange' case of the **Surge** application, where the difference in execution time between **MOAP-Diff** and **Deluge** amounts to only 0.55 seconds. **FlexCup Diff** is actually slower than **FlexCup Basic** in this example with the processing effort outweighing the transmission savings.

Energy Consumption. Fig. 4 shows the amount of energy in millijoules consumed by the four code update mechanisms during the three phases of the code updates. The measurements confirm the good performance of **FlexCup** compared to the other approaches, showing that in the best case **FlexCup** consumes only an eighth of the energy of **Deluge** and **MOAP-Diff**. On the other hand, the results cannot confirm the relatively good performance of **MOAP-Diff** compared to **Deluge** observed for the execution times of the code updates. Energy-wise, **MOAP-Diff** performs worse than **Deluge** in three out of the six cases. This is mainly due to the relatively inefficient implementation of **MOAP-Diff** which uses a lot of access operations to the external flash memory. These access operations are very energy expensive on the MICA2 hardware.

The expensive implementation of **MOAP-Diff** also explains the inferior performance of **FlexCup Diff**, which uses the **MOAP-Diff** algorithm for extracting its component data. It remains to be investigated whether a more efficient implementation of the diff approach is able to retain more of the advantage achieved during the transmission phase and to improve on the results of **FlexCup Basic**.

Nevertheless, our experiments show that **FlexCup Basic** and **FlexCup Diff**, although similar in energy consumption and execution time, use the sensor node hardware in different ways. In general, **FlexCup Basic** transmits more data than **FlexCup Diff**, but the latter has extra overhead regarding the decoding of the binary component to be installed in program memory. Thus, depending

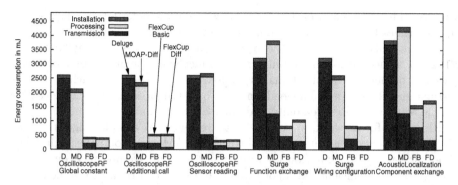

Fig. 4. Energy consumption of the code updates

on the physical characteristics of the external flash memory and radio components, it might be preferable to use `FlexCup Basic` instead of `FlexCup Diff`, or vice versa.

An additional lesson that can be learned from the results in Fig. 3 and 4 is that counting the number of bytes a code update algorithm needs to transmit does not necessarily give information about the time and energy efficiency of the algorithms. All relevant factors, including processing and flash memory access costs, need to be part of the evaluation.

4.4   Advantages and Limitations of FlexCup

`FlexCup` exhibits several advantages compared to other code update mechanisms. First of all, it allows for greater *flexibility* in the exchange of application and system software components at runtime, thereby offering functionality required by *adaptive system software* like `TinyCubus`. Second, `FlexCup` is able to reduce the number of bytes transferred to each sensor node and to minimize the amount of energy needed for the processing of code updates, which immediately translates into a *better overall energy consumption*.

One limitation of `FlexCup` is its use of external flash memory for the storage of meta-data and the use of program memory for the storage of the `FlexCup` program code. Both are only possible if there is enough free space available after fulfilling the requirements of the application. Like other code update mechanisms, `FlexCup` also has to deal with the access characteristics of the platform's flash memory. Especially the problem of wear levelling in flash memory remains to be addressed.

5   Conclusions and Future Work

In this paper we have presented `FlexCup` a flexible code update mechanism for sensor networks that offers the functionality and performance required by adaptive system software. We have evaluated `FlexCup` by analyzing several realistic code updates with the help of emulation tools calibrated on real sensor nodes.

Compared to related approaches, `FlexCup` was able to perform the same updates up to 8 times faster while consuming only an eighth of the energy.

We have also shown that the overall code image size of `TinyCubus` and `FlexCup`, as needed for the reconfiguration functionality required by more complex sensor network applications, is comparable to other approaches such as `Deluge` and Reijers' and Langendoen's diff-based algorithm, although `FlexCup` is able to provide more flexibility and adaptation capabilities.

Regarding future work, we would like to explore more complex algorithms for the management of flash memory and reserved RAM space to further reduce the time and energy consumption for linking in `FlexCup`. We are also considering the use of more efficient diff algorithms that would contribute to reducing the amount of energy needed for the execution of the diff scripts in `FlexCup Diff`. Finally, it would also be interesting to evaluate the influence of different hardware properties on our implementation by porting `FlexCup` to other platforms such as the EYES sensor nodes.

References

1. Marrón, P.J., Lachenmann, A., Minder, D., Hähner, J., Sauter, R., Rothermel, K.: TinyCubus: A flexible and adaptive framework for sensor networks. In: Proc. of the 2nd European Workshop on Wireless Sensor Networks. (2005) 278–289
2. Hill, J., Szewczyk, R., Woo, A., Hollar, S., Culler, D., Pister, K.: System architecture directions for networked sensors. In: Proc. of the 9th Intl. Conf. on Architectural Support for Programming Languages and Operating Systems. (2000) 93–104
3. Gay, D., Levis, P., von Behren, R., Welsh, M., Brewer, E., Culler, D.: The nesC language: A holistic approach to networked embedded systems. In: Proc. of the ACM SIGPLAN 2003 Conf. on Programming Language Design and Implementation. (2003) 1–11
4. Dunkels, A., Grönvall, B., Voigt, T.: Contiki – a lightweight and flexible operating system for tiny networked sensors. In: Proceedings of the First IEEE Workshop on Embedded Networked Sensors 2004 (IEEE EmNetS-I). (2004)
5. Levis, P., Culler, D.: Maté: A tiny virtual machine for sensor networks. In: Proc. of the 10th Int. Conf. on Architectural Support for Programming Languages and Operating Systems. (2002) 85–95
6. Liu, T., Martonosi, M.: Impala: A middleware system for managing autonomic, parallel sensor systems. In: Proc. of the 9th ACM SIGPLAN Symp. on Principles and Practice of Parallel Programming. (2003) 107–118
7. Heinzelman, W.B., Murphy, A.L., Carvalho, H.S., Perillo, M.A.: Middleware to support sensor network applications. IEEE Network 18 (2004) 6–14
8. Hui, J.W., Culler, D.: The dynamic behavior of a data dissemination protocol for network programming at scale. In: Proc. of the 2nd Intl. Conf. on Embedded Networked Sensor Systems. (2004) 81–94
9. Stathopoulos, T., Heidemann, J., Estrin, D.: A remote code update mechanism for wireless sensor networks. Technical Report CENS-TR-30, University of California, L.A. (2003)
10. Reijers, N., Langendoen, K.: Efficient code distribution in wireless sensor networks. In: Proc. of the 2nd ACM Intl. Conf. on Wireless Sensor Networks and Appl. (2003) 60–67

11. Jeong, J., Culler, D.: Incremental network programming for wireless sensors. In: First IEEE Comm. Soc. Conf. on Sensor and Ad Hoc Communications and Networks. (2004)

12. Tridgell, A.: Efficient Algorithms for Sorting and Synchronization. PhD thesis, The Australian National University (1999)

13. Koshy, J., Pandey, R.: Remote incremental linking for energy-efficient reprogramming of sensor networks. In: Proc. of the 2nd European Workshop on Wireless Sensor Networks. (2005) 354–365

14. Yeh, T., Yamamoto, H., Stathopolous, T.: Over-the-air reprogramming of wireless sensor nodes. UCLA EE202A Project Report (2003) http://lecs.cs.ucla.edu/~thanos/EE202a_final_writeup.pdf.

15. Polley, J., Blazakis, D., McGee, J., Rusk, D., Baras, J.S.: ATEMU: a fine-grained sensor network simulator. In: Proc. of the First IEEE Communications Society Conference on Sensor and Ad Hoc Communications and Networks. (2004)

Transforming Protocol Specifications for Wireless Sensor Networks into Efficient Embedded System Implementations

Gerald Wagenknecht, Daniel Dietterle, Jean-Pierre Ebert, and Rolf Kraemer

IHP microelectronic GmbH, Wireless Communication Systems,
P.O. Box 1466, 15204 Frankfurt (Oder), Germany
{wagenknecht, dietterle, ebert, kraemer}@ihp-microelectronics.com
http://www.ihp-microelectronics.com

Abstract. In this paper, we present an efficient way how protocols modelled in SDL (Specification and Description Language) can be transformed into efficient implementations for resource-constrained wireless sensor nodes. We will show how SDL concepts such as processes, timers, or signals can be mapped to operating system concepts provided by the Reflex operating system. Our approach is based on optimized, automatically generated C code derived from the Telelogic TAU SDL Suite that can be left as is. The overhead caused by our SDL run-time environment is minimal, thus making it applicable in embedded systems. By pre-allocating memory for SDL signals it is possible to completely avoid dynamic memory allocation. We will also highlight some SDL modelling guidelines that help to avoid common SDL implementation overhead.

1 Introduction

Wireless sensor networks (WSN) have attracted much research effort in recent years. Typical WSN applications target several months or years of unsupervised operation. Applications as well as communication protocols for WSNs are becoming increasingly complex as the processing capabilties of sensor nodes grow. There is a strong need for reliable software when WSNs shall become economically successful.

The material presented here are results of work within the scope of the BASUMA (Body Area System for Ubiquitous Multimedia Application) project [4]. Here, we are designing a wireless communication platform for sensor nodes located on and around the human body. Though not using multi-hop communication as often assumed in WSNs, most of the implementation challenges in wireless sensor node design appear also in our scenario.

In particular, reliability is a major concern for us as the BASUMA system shall be used for autonomous, long-term health monitoring. The medium access control (MAC) protocol proposed for the BASUMA communication system is modelled in SDL. A 32-bit open-core processor, the LEON2 processor, was selected for the BASUMA platform. On this processor, the real-time operating

K. Römer, H. Karl, and F. Mattern (Eds.): EWSN 2006, LNCS 3868, pp. 228–243, 2006.
© Springer-Verlag Berlin Heidelberg 2006

system (OS) Reflex [5] from Brandenburg University of Technology Cottbus is running. Reflex is a tiny, data-flow oriented OS for deeply embedded systems. Although quite similar to TinyOS [7], we believe it is better tailored for reliable systems because of its earliest-deadline-first process scheduling strategy. Process priorities can be expressed by shorter deadlines. This way, it is much easier and less error-prone to implement time-critical functions, something that requires much effort in TinyOS.

SDL [1] — a high-abstraction level formal description language — has long been used for modelling, simulation, and verification of communication protocols ([8], [9], [10]). Formal verfication can be employed to design reliable systems.

However, SDL should not only be used for system *modelling and verification*. SDL models should be also the basis for tailored, efficient sensor node *protocol implementations*. There is a range of tools for automatic C/C++ code generation, real-time operating system integration, and even hardware synthesis from SDL models available from both academia and industry. A well-known commercial tool is Telelogic TAU SDL Suite [2].

Software developed with SDL is still not efficient and small enough to be utilized in embedded systems with severe processing and storage limitations as we are faced with in todays wireless sensor nodes. Reasons for this are some SDL concepts and data types that incur high implementation overhead as well as an inefficient SDL run-time environment.

By restricting ourselves to a subset of the SDL language for system modelling and by replacing the SDL run-time environment with a thin operating system integration layer, we achieve tiny SDL-based software implementations with little overhead, nonetheless preserving the SDL semantics. The integration layer has been designed specifically for the Reflex OS, but can be adapted to any other OS. It is combined with the C code generated by the Telelogic TAU SDL tool through the definition of C macros that are part of the generated code. Our approach is called tight integration in the Telelogic documentation [2].

This paper is organised as follows: Section 2 introduces briefly the BASUMA communication system and the protocol that will be implemented using our integration approach. Section 3 describes the basic concepts of SDL so much as required for an understanding of this paper. Likewise, Section 4 gives an overview of the Reflex OS. The main part of this paper, Section 5 is dedicated to a detailed presentation of the integration approach of the generated C code into Reflex. After that, limitations of our approach as well as modelling guidelines for SDL software designers for embedded systems are given in Section 6. Our results are presented in Section 7. Finally, in Section 8 the paper is summarized and conclusions are drawn.

2   BASUMA Wireless Communication Platform

BASUMA [4] (Body Area System for Ubiquitous Multimedia Applications) is a research project started in 2004 that has the objective to develop a platform for wireless communication around the human body. This platform will consist

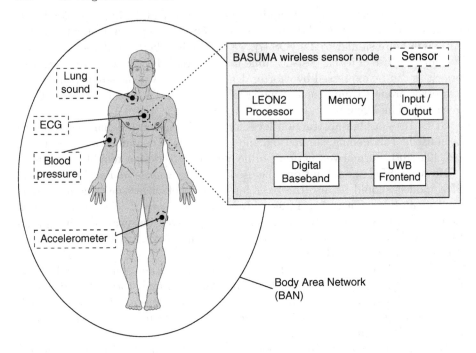

Fig. 1. Body area network and BASUMA hardware architecture

of hardware and software components that are specifically designed for small, low-power devices.

The capabilities of the BASUMA platform are to be demonstrated with a medical application. A number of battery-powered sensor nodes measuring various bioparameters, such as heart rate, temperature, or ECG are attached to the human body and form a wireless network. This body area (sensor) network (BAN) forms the basis for long-term monitoring of chronically ill patients. The signals measured by the sensor nodes are locally analyzed (preprocessed) and evaluated within the node or network, and communication with a remote medical center is only initiated, if necessary. An application scenario and the BASUMA hardware architecture are shown in Fig. 1.

All nodes in the BAN are in communication range of each other, hence multi-hop communication is not required. We investigate ultra-wide band (UWB) technology as the means of communication. We assume IEEE 802.15.3 MAC protocol [3] as very suitable for medical applications due to its offered functionality such as reserved time slots, power management, security features, and network coordinator handover. We have reduced the complexity of the protocol by omitting not required functions. The MAC protocol was modelled in SDL and simulated using Telelogic TAU SDL Suite. A description of our SDL model can be found in [12].

The validated SDL model should be the basis for the MAC protocol implementation by an automatic transformation. The effort of re-implementing the protocol in C/C++ would be too high and error-prone compared to an optimisation approach where inefficient SDL concepts in the model are replaced by equivalent functions with less overhead. Additionally, the time to achieve a fully tested implementation is considerable shortened. Here, instead of using an SDL run-time environment, we tightly integrate the SDL model with the underlying OS. This approach is described in the following sections in more detail.

3   Specification and Description Language (SDL)

In a way, SDL can be considered as a programming language with a graphical user interface that offers high-abstraction level programming elements to the designer. It was standardised by ITU-T in Recommendation Z.100 [1]. SDL models can be simulated, which allows verification of system functionality during an early stage in the design flow.

In this section, we will first introduce the basic concepts of the language and, later, describe how SDL models can be implemented using Telelogic TAU SDL Suite.

3.1   Basic Concepts

The SDL description of system behavior is based on *communicating extended finite state machines (CEFSM)* that are executed concurrently. State machines are represented by SDL *processes*. Processes communicate with each other and the system environment by exchanging *asynchronous signals* that may carry any number of parameters. SDL also provides *timers* that can be configured to generate signals at defined points in time. Each process in an SDL system contains a FIFO (First-In-First-Out) input buffer (with infinite space) into which the received signals and timer events are queued. This is shown in Fig. 2 (a).

SDL models are hierarchically structured. The system level, which is the top level, consists of blocks connected via channels. Channels are used as signal carriers. Each block may contain any number of sub-blocks. The lowest level sub-block contains the actual processes. A process may have local variables and may contain procedures. Processes communicate within the same or across different blocks via signal routes. Procedures are the lowest level in the functional hierarchy and have their own local scope.

In Fig. 2 (b), a typical SDL transition is shown. Transitions are triggered by receiving a signal from the signal input queue of the process. During state transition, the SDL process may perform computations, send any number of signals to other processes, set/reset timers, call procedures, and, finally, settle in the next state. Only then, a new signal can be consumed from the head of the input queue. If no transition is specified for a received signal, it is simply discarded. It is also possible, and often used in system modeling, to use the SAVE symbol in order to defer the reception of a particular signal from the queue. This means, that the saved signal is not removed from the input queue, but the next signals in the queue can be processed instead.

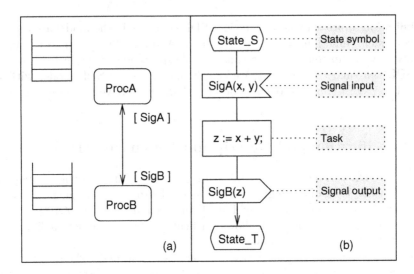

Fig. 2. (a) SDL processes with signal route and emphasised input queue. (b) Sample SDL transition.

3.2   Code Generator and OS Integration Approach of Telelogic TAU SDL Suite

Telelogic TAU SDL Suite [2] is a tool that allows modelling, simulating, validating, and implementing SDL systems. The CAdvanced code generator translates the SDL model into C code. This C code contains definitions of the required SDL structures such as processes, signals, etc., but also the state machine implementations of the SDL processes in the so-called PAD (process activity description) function. In this function, SDL transitions are triggered depending on the current state and signal input.

```
YPAD_FUNCTION(yPAD_z01_ProcB) {
    ...
    switch(yVarP->RestartAddress) {
    ...

    //INPUT SigIn
    case 1:
        ...

    //OUTPUT SigOut
    case 4:
        ALLOC_SIGNAL(SigOut, ySigN_z2_SigOut,
            TO_PROCESS(Prs1, yPrsN_z00_ProcA), XSIGNALHEADERTYPE)
        SDL_2OUTPUT(xDefaultPrioSignal, (xIdNode *)0, SigOut,
            ySigN_z2_SigOut, TO_PROCESS(Prs1, yPrsN_z00_ProcA),
            0, "SigOut")

    //NEXTSTATE State_T
    case 5:
        SDL_NEXTSTATE(State_T, z001_State_T, "State_T")
        ...
```

Fig. 3. Fragment of generated code by CAdvanced for the PAD function

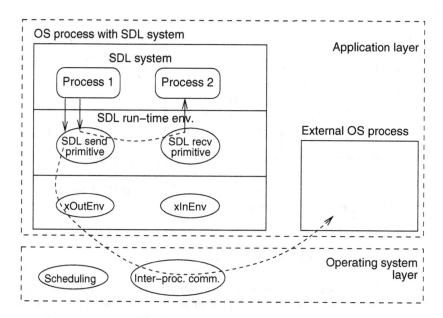

Fig. 4. Light Integration approach

The generated code is independent of the underlying OS. It can be the basis for a system simulation or implementation. This is achieved by using C macros wherever a run-time environment specific implementation is required. By defining these C macros in an appropriate way, the generated code is turned into a simulation or OS-specific implementation. An example of the code generator output for a PAD function is shown in Fig. 3.

Telelogic TAU supports three integration models for creating an application from an SDL system description. Here, we will focus on the Light Integration and the Tight Integration approach. With Light Integration, there is an OS-independent run-time environment that provides, for instance, functionality for process scheduling, signal exchange and queueing, or timer handling. Together with all SDL processes of the system, it runs in its own OS process. Environment functions form the interface between the SDL system and other OS processes. The Light Integration approach is shown schematically in Fig. 4.

While porting to a new OS is made relatively simple with the Light Integration approach, it causes some overhead due to its run-time environment, since scheduling and some form of inter-process communication are also common OS services. Therefore, in order to avoid redundancy, the Tight Integration approach does without the run-time environment. All SDL processes are running as separate OS processes. Signal exchange and scheduling is performed by using the native OS services. This is depicted in Fig. 5.

For an integration of SDL systems with Reflex, the OS we chose for our sensor nodes, we have adopted the Tight Integration approach because of its reduced memory footprint. This involved the definition of a number of C macros that are present in the generated code and some additional support functions. Note, that

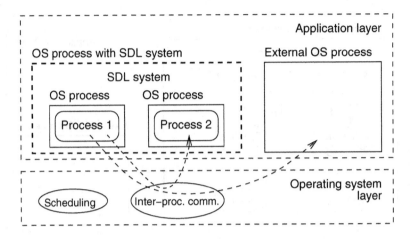

Fig. 5. Tight Integration approach

the approach is general and therefore utilizable with other embedded system OSs such as TinyOS. In Section 5 we present in detail how we used the services offered by the Reflex OS as a substitute for the SDL run-time environment. Before that, a brief introduction into Reflex is needed and can be found in the following section.

4   Reflex

Reflex (Real time Event Flow EXecutive) [5] is a small operating system for deeply embedded devices. It mainly consists of a scheduler and a general interrupt handling mechanism. Reflex provides programming abstractions that were specifically designed to support data-flow oriented applications, for instance processing of sensor signals [6]. With the exception of some hardware-specific initialization routines, the OS is written completely in C++. It has been ported to a number of 8-bit microprocessors and, recently, to the LEON2 processor, an open-core 32-bit SPARC instruction set processor. The LEON2 port requires about 4 kbytes of memory.

In Reflex, there are two kinds of activities: schedulable and non-schedulable activities. The non-schedulable ones are interrupt handlers triggered by hardware events. Schedulable activities are posted by interrupt handlers or other activities and are managed by the scheduler. Each schedulable activity is derived from a base class and provides a `run()` function that is called by the scheduler to start the activity.

The scheduler schedules activities according to an earliest-deadline-first (EDF) strategy. Running activities can only be preempted by interrupts. In case that the interrupt handler posts an activity with an earlier deadline than the interrupted activity, the scheduler will start this new activity. Only after its completion, the interrupted activity is resumed. This behaviour has got the advantage that a single stack for the whole application is sufficient.

In comparison with TinyOS [7] — the operating system most often used for wireless sensor nodes — software development based on Reflex is made much easier in some respects. While TinyOS tasks run to completion before any other task is scheduled, time-critical activities in Reflex will interrupt a lower-priority activity. Such a behaviour is difficult to achieve in TinyOS. A possible solution is to break tasks into smaller chunks, so that the processor is never occupied with a task for a longer period of time and a task switch can take place. In essence, all tasks in a system need to collaborate to ensure that time-critical tasks get scheduled in time. This tight coupling impedes re-use of system components.

Furthermore, TinyOS applications are written in the nesC language. As has been reported in the literature [11], debugging applications is made much more complicated compared with the traditional C/C++ approach.

5   Integration of SDL Systems in Reflex

In this section, we will describe our approach towards a mapping of SDL concepts to the programming abstractions and services offered by Reflex. This approach is based on the generated code for the SDL system from the Telelogic TAU tool. Therefore, we will also immerse into some C macros that are in the code and must be defined for an OS-specific integration.

5.1   SDL Processes and Reflex Activities

In our approach, each *SDL process* is mapped directly to a *Reflex activity*. As introduced before, the behaviour of SDL processes is contained in their PAD (process activity description) functions. When the SDL process receives an input signal, a new transition is triggered and the PAD function called. This corresponds very well to how activities are handled in Reflex.

Therefore, our solution is to create a wrapper object for each SDL process instance. This wrapper object is a Reflex activity and has the SDL process representation — a C structure in the generated code — associated with it. From the activity's run() function, the PAD function of the associated process is called when the activity is started. This relationship is shown in Fig. 6.

5.2   Communication Between Processes

SDL processes communicate via signals. When modelling a SDL system, it is not required to explicitly state the receiver of a signal, rather the system will determine from the static signal routes, which process shall receive the signal. However, this route finding operation causes overhead as it is performed at run-time when a signal is sent without an explicit destination. In our approach, since we are targeting sensor nodes, only direct addressing is allowed, that is for each signal output the receiver process must be stated.

A global *symbol table* stores the identifiers of all processes. The symbol table is managed by a system object (see Section 5.3). The sending process gets the reference of the receiving process from the symbol table calling the GetPrsId()

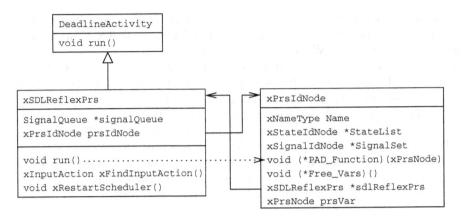

Fig. 6. Process wrapper class (*xSDLReflexPrs*) and associated SDL process representation

function. With this reference, it gets access to the input queue and outputs the signal using the **SendSig()** function.

The hierarchical SDL system structure (system, blocks, processes) will no longer exist, as it is not relevant for the implementation and would mean a waste of memory resources.

Each process wrapper object manages its own FIFO signal queue (see Fig. 7). Sending a signal to a process involves adding the signal to the queue of the receiver process. The signal queue is implemented as a trigger variable, a special programming concept in the Reflex OS. Trigger variables are attached to an activity object, writing to the trigger variable causes scheduling of the activity object. This way, the **run()** function and, consequently, the PAD function are called and the signal is consumed from the input queue.

5.3 System Initialisation

We have introduced an SDL *system object* that is responsible for the creation and initialisation of processes. This happens at the start of the application and not dynamically during process execution (see Section 6). The system creates processes by calling the function **CreatePrs()**. With the function **RegPrsId()**,

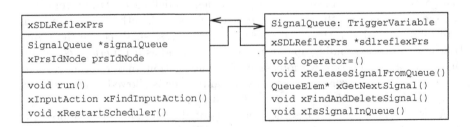

Fig. 7. The *SignalQueue* class

processes register themselves in the symbol table. The system object is a Reflex activity. It also owns a queue for SDL timers, that are described in more detail in the following Section 5.4.

5.4   Timers

In SDL it is possible to set and reset timers and to check whether a particular timer is active. In the generated code, C macro calls are included for these operations. We have provided our own definitions for these macros.

In our integration approach, SDL timers are managed by the system object, which has got a timer queue. In this queue, all timers of all processes are ordered according to their expiration time. If a timer expires, it is transformed into a signal and written into the signal queue of the according process. This causes the process to be scheduled. The system object is notified with every tick of the system clock by calling its `Tick()` function. These ticks are generated by the interrupt handler of the system clock. When the system's `Tick()` function is executed, the current system time is read and any expired timers are transformed into signals.

The system object handles timer reset, as well. This means removing the timer from the timer queue. Additionally, the input queue of the process is browsed to remove the timer signal, in case the timer has expired already and was not yet consumed.

5.5   Communication with the Environment

The SDL processes communicate with the environment directly via signals using the `SigOutput()` function. The environment is derived from the SDL process wrapper class, this means that it is a Reflex activity and has its own signal queue. However, since its behaviour is not specified in the SDL model, there is no associated SDL process and, hence, no PAD function. The unique identifier of the environment in the symbol table is `xEnv`.

Communication from the environment to other processes follows the same scheme as introduced in Section 5.2 by calling `SigOutput()`. The identifier of the receiving process has to be specified.

The behavior of the environment is not specified in the model. It can be used as an interface to the lower layers of the application as shown in Fig. 8. If a sensor or another device triggers an interrupt, an interrupt handler can transform this interrupt into a signal and send it to the right process. Similarly, processes can communicate via the environment with drivers and trigger actuators.

5.6   Source Code Example

Now, our implementation shall be described by means of a small source code example. It is based on the state machine fragment and code generator output presented in Fig. 3 and shown again in Fig. 9.

The generated code contains the PAD function, where all state transitions are implemented. Here, we look at one part of a transition where the process sends

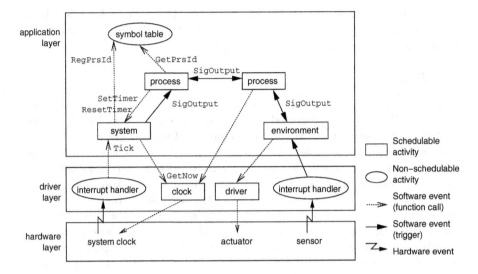

Fig. 8. Interactions between the SDL system and the Reflex OS

a signal (`SigOut`) to process `ProcA`. The signal will be allocated (`ALLOC_SIGNAL`) and then sent (`SDL_2OUTPUT`) to the receiving process (`TO_PROCESS`). After this, the process goes into the next state (`SDL_NEXTSTATE`).

The macro `ALLOC_SIGNAL` defines the memory allocation of the signal:

```
#define ALLOC_SIGNAL(SIG_NAME, SIG_IDNODE, RECEIVER, SIG_PAR_TYPE) \
    OUTSIGNAL_DATA_PTR = ((xSDLReflexPrs*) RECEIVER)->
                        AllocSignal(SIG_NAME, SIG_IDNODE);
```

Sending a signal includes two more steps: finding the receiver process and writing the signal into the input queue. The former is implemented by the macro `TO_PROCESS`:

```
#define TO_PROCESS(PROC_NAME, PROC_IDNODE) \
    ((xSDLReflexPrs*) symbolTable[PROC_NAME])->prsIdNode->prsVar
```

The unique name of the process (`ProcA`) serves as an index for the symbol table where the reference of the process activity is stored. With this reference, access

```
                        //OUTPUT SigOut
                        case 4:
                            ALLOC_SIGNAL(SigOut, ySigN_z2_SigOut,
                            TO_PROCESS(Prs1, yPrsN_z00_ProcA), XSIGNALHEADERTYPE)
    SigOut               SDL_2OUTPUT(xDefaultPrioSignal, (xIdNode *)0, SigOut,
    TO ProcA             ySigN_z2_SigOut, TO_PROCESS(Prs1, yPrsN_z00_ProcA),
                            0, "SigOut")

    State_T              //NEXTSTATE State_T
                        case 5:
                            SDL_NEXTSTATE(State_T, z001_State_T, "State_T")
```

Fig. 9. Fragment of generated code in the PAD function

to its input queue is possible. In the second step, the signal will be written into the input queue:

```
#define SDL_2OUTPUT(PRIO, VIA, SIG_NAME, SIG_IDNODE, RECEIVER,
                    SIG_PAR_SIZE, SIG_NAME_STRING) \
  xSigOutput((xSignalNode) OUTSIGNAL_DATA_PTR, SIG_IDNODE,
             VarP, RECEIVER);
```

The function `xSigOutput()` composes the signal and writes the signal into the input queue. The first two parameters are the structur of the signal. The third parameter `VarP` is a reference to the sending process. The symbol `RECEIVER` is a reference to the receiving process. Now the process goes to the next state. The macro `SDL_NEXTSTATE` defines this:

```
#define SDL_NEXTSTATE(STATE_NAME, STATE_IDNODE, STATE_NAME_STRING) \
  xGetNextState(VarP, STATE_IDNODE); \
  return;
```

The function `xGetNextState()` gets the ID of the following state (`z001_STATE_T`). This ends the transitions. The PAD function call returns and the handling of the process is completed.

5.7   Static Allocation of Signals

Dynamic memory management is often not needed or desired for embedded systems design, because it is inefficent in terms of time and space. Instead, one common approach is to manage pools of pre-allocated buffers of equal size. This can be implemented with less overhead and requires a-priori knowledge about the pool size to be used.

When sending a signal to a process in the SDL system, a signal buffer must be allocated first, so that signal parameters can be set. In the original SDL run-time environment, this involves dynamic memory allocation.

We have chosen a different approach to be more efficinet: The provision of a signal buffer is the responsibilty of the receiving process. The process can either dynamically allocate the requested memory space when dynamic memory management is available — or take the buffer from a pool of pre-allocated signals. At compile time, the pool size is fixed and memory is reserved for it.

Static allocation requires an careful analysis of the SDL system to identify required pool space. The SDL system will expect in any case that a signal could be successfully allocated or it will lead to a system failure.

However, when sending a signal from the environment into the SDL system, it is possible that the SDL system cannot handle any more input signals and returns no valid buffer to the environment. In this case, the signal cannot be sent and the environment needs to handle the situation appropriately. This could happen, for example, in a communication protocol model when no more received packets can be processed and must be dropped or buffered for some time. It is the responsibility of the programmer of the environment functions to handle the case that no valid signal buffer was returned in order to avoid system failure.

6   Limitations and SDL Modelling Guidelines

The most important features of the SDL language are implemented and can be used for system modelling, but there are unavoidable limitations:

- It is not possible to use processes with multiple instances and to create process instances dynamically. Only processes with a single instance are supported in our implementation.
- There are different possibilities in SDL to send a signal. One can specify the signal route (key word: VIA) or trigger a spontaneaus transition using the key word NONE. There are only two possibilities in our approach to send a signal. One need to specify the receiver. Either one specifies the receiver by using its unique name or one uses the identifier of the process. The reason for the restriction are the inefficient SDL runtime calculations of the receiver using the VIA function.

There are some further guidelines and recommendations for an SDL system modeller:

- Avoid (remote) procedures. They are cumbersome. If possible, use external C procedures and call the C function from SDL. Of course, this limits the ability to verify the formal protocol description.
- Avoid certain SDL predefined types such as Octet_String, Bit_String. Use the corresponding XNOUSE compiler flag.
- Avoid copying parameters.

7   Implementation Results

In this section, we will show some experimental results of our work, in particular the system performance and the usage of memory space.

7.1   Performance

Our approach will be compared with the original run-time environment from Telelogic TAU SDL Suite running on the operating system eCos (Light Integration). Both systems are compiled with the sparc-elf-gcc cross-compiler and executed on a LEON2 processor.

To measure the performance, a small communication system was modelled, containing two processes that exchange a number of signals (1000, 3000, and 8000). Execution time will be measured between the Start signal from the environment (indicating the start of the signal exchange) and the Stop signal sent to the environment (indicating the end of the signal exchange). The system clock accuracy in the measurement was 10 millicesonds. The measured performance results are summarised in Table 1.

The execution time of our Tight Integration approach is notable 40% of the execution time of the original run-time environment. This equals a performance increase by a factor of 2.5.

Table 1. System performance with two communicating processes

Number of signals	Own approach	Telelogic TAU RTE
1000	0.050 s	0.120 s
3000	0.140 s	0.360 s
8000	0.400 s	0.980 s

Signal exchange is a common operation in all SDL systems. A complex MAC protocol model will consist of more processes than just two. First experiments with a larger number of SDL processes have confirmed the same order of magnitude performance improvement.

7.2 Memory Consumption

Here, we report on the required memory space for our integration approach. The sizes of the text, data, and bss sections of the object files are given in Table 2. They have been collected for a LEON2 compilation and broken down into the categories Reflex OS, integration layer, and sample SDL system. The code for the SDL system consists of the generated C code and system-specific wrappers containing, among other things, signal pools. We have used the sparc-elf-gcc 3.2.3 cross-compiler with optimisation level set to -O2.

The text segment contains the program code and is read-only. The data and bss segments contain global variables and uninitialised data, such as stack space. They are not read-only. The last row in Table 2 shows the memory space required for the executable application (SDLDemo.elf). This includes the Reflex OS, the integration layer, as well as the SDL system. The application is linked only with libgcc — a shared library of support routines used by the gcc compiler's runtime.

Table 2. Code sizes for a demonstration system

	text	data	bss
Operating system:	9852*	272	148
Integration layer:	4592	236	16
SDL System			
Generated code:	1172	472	160
System-specific wrappers:	1892	184	136
SDLDemo.elf			
(linked with libgcc):	20056	704	460

* This number includes 4 kbytes for the interrupt handler table (256 interrupts x 16 bytes) and about 1 kbyte for debug output routines. Since only few interrupts are required, the code size can be dramatically reduced.

8 Conclusions

In this paper, we have presented an efficient integration of SDL systems with the operating system Reflex. Our work is based on the C code generator of Telelogic

TAU SDL Suite. We have demonstrated its feasibility for resource-constrained embedded systems such as the BASUMA platform, which is a wireless sensor node, enabling SDL-based software development for this class of devices. This leads to verified and reliable systems that can be used for long-term, unsupervised applications. So far, we have not yet thoroughly tested and verified our implementation. This would be required before it can be applied to real commercial or safety-critical systems. We are in the process of implementing a 802.15.3 MAC protocol, that we modelled already in SDL for a body area sensor network based on our presented work.

Acknowledgments

This work was partly funded by the German federal ministry of economics and labour (BMWA) under grant no. 01 MT 306.

References

1. ITU-T: ITU-T Recommendation Z.100 (11/99). SDL: Specification and Description Language (1999)
2. Telelogic AB: Telelogic Tau SDL Suite (2004) Available from
   http://www.telelogic.com/products/tau/sdl
3. IEEE Standard 802: Part 15.3: Wireless Medium Access Control (MAC) and Physical Layer (PHY) Specifications for High Rate Wireless Personal Area Networks (2003)
4. BASUMA - Body Area System for Ubiquitous Multimedia Applications. Available from http://www.basuma.de
5. Nolte, J.: Reflex - Realtime Event FLow EXecutive (2005) Available from
   http://www-bs.informatik.tu-cottbus.de/38.html?&L=2
6. Walther, K., Hemmerling, R., Nolte, J.: Generic Trigger Variables and Event Flow Wrappers in Reflex. In: ECOOP — Workshop on Programming Languages and Operating Systems (2004)
7. Hill, J., Szewczyk, R., Woo, A., Hollar, S., Culler, D., Pister, K.: System Architecture Directions for Networked Sensors. In: Architectural Support for Programming Languages and Operating Systems (2000)
8. Graney, M.: Speeding Up Wireless Standards Development. In: CommsDesign (2000). Available from
   http://www.commsdesign.com/main/2000/09/0009stand.htm
9. Drosos, C., Zayadine, M., Metafas, D.: Embedded real-time communication protocol development using SDL for ARM microprocessor. In: Dedicated Systems Magazine **Q1** (2001) 37-43
10. Hännikäinen, M., Knuutila, J., Hämäläinen, J., Saarinen, J.: Using SDL for Implementing a Wireless Medium Access Control Protocol. In: IEEE International Symposium on Multimedia Software Engineering. IEEE Computer Society (2000) 229-236
11. Beutel, J., Dogan, A.: Using TinyOS on BTnodes. In Römer, K. (ed.): 4. GI/ITG KuVS Fachgesprch "Drahtlose Sensornetze". Technischer Bericht TR 481, Departement Informatik, ETH Zürich (2005) 6-10

12. Dietterle, D., Bababanskaja, I., Dombrowski, K., Kraemer, R.: High-Level Behavioral SDL Model for the IEEE 802.15.3 MAC Protocol. In Langendörfer, P., Liu, M., Matta, I., Tsaoussidis, V. (eds.): Proc. of the 2nd International Conference on Wired/Wireless Internet Communications (WWIC). Lecture Notes in Computer Science, Vol. 2957. Springer-Verlag, Berlin Heidelberg New York (2004) 165-176

Extending Network Lifetime Using an Automatically Tuned Energy-Aware MAC Protocol

Rebecca Braynard, Adam Silberstein, and Carla Ellis*

Department of Computer Science, Duke University, Durham, NC 27708, USA
{rebecca, adam, carla}@cs.duke.edu

Abstract. Sensor network devices have limited battery resources primarily consumed by radio communication. Network nodes play different communication roles and consequently consume different amounts of energy. Nodes with heavier communication burdens prematurely deplete their batteries and potentially partition the network such that other nodes are unable to communicate despite having energy remaining. We have developed SEESAW, an asynchronous and asymmetric MAC protocol that balances the energy consumption among nodes with differing loads, and thus prolongs network lifetime. Balancing is possible through SEESAW mechanisms that allow heavily burdened nodes to shift some of the effort of maintaining communication to more lightly loaded neighboring nodes. We show how to exploit the flexibility of asynchrony and asymmetry to balance energy consumption across the network, and develop methods for automatically tuning each node to achieve this.

1 Introduction

Sensor networks are constrained by limited battery power resources, of which the primary consumer is the radio. Sensor nodes may play different communication roles and consequently consume different amounts of energy. Thus, nodes carrying a heavier burden of communication may prematurely deplete their batteries and partition the network such that other nodes cannot communicate despite having energy remaining. We address the specific goal of extending the effective sensor network lifetime, defined as time prior to the first node dying. The nodes likely to play a critical role in maintaining connectivity and delivering the sensor data are those at greatest risk for depletion. We have developed SEESAW, an asynchronous and asymmetric MAC-layer protocol that balances energy consumption among nodes to prolong network lifetime.

Figure 1 illustrates the problem using a three node topology with source, s, forwarder, f, and destination, d. The energy consumption of multihop communication is given in the bar charts for two different protocols. In each plot, the lower bar components represent the energy to transmit and receive sensor data, while the upper components represent energy consumed by protocol overhead. Data

---

* This work has been supported, in part, by NSF grant 0204367.

K. Römer, H. Karl, and F. Mattern (Eds.): EWSN 2006, LNCS 3868, pp. 244–259, 2006.

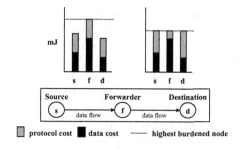

Fig. 1. Offloading protocol overhead from high loaded nodes to light loaded neighbors can increase system lifetime

cost for each node is necessarily equal between the two plots because the same data is exchanged. A horizontal line marks the most heavily consuming node, the first to die from battery depletion. In this example that is f, by virtue of its sending and receiving. Minimizing the maximum energy consumption across all nodes maximizes the time until some node dies.

A solution is illustrated by the right plot in Figure 1. Since data costs are fixed, the protocol overhead must be the focus of energy management efforts. On the left, overhead is equal at each node. The idea is to shift some of the protocol burden onto s and d to reduce the protocol cost at f. This decreases the total energy consumption at f and increases consumption at s and d, leading to balanced energy consumption among them. This better utilization of network energy supplies results in increased time until the first node dies, thus extending network lifetime. In fact, with complete balance, all nodes die together, leaving no unused energy. In some cases, due to the workload and topology, perfect energy consumption balance cannot be achieved. In these, SEESAW balances the heaviest consumers, while avoiding excess consumption at lightly loaded nodes.

An important mechanism for controlling consumption is exploitation of power-saving radio states. Wireless radios provide a number of possible power states [10,17,18], including *off*, *sleeping* (0.015mW), *idle* or listening (14.4mW), *receiving* (14.4mW) and *sending* (36mW). Furthermore, changing state to save energy comes at a cost [6]. For example, changing from *sleeping* to *idle* costs a node about twice the *idle* power for about 800 μseconds [4,12]. Nodes could easily waste energy by switching between power states too often. Our challenge is to design a protocol that leverages these states while still providing the connectivity to meet desired performance levels.

The energy used for sending and receiving is dictated by the data traffic generated by the sensor application. While a radio in the *idle* state does not actively process packets, it is listening – able to detect a transmission and begin receiving. Without changing the application's data demands,[1] reducing *idle* time offers the most promising opportunities to improve energy use. In particular, a node wastes energy while listening for a transmission when none is forthcoming,

---

[1] Application-specific techniques to filter, aggregate, and otherwise reduce sensor data are valuable but orthogonal to this work.

while listening through a transmission not intended for it, and in the overhead of dealing with collisions. These are opportunities to exploit the *sleeping* state at the cost of possibly missing transmission attempts.

SEESAW[2] is an asymmetric protocol designed to achieve flexible overhead distribution. An asymmetric protocol allows nodes to utilize different *idle/sleeping* duty cycle schedules. By not forcing nodes to have identical schedules, nodes are better able to adapt to their environments (e.g., adjusting to local traffic). SEESAW is also an asynchronous protocol; nodes are not globally coordinated, nor do they rely upon a shared timing mechanism. Asynchronous protocols avoid the communication overhead involved in synchronizing clocks solely for the purpose of connectivity. We claim an asynchronous and asymmetric protocol provides the flexibility to shift the burden of maintaining communication among neighbors.

Contributions

We a) investigate SEESAW's ability to extend network lifetime until the first node failure, b) show the impact of asymmetry in protocol parameter settings on balancing energy consumption, c) automatically tune parameter settings to achieve balance, and d) have built a sophisticated simulator, validated by reproducing results from our implementation in TinyOS on Mica2 Motes, and related protocol published results. As a preview of our results, we show:

- Asymmetry in duty cycles can be effectively exploited to balance energy consumption across nodes.
- The flexibility of SEESAW's asymmetry and asynchrony, SEESAW, does not incur significant energy or performance costs compared to other MAC protocols, which would otherwise inhibit its practical effectiveness.
- Protocols parameters can be successfully tuned by automated methods, showing that its flexibility can be leveraged in practice.

The paper is organized as follows: Section 2 provides related work. In Section 3, we present SEESAW. In Section 4, we propose SEESAW parameter tuning methods. We evaluate our protocol mechanisms and tuning techniques in Section 5. Lastly, we conclude in Section 6.

2   Background in Energy Savings in Wireless Protocols

Collisions produce extra traffic and waste energy. A node in a contention-based network may not directly detect another transmission within its own range [1]. The classic solution is the distributed coordination function of IEEE 802.11 and the RTS-CTS (Request To Send-Clear To Send) handshake [7]. This approach continues to be adapted as a protocol foundation, SEESAW included. The TDMA alternative (e.g. [14]) allows nodes to communicate with a reduced chance of

---

[2] SEESAW comes from the analogy of two children of different weights cooperating to play on a teeter totter by asymmetrically adjusting their distances from the fulcrum.

collisions by designating time slots. Overhearing transmissions intended for other nodes while in idle listening mode represents another form of wasted energy. The idea of overhearing avoidance, presented in PAMAS [13], allows nodes to determine if a packet is for them and, if not, to disable their radio for the duration of the packet to reduce energy wasted receiving a packet for another node.

Coordinating between nodes by predictive schemes [19] or scheduling through advertising data paths [20] can enable nodes to sleep more often and reduce the number of transmission attempts when coordinating communication.

Flexible Power Scheduling (FPS) [5] uses a two-level architecture for saving energy while supporting varying demand. At the network layer, the distributed protocol provides coarse-grained scheduling to plan data flow communication, allowing nodes to sleep during idle times. At the MAC layer, finer-grained scheduling is used to handle channel access. FPS uses the combination of slots, cycles and reservations in a time division protocol to coordinate communication between neighbors in a tree to forward data toward a sink. The node schedules are adaptive based on supply and demand of data flows in the neighborhood. While the protocol provides opportunities to save energy in idle slots, nodes with higher demand (e.g., forwarding nodes) will still have higher duty cycles.

S-MAC [17,18] incorporates *virtual clusters* to coordinate node sleep schedules, and message passing to reduce latency from contention. This involves fragmenting packets into smaller packets forming a burst, with one RTS-CTS exchange, much like fragmentation in 802.11. S-MAC does not attempt to reduce the energy consumption of the vital, forwarding nodes. Building upon S-MAC is another protocol, T-MAC [16], which adds the concept of a threshold for idle time during an active cycle. If an event does not occur within a threshold, the radio transitions back to the sleep state earlier, decreasing power consumption. While this does vary node schedules, nodes are still expected to be active based upon a set schedule so that neighbors can predict their cycle. This makes the protocol not truly asymmetric in the sense that we describe.

Asynchronous protocols [15,8,9] are motivated by clock synchronization overhead. Tseng, et al. [15], present three power management protocols applying to the power-save mode of IEEE 802.11 mobile ad hoc networks. Polastre, et al. [9], introduce B-MAC, an asynchronous-symmetric protocol for low power listening. B-MAC nodes periodically check for transmissions using a defined interval. To ensure that receiving nodes will receive a transmission, B-MAC senders transmit a preamble that takes longer than the check interval, alerting neighboring nodes of an upcoming data transmission. Every time a node needs to send data, it must first send the preamble. For senders, *sources* and *forwarders*, this requires an increased burden when compared to the *sinks* that do not transmit preambles. Z-MAC [11] is a hybrid protocol that dynamically adapts to contention levels at nodes. It is built upon B-MAC to behave like a CSMA protocol under low contention and incorporates a loosely synchronized TDMA schedule to prioritize transmissions under higher contention. The primary effect on energy comes from reducing collision overhead at high contention.

Unlike previous asynchronous protocols using duty cycles greater than 50% to guarantee overlapping neighbor awake times, SEESAW decouples advertisements from the listening duty cycle, allowing for more flexibility.

3   Seesaw Protocol

SEESAW extends system lifetime by balancing node energy consumption in a wireless network. To achieve this, it utilizes three main features: probabilistic communication, decoupled advertising and listening, and batching. These are enabled by four node parameters, a combination of asynchrony and asymmetry, and three packet types. Probabilistic communication means we cannot *guarantee* that communication will occur in the time of one interval, but, by relaxing this requirement, we allow nodes to tailor their schedules to their workloads.

3.1   Description

SEESAW has three main packet types: Ad, Accept and Data. Ads advertise data to their next hop. Data packets hold application data to be sent. Accept packets have two purposes; they establish a connection between nodes for sending Data packets, and provide a means for acknowledging Data packets. To prevent overhearing transmissions, Accept and Data packets have the bytes to transmit listed in their headers. This allows neighboring nodes to sleep for the remainder of the transmission to avoid wasting energy.

We provide a node action overview and discuss a simple example. Consider three node types: *senders, forwarders* and *destinations*, as shown in Figure 1 as s, f and d. In reality, each node can take any of the duties, even simultaneously. All nodes invoke the same algorithm, but act based on their parameters. During an interval, according to their respective listening times and ad rates, nodes listen for Ads and, if they have data to transmit, advertise. Data are collected at s, filling a buffer until it reaches the batch size. s then advertises to the next hop with Ads evenly spaced throughout the interval. Meanwhile, f fulfills its listening time requirement. When s sends an Ad that overlaps with f's listening, data transfer begins (assuming no collisions). To reduce the hidden terminal problem, nodes utilize virtual carrier sense and backoffs after sleeping using the time it takes to transmit both a Data and an Accept packet. When s receives an Accept packet from f, it responds with a Data packet. Each Data packet is reciprocated with an Accept packet until *batchsize* Data packets have been sent. This same process repeats between f and d, since the data are meant for d.

Figure 2 shows the three nodes: s is the source (left), f is the forwarder (middle) and d is the destination (right). While this is only 0.78 seconds of a simulation, it illustrates SEESAW. s transitions to listen at point A and waits to send an Ad. Since f is sleeping, the Ad is missed and s transitions to sleep. At B, s wakes up and sends another Ad. Since f is listening, it receives the second Ad and establishes the connection. The batch is transmitted at C. After the batch is sent, f tries to send an Ad, but d is sleeping and misses it, and f then goes to sleep. f wakes and attempts another Ad at D, but again, d is sleeping. Finally,

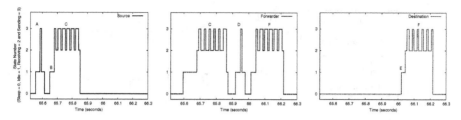

Fig. 2. State information from a portion of a SEESAW simulation run

d wakes up at E and receives the next Ad from f. The batch is transmitted at F and the data are delivered to d.

3.2   Parameters

Node Interval (i): Each node has an interval of i seconds. The length of i influences system performance. Short node intervals can reduce latency, however, they also increase the number of radio state transitions, reducing energy efficiency. Note that SEESAW does not rely upon precise time synchronization between nodes, which reduces system control overhead. Clock rates of different nodes need only be relatively stable to maintain i.

Listening Time (l): Within each interval, nodes listen for a continuous time, L, of at least (li), where $0.0 \leq l \leq 1.0$. As expected, the closer l is to 0.0, the more energy is conserved, while the closer l is to 1.0, the more energy is consumed, but with the boon of reducing latency. SEESAW allows nodes to adopt different l values, making it an asymmetric protocol. l at a node x is $l(x)$.

Number of Advertisements (a): Nodes with data to send notify the next hop using Ad packets sent during each interval. The number of Ads sent is determined by a. While Ads can be sent any time during the interval (i.e. without synchronization), they should be spaced uniformly over the interval, independent of the active time spent listening for transmissions. Again, there is a tradeoff between latency and energy consumption. The more Ads a node transmits, the more energy is consumed, not only at the sender, but also at neighboring nodes able to overhear the transmission. a at node x is denoted as $a(x)$.

Batch Size (B): The number of Data packets in each batch also influences the tradeoff. The higher a data rate, the faster a node reaches B, reducing buffering latency. Depending on the application, different batch sizes may be tolerated, or even encouraged, to conserve energy. Higher batch sizes lower control overhead and overheard transmissions. Batching also allows neighboring nodes to make fewer transitions and remain asleep longer using overhearing avoidance mechanisms. B at node x is $B(x)$.

3.3   Advertisement Reception

Like the IEEE 802.11 RTS/CTS exchange, nodes advertise data to the packet's next hop. An Ad can be sent any time with a free medium, but, for it to be answered with an Accept, the next hop must be listening to receive it and reply.

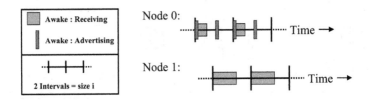

Fig. 3. Two i subset time subset for each of two *unsynchronized* nodes

Given a node x with data to send to a node y, x advertises the data $a(x)$ times each interval of i seconds. Destination y is awake to hear a transmission, including from x, for a time of length $i * l(y) = L$. y must be awake to receive the advertisement from x; however, we do not require that x and y have synchronized duty cycles. Thus, it is possible for multiple intervals to pass before x successfully notifies y of the pending traffic. We determine a lower bound on the probability that y hears x's advertisement in the absence of other traffic.

Any two adjacent intervals of node x are guaranteed to overlap with one continuous awake cycle by node y, given that all nodes share the same size interval. This is depicted in Figure 3, which shows two unsynchronized intervals for nodes 0 and 1. The top line shows the behavior of node 0, as sender, advertising twice per interval. This pair of intervals at 0 overlaps one continuous awake cycle on 1. In other words, in the time two intervals pass at 0, at least one full interval passes at 1. If the listening time at 1 is longer than the time between Ads at 0, an Ad must arrive during a listening period at 1. There may be other overlapping Ads and listening periods, but these only increase the probability that 1 successfully receives the Ad by 0.

We give a lower bound on the probability that node y hears an advertisement from node x, called $P(y \text{ rcv Ad})$, within a $2i$ time interval.

$$
\begin{aligned}
P(y \text{ rcv Ad}) &\geq \frac{listening\_time(y) * num\_ads(x)}{time} \\
&\geq \frac{(l(y) * i) * (2a(x))}{2i} \\
&\geq \begin{cases} l(y) * a(x) & \text{if } l(y) * a(x) \leq 1 \\ 1 & \text{otherwise} \end{cases}
\end{aligned}
$$

If the goal is to conserve energy at y, we should reduce $l(y)$, meaning $a(x) \rightarrow \infty$ and $l(y) \rightarrow 0$. Of course, state transition and transmission costs bound the frequency at which x can advertise its packets.

4 Parameter Tuning

To exploit its flexibility, SEESAW must be accompanied by a self-tuning methodology. We require that nodes communicate with their neighbors to determine adjustments for their own advertising and listening rates. Ideally, given a stable pattern of data traffic, these tuning decisions, made in a decentralized manner at each node, should eventually lead to an optimal network state where the time until a single node exhausts its energy is maximized.

We make two contributions toward this goal. We begin with a centralized, off-line method of encoding a quadratic programming model to find optimal settings of node parameters. The solution demonstrates the feasibility of automatic tuning and its effectiveness corroborates our understanding of how settings affect energy consumption. We then present an online algorithm.

4.1   Offline

The set R contains all directed edges (x, y), such that x communicates with y. Table 1 defines the functions that describe behavior at each node. More details on their derivations appear in [3]. $\alpha(x)$ is the total expected energy cost at node x to advertise to each receiver y_n such that $(x, y_n) \in R$, given its listening rate of $l(y_n)$. The higher $l(y_n)$, the sooner x establishes communication and can stop advertising. Therefore, the cost of advertising is based both on the chosen advertising rate at the sender and the listening rates at the receivers. x may also receive data. $\lambda(x)$ gives the energy cost at x to listen based on its $l(x)$. $\delta(x)$ gives the energy cost at x to send and/or receive its data load.

We develop a quadratically-constrained quadratic program that maximizes the time until any node dies.

Maximize

(1)
$$\min_{\forall\, m}\{\frac{e(x_m)}{(\alpha(x_m) + \lambda(x_m) + \delta(x_m)}\}$$

(2)
$$a(x_m) * l(y_n) \geq S \ \forall\, (x_m, y_n) \in R$$

Line (1) states the optimization objective. Each node's time until its energy is exhausted is calculable from its starting energy and total consumption rate. The goal is to maximize the minimum of these. Line (2) encodes the constraint that along all edges, all communication must be completed at a minimum expected service level of S, the inverse of the expected number of intervals until communication is achieved. The solution to this program gives advertising and listening rates for each node that when applied, as described in Section 5.3, achieve our goal of maximizing the time before any node exhausts its battery.

Table 1. Objective function notation

Consumption Components	
$e(x)$	energy at node x (mJ)
$\alpha(x)$	Avg advertising energy at x (mJ/s)
$\lambda(x)$	Avg listening energy at x (mJ/s)
$\delta(x)$	Avg data transfer energy at x (mJ/s)

Table 2. Parameter changes for assisting neighbors

mW % Diff	a Change	l Change
> 60%	+4	*1.6
> 40%	+3	*1.4
> 20%	+2	*1.2
> 10%	+1	*1.1
> 5%	+1	*1.01
less	a	*1.001

4.2 Online

In practice nodes must automatically tune their values. We present a simple gradient descent algorithm that balances energy consumption, using only local information. Nodes utilize header information in Accept and Data packets.

A receiver, y, lists $l(y)$ along with an energy consumption value (average mW). A sender, x, lists $a(x)$ and its average consumption. Nodes store their neighbors' energy header information for those with which they communicate, and use it to determine if changes are needed in their own settings. This information encodes relationships. If a node stores an a for a neighbor, it is a receiver for it; if it stores an l, it is a sender.

After each interval, each node invokes a function to determine if it should adjust its parameters. This involves looping through its neighbor information and comparing the consumption between each neighbor and itself. If the maximum difference among these is higher than a user-defined threshold (2% in our experiments) the node adjusts its parameters. Actions are role-specific. If a node determines it must assist a neighbor and absorb protocol overhead, it changes its respective a and/or l value based on its communication role and the values in Table 2. These increases allow neighboring nodes to reduce their a and l values to the minimum given a service level. In experiments we require $a(x)*l(y) \geq 1.2$. For example, if x is a receiver for y and it needs to assist y based on a 10% difference in average mW, it would increase $l(x)$ by 10%. This action allows y to decrease $a(y)$ after the next batch.

5 Evaluation

This section answers three questions. Will the additional overhead required by an asynchronous-asymmetric protocol be prohibitive in terms of consumed energy and packet delivery performance? Will SEESAW's flexibility allow us to tune parameters to achieve a variety of network-wide energy goals including balancing energy consumption? Can tuning be automated?

To evaluate SEESAW, we developed a discrete event simulator, SENSIM, able to provide energy consumption detail, including radio state transition costs (time and energy). Using simulator parameters for the Mica2 Mote radio characteristics (Section 1) and the published S-MAC and B-MAC parameters, we reproduced results presented in [18,9]. This is omitted here, but available in [3].

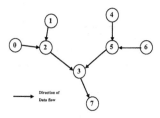

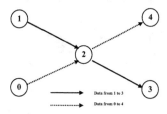

Fig. 4. Sink Topology   **Fig. 5.** Cross Topology

We implemented SEESAW in TinyOS on Mica2 Motes and used its measurements to validate SEESAW simulation results. Again, these results are in [3]. To summarize, though, despite not modeling all real-world factors, the SENSIM results correspond to those produced running on the Mica2 Mote hardware. The remainder of this paper presents results produced with SenSim.

5.1 Is an Asymmetric and Asynchronous Protocol Too Costly?

SEESAW provides flexibility, however, these mechanisms are not free. In this section we compare the energy consumption of our asynchronous-asymmetric protocol to published protocols based on the other three combinations of (A)Synchrony and (A)Symmetry. We measure total system and per packet energy consumption, number of delivered packets, and latency.

We use the sink topology in Figure 4 with source nodes 0, 1, 4 and 6, sending data (50B packets) through forwarder nodes 2, 3 and 5, to destination node 7. Sources generate 30 packets and tests run for $30 * generation\_interval$ seconds.

We perform two sets of experiments, one with base protocols and the second with enhancements. Both sets use a protocol to represent each of four permutations: SS (Synchronous-Symmetric), AS, SA and AA. In the first set, the SS and SA protocols are based upon S-MAC, however, we eliminated the need for SYNC packets by allowing the nodes to utilize simulator time, reducing their overhead. For the SA protocol, nodes have different duty cycles as proposed in [18] (i.e. asymmetric schedules): nodes 0, 1, 4 and 6 use 1% duty cycles, nodes 2 and 5 use 8%, node 3 uses 5% and node 7 uses 20%. For SS, we use 10% duty cycles, as in [18]. The AS protocol is based upon the *Overlapping Duty Cycles* protocol [15] that guarantees overlapping active cycles with neighbors by having nodes awake > 50% of the interval. In these experiments, we use an awake period of 55% of the interval and 10 Ads are transmitted within that active period. The final protocol, AA, is SEESAW, with (a, l) settings as follows: sources $(12, 0.0)$, forwarders 2 and 5 $(8, 0.1)$, forwarder 3 $(6, 0.13)$ and sink $(0, 0.2)$. All SEESAW nodes have $B = 1$.

The second experiment set incorporates protocol enhancements and repeats the design. We incorporate *adaptive listening* in S-MAC and batching to SEESAW (B values: sources $B = 1$, forwarders 2 and 5 $B = 2$, forwarder 3 and sink $B = 4$). For the AS protocol, B-MAC [9] replaces the > 50% protocol. For B-MAC, we use the recommended values described in [9]. The node check interval is 0.1

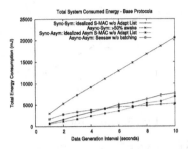

Fig. 6. Base: Total system energy

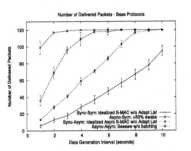

Fig. 7. Base: Delivered packets

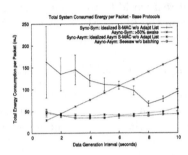

Fig. 8. Base: Energy per packet

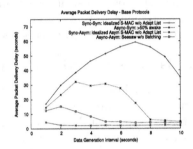

Fig. 9. Base: Avg packet latency

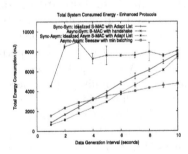

Fig. 10. Better: Total system energy

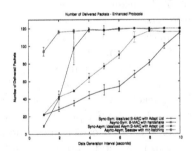

Fig. 11. Better: Delivered packets

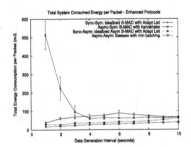

Fig. 12. Better: Energy per packet

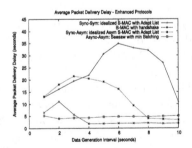

Fig. 13. Better: Avg packet delay

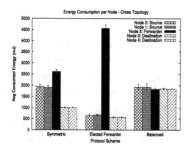
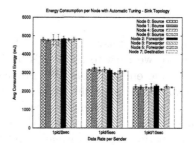

Fig. 14. Three target scenarios   **Fig. 15.** Balanced consumption - CPLEX

seconds and the preamble is 271B. All other protocols (base included) use the recommended node interval of 1.15 seconds [18].

Figure 6 shows the four base protocols and their total system energy consumption. The x-axis varies the data generation interval (time between data packet creation). Due to the necessity of long active cycles, the AS protocol has the highest consumption, however, it also has the best performance for the number of packets delivered and latency (Figures 7 and 9). The two S-MAC-based protocols and SEESAW have comparable energy consumption, but perform differently for packet delivery. S-MAC without *adaptive listening* is restricted in the amount of data it can deliver, and at what speed (packets are buffered at intermediate nodes in the network). Looking more closely at SEESAW (AA), for data generation intervals of about 1-6 seconds, we see it has higher consumption than the two protocols based on S-MAC. But if we look at Figure 7, we see this increased energy consumption is due to SEESAW's ability to deliver more packets. It consumes more energy because it does more work. In Figure 8, for data generation intervals of greater than 2 seconds, SEESAW has the lowest per packet energy consumption. With data generation intervals of 1 and 2 seconds there is contention at the sources, so Ad packets may collide. Utilizing batching reduces control overhead and, therefore, contention.

The protocol enhancements reduce energy consumption (Figure 10) and improve performance. For data packet delivery (Figure 11) we see that the protocols based on S-MAC and SEESAW improve. Figure 12 shows the per packet energy consumption, this time with a small amount of batching. SEESAW has the lowest energy consumption per packet for all data generation intervals tested. Turning to the data packet delivery latencies (Figure 13) we see SEESAW delivers the data with delays close to that of the AS protocol and is faster than both of the S-MAC-based protocols, even with data buffering. B-MAC provides lower latencies because of the small (100 ms) check interval. We could increase the check interval for B-MAC to 1.15 seconds, like the other protocols, however, this would require senders transmit longer preambles and consume more energy. Instead, we use the parameters recommended by their authors.

Despite having nodes do extra advertising to coordinate transmissions due to asynchrony, SEESAW is competitive with the SS, SA and AS protocols. SEESAW utilizes its four parameters to quickly deliver data without consuming comparably more energy.

5.2   Utilizing Flexibility

Having shown an asynchronous and asymmetric schedule can competitively deliver data, we turn to SEESAW's flexibility. Can SEESAW be tuned to achieve system-wide energy goals? We provide a base case with a Symmetric scheme where all nodes have the same settings. We also demonstrate SEESAW's ability to tailor itself to benefit a backbone-like scheme, Elected Forwarder, where the nodes are heterogeneous, with forwarding nodes having larger, possibly unlimited energy supplies. Finally, we demonstrate SEESAW's ability to balance consumption in a network of homogeneous nodes.

Each test is run on the cross topology 5 times, in Figure 5, with averages and standard deviations shown. Each source generates a packet every 5 seconds and tests run for 600 seconds. For the Symmetric scheme, all nodes have $a = 10$ and $l = 0.1$. In the Elected Forwarder scheme, the (a, l) settings are as follows: sources $(6, 0.0)$, forwarders $(18, 0.2)$, and sinks $(1, 0.05)$. The final scheme, Balanced, settings are sources $14, 0.0)$, forwarders $(7, 0.08)$ and sinks $(1, 0.19)$.

Figure 14 demonstrates how SEESAW's flexibility meets the target system-wide goals for the scenarios. The data latencies are approximately the same, but the nodes have varied energy consumption. In the Symmetric scheme, nodes all have the same schedule, despite having different roles. The destinations (3 and 4) have the lowest consumption, since receiving is less expensive than sending. In the Elected Forwarder scheme, the forwarder (2) provides connectivity with a high l value, resulting in greater consumption, letting remaining nodes have low consumption. In the final scheme, Balanced, consumption across all nodes is balanced, so they exhaust their batteries at the same time.

Each parameter differently affects the energy of a node and its neighbors, and latency. Due to space restrictions, figures exploring tuning capabilities of the four parameters are omitted, but available in [2]. Additionally, we performed 24-hour clock stability tests on Mica2 Motes and interval length sensitivity experiments for SEESAW and determined it is robust to any differences in interval lengths likely to be encountered [2].

5.3   Tuning

SEESAW's flexibility lets us tune parameters to meet consumption goals, but is only useful if parameters can be automatically tuned. In this section, we show an offline algorithm generates effective advertising and listening values.

Table 3. CPLEX a, l values for 3 rates

Node Type ID(s)	1pkt/2s		1pkt/5s		1pkt/10s	
	a	l	a	l	a	l
Source 0,1,4,6	15	.021	16	.021	19	.021
Forwarder 2,5	10	.09	12	.09	15	.07
Forwarder 3	6	.13	8	.11	9	.09
Sink 7	1	.27	1	.19	1	.14

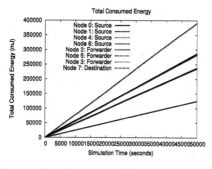 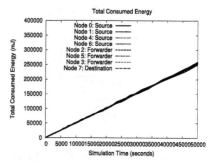

Fig. 16. Cumulative energy consumption with static settings

Fig. 17. Cumulative energy consumption for each node with auto tuning

Offline. We implemented the quadratic program from Section 4.1 using CPLEX 8.1. We built an integer approximation of it by discretizing settings for $a(x)$ and $l(x)$, and generating expected energy cost tables for all possible setting combinations. We run this program for the sink topology with three data rates. We then apply the solution in SENSIM by assigning the returned settings (Table 3) to the respective nodes, and simulate for 1000 seconds. The results, Figure 15, show balanced consumption at each node for the three data rates. The program shows it is possible to automatically achieve balanced consumption.

Online. Finally we come to the question of whether SEESAW nodes can automatically tune their own parameters to balance system-wide energy consumption, given only local information. In a 50,000 second test, we use the algorithm presented in Section 4.2 with the the sink topology and a 2 second data generation interval for each source. Nodes start with symmetric settings ($a = 12$ and $l = 0.1$). We compare delivery performance and total consumption for each node to a run with static parameters. In the static parameter test, the sink receives 99,990 packets with an average delay of 5.35 seconds. With automatic tuning, the sink receives 99,991 packets with an average delay of 4.50 seconds. Figures 16 and 17 show node energy consumption in mJ. Average node consumption is 255,212 mJ +/- 1.2% compared to the static run with an average of 265,974 mJ +/- 27.9%. Without balancing, node 3 has the highest energy consumption and the node 7 the lowest. When 3 depletes its batteries, the network will be partitioned. The consumption among the nodes is much more balanced, so all nodes will fail at roughly the same time, increasing the time until a node fails. Note that in Figure 16, node 3 consumes almost 400,000 mJ while in Figure 17 all nodes consume about 250,000 mJ, demonstrating about a 37% improvement. The nodes determine parameter settings similar to those produced using the offline algorithm, Table 4. Despite nodes having vastly different data communication responsibilities, their energy consumption is balanced.

Table 4. Online tuning parameter values

Node Type ID(s)	online		offline	
	a	l	a	l
Source 0,1,4,6	16,15,15,16	.021 (all 4)	15 (all 4)	.021 (all 4)
Forwarder 2,5	11,13	.098,.09	10	.09
Forwarder 3	5	.13	6	.13
Sink 7	1	.279	1	.27

6   Conclusions and Future Work

We have presented SEESAW, an asynchronous and asymmetric MAC protocol
for wireless sensor networks that offers flexibility to tailor energy consumption
on a per-node basis. In particular, we address the problem that different nodes
may consume very different amounts of energy and the nodes with the heaviest
burdens of communication are often in a position to disrupt the sensor network
most seriously when they die. When this happens, the network may become
partitioned such that other nodes are unable to communicate despite having
energy remaining. Our solution is to balance the energy consumption among
nodes with differing communication loads to prolong network lifetime. Balancing is possible through mechanisms that allow heavily burdened nodes to shift
protocol overhead to more lightly loaded neighboring nodes.

Our contributions include simulation results showing SEESAW's flexibility does
not incur significant energy or performance costs compared to other MAC protocols, and that SEESAW can be effectively used to achieve balanced energy
consumption. We develop offline and online methods for automatically tuning
the parameters to extend system lifetime. Future work includes developing more
sophisticated online tuning algorithms and more extensive evaluations in both
our simulator and TinyOS implementation.

References

1. V Bharghavan, A Demers, S Shenker, and L Zhang. MACAW: a media access
   protocol for wireless LAN's. In *Proc of the conference on Communications architectures, protocols and apps*, 1994.
2. Rebecca Braynard, Shobana Ravi, and Carla Ellis. Exploring the design of an
   asynchronous and asymmetric MAC protocol. In *International Workshop on Measurement, Modeling, and Performance Analysis of Sensor Networks*, July 2005.
3. Rebecca Braynard, Adam Silberstein, and Carla Ellis. Extending network lifetime
   using an automatically tuned energy-aware mac protocol. Technical Report CS-
   2005-05, Duke University Department of Computer Science, 2005.
4. P Havinga and G Smit. Energy-Efficient TDMA Medium Access Control Packet
   Scheduling. In *Asian International Mobile Computing Conference AMOC 2000*,
   Nov 2000.
5. B Hohlt, L Doherty, and E Brewer. Flexible power scheduling for sensor networks.
   In *IPSN'04*, 2004.

6. E Jung and N Vaidya. A power control MAC protocol for ad-hoc networks. In *Proc of ACM MOBICOM*, 2002.

7. P. Karn. MACA - A New Channel Access Method for Packet Radio. In *ARRL/CRRL 9th Comp Net Conf*, 1990.

8. M McGlynn and S Borbash. Birthday Protocols for Low Energy Deployment and Flexible Neighbor Discovery in Ad Hoc Wireless Networks. In *2nd Intl Symposium on Mobile Ad Hoc Networking and Computing*, 2001.

9. J Polastre, J Hill, and D Culler. Versatile low power media access for wireless sensor networks. In *SenSys*, 2004.

10. RF Monolithics Inc. ASH Transceiver TR3000 Data Sheet.

11. I Rhee, A Warrier, M Aia, and J Min. Z-MAC: A hybrid MAC for wireless sensor networks. In *SENSYS'05: Proceedings of the 3rd ACM Conference on Embedded Networked Sensor Systems*, Nov 2005.

12. T Simunic, H Vikalo, P Glynn, and G De Micheli. Energy efficient design of portable wireless systems. In *Proc of the 2000 international symposium on Low power electronics and design*, 2000.

13. S. Singh and C. Raghavendra. Power efficient MAC protocol for multihop radio networks. In *Proc of IEEE PIRMC'98 Vol 1*, Sep 1998.

14. K Sohrabi, J Gao, V Ailawadhi, and G Pottie. Protocols for Self-Organization of a Wireless Sensor Network. In *Proc of the 37th Allerton Conference on Communication, Computing and Control*, September 1999.

15. Y Tseng, C Hsu, and T Hsieh. Power-Saving Protocols for IEEE 802.11-Based Multi-Hop Ad Hoc Networks. In *Proceedings of INFOCOM*, 2002.

16. T van Dam and K Langendoen. An Adaptive Energy-Efficient MAC protocol for Wireless Sensor Networks. In *SenSys*, 2003.

17. W. Ye, J. Heidemann, and D. Estrin. An Energy-Efficient MAC Protocol for Wireless Sensor Networks. In *IEEE INFOCOM*, 2002.

18. W Ye, J Heidemann, and D Estrin. Medium access control with coordinated adaptive sleeping for wireless sensor networks. *IEEE/ACM Trans. Netw.*, 2004.

19. R Zheng, J Hou, and L Sha. Asynchronous wakeup for ad hoc networks. In *Proc of the 4th ACM Intl symposium on Mobile ad hoc networking and computing*, 2003.

20. R Zheng and R Kravets. On-demand Power Management for Ad Hoc Networks. In *Proc. IEEE INFOCOM*, 2003.

Sift: A MAC Protocol for Event-Driven Wireless Sensor Networks*

Kyle Jamieson[1], Hari Balakrishnan[1], and Y.C. Tay[2]

[1] MIT Computer Science and Artificial Intelligence Laboratory,
The Stata Center, 32 Vassar St., Cambridge, MA 02139
jamieson@csail.mit.edu, hari@csail.mit.edu
[2] Department of Computer Science, National University of Singapore,
Kent Ridge 117543, Republic of Singapore
tay@acm.org

Abstract. Nodes in sensor networks often encounter *spatially-correlated contention*, where multiple nodes in the same neighborhood all sense an event they need to transmit information about. Furthermore, in many sensor network applications, it is sufficient if a subset of the nodes that observe the same event report it. We show that traditional carrier-sense multiple access (CSMA) protocols for sensor networks do not handle the first constraint adequately, and do not take advantage of the second property, leading to degraded latency as the network scales in size. We present *Sift*, a medium access control (MAC) protocol for wireless sensor networks designed with the above observations in mind. We show using simulations that as the size of the sensor network scales up to 500 nodes, Sift can offer up to a 7-fold latency reduction compared to other protocols, while maintaining competitive throughput.

1 Introduction

Every shared wireless communication channel needs a medium access control (MAC) protocol to arbitrate access to the channel. Over the past several decades, many MAC protocols have been designed and several are in operation in wireless networks today. While these protocols work well for traditional data workloads, they are inadequate in emerging wireless sensor networks where the nature of data transmissions and application requirements are different. This paper argues that wireless sensor networks require a fresh look at MAC protocol design, and proposes a new protocol that works well in this problem domain by taking advantage of application requirements and data characteristics. We start with an example of a real sensor network.

Machine room monitoring. A fire in a basement machine room of the computer science building triggers a number of redundant temperature and smoke sensors to begin reporting the event. They all simultaneously become backlogged with the sensor reports and

---

* This material is based upon work supported by the National Science Foundation under Grant Nos. CNS-0205445 and CNS-0520032. Any opinions, findings, and conclusions or recommendations expressed in this material are those of the author(s) and do not necessarily reflect the views of the National Science Foundation.

K. Römer, H. Karl, and F. Mattern (Eds.): EWSN 2006, LNCS 3868, pp. 260–275, 2006.

use a MAC protocol to arbitrate access to the medium. Higher-level applications need some number of event reports that is less than the number of reporting sensors.

From these example, we make the following observations:

1. *Many sensor networks are event-driven and have spatially-correlated contention.* In most sensor networks, multiple sensors are deployed in the same geographic area, usually for fault-tolerance and reliability. In addition to sending periodic observations, when an event of interest happens, the sensing nodes that observe the event send messages reporting the event. The result is *spatially-correlated contention.* Multiple sensors sharing the wireless medium all have messages to send at almost the same time because they all generate messages in response to the same event.

2. *Not all sensing nodes need to report an event.* In sensor network applications such as the machine room example above, not all the nodes that sense an event need to report it. It is enough for a subset of the event reports to reach the data sink.

3. *The density of sensing nodes can quickly change.* In many sensor networks, the size of the set of sensing nodes changes quickly with time, e.g., when a target enters a field of sensors. The potential for sensor nodes to continue decreasing in size [1] leads us to believe that the number of sensing nodes could quickly become very large. As a result, we need a MAC protocol that not only handles spatial correlations, but also adapts well to changes in the number of contending nodes.

These three observations lead to a problem statement for wireless sensor MAC protocol design that is different from classical MAC design. Specifically, in a shared medium where N nodes sense an event and contend to transmit on the channel at the same time, our goal is to design a MAC protocol that minimizes the time taken to send R of these messages without collisions. Notice that when $R = N$, this becomes the throughput-optimization problem that classical MAC protocols are designed for. When $R < N$, what we seek is a protocol that allows the first R winners of the contention protocol to send their messages through as quickly as possible, with the remaining $N - R$ potential transmitters suppressing their messages once R have been sent. In the rest of this paper, we denote the number of nodes that have data to send as N, and the number of reports that the sink needs as R.

At their core, all randomized carrier-sense multiple access (CSMA)-based MAC protocols attempt to adapt to the active population size of contending nodes. Typically, each node maintains a slotted *contention window* with collisions (i.e., unsuccessful transmissions) causing the window to grow in size, and successful transmissions causing it to shrink. Each node transmits data at a slot picked uniformly at random within the current contention window. This approach does not work well when we are interested in the first R of N potential reports, and has problems scaling well when N suddenly grows. The result is degraded response latency.

Our protocol, *Sift*, is based on the intuition that when we are interested in low latency for the first R reports, it is important for the first few successful slots to be contention-free. To tightly bound response latency, we use a *fixed-size* contention window, but a non-uniform, geometrically-increasing probability distribution for picking a transmission slot in the window.

We give theoretical justification for Sift's choice of geometrically-increasing probability distribution and show using simulations that Sift can offer up to a 7-fold latency reduction as the number of sensors in one radio range scales up to 500 nodes. We also show that Sift delivers slightly worse throughput than other CSMA protocols when N is small, and slightly better throughput when N is large. Finally, we describe the theoretically-optimal non-persistent CSMA MAC when one report of each event is enough, and show that Sift's latency approaches optimal.

2   Sift Design

Sift is a non-persistent CSMA wireless MAC protocol. In such protocols, the time immediately after any transmission is divided into CW contention slots, whose duration is usually several orders of magnitude smaller than the time it takes to send a data packet. Immediately after a transmission or collision, each station picks a random contention slot $r \in [1, CW]$. During the contention slots prior to r, each station carrier senses the medium, and aborts or delays its pending transmission if it hears the beginning of another transmission. At contention slot r, the station begins its transmission. If two nodes pick the same slot, they both transmit at the same time, causing a collision. Wireless nodes infer that a collision has occurred by the absence of a link-level acknowledgment. When a collision occurs, most CSMA protocols specify that the colliding nodes double their value of CW. This is known as *binary exponential backoff* (*BEB*). 802.11 [2], B-MAC [3], S-MAC [4], and MACAW [5] are all based on BEB.

By increasing CW, most other CSMA protocols attempt to adapt to the current active population size to make a collision-free transmission more likely. There are two problems with this method. First, it takes time for CW to increase to the right value when the active population (N) becomes large, such as when an event is observed by many sensors after a previously-idle period. Second, if CW is already large (because of traffic congestion that has just subsided) and N is small, then such protocols waste

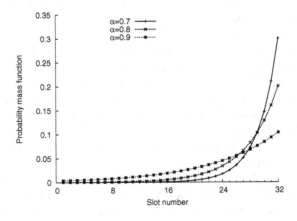

Fig. 1. The probability distribution for the contention slot number that each Sift station chooses. We show various values of α, the parameter of the distribution.

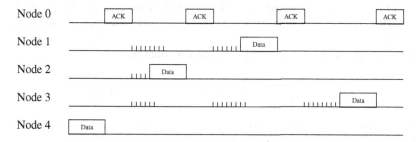

Fig. 2. A timeline of five nodes running the Sift protocol with $N = R = 4$. Nodes 1–4 each send one packet to Node 0. Every time the medium becomes idle, stations re-select a slot at random according to the Sift distribution (Figure 1) before transmitting in that slot. The small bars signify contention, and the number of small bars signifies which slot each station picked.

bandwidth "backing off." Furthermore, CW is usually chosen to ensure that all active nodes get a chance to send their data, whereas we are interested in the collision-free transmission of the first R of N potential reports of some event.

In contrast to previous protocols, Sift uses a small and fixed CW. Of course, nodes can no longer pick contention slots from a uniform distribution, because this would lead to collisions for even moderate values of N. The key difference between Sift and previous CSMA-based wireless MAC protocols is that the probability of picking a slot in this interval is not uniform. Instead, with a carefully-chosen fixed CW and fixed probability distribution, we will show that Sift can perform well in a sensor network.

The following intuition leads us to propose the *geometrically-increasing* probability distribution for picking a contention slot, shown in Figure 1. When N is large, most nodes will choose medium to high slot numbers to transmit (see Figure 1), but a small number will choose low slot numbers, making a collision-free transmission likely in a low slot number. When N is medium, most nodes will choose high-numbered slots, making a collision-free transmission likely in a medium slot number. Finally, when N is small, a collision-free transmission is likely in a high slot number[1]. Thus, for any N, and no matter how fast N changes, a collision-free transmission is likely. We make this intuition precise in Section 2.1.

Figure 2 shows an example run of the Sift MAC protocol. Note that when the transmission or collision finishes, all competing Sift nodes select *new* random contention slots, and repeat the process of contending over the fixed contention window.

In the rest of this section we describe Sift's probability distribution and compare it to an optimal (for $R = 1$) non-persistent CSMA. We then give a formal protocol specification, and qualitatively compare Sift to other contention window-based CSMA protocols.

2.1   The Sift Probability Distribution

Suppose each sensor picks a slot $r \in [1, CW]$ with probability p_r. We say that slot r is *silent* if no sensor chooses that slot, and there is a *collision* if more than one sensor

---

[1] This is the motivation behind the name *Sift*: the non-uniform probability distribution "sifts" the (collision-free) winners from the entire contending set of nodes.

chooses that slot. Also, a sensor *wins in slot* r if it is the only one to choose slot r, and all others choose later slots. Finally, there is *success* if some sensor wins some slot in $[1, CW]$.

Sift uses the truncated, increasing geometric distribution

$$p_r = \frac{(1 - \alpha)\alpha^{CW}}{1 - \alpha^{CW}} \cdot \alpha^{-r} \quad \text{for } r = 1, \ldots, CW, \tag{1}$$

where $0 < \alpha < 1$ is a parameter. For these values of α, p_r increases exponentially with r, so the later slots have higher probability.

To motivate this choice, view each sensor's choice of which slot to pick as a decision procedure with CW stages. Each node starts in stage 1 with some overestimate N_1 of N and chooses slot 1 with a small probability.[2] If no sensor chooses slot 1, that is an indication that N_1 is an overestimate of N, so each node updates its guess of the population size by decreasing N_1 to N_2, and proceeds to choose slot 2 with a different probability in stage 2. If slot 2 is also silent, this guess is reduced to N_3 in stage 3, and so on; in general, N_r is the updated guess after there is silence in slots $1, \ldots, r - 1$. In previous work [6], we have shown that a near-optimal choice of α for a wide range of population sizes is $\alpha = N_1^{-\frac{1}{CW-1}}$.

The points in Figure 3 plot the result of an experiment in which N sensors choose slots using the distribution in Equation 1 with $\alpha = 512^{-\frac{1}{31}} \approx 0.818$. Each point in the graph represents one run with N sensors. Note that although we engineered the Sift probability distribution for a maximum number of sensors $N_1 = 512$, performance degrades gracefully when the true number of contending stations exceeds 512. This degradation happens because the first slot starts to get picked by more than one sensor, resulting in a collision. We ran the same simulation with α set to various values in the range $[0.7, 0.9]$. Our results verified that we had chosen the correct α, and that over this range, the success rate is not sensitive to the exact choice of α.

Figure 3 also shows that although the sensors do not know N and use a fixed distribution p_r, the probability of a successful transmission is constantly high for a large range of N. In the next section, we will see that this probability of success is in fact close to the maximum that is achievable even if the sensors knew N and used a distribution tuned for N. We emphasize that we introduced N_r and p'_r here for explanatory purposes only, as a way of understanding our choice of p_r. In particular, nodes running Sift do not maintain an explicit estimate of N_r.

2.2 Comparison with an Optimal Protocol

Suppose each contending station had perfect knowledge of the true number of contending stations at the instant it started contending for the shared medium, and picked a contention slot in which to transmit at the beginning of the contention period, with no

---

[2] N_1 is a fixed parameter that defines the maximum population size Sift is designed for. All practical MACs have such a parameter; for example 802.11 limited the maximum contention window size to 1024 for commodity hardware at the time this paper was written. In Section 2.2, we show that above this population size, Sift's performance degrades gracefully.

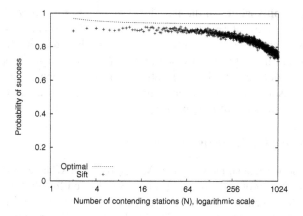

Fig. 3. A comparison between Sift with $\alpha = 0.818$ and $CW = 32$, and an optimal protocol, with $CW = 32$. The optimal protocol has full knowledge of N; Sift has no knowledge of N. The Sift distribution shown above was engineered for a maximum value of $N = 512$ nodes, but its performance degrades gracefully when N exceeds that figure.

other information provided to it during the contention period.[3] In related work [6], we derive the distribution p^* that optimizes the probability of a successful transmission.

Figure 3 shows the success probability of the Sift distribution as well as the theoretical success probability of the optimal distribution. When $R = 1$, the Sift distribution (which does not know N) performs almost as well as the optimal distribution (which needs to know N). As we argued in Section 1, it is most often the case that N is unknown and hard to predict.

The RTS/CTS Exchange. For large packet sizes (those above a tunable threshold), Sift uses the RTS/CTS exchange in the same way as IEEE 802.11 [2]. Instead of using the Sift distribution to compete on data packets, we use it to compete on sending the RTS packet. Since sensor network workloads mostly contain short packets, we evaluate the Sift's performance in Section 3 and 802.11 with RTS/CTS disabled, sending short data packets. In Section 3.4 we run some experiments with RTS/CTS enabled, sending large data packets.

Hidden Terminals. Modern spread-spectrum radios have a carrier-sensing range approximately twice that of their transmission range [2, 7], making it more likely that a node will carrier-sense a transmission that can interfere at the receiver of its transmission. This lessens the frequency of hidden terminals. For large packets, Sift uses the RTS/CTS exchange to avoid collisions between hidden terminals. In the case of collisions between small data packets among hidden terminals, senders can arbitrate as CODA [8] proposes, or can vary their transmit phases with respect to one other to avoid collisions [9]. We evaluate Sift under hidden terminal conditions in Section 3.5.

---

[3] These conditions exclude non-contention-window-based protocols like tree-splitting contention resolution. We address such protocols in related work [6].

Implementing Suppression. In the introduction, we described a workload in which sensors suppress their event reports after some number of reports R have been sent. In some scenarios, such as the last hop to a base station, this suppression is not hard to implement: sensors listen to the base station for R acknowledgment packets (ACKs) from data packets delivered to the base station. In general, when not at the last hop to a base station, sensors listen for R events timestamped within some time interval away from the event of interest before suppressing their event report.

2.3   Exploring the CSMA Design Space

Current sensor network designs (such as B-MAC [3], the MAC layer of TinyOS[4]) use a fixed-window CSMA protocol, choosing contention slots uniformly at random. The advantage of this design choice is simplicity, and good performance under most practical sensor network deployment scenarios. The disadvantage of this design choice is a lack of scalability under highly-correlated traffic or large numbers of sensor nodes.

Bharghavan *et al.* proposed MACAW [5], a MAC protocol for wireless local-area networks. MACAW uses BEB (described at the beginning of Section 2), and so without some way to share information about the state of the wireless medium, MACAW would suffer from the well-known Ethernet capture problem: a station that just transmitted resets its contention window to the minimum value, and is thus more likely to transmit again in subsequent competitions. MACAW's solution to this belongs to a class of techniques that we term *shared learning*. Stations *copy* the CW value of a station that transmits to their own CW value, and modify BEB so that instead of resetting CW after a successful transmission, decreases it linearly (a multiplicative increase, linear decrease policy).

Instead of shared learning, 802.11 [2] uses *memory* to solve the fairness problem. When stations begin to compete, they set a countdown timer to a random value picked uniformly from the contention window CW. When the medium becomes busy, the station pauses the countdown timer. When the medium becomes idle and the station wants to compete again, 802.11 resumes its countdown timer. When the countdown timer expires, the station begins its transmission.

In 802.11, a station that successfully transmits resets its CW to a small, fixed minimum value of CW. Consequently, the station has to rediscover the correct CW, wasting some bandwidth.

Table 1. Some design parameters in the contention window-based CSMA space. Sift requires neither shared learning, a variable-sized contention window, nor memory to perform well.

Protocol	Contention window	Shared learning?	Memory?	Distribution
BEB	Variable	No	No	Uniform
802.11	Variable	No	Yes	Uniform
MACAW	Variable	Yes	No	Uniform
802.11/copy	Variable	Yes	Yes	Uniform
B-MAC, S-MAC	Fixed	No	No	Uniform
Sift	**Fixed**	**No**	**No**	**Reverse-exponential**

---

[4] See http://tinyos.net.

One might think that shared learning could help the problem of high rate of change of N with respect to time. The spurious intuition behind this is that when a node is successful in its transmission, it might have found the correct value of CW for all nodes to use. 802.11 with shared learning, which we term *802.11/copy*, still suffers when N increases quickly. We substantiate this claim in Section 3.

Table 1 summarizes the design parameters we have reviewed. From the table, it is clear that Sift explores a novel region of the contention window-based MAC design space. We now show that this particular point in the design space results in good performance in sensor networks with respect to throughput, latency, and fairness.

3   Performance Evaluation

In our experiments, we compare Sift configured with $CW = 32$ and $\alpha = 0.818$ to 802.11 and 802.11/copy (defined in Section 2.3). We choose the 802.11 family because it is a practical CSMA protocol whose mechanism for adapting to the number of transmitting stations (BEB) has been included, unmodified, in several proposals for the MAC layer of a sensor network [4, 9].

We run experiments using version 2.1b9 of the *ns-2* [7] network simulator, with all nodes within range of a common base station. We modify all the MACs in our experiments to perform suppression: if a sensor hears R acknowledgments for motion event $\mathcal{E}$ from the base station, it suppresses its report of $\mathcal{E}$ and removes $\mathcal{E}$'s packet from its transmit queue. For experiments with small data packets (40 bytes), we compare Sift, 802.11 *without* RTS/CTS, and 802.11/copy *without* RTS/CTS. For the fairness experiments in Section 3.4, where data packets are 1500 bytes long, we enable RTS/CTS for both Sift and the 802.11 protocols. All experimental results average 20 runs using different random seeds for each run, except the fairness experiments in Section 3.4 which average 5 runs.

3.1   Event-Based Workloads

Constant-bit-rate (CBR) or TCP flows do not suffice to evaluate protocols for sensor networks, because they capture neither the burstiness inherent in the network, nor some underlying physical process that the network should be sensing. We therefore propose two event-based workloads to evaluate our design.

Trace-Driven Event Workload. We model a sensor network that detects the presence of people or cars in a region of a busy street. Rather than deploying this sensor network, we acquire video from a camera pointed at a busy street and log motion events to a database. This data captures the physical process of person and car inter-arrival times on the street. We call this the *trace-driven event* workload.

To run an experiment with this trace-driven workload, we create an *ns-2* scenario where sensors are placed uniformly at random on a two-dimensional plane. At the time given by each motion event in the database, all sensors within d_{report} meters of the location of that event send a 40 byte report packet, suppressing their reports after R have been sent.

Constant-Rate Event Workload. In some experiments, we measure the network not in the steady-state, but in a dynamic situation where the network has quiesced, then N nodes sense an event and report that event, suppressing their reports after R have been sent. Event reports are 40 bytes in size. We call this the *constant-rate event* workload.

3.2   Latency Experiments

We begin by evaluating latency under the constant-rate event workload. To capture varying propagation delays in the environment, variations between sensor electronics, and uncertainty in software system delays on the sensor nodes themselves, we add a random delay in $[0, 1]$ ms to the time that each sensor sends its event report. We measure the time for the base station to receive the first, median, and 90th percentile event report. We plot these times as a function of N.

Figure 4 shows the results of this experiment. When N is small, the minimum 802.11 contention window size is large enough to quickly resolve contention between the nodes. As N grows, however, the 802.11 and 802.11/copy contention window needs to grow before even one event report can be successfully sent (see the bottom of the error bars in Figure 4), while Sift's fixed contention window resolves contention in constant time with respect to N. Turning to the median and 90th percentile event reporting times, we see that Sift also improves latency for these measures as well, up to $N = 256$. This is primarily due to Sift's improvement in the first event reporting time, but it also shows that Sift can deliver enough throughput to keep up with 802.11 and 802.11/copy as it sends subsequent event reports.

802.11/copy does not improve performance much because some stations transmit before they have estimated the optimal CW value, broadcasting values of CW that are too low. As a result, CW cannot increase quickly enough when N is large. Sift does not need any time to adapt to large N, and so performs well over a large range of N. Figure 4 shows that as N increases, Sift achieves a seven-fold latency reduction over 802.11.

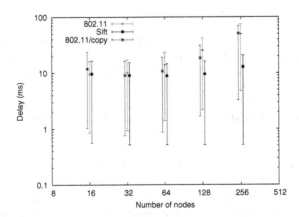

Fig. 4. Latency as a function of N (number of sensors reporting an event). 16 reports are required ($R = 16$). We show the time that the first (bottom of error bar), median (point in error bar), and 90th percentile (top of error bar) event report was received at the base station. This experiment uses the constant-rate event workload, and all three protocols use suppression.

3.3   Throughput Experiments

We now compare the throughput of Sift, 802.11, and 802.11/copy under a variety of workloads that saturate the capacity of the wireless medium.

Trace-Driven Events. Using our trace-driven workload, we measure the time each protocol takes to deliver R reports for each motion event, varying R. N also varies, depending on how many of the 128 total nodes are within range of each motion event, but averages 100. Since the traffic pattern is bursty, when R grows (and the number of reports suppressed shrinks), we quickly reach the capacity of the medium. When this happens, interface queues at the senders start to build up, and latency sharply increases. To examine the capacity of the medium using Sift versus using 802.11, we increased the upper bound on the interface queue length by an order of magnitude, from 50 packets to 500 packets. We then measured the latency to receive R events for Sift, 802.11, and 802.11/copy. Figure 5 shows the results of this experiment. As expected, when R is small, Sift has lower latency than either 802.11 or 802.11/copy, because it can resolve contention faster than a BEB protocol. Furthermore, noting the position of the knee of each curve, Sift can continue delivering low-latency events for higher values of R because it can deliver higher throughput under the varying values of N that this workload generates.

Constant-Rate Events. Now we measure the time it takes to receive R events when N is fixed at 128. Figure 6 shows that Sift achieves better throughput than 802.11 under this workload. The reason for this is again that Sift does not have to track the sudden change in N like BEB does.

The Sift Performance Space. In Figure 7, we explore the Sift performance space when we vary both N and R. Consider first the five bottom-most curves ($R = 1, 2, 4, 8, 16$)

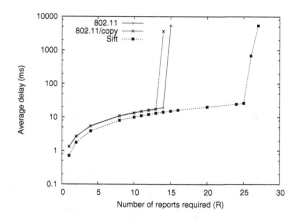

Fig. 5. Average delay as a function of R (number of reports required) for each camera motion event. The sensor range in this experiment is fixed at 20 meters ($d_{report} = 20$), and there are 128 nodes in this experiment. N is a function of event location, as explained in the text. This experiment uses the trace-driven event workload, and all three protocols use suppression.

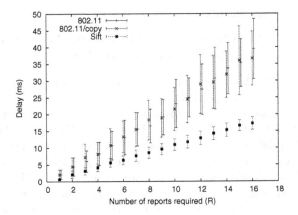

Fig. 6. Average and standard deviation latency to receive R event reports when 128 sensors report an event ($N = 128$). All sensors detect the event at the same time. This experiment uses the constant-rate event workload, and all three protocols use suppression.

with zero slope. They show that no matter how many stations report an event (N), Sift can deliver $R = 1, 2, 4, 8,$ or 16 messages with a small, constant latency. Now consider the remaining curves ($R = 24, 32, 64$) in Figure 7, which have a non-zero slope. They show that once R becomes greater than or equal to 24 messages, Sift requires more time to deliver R messages as N grows. Thus to a point, Sift scales well *simultaneously* with respect to R and N.

3.4   Fairness Experiments

We now examine whether Sift fairly allocates bandwidth between stations. It has been shown that 802.11 does not, but that minor changes to 802.11 can yield a fair

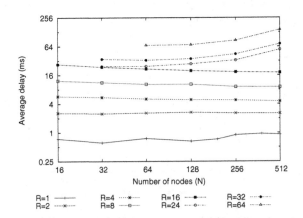

Fig. 7. Average delay of Sift event reports as a function of N (number of sensors reporting an event). We show curves for various values of R (number of reports required). Note that $R \leq N$. This experiment uses the constant-rate event workload with suppression.

protocol [10]. We duplicate the experimental setup given by the authors of the distributed fair scheduling (DFS) protocol [10]. We place some even number of nodes in the same radio range, and set up a traffic pattern where each node is either a traffic source or a traffic sink. The packet size is 1500 bytes, and the RTS/CTS exchange is enabled for both 802.11 and Sift. We ensure that each node is backlogged so that the offered load exceeds the available wireless capacity.

Figure 8 shows the throughput achieved by each node in six seconds as a function of the node number. Note that as expected, 802.11/copy outperforms 802.11 in terms of fairness. Also notice that Sift outperforms 802.11 in terms of fairness. Sift does not in fact achieve a perfectly-fair bandwidth allocation. We expect that this is not a major issue, since sensor networks will contain many redundant nodes reporting similar observations about the environment. However, due to the simplicity of Sift, we expect that a similar approach to DFS could be applied to Sift should fairness become an issue.

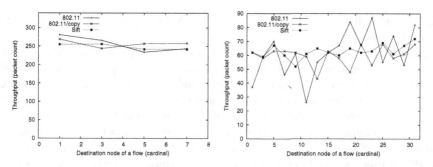

Fig. 8. Fairness comparison of 802.11 and Sift. Left: eight nodes; right: 32 nodes. In each experiment there are half as many flows as there are nodes. This experiment uses a CBR workload, without suppression. RTS/CTS is enabled for all three protocols.

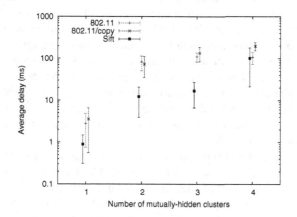

Fig. 9. Latency comparison between Sift and 802.11 in the presence of varying numbers of hidden terminals. This experiment uses an event-based workload with suppression. RTS/CTS is disabled, and each packet is 40 bytes in length.

3.5   Hidden Terminal Experiments

We now compare Sift with 802.11 and 802.11/copy in the presence of hidden terminals. In this experiment, we arrange $N = 128$ nodes in closely-spaced clusters around the base station to which they send event reports. Nodes in each cluster can carrier-sense each others' transmissions, and defer and suppress accordingly. Nodes in separate clusters cannot carrier-sense each others' transmissions: they are hidden terminals with respect to each other. We vary the number of clusters around the base station, and measure the time to receive $R = 1$ report. Figure 9 shows that as the number of hidden terminals increases, latency increases due to a significantly-increased number of collisions. Sift performs better than 802.11 in hidden terminal situations because it does not incur the penalty of contention-window doubling when a collision occurs.

4   Related Work

We compared Sift to 802.11, B-MAC, and MACAW in Section 2.3. We now review more related work.

There have been a number of proposals [11–14] for controlling the flow of information in a sensor network at the application layer. While these proposals are essential, they are orthogonal to the choice of MAC layer, and that choosing an appropriate MAC is important for the performance of a sensor network.

Cai et al. [15] propose CSMA with a truncated polynomial distribution over a fixed contention window. There are several significant differences between their proposal and Sift. First, Sift uses the exponential distribution, which is close to optimal over all possible distributions, as described in Section 2.2. Furthermore, Cai et al. optimize only over the polynomial distributions, not over all possible distributions. Finally, Sift was designed and evaluated in an event-based workload (see Section 3), while Cai et al. evaluate their proposal using a Poissonian workload.

Like Sift, the HIPERLAN standard [16] for wireless LANs uses a truncated geometric probability distribution in the "elimination" phase of its contention protocol. Cho et al. [17] describe and analyze HIPERLAN's MAC protocol in detail. Sift uses traditional CSMA, where immediately following a busy channel, the first station to break the silence wins access to the medium. In contrast, HIPERLAN stations transmit noise bursts of varying length after the medium becomes idle, and the station that ceases its noise burst *last* wins access to the medium. Sift compares favorably with HIPERLAN for two reasons. HIPERLAN's noise bursts raise the overall noise floor of the network when there are many stations, and consume more power than listening for the same amount of time on most radio hardware.

Mowafi and Ephremides [18] propose Probabilistic Time Division (PTD), a TDMA-like scheme in which stations transmit in each TDMA slot with a given probability. Each station chooses one TDMA slot in each round with a fixed probability a. By tuning a, PTD achieves a compromise between TDMA and pure random access. Our proposal differs from PTD because we compute an optimal probability distribution on *contention slots*, which in practice are several orders of magnitude smaller than TDMA data slots.

Rhee *et al.* propose Z-MAC [19], a MAC for sensor networks that combines the strengths of TDMA and CSMA. Sift stands out from Z-MAC because Sift's probability distribution reduces the likelihood of collisions compared to CSMA's uniform distribution. Z-MAC is one of many examples of a MAC protocol that could incorporate Sift's probability distribution to improve performance.

Tan and Guttag [20] demonstrate that 802.11 nodes use globally-inefficient transmission strategies that lead to degraded aggregate throughput. They propose changes to 802.11's backoff window that increase network capacity. Sift has the orthogonal goal of minimizing response latency of a wireless network.

Woo and Culler [9] compare the performance of various contention window-based MAC schemes, varying carrier sense time, contention window size increase/decrease policies, and transmission deferral policies. All of their protocols use contention windows with the uniform distribution. They find that CSMA schemes with a fixed-size window are the most energy-efficient, since nodes spend the least time listening. This further motivates the case for Sift, because Sift uses a fixed-size contention window. Woo and Culler also find that fixed-size contention window protocols perform well in terms of throughput.

S-MAC [4] is a MAC protocol designed for saving energy in sensor networks. It uses periodic listen and sleep, the collision avoidance facilities of 802.11, and overhearing avoidance to reduce energy consumption. LEACH [21] is designed for sensor networks where an end-user wants to remotely monitor the environment. It includes distributed cluster formation, local processing to reduce global communication, and randomized rotation of the cluster-heads to extend system lifetime. PAMAS [22] reduces energy consumption by powering off nodes when they are about to overhear a transmission from one of their neighbors. While S-MAC, LEACH, and PAMAS govern medium-access to some degree they do not address the contention portion of a medium-access protocol. Since Sift is a CSMA protocol, it can be implemented concurrently with these protocols.

There have also been a number of proposals [23–25] for topology-control in wireless networks. Although their goal is energy savings, if topology formation protocols could be adapted to take into account the number of sensor reports required, it might be possible to provide an alternate solution to our problem; we leave this idea as future work. We note that Sift can be used as a building block in the underlying MAC to arbitrate access between the large numbers of nodes that need to rendezvous at the same time and elect coordinators.

5   Conclusion

We have presented Sift, a MAC protocol for wireless sensor networks that performs well when spatially-correlated contention occurs and adapts well to sudden changes in the number of sensors that are trying to send data. Sift is ideal for sensor networks, where it is often sufficient that any R of N sensors that observe an event report it, with the remaining nodes suppressing their transmissions. The key idea in Sift is to use a geometrically-increasing probability distribution within a fixed-size contention window, rather than varying the window size as in many traditional MAC protocols.

Using trace-driven experiments, we have shown that Sift outperforms 802.11 and other BEB-based protocols both when the ratio R/N is low, and when both N and R are large. For $R = 1$, we have identified the optimal non-persistent CSMA protocol, and shown that Sift's performance is close to optimal.

References

1. Kahn, J., Katz, R., Pister, K.: Mobile Networking for Smart Dust. In: Proc. of the ACM MOBICOM Conf., Seattle, WA (1999) 271–278
2. IEEE 802.11 Standard: Wireless LAN Medium Access Control and Physical Layer Specifications (1999)
3. Polastre, J., Hill, J., Culler, D.: Versatile Low Power Media Access for Wireless Sensor Networks. In: Proc. of the ACM SenSys Conf., Baltimore, MD (2004) 95–107
4. Ye, W., Heidemann, J., Estrin, D.: An Energy-Efficient MAC Protocol for Wireless Sensor Networks. In: Proc. of the IEEE INFOCOM Conf., New York, NY (2002) 1567–1576
5. Bharghavan, V.: MACAW: A Media Access Protocol for Wireless LANs. In: Proc. of the ACM SIGCOMM Conf., London, UK (1994) 212–225
6. Jamieson, K., Tay, Y.C., Balakrishnan, H.: Sift: a MAC Protocol for Event-Driven Wireless Sensor Networks. Technical Report MIT-LCS-TR-894, Massachusetts Institute of Technology (2003)
7. USC ISI: ns-2 Notes and Documentation (2002) http://www.isi.edu/nsnam/ns.
8. Wan, C.Y., Eisenmen, S., Campbell, A.: CODA: Congestion Control in Sensor Networks. In: Proc. of the ACM Sensys Conf., Los Angeles, CA (2003) 266–279
9. Woo, A., Culler, D.: A Transmission Control Scheme for Media Access in Sensor Networks. In: Proc. of the ACM MOBICOM Conf., Rome, Italy (2001) 221–235
10. Vaidya, N., Bahl, V., Gupta, S.: Distributed Fair Scheduling in a Wireless LAN. In: Proc. of the ACM MOBICOM Conf., Boston, MA (2000) 167–178
11. Intanagonwiwat, C., Govindan, R., Estrin, D.: Directed Diffusion: A Scalable and Robust Communication Paradigm for Sensor Networks. In: Proc. of the ACM MOBICOM Conf., Boston, MA (2000) 56–67
12. Madden, S., Franklin, M., Hellerstein, J., Hong, W.: TAG: a Tiny AGregation Service for Ad-Hoc Sensor Networks. In: Proc. of the USENIX OSDI Symp., Boston, MA (2002) 131–146
13. Ye, F., Luo, H., Cheng, J., Lu, S., Zhang, L.: A Two-Tier Data Dissemination Model for Large-Scale Wireless Sensor Networks. In: Proc. of the ACM MOBICOM Conf., Atlanta, GA (2002) 148–159
14. Ratnasamy, S., Karp, B., Yin, L., Yu, F., Estrin, D., Govindan, R., Shenker, S.: GHT: A Geographic Hash Table for Data-Centric Storage. In: Proc. of the ACM WSNA Workshop, Atlanta, GA (2002) 78–87
15. Cai, Z., Lu, M., Wang, X.: Randomized Broadcast Channel Access Algorithms for Ad Hoc Networks. In: Proc. of the IEEE Intl. Conf. on Parallel Processing. (2002) 151–158
16. European Telecommunication Standard: HIgh PErformance Radio Local Area Network (HIPERLAN) Type 1; Functional Specification (1996)
17. Cho, K.O., Shin, H.C., Lee, J.K.: Performance Analysis of HIPERLAN Channel Access Control Protocol. Proc. of the ICICE Trans. on Comm. **E85-B** (2002) 2044–2052
18. Mowafi, O., Ephremides, A.: Analysis of a Hybrid Access Scheme for Buffered Users—Probabilistic Time Division. IEEE Trans. on Software Engineering **8** (1982) 52–60
19. Rhee, I., Warrier, A., Aia, M., Min, J.: Z-MAC: A Hybrid MAC for Wireless Sensor Networks. In: Proc. of the ACM SenSys Conf., San Diego, CA (2005) 90–101

20. Tan, G., Guttag, J.: The 802.11 MAC Protocol Leads to Inefficient Equilibria. In: Proc. of the IEEE INFOCOM Conf., Miami, FL (2005) 1–11
21. Heinzelman, W., Chandrakasan, A., Balakrishnan, H.: Energy-Efficient Communication Protocol for Wireless Microsensor Networks. In: Proc. of the 33rd Hawaii International Conf. on System Sciences (HICSS). (2000)
22. Singh, S., Woo, M., Raghavendra, C.: Power-Aware Routing in Mobile Ad Hoc Networks. In: Proc. of the ACM MOBICOM Conf., Dallas, TX (1998) 181–190
23. Chen, B., Jamieson, K., Balakrishnan, H., Morris, R.: Span: An Energy-Efficient Coordination Algorithm for Topology Maintainence in Ad Hoc Wireless Networks. In: Proc. of the ACM MOBICOM Conf., Rome, Italy (2001) 85–96
24. Wattenhofer, R., Li, L., Bahl, V., Wang, Y.M.: Distributed Topology Control for Wireless Multihop Ad-hoc Networks. In: Proc. of the IEEE INFOCOM Conf., Anchorage, AK (2001) 1370–1379
25. Xu, Y., Heidemann, J., Estrin, D.: Geography-Informed Energy Conservation for Ad Hoc Routing. In: Proc. of the ACM MOBICOM Conf., Rome, Italy (2001) 70–84

f-MAC: A Deterministic Media Access Control Protocol Without Time Synchronization

Utz Roedig, Andre Barroso, and Cormac J. Sreenan

Mobile and Internet Systems Laboratory (MISL),
Computer Science Department, University College Cork (UCC), Ireland
{u.roedig, a.barroso, c.sreenan}@cs.ucc.ie

Abstract. Nodes in a wireless network transmit messages through a shared medium. Thus, a Media Access Control (MAC) protocol is necessary to regulate and coordinate medium access. For some application areas it is necessary to have a deterministic MAC protocol which can give guarantees on message delay and channel throughput. Schedule based MAC protocols, based on time synchronization among nodes, are currently used to implement deterministic MAC protocols. Time synchronization is difficult and costly, especially in energy constrained sensor networks. In this paper the f-MAC protocol is presented which can give guarantees regarding message delay and channel throughput without the requirement of time synchronization among nodes. The various trade-offs of f-MAC are analysed and discussed and application areas that would benefit from f-MAC are presented.

1 Introduction

Nodes in a wireless network transmit messages through a shared medium. Thus, some form of organization among the nodes is necessary to enable an effective usage of the shared resource. This organization is implemented by a Media Access Control (MAC) protocol that each node has to obey. Currently a number of varying MAC protocols with different properties and requirements exist. These properties might be high data throughput or transmission delay guarantees. Requirements might be time synchronization among all nodes or the capability of detecting a busy channel (carrier sense).

Most MAC protocols used in wireless networks today can be divided into two major classes: *contention* and *schedule* based MAC protocols. Both types differ in their properties and requirements.

A contention based MAC protocol is relatively simple to implement since there is no coordination necessary among the nodes. A node simply detects if the channel is currently used by another node; if not, the message is transmitted. If the channel is busy, the node backs off and tries again after some time. The problem of such a MAC protocol is that no worst-case guarantees can be given regarding throughput or maximum transmission delay. However, many application areas, for example medical applications, require strict guarantees.

K. Römer, H. Karl, and F. Mattern (Eds.): EWSN 2006, LNCS 3868, pp. 276–291, 2006.

A schedule based MAC protocol is more difficult to implement because accurate time synchronization among neighbouring nodes is required. Each node uses a dedicated time slot to transmit messages. As fixed time slots are used, guarantees regarding bandwidth and message delay can be given. The main problem of such a MAC protocol is the complexity introduced by time synchronization. Especially in highly constrained sensor networks the synchronization overhead might not be acceptable.

This paper presents the f-MAC protocol which overcomes the aforementioned restrictions. The protocol has, among other benefits shown in the paper, the following main features:

1. Bandwidth and delay guarantees are provided.
2. Time synchronization among nodes is not necessary.

The f-MAC protocol uses a *framelet* approach: fixed sized frames are retransmitted a fixed number of times with a specific frequency. Thus, the abbreviation f-MAC is used to refer to the presented protocol. As it will be shown in the paper, the capability of giving guarantees is traded for a lower bandwidth and higher transmission delay. However, for many application areas this is acceptable as hard guarantees are considered to be the most important design goal.

The remaining paper is organized as follows. In Section 2, the functionality and requirements of f-MAC are described. In Section 3 basic properties such as bandwidth and transmission delay are investigated analytically and by experiment. Section 4 compares the delivery probability of a simple random MAC with f-MAC. Section 5 describes cluster forming issues in larger f-MAC based networks. Section 6 shows application areas that benefit from the use of f-MAC. In Section 7 related work is discussed. Section 8 concludes the paper.

2   f-MAC Concept

In this section, the basic concept of f-MAC is presented. f-MAC uses a framelet approach as it is described in detail in [1].

2.1   The Framelet Approach

In the framelet approach, the same message is transmitted several times using small, fixed sized data packets. Each data packet of the transmission is called a framelet. A message transmission via the framelet approach is depicted in Fig. 1. The transmission duration of a framelet is denoted as d. Each transmission consists of r framelets and the framelets are sent with a frequency of $f = 1/t$.

Certain types of ultra low-power transceivers, such as the Nordic nRF2401 [3], the Chipcon CC2420 [5] or the nanoNET TRX [4], are able to transmit small, fixed sized packets at a high speeds of typically 1Mb/s. These transceiver types are currently used in sensor networks and are capable of supporting the framelet approach.

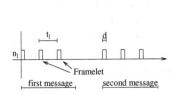

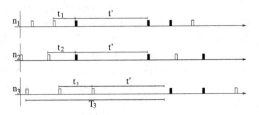

Fig. 1. Framelet transmission   **Fig. 2.** f-MAC operation

A framelet approach is normally used to increase transmission reliability or to allow a power efficient operation of the transceivers (see [1, 2], implementation of duty cycles). As the same information is transmitted several times, the available bandwidth is reduced. However, in many cases reliability and especially power efficiency is considered more important than a high throughput.

2.2   Collision Handling Using Framelets

Instead of using the framelet approach to increase transmission reliability or to allow power efficient transceiver operation, it can be used to deal with the problem of collisions. If several nodes in the same radio range transmit data via a set of framelets, collisions can still occur. However, if each node uses a specific unique framelet transmission frequency f_i, it is possible to ensure that one framelet of a set is always received, even if collisions are not prevented. This is the basic idea behind the f-MAC protocol and is explained in detail in the next paragraph.

2.3   Framelet Media Access Control

In f-MAC, no collision detection or time synchronisation between the nodes is used. The number of framelets per message and the framelet frequencies are selected such that it is guaranteed that at least one framelet per message is delivered without collision. f-MAC defines the following simple transmission policy:

Rule#1   Each node has to transmit messages as framelets. The framelet length d is defined by the f-MAC base unit δ as follows:

$$d = \delta/2 \tag{1}$$

Rule#2   The number of framelets r per message is defined by the number of nodes N in transmission range.

$$r = N \tag{2}$$

Rule#3   Each node n_i has to use a specific framelet frequency $f_i = 1/t_i = 1/(k_i \cdot \delta)$. The $k_i \in N^+$ must satisfy the following equation:

$$k_i \cdot (r-1) < LCM(k_i, k_j) \quad \forall k_i < k_j \; 1 \le i, j \le N \tag{3}$$

Rule#4   After the start of the transmission of the last framelet of a message, a node must wait at least the time t' before a next message can be transmitted. t' is computed as:

$$k_{max} = \max_{0 \leq i \leq N}\{k_i\}$$

$$t' = (k_{max} \cdot (r-1) + 1) \cdot \delta \qquad (4)$$

From the previous described rules it can be deduced that a node n_i needs in the worst case the following time T_i to transmit a message:

$$T_i = (r-1) \cdot t_i + t' \qquad (5)$$

Example. Fig. 2 shows an example with three nodes ($N = 3$). The number of framelets is therefore $r = 3$. A possible[1] set of k_i satisfying Equation (3) is $k_1 = 4$, $k_2 = 5$ and $k_3 = 6$. According to Equation (4), the nodes use $t' = 13 \cdot \delta$. In the example it is assumed that n_2 starts first at an arbitrary time with a message transmission. Shortly after, n_3 and then n_1 start a transmission as well. In the example, framelet#3 of n_1 and n_2 collide. However, all other remaining framelets of each node's ongoing transmissions can be transmitted successfully. After the time t' of node n_1 and n_2 expires, both nodes start immediately a new transmission. Here framelet#1 of n_1 and n_2 collide and are destroyed. However a framelet of each transmission can be subsequently submitted successfully. n_3 sends a message some time after its waiting period t' is over. Framelet#1 of this transmission collides with framelet#2 of the ongoing transmission of node n_1. Framelet#2 of the transmission of n_3 collides with the framelet#3 of n_2. However the last framelet of n_3's transmission is successfully transmitted.

2.4   Validation

The previous stated example shows that the transmission scheme is feasible under certain conditions. However, it has to be shown that the transmission scheme is successful for all possible time shifts between the nodes.

Lemma 1. *If node n_i sends u ($u \in N^+$) consecutive messages $m_{i,u}$ and node n_j sends v ($v \in N^+$) consecutive messages $m_{j,v}$, only framelets of exactly one message $m_{i,u}$ can collide with framelets of exactly one message $m_{j,v}$.*

Proof. Assume for the sake of contradiction that framelets of message $m_{i,u-1}$ and $m_{i,u}$ with $u \neq 1$ collide with message $m_{j,v}$. For this to happen, the following equation must be fulfilled (see Equation 5):

$$t' < (r-1) \cdot t_j + \delta$$

---

[1] This set of k_i is possible, but not optimal. The optimal set of k_i is shown in Section 3.

The origin of this inequality can be described using the example shown in Fig. 2. The inequality describes the case where a message transmission of n_2 does fit between two consecutive transmissions of n_1. This inequality can be simpified the following way:

$$(k_{max} \cdot (r - 1) + 1) \cdot \delta < (k_j \cdot (r - 1) + 1) \cdot \delta \Rightarrow k_{max} < k_j$$

According to f-MAC Rule#4 and Equation 4, this statement can not be fulfilled and thus contradicts the initial assumption.

Lemma 2. *If node n_i and node n_j transmit a message, no more than one framelet of these two message transmissions can collide.*

Proof. Assume that more than one framelet of the transmission collide. Therefore, after one collision happened, n_i and n_j must send again a framelet at the same time. This can only be achieved if k_i and k_j have a least common multiplier within the period k_i is sending its framelets. This can be expressed as follows:

$$LCM(k_i, k_j) < k_i \cdot (r - 1) \quad \forall k_i < k_j \; 1 \leq i, j \leq N$$

This statement obviously contradicts Rule#3 and Equation 3 and thus contradicts the initial assumption.

Theorem 1. *At least one framelet of any message transmission will be transmitted collision-free (f-MAC theorem).*

Proof. According to Lemma 1 and 2 only one framelet collision per message transmission between two nodes can occur. According to f-MAC Rule#2 and Equation 2 exactly $r = N$ framelets are transmitted. Thus, even under worst case conditions, only $N - 1$ framelets can be affected by a collision as a node cannot produce a collision with itself.

3   f-MAC Properties

Two important properties of a MAC protocol are the message delay and the available bandwidth. For most MAC protocols, the figures of these properties vary with the number of nodes that participate in a collision domain. This is observed as well within f-MAC and analyzed within this section.

Regarding message delay it has to be noted that an upper bound can be computed. This is the main feature and design goal of f-MAC. Many available MAC protocols do not allow us to compute such a deterministic bound. For example collisions might occur and random back-off times are used.

Regarding bandwidth it has to be pointed out that f-MAC's design goal is not an optimisation of the channel utilisation. In fact, the channel utilisation is reduced to enable strict guarantees for the message delay. Therefore, f-MAC has a naturally poor channel utilisation.

3.1 Worst Case Message Delay

The upper bound for the message delay between two nodes is given by the time T_{max}. T_{max} is computed the following way using Equation 5:

$$T_{max} = \max_{0 \leq i \leq N} \{T_i\} \qquad (6)$$

f-MAC ensures that after a delay of T_{max} a message is delivered between two arbitrary nodes. This is the worst-case delay bound for all nodes. If just one specific node is investigated, it might be possible to give a better upper bound of the message delay. This is possible as some nodes are able to transmit messages faster than others (They have a $T_i < T_{max}$). Thus, the worst case delay bound T_{min} for the fastest node of the set is defined as:

$$T_{min} = \min_{0 \leq i \leq N} \{T_i\} \qquad (7)$$

To analyse how the times T_{min} and T_{max} increase with the number of nodes, a program was implemented to determine the combination of k_i for a given N that leads to a minimal T_{max}. The result of this computation is shown in Table 1 and T_{min} and T_{max} are shown graphically in Fig. 3 (The value T_{av} is explained and obtained by simulation in Section 3.3).

As shown, the worst case delay bound increases exponentially with the number of nodes that are in the same collision domain. Obviously, the number of nodes used in one collision domain has a dramatic impact on the transfer delay. Thus, f-MAC might not be useful in highly populated networks.

It also has to be noted that the gap between T_{min} and T_{max} increases with the number of nodes. Some nodes are able to send messages faster than others. This feature might be useful in cases where specific nodes have to deal with a high traffic load.

Example. If, for example, $N = 5$ nodes are selected and a Nordic nRF2401 transceiver [3] with a message size of $b = 32$ bytes and a transmission speed of $1 Mbit/s$ is assumed, the following value for the transfer delay bound is obtained:

$$\delta = 2 \cdot 0.25 \; ms = 0.5 \; ms \Rightarrow T_{max} = 89 \cdot 0.5 \; ms = 44.5 \; ms$$

Table 1. Sets satisfying the f-MAC condition

N	Set k_i	T_{min}	T_{max}	T_{av}
2	$\{2,3\}$	6δ	7δ	3δ
3	$\{2,3,5\}$	15δ	21δ	8δ
4	$\{3,4,5,7\}$	31δ	43δ	16δ
5	$\{3,5,7,8,11\}$	57δ	89δ	32δ
6	$\{5,7,8,9,11,13\}$	91δ	131δ	50δ
7	$\{5,7,8,9,11,13,17\}$	133δ	205δ	70δ
8	$\{5,9,11,13,14,16,17,19\}$	169δ	267δ	101δ

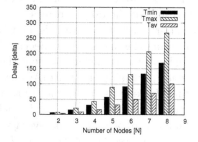

Fig. 3. Transmission delay T_{min} and T_{max} and T_{av}

3.2   Bandwidth

The available bandwidth B_i between two arbitrary nodes is given by the time T_i and the fixed framelet size b in byte.

$$B_i = \frac{b}{T_i} \qquad (8)$$

The available maximum bandwidth B_{max} (at the node using the smallest k_i) and minimal available bandwidth B_{min} can thus be calculated using T_{min} and T_{max}. The available bandwidth decreases exponentially as it depends on the exponentially increasing message delay bound T_i.

Example. If, for example, $N = 5$ nodes are selected and a Nordic nRF2401 transceiver [3] with a message size of $b = 32$ bytes and a transmission speed of $1 Mbit/s$ is assumed, the following value is obtained:

$$B_{min} = \frac{32\ byte}{44.5\ ms} = 7.2\ \frac{kbit}{s}$$

In this example, the maximum bandwidth is available for the node with $k_i = 3$. In this case T_{min} is:

$$T_{min} = (r - 1) \cdot t_i + t'_i = 4 \cdot 03 \cdot \delta + 45 \cdot \delta = 57 \cdot \delta \Rightarrow B_{max} = 11.23\ \frac{kbit}{s}$$

This small example shows that some nodes have a $T_i < T_{max}$ and therefore have a higher bandwidth available.

3.3   Average Message Delay

As previously described, f-MAC guarantees that a message is delivered within the time T_{max} between arbitrary nodes. However, as each message transmission consists of several framelets, it is likely that the destination node will receive a message earlier than T_{max}. In the previous paragraphs, the worst case upper bound for the message transfer delay was calculated. In this section, the average message transfer delay T_{av} between nodes is determined by simulation for specific traffic patterns.

If a node wants to transmit a message using the f-MAC protocol, three factors contribute to the observed message delay. First, the node n_i might have to wait for a portion of t' before it is allowed to start the transmission of the framelets containing the message (see Section 2.3, f-MAC rules). Second, it depends which framelet of the framelet trail sent the receiver gets first. Third, the transfer delay depends on the k_i of the f-MAC set the node is using to transmit. A node with a small k_i repeats the framelets relatively fast and thus the receiver has a high chance to catch an uncollided framelet early.

One can expect that the average message transfer delay T_{av} is less than the guaranteed message delivery time T_{max}. Obviously, the resulting average message transfer delay depends on the network configuration used and the particular traffic pattern.

Experiment. The f-MAC protocol was implemented within a simulation environment. The *ns2* network simulator was used for the experimental evaluation.

For the experiment, N nodes ($2 \leq N \leq 8$) are setup to transmit to one base station (star topology). All N nodes are in the communication range of each other and the base-station.

For the experiment, a Nordic nRF2401 transceiver [3] with a message size of $b = 32$ bytes and a transmission speed of $1 Mbit/s$ is assumed. Thus $\delta = 0.5\ ms$ is used. Each of the N nodes creates new messages according to a Poisson distribution. The arrival rate λ is the same at each node. Throughout all experiments, an arrival rate of a quater of the maximum possible rate, determined by the minimum available bandwidth B_{min} is used.

The experimentally obtained values of T_{av} are shown together with the analytically obtained results of T_{min} and T_{max} (see Section 3.1) in Table 1 and Fig. 3. As expected, the experiments show that the average message transfer delay is considerably better than the guaranteed maximum message transfer delay. If the arrival rate λ is increased, the transfer delay T_{av} increases as more single framelet collisions occur. As expected, T_{av} is always - regardless of the λ selected - smaller than T_{max}.

Furthermore, the experiments show that the communication among all nodes can take place without any collision. The experiments show as well that the f-MAC protocol implementation is relatively simple. To complete a full f-MAC implementation, only 100 lines of C++ code were necessary. This simplicity makes the MAC protocol useful for implementation in the very constrained sensor network environment.

3.4   Findings

The guaranteed upper bound for the message delay and the available bandwidth depend heavily on the node density in the network. More specificly:

1. The available bandwidth drops exponentially with the number of nodes.
2. The worst case delay increases exponentially with the number of nodes.

Therefore, it can be concluded that f-MAC is beneficial in sparsely populated networks where each node has only a few neighbours.

However, the experiments show that in realistic traffic scenarios, the worst case is not necessarily equal to the average operational case. Therefore the average message delay T_{av} is significantly smaller than the worst case message delay T_{max}.

4   Delivery Probability Analysis

f-MAC provides 100% message delivery if it is assumed that messages are only lost due to collisions. In this section, the collision probability of a simple random transmission scheme is investigated. It is analysed how close such a simple MAC protocol will get to the design goal of 100% collision-free message delivery.

Under real world conditions, even a collision-free protocol can not guarantee 100% message delivery as the wireless channel is lossy[2]. Thus, one could argue that a MAC protocol does not need to be 100% collision-free; it would be enough if the probability of a message loss is not significantly increased by an additional collision probability. It is therefore of interest to know how a more primitive MAC protocol with properties similar to f-MAC performs regarding its collision probability. The comparison allows us to assess the operation conditions that justify the use of f-MAC instead of a more simple solution.

4.1   Random Transmission Scheme

The MAC protocol used for comparison with f-MAC is similar to the MAC protocol described and analysed in detail in [13].

The protocol is selected because it uses a framelet approach comparable to f-MAC. Different to f-MAC, the transmitted r framelets are distributed in a random fashion within the time interval T_{RS}. The time interval T_{RS} is divided in r subintervals. A framelet of the current message is submitted within each subinterval. The transmission time of the framelet in the subinterval is given by a uniformly distributed random variable on $[0, (T_{RS}/r) - \delta/2]$ (Fig. 4).

The resulting MAC protocol is simpler than f-MAC as no coordination (careful determination of the k_i) among neighbouring nodes is needed. Bandwidth and delay bounds of the protocol are equal to f-MAC if $T_{RS} = T_{max}$ is selected. Basically, the collision-free behaviour of f-MAC is traded for simplicity of the described random MAC.

Table 2. Delivery probability P of the random transmission scheme

N	T_{max}	P_{ST}	P_{BT}
2	7δ	0.651428	0.640000
3	21δ	0.944530	0.858846
4	43δ	0.984797	0.944530
5	89δ	0.998696	0.989094
6	131δ	0.999716	0.995770
7	205δ	0.999975	0.999134
8	267δ	0.999995	0.999667

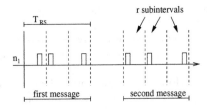

Fig. 4. Random transmission scheme

4.2   Traffic Analysis

f-MAC attains a message delivery probability equal to 1 if it is assumed that only collisions will be responsible for packet losses. If N nodes are contending for transmission, then f-MAC requires each node to transmit $r = N$ framelets and every message will have been delivered after T_{max}. With the random transmission

---

[2] It has to be noted that TDMA based protocols also have to deal with lossy media and are therefore unable to provide a 100% delivery probability.

scheme, a message is transmitted within the time T_{RS} but the message could be lost due to collisions. Thus, the probability P of a successful transmission is less than 1 ($P < 1$).

Saturated Traffic. In this comparison it is assumed that N nodes contending for the media are sending messages with the maximum available rate. If f-MAC is used in this traffic scenario, a message is sent every T_i seconds, depending on the nodes specific k_i. If the random scheme is used, every node is sending a message every T_{RS} seconds. To enable a fair comparison - both schemes provide the same bandwidth - the following value for T_{RS} is selected: $T_{RS} = T_{max}$. In this scenario, f-MAC attains a message delivery probability equal to 1. For the analytic analysis it is assumed that all nodes start the transmission of messages at the same point in time. In this case, the random transmission scheme attains a transmission probability that can be calculated the following way:

$$P(T_{RS}) = 1 - \left(1 - \left(\frac{\frac{T_{RS}}{N} - \delta}{\frac{T_{RS}}{N} - \frac{\delta}{2}}\right)^{2N}\right)^N \tag{9}$$

The probability depends on the number of nodes that are in communication range of a potential message receiver. The delivery probability $P_{ST} = P(T_{RS} = T_{max})$ is shown in Table 2. For small N, the delivery probability is significantly lower than 100%. In this operation area, the usage of the more complicated f-MAC sceme instead of the imsple random scheme is justified.

Bursty Traffic. In this traffic scenario, it is assumed that sporadically an event triggers N nodes to send a message to a receiver (similar to the application example described in Section 6). The time between events is assumed to be far larger than T_{max}. Consequently, the channel will be temporarily saturated as nodes contend for transmission. Such a channel usage is for example likely if the nodes are sensor nodes. The sensor nodes in one area of the field might be triggered by the same event that all nodes are set-up to monitor.

If f-MAC is used in this case, messages are guaranteed to be delivered after the time: $(r - 1) \cdot t_i + \delta/2$ (the waiting time t' must not be considered, as it is assumed that messages of previous events have been completely processed by the system). For comparison purposes, the same delivery time should be achieved by the random scheme. Thus, $T_{RS} = (r - 1) \cdot t_{max} + \delta/2$ is selected.

The delivery probability P_{BT} can be calculated using Equation (9). $P_{BT} = P(T_{RS} = (r - 1) \cdot t_{max} + \delta/2)$ is shown in Table 2. Here again, the delivery probability for small N is significantly lower than the 100% achieved by the f-MAC protocol.

4.3   Findings

In the real world, collision-free is not equal to 100% message delivery probability. Channel loss by interference will occur as well. However, in sparsely populated networks (small N), the probability of a message loss by collision can be considerable if a simple MAC protocol is used. f-MAC can reduce the number of message losses significantly as only message losses due to lossy links occur. Thus, f-MAC can be considered useful in sparsely populated networks with bursty traffic patterns if the link quality is not too bad.

5   f-MAC Clusters

The f-MAC scheme described previously allows only a collision-free delivery if all nodes participate in the scheme. Thus, if a large number of nodes have to communicate (e.g. many wireless sensors in a sensor field), the following problem arises. The number of framelets per transmission r is equal to the number of nodes N in the field. Additionally, k_{max} might be a high number so that Rule#3 can be satisfied. This will result in a large T_{max} which finally defines the upper bound for transmission latency and the lower bound for bandwidth.

This problem can be attenuated by forming clusters. In most cases, not all nodes will be within the transmission range of all other nodes. Alternatively, the transmission power of the nodes can be dynamically adjusted such that only a few nodes are in transmission range of each other. Thus, the f-MAC scheme can be applied in localized areas that are formed by nodes that are within each others radio range.

5.1   Cluster Example

An example is depicted in Fig. 5. All nodes are assumed to have the same radio range R. Thus, n_1, n_2 and n_3 are within each others radio range and form cluster C_1. Within the cluster, the different k_i have to be selected according Rule#3. For example $k_1 = 3$, $k_2 = 5$ and $k_3 = 7$ can be used. Within cluster C_2, which comprises the next set of nodes that are in each others radio range, the k_i have to be selected. As n_2 is member of 2 different clusters, it will use the already selected $k_2 = 5$. n_5 and n_6 can not select the same k_i used by n_1 and n_3 due to the hidden terminal problem. If for example n_5 would use $k_5 = 3$, messages sent by n_1 and n_5 to n_2 might collide at n_2. Thus, cluster C_1 and C_2 must obey the f-MAC rule set together. After computing the equations in Rule#3, the following set of k_i can be chosen for the clusters: $k_1 = 3$, $k_2 = 5$, $k_3 = 7$, $k_4 = 8$, $k_5 = 11$. Now, in C_1 and C_2 $k_{max} = 11$ is obtained and the upper bound for the transmission delay is $T_{max} = 89 \cdot \delta$. Cluster C_3, containing another three nodes (n_5, n_6, n_7) can now be added in a more simplistic way. $k_5 = 11$ can be maintained, for n_6 $k_6 = 3$ can be selected as n_1 is not in the collision domain of C_3. For the same reason, $k_7 = 7$ can be selected for n_7. Now the clusters are setup and can be used with the f-MAC protocol.

5.2   Cluster Forming

Obviously, a method is necessary to form clusters and compute the k_i after a field is first set-up. This can be done statically after deployment, or a dynamic

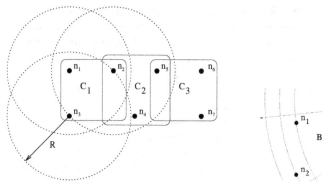
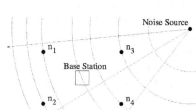
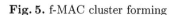

Fig. 5. f-MAC cluster forming   **Fig. 6.** Noise-event detection

protocol for cluster forming has to be used. This paper focus on the investigation of the basic features of f-MAC and therefore cluster forming techniques are not discussed in this paper.

6   f-MAC Application Areas

The two exemplary application areas described in this Section benefit from the use of f-MAC.

The first application is the use of f-MAC to realise deterministic sensor networks. As f-MAC provides hard guarantees on the information transfer delay, it can be used as one building block of a sensor network that can guarantee proper functioning in all possible operation cases. The second application is the use of f-MAC to realise a sensor network that is used for time critical event detection.

For both described areas other solutions than f-MAC exist. However, for some characteristics of the described applications, f-MAC represents the better solution.

6.1   Worst Case Dimensioning

Application areas for wireless sensor networks may encompass production surveillance, road traffic management, medical care or military applications. In these areas it is crucial to ensure that the sensor network is functioning even under worst case circumstances.

Analytical tools such as network calculus can be used to determine the numerical range of network properties such as message transfer delay and node buffer requirements [7]. It is then possible to dimension the sensor nodes in a way such that all possible (even the worst cases) traffic scenarios can be supported by the network. Supported means here that the specifications regarding message transfer delay or node buffer requirements stay within the defined bounds at any time.

To implement a sensor network that complies with the analytically determined specifications, deterministic network components are necessary. For example it is necessary to give a maximum upper bound for the message forwarding delay. Hence it is necessary to have a deterministic MAC layer. Contention based MAC protocols do not provide these guarantees. Collisions may occur and a back-off time is necessary. It is not possible to give an upper bound for the amount of back-offs that are necessary to transmit a message successfully. Thus, scheduled based MAC protocols are used if deterministic behaviour of the MAC protocol is required. These protocols have the desired deterministic behaviour but need a complicated and energy expensive time synchronisation among the nodes.

f-MAC provides the necessary deterministic behaviour in the MAC layer without costly time synchronisation. Thus, f-MAC can be seen as a building block for wireless sensor networks with deterministic behaviour.

6.2   Time Critical Event Detection

Sensor networks are often used to observe time critical events. For these kind of measurements it is necessary to associate measurements with the accurate point in time when they were taken. Particularly, if all measurements are analyzed at one point (e.g. a base station), it must be known at which point in time the measurements were taken. The example of such an application is shown in Fig. 6. The figure shows a base station and 4 sensors. The sensors are used to detect a specific acoustic event (e.g. a loud bang). Immediately after detection of the event a message is generated and sent to the base station. If the base station knows now when each of the sensors detected the event, it can calculate the position of the noise source. This is possible because the sound wave needs different times to reach each of the sensors.

Each sensor node places a time-stamp in each message sent towards the base station. Either a time synchronisation among the nodes is used or the base station determines the time offset of each node after the measurement was reported [6]. However, time synchronisation among nodes might not be possible or is too costly and the determination of time offsets after event detection needs additional protocol steps.

To work around these problems, f-MAC can be used. Each node detecting an event can immediately send a message to the base-station. The base station can then, knowing which framelet of a transmission was received and which k_i was used, compute the time when the event was detected. This is possible as f-MAC provides a deterministic message delay. In this case no time synchronization among the nodes or additional protocol steps are necessary. Another advantage of using f-MAC for the described application is the fact that collisions can be handled. The detection of the acoustic event is very close together in time at each sensor. Therefore, if a contention based MAC protocol would be used, collisions would occur and the nodes would need to deal with this problem as well. This will increase the hardware complexity of the sensor node; an f-MAC sensor is simpler as it only has to send the framelets (no carrier sensing feature is necessary).

For the given application scenario, f-MAC provides a simpler alternative solution.

7   Related Work

MAC protocols for sensor networks can be coarsley classified in two groups: contention based and schedule based. Examples of contention based protocols are S-MAC [8] and T-MAC [9]. Representatives of the schedule based approach are TRAMA [10] and μ-MAC [11]. The primary design goal of most MAC protocols for the area of wireless networks is energy efficiency and channel utilization. The primary design goal of the presented f-MAC protocol in contrast is a deterministic, collision-free behavior without time synchronization.

f-MAC shares with the contention based approach the lack of coordination between contending nodes for shared medium access. However, f-MAC differs from the cited contention based approaches because it is able to prevent message losses due to collisions with 100% guarantee. Schedule based protocols are are able to ensure collision-free communication but they invariably require some form of coordination between nodes. Mainly, time synchronisation among nodes is used which is not required in in the presented f-MAC protocol.

The Bitmac [12] protocol differs from the previously described, classical protocols and has similar properties and design goals as the presented f-MAC. Simmilar to f-MAC, collisions are not seen as "bad thing". If several nodes transmit a bit at the same time, the transmission collides and the receiver gets the bitwise OR of the transmission. This feature can be used for specific applications in sensor networks. Additionally Bitmac has, similar to f-MAC, a deterministic behaviour. In difference to f-MAC, Bitmac requires synchronisation (time-division multiplexing) among nodes.

8   Conclusion

The paper presented the f-MAC protocol that allows the implementation of a deterministic MAC layer without the need of time synchronization among the nodes. The protocol is collision-free and thus gives hard guarantees on message transfer delays and available bandwidth. The price for the deterministic behavior is a low channel utilization. However, some application scenarios might require a deterministic behavior and not necessarily a high throughput.

As shown, the message transfer delay increases exponentially with the number of nodes present in the same collision domain. Similarly, bandwidth degrades exponentially with the number of nodes in the same collision domain. Therefore, in most cases, f-MAC is only useful in sparsely populated networks.

The protocol is relatively simple to implement and therefore useful in areas where nodes are resource constrained. A timer is necessary within each node to implement the protocol. This timer is needed to time the transmission of the framelets and to measure when a next message can be transmitted. This timer has to be accurate only during the relatively short transmission time of one message. Thus, relatively simple clocks can be used which helps an implementation of f-MAC in constrained environments.

As the delivery of at least one framelet of a message is guaranteed, a node does not have to perform a carrier sense. This is advantageous in a wireless environment as a reliable carrier sensing mechanism is difficult to implement. Additionally, the protocol deals with the hidden terminal problem. Two nodes which are not in radio range of each other can send simultaneously to a third node without additional protocol mechanisms (e.g. a CTS/RTS mechanism).

If power consumption has to be optimised within a network, f-MAC can be tuned in a way that duty cycles are implemented. In this case a message is repeated j times by a node (a message is sent j times using r framelets for each message transmission). The receiver can then alter between a short energy intensive listen period and a long energy saving sleep period (sleeping $j-1$ times, awake 1 time). In this case, the message delay is increased by the factor j.

Clustering is necessary if f-MAC is used in a larger network. The cluster configuration might be obtained by a clustering protocol or via static configuration. Within a mobile environment, this might lead to an unacceptable communication overhead to maintain a cluster structure. Therefore, f-MAC might be only suitable for a non mobile network environment.

Consolidated, f-MAC is useful in constrained, static and sparsely populated networks where guarantees on the message transport delay are required.

The f-MAC protocol was implemented within a simulation environment and it was shown that the protocol has a low complexity and is therefore suitable in the sensor network environment. Currently we are incorporating the protocol in our sensor platform to evaluate the protocol in a real environment.

Acknowledgments

The support of the Informatics Research Initiative of Enterprise Ireland is gratefully acknowledged.

References

1. B. O'Flynn, A. Barroso, S. Bellis, J. Benson, U. Roedig, K. Delaney, J. Barton, C. Sreenan, and C. O'Mathuna. The Development of a Novel Miniaturized Modular Platform for Wireless Sensor Networks. In Proceedings of the IPSN Track on Sensor Platform, Tools and Design Methods for Networked Embedded Systems (IPSN2005/SPOTS2005), Los Angeles, USA, April 2005.
2. S. Mahlknecht and M. Boeck. CSMA-MPS: A Minimum Preamble Sampling MAC Protocol for Low Power Wireless Sensor Networks. In Proceedings of the 5th IEEE International Workshop on Factory Communication Systems (WFCS2004), Vienna, Austria, September 2004.
3. Nordic Inc. nRF2401 Single Chip 2.4GHz Radio Transceiver Data Sheet, 2002.
4. NannoNET. nanoNET TRX Transceiver Data Sheet, http://www.nanotron.com.
5. Chipcon. CC2420 Transceiver Data Sheet, http://www.chipcon.com, 2004.

6. G. Simon, M. Maroti, A. Ledeczi, G. Balogh, B. Kusy, A. Nadas, G. Pap, J. Sallai, K. Frampton: Sensor Network-Based Countersniper System, SenSys 04, Baltimore, USA, November 2004
7. J. Schmitt and U. Roedig. Sensor Network Calculus - A Framework for Worst Case Analysis. In Proceedings of the International Conference on Distributed Computing in Sensor Systems (DCOSS05), Marina del Rey, USA, June 2005.
8. W. Ye, J. Heidemann, and D. Estrin. An energy-efficient MAC protocol for wireless sensor networks. In Proceedings of the IEEE Infocom 2002 (INFOCOM2002), New York, USA, June 2002.
9. T. van Dam and K. Langendoen. An adaptive energy-efficient mac protocol for wireless sensor networks. In Proceedings of the First ACM Conference on Embedded Networked Sensor Systems (SenSys 2003), Los Angeles, USA, November 2003.
10. V. Rajendran, K. Obraczka, and J. Garcia-Luna-Aceves. Energy-efficient, collision-free medium access control for wireless sensor networks. In Proceedings of the First ACM Conference on Embedded Networked Sensor Systems (SenSys 2003), Los Angeles, USA, November 2003.
11. A. Barroso, U. Roedig, and C. J. Sreenan. u-MAC: An Energy-Efficient Medium Access Control for Wireless Sensor Networks. In Proceedings of the 2nd IEEE European Workshop on Wireless Sensor Networks (EWSN2005), Istanbul, Turkey, January 2005.
12. M. Ringwald and K. Roemer. BitMAC: A Deterministic, Collision-Free, and Robust MAC Protocol for Sensor Networks. Proceedings of 2nd European Workshop on Wireless Sensor Networks (EWSN 2005), Istanbul, Turkey, January 2005.
13. B. Davidson and C. Bostian. A One-Way Packet Communication Channel with Retransmissions. SIGMOBILE Mobile Computing and Communication Review, vol. 2, no. 1, 1998.

A Measurement-Based Analysis of the Interaction Between Network Layers in TinyOS

Umberto Malesci[1,2] and Samuel Madden[1]

[1] MIT CSAIL, Cambridge, MA 02139
{umberto, madden}@csail.mit.edu
[2] Fluidmesh Networks, Inc., Boston, MA 02111
umberto.malesci@fluidmesh.com

Abstract. There have been a number of recent proposals for link and network-layer protocols in the sensor networking literature, each of which claims to be superior to other approaches. However, a proposal for a networking protocol at a given layer in the stack is typically evaluated in the context of a single set of carefully selected protocols at other layers. Because of the limited data available about interactions between different protocols at various layers of the stack, it is difficult for developers of sensor network applications to select from amongst the range of alternative sensor networking protocols. This paper evaluates the interaction between several protocols at the MAC and network layers measuring their performance in terms of end-to-end throughput and loss on a large testbed. We identify some common sources of poor performance; based on this experience, we propose a set of design principles for the designers of future interfaces.

1 Introduction

The sensor network community has proposed a number of different networking protocols for routing [14, 21], media access [4, 5, 8, 16, 17], and power management [6, 8, 16, 17]. Despite significant innovation in each of these areas, there has been little work addressing the interaction of protocols across areas into a single network stack. Published papers typically propose changes in one abstraction (e.g., a new MAC layer) while using some "default" implementation of the other abstractions (e.g., using the "standard" multihop routing protocol in TinyOS) and evaluating on a particular topology and a particular workload. This approach has led to a large number of competing protocol proposals which are difficult to compare with one another due to varying choices made by authors about appropriate defaults, application workloads, and network topologies. This makes it hard for an application designer to select the best set of protocols for his or her application and impossible for other researchers to understand whether claimed differences between protocols are simply due to artifacts in one experimenter's setup or are true differences between protocols.

In this paper, we focus on the TinyOS [7] operating system, because source code for many different protocol implementations is widely available and because it appears to be the current platform of choice for sensor network research. In TinyOS, problems related to the interactions between protocols are aggravated by significant disagreement in the community about how functionality should be spread across

K. Römer, H. Karl, and F. Mattern (Eds.): EWSN 2006, LNCS 3868, pp. 292–309, 2006.

different network 'layers'. Lines between layers are blurred, making innovation difficult and mixing and matching of implementations tricky as interfaces are poorly specified. As an example, consider per-link acknowledgments and retransmissions, which are widely regarded as an important feature for reducing loss in sensor networks. Different designers implement these features in different parts of the network stack. Retransmissions due to negative or failed acknowledgments can be implemented at either the link or network layers, as can duplicate suppression. Placement of these operations is not consistent across implementations; for example, the B-MAC [17] link/MAC protocol implements acknowledgments but assume that retransmissions and not duplicate suppression should be implemented in the layers above, whereas the S-MAC protocol implements all three. If a researcher wants to design a new 'network' layer, he must choose which of ACKs, retransmissions, and duplicate suppression to implement. These choices will invariably tie his implementation to a particular MAC layer and limit the generality and impact of his work; worse yet, due to unstated assumptions in various implementations, he may believe his protocol will work with a particular MAC layer only to find it does not. If the abstraction boundaries between layers were more cleanly implemented and specified, these issues would not arise.

In this paper, we present a systematic study of the performance (in terms of network loss rate) of different combinations of MAC, routing, forwarding, and power management protocols that have been previously proposed in the literature. Our aim is to provide measurements that will enable a first step towards fixing these problems with the network protocols in TinyOS by:

1. Benchmarking several widely published protocols with the same application workload and on the same network topology.
2. Highlighting the significant differences between different implementations protocols that are ostensibly at the same 'layer'.
3. Illustrating a number of examples where interactions between different layers lead to significant performance degradation.
4. Recommending combinations of protocols for particular application workloads.
5. Illustrating that no one protocol at any of these layers strictly dominates any other protocol (despite claims to the contrary in the literature), and that there are many hidden assumptions and subtle issues with even widely used network protocols.

The purpose of this paper is not to proscribe a specific layering or to suggest that one implementation is better than another. Rather, we aim illustrate some of the limitations of the current state of software in TinyOS so that the community can move towards a cleaner set of interfaces that support greater protocol diversity and allow application developers to make more informed choices about the appropriate selection of networking protocols.

2 Sensor Network Architecture

A common architecture and set of abstractions has emerged for the network stack for wireless sensor networks. As in most network architectures, the basic abstraction is the layer. However, the TinyOS network stack differs from the traditional Internet stack in several ways:

- Layers make abundant use of cross-layering in order to increase throughput and decrease power consumption [10].
- Power management is present in many different forms in several layers.

The network stack in TinyOS can be broken into four major layers: the physical layer, the link/MAC layer (to keep consistent with the naming using in many publications, we refer to this simply as the MAC layer in the remainder of this paper), the forwarding/routing layer (we refer to this as the routing layer in the remainder of this text), and the application layer. Moreover, the network stack also performs other two major services that are not present in Internet routing: power management and link-quality estimation.

This paper mainly focuses on the analysis of the interaction between MAC layer, routing layer, and power management taking into consideration the application-specific requirements.

2.1 MAC Layer

As far as the Medium Access Control (MAC) protocol is concerned, the major distinction is between the use of TDMA or CSMA to negotiate channel access. In this paper, we focus on CSMA-based implementations, because, although several TDMA protocols have been proposed [4], they are not available in implementations that are easily integrated with existing multi-hop forwarding and routing protocols.

The different MAC protocols developed for sensor network also differ in the additional services that they provide. For example, some MAC protocols, such as S-MAC [8, 16], also perform link level acknowledgment and retransmission and hidden-terminal avoidance via RTS/CTS. Moreover many MAC protocol also take care of power management for the entire network stack [8, 16, 17]. However, the needs of the application layer are not always considered when the MAC protocol takes care of power management. For example, often the application needs require the mote to wake up and sense the environment at specific times and rates that are not the same as the forwarding needs of the communication stack.

Contention-Based Approaches

Contention-based approaches rely on protocols that detect and avoid packet-collisions. Packet-collisions are detected by means of acknowledgment packets and can be partially avoided using RTS/CTS (Request-To-Send/Clear-To-Send) packets as well as exponential back-off on resend when a collision occurs. The major advantages of contention-based MAC protocols are:

- No need for a very precise time-synchronization between the devices [8].
- Flexibility in terms of both changes in the network topology and changes in the data-rates.

On the other hand, the major disadvantages of contention-based MAC protocols are related to the possible contention for the medium and to the lack of innate energy management mechanisms:

- Collisions increase the number of retransmissions and decrease channel capacity.
- They require the use of RTS/CTS packets to avoid collisions or per-link acknowledgment packets to determine if a collision occurred.

- Power management is difficult. Inserting a duty cycle in CSMA-based protocols requires both time-scheduling and time-synchronization. Without such mechanisms, motes always listen to the channel, wasting energy [5].

Power management is often performed in the MAC layer and there are several contention-based protocols designed for sensor networks that introduce duty-cycles in order to save energy [5, 7, 8].

TDMA-Based Approaches

Though we do not experimentally evaluate TDMA, we briefly survey its merits because it has some attractive properties that potentially make it useful in sensor networks. In TDMA, a single radio-frequency channel is divided into multiple time slots. Each time slot is assigned to a different device (e.g. mote) that requires access to the medium. The two main strengths of the TDMA-based approach are that it eliminates packet collisions since every device transmits during a different time slot and that it provides a built-in power management scheme since devices only need to be "on" in slots when they are sending or receiving data [4].

The major disadvantages of the TDMA approach in sensor networks is that it requires precise time synchronization and provides a fixed, inflexible bandwidth allocation to every node.

In addition to pure TDMA, Hohlt et al [6] propose a hybrid solution, where transmission is scheduled using time slots, but medium contention and packet collisions are still possible. This hybrid approach reduces medium contention by assigning different time slots to different clusters of motes, while simultaneously avoiding complexities in terms of time-synchronization that a full TDMA solution would require. However, the current implementation only allows a one-way communication toward the root of the routing tree and it therefore cannot be deployed with many data-collection applications, such as TinyDB [9], that need broadcast and multicast communication as well. Hence, we could not evaluate it in this study.

2.2 Routing Layer

Multi-hop protocols are widely used in sensor networks because, by multi-hopping, nodes are able to send data-packets beyond the transmission range of a single low-power radio.

In tree-based multi-hop routing, every node in the network keeps a neighborhood table containing the best neighbor nodes that it can use to route packets toward the root of the tree. A node has a parent that it uses to route packets toward the root; the routing protocol decides which neighbor node should play this role and when it should switch parents. The most recent multi-hop protocols base routing decisions on the number of hops and on the estimated link quality [14, 15, 21].

Some services such as link-level retransmission and link-quality estimation are performed in the routing layer in some implementations and in the MAC layers in other implementations. This irregularity regarding the placement of key services inside the network stack makes designing a new, general-purpose implementation of a specific network layer difficult, as the layer will have to make assumptions about the services provided by other layers that will invariably tie it to one set of accompanying implementations. For example, some routing protocols rely heavily on snooping packets addressed to other nodes [14]. Therefore, power management schemes implemented in the MAC layer that save energy by decreasing overhearing will break when used with such routing protocols.

This tight and non-standardized correlation between the services required by the routing protocol and the services provided by the underlying MAC layer make many implementations difficult to reuse across multiple implementations; in Sections 4 and 5, we illustrate a number of such problems that exist in practice today, and discuss some design options for remedying these problems in Section 6.

2.3 Power Management

Many sensor network applications require the network to survive several months or years in the field without changing batteries. To achieve such lifetimes, it is necessary to keep devices in a low-power ("sleeping") state most of the time. The devices wake up only when they need to perform a particular task, such as sensing or receiving and transmitting data. This duty cycling needs to adapt to different application-specific data rates and to variable network sizes.

Power management is often performed in the MAC layer and there are several contention-based protocols designed for sensor networks that introduce duty-cycles in order to save energy [5, 8, 16, 17]. Some protocols, such as B-MAC, implement a power management scheme (called "low-power listening" by the B-MAC designers) that increases packet preamble length (and hence transmission costs) but decreases idle-listening costs by requiring nodes to listen for packet transmissions only once per preamble period. Note, however, that this approach does not solve the "problem" of nodes consuming power listening to packets addressed to other nodes.

Other protocols, such as S-MAC [8, 16] or T-MAC [5], employ a listen/sleep duty-cycle, creating a cluster of neighboring nodes that share the same schedule and therefore wake up and go to sleep all at the same time.

Another commonly used power management scheme for sensor nets, used in the TASK/TinyDB system [1], works at the application layer and divides the time into two frames; an active frame and a sleeping frame. In the active frame, motes transmit and route the data-packets that were queued during the sleeping frame. Due to the large size of the two frames, this approach does not need very precise time-synchronization. However, it is not very flexible because the size of the frames is fixed and does not adapt to either the network size or to the traffic characteristics.

3 Studied Implementations

We focused our effort in working with routing, MAC and power management protocols that have been implemented using the TinyOS platform. Unfortunately only a small percentage of all the protocols that have been proposed in the literature have a mature and robust enough implementation that can be integrated and used on a real test bed. Therefore, we had to limit the research are to two different MAC protocols (B-MAC [17] and S-MAC [8, 16]) and three different routing protocols (/lib/Route, MINTRoute and ReliableRoute [14]). Both B-MAC and S-MAC implement a power management scheme integrated with the MAC layer, therefore in our experiments changing MAC protocol meant also changing power management scheme. Within each protocol variant, we look at performance differences with and without power management.

3.1 MAC Protocols

B-MAC and S-MAC are the most mature and widely used MAC protocols within the TinyOS project. They are both based on packet-collision avoidance schemes and they both integrate a power management scheme within the MAC protocol. However, they differ greatly in their architecture, in the additional services they provide, and in the techniques they use to achieve energy-efficient operations.

B-MAC

The standard TinyOS MAC protocol is a contention-based protocol called B-MAC [17]. As discussed above, B-MAC provides power management via low-power listening; the "recommended" preamble length in B-MAC is 100ms [17], which is the value we use here. B-MAC has been shown to outperform other MAC protocols in previous studies [17], and has been carefully tuned for the radio used in Mica2 motes like those in our deployment.

On Mica2 nodes with CC1000 radios, B-MAC supports synchronous acknowledgments that require only a few extra bit-times on the end of each packet to transmit. This depends on the ability of the sender and receiver to quickly switch roles at the end of a packet transmission and remain synchronized before any additional sender can sense an idle channel and begin transmitting.

B-MAC does not perform link-level retransmission or hidden terminal avoidance using RTS/CTS schemes. The designers assume that such protocols will be implemented at higher layers if necessary.

In B-MAC, every mote overhears every packet transmitted; this allows high-layer network protocols to employ snooping for link-quality estimation [14] and in-network processing [9].

The designers of B-MAC do not assume that a single set of parameters will work with every possible application and they do not try to make B-MAC oblivious to the protocols that run above it. Instead, B-MAC offers control to the protocols that sit on top of it, allowing to the routing and application layers to change parameters like the low-power listening duration or the number and type of retransmissions used. The idea is to enable cross-layer optimization without imposing a particular API on end users. Unfortunately, as far as we know, most implemented routing layers do not make use of this cross-layer tuning API.

The authors of BMAC [17] claim that their protocol consistently delivers 98,5% of packets. Our results show that, in fact, such low loss rates are only possible under optimal conditions, and that, in many cases, BMAC performs far worse, delivering a relatively small fraction of packets even under lightly loaded conditions.

S-MAC

S-MAC [8, 16] is a contention based MAC protocol that adds into the MAC layer power management, link-level retransmission, duplicate packet suppression, hidden terminal avoidance using RTS/CTS, and link-quality estimation.

The power management scheme is based on shared schedules between "neighborhoods" of small groups of motes. Some motes follow more than one schedule simultaneously and therefore are able to forward packets from one neighborhood to another.

The S-MAC power management scheme tries to minimize energy consumption by decreasing the overhearing of other motes' transmissions. Motes sleep when they detect a transmission not addressed to them, and neighborhoods deactivate during times when they are not actively scheduled.

Unlike B-MAC, S-MAC does not provide any way for the higher layers to change its MAC parameters but assumes, as in Internet routing, that every layer can be completely separated and independent from the others.

3.2 Routing Protocols

The three different routing protocols we tested differ in terms of both the routing algorithm and the services they provide. /lib/Route seeks to minimizes the number of hops that each packet traverses. On the other hand, MINTRoute and ReliableRoute route packets based on link-quality estimates that seek to maximize the probability of a packet being delivered.

/lib/Route. Route was the standard routing protocol in TinyOS 1.1.0; it has been supplanted by MINTRoute. Route performs link-quality estimates but bases routing decisions mainly on hop count, using link-quality estimates simply as a threshold to prune very low quality links.

MINTRoute. MINTRoute is the new standard routing protocol for TinyOS. Unlike /lib/Route, MINTRoute bases its routing decisions mainly on link-quality estimates rather than minimum hop count. The quality estimates for sending and receiving are used to select a parent that will minimize the expected number of transmissions to reach the root of the network. The literature [1, 14, 15, 21] reports better performance using link quality estimates rather than minimum hop count. Moreover, MINTRoute adds to /lib/Route a topology stabilization mechanism in order to avoid frequent parent switching.

MINTRoute's design and implementation involves several hidden assumptions that make it inappropriate under certain conditions. For example, MINTRoute assumes the capability to snoop every neighbor's packets. This makes using MINTRoute with a MAC that doesn't conform to this specification (such as S-MAC) problematic; we discuss this issue further in Section 5.

ReliableRoute. ReliableRoute uses the same routing algorithm as MINTRoute but implements link-level retransmissions. However, it does not implement duplicate suppression; to provide valid end-to-end throughput results, we implemented a duplicate suppression algorithm for purposes of our experiments. By default ReliableRoute performs up to 5 link-level retransmissions. In our experiments we decreased the maximum number of retransmissions to 3 in order to achieve consistency with S-MAC which also performs up to 3 retransmissions by default.

ReliableRoute performs packet retransmissions based on acknowledgement information that it expects the MAC layer to provide and therefore does not work with any MAC protocol, such as S-MAC, that does not conform to this specification.

3.3 Application Workload

Our experiments use a workload similar to that of many environmental monitoring applications like TinyDB [9] or Surge (a simple TinyOS application designed to collect readings from all motes in a network at a fixed rate).

Environmental monitoring applications, broadly speaking, have low, fixed data rates, require relatively long-lived deployments, do not require reliable data delivery, are tolerant of a high degree of latency, are generally many-to-one (e.g., can use tree-based routing.) As our work is mainly focused on sensor networks for data collection, we use several different workloads of this type. In particular, we use different routing and MAC layers under the Surge application.

4 Evaluations and Experiments

In this section, we study the performance of the different MAC and routing protocols under different application workloads. All our results are based on experiments run on a 61-a Mica2 [18] and Cricket [19] test bed which covers about 20,000 square feet and 8-10 network hops. Although both types of motes are able to run the same executables, in order to ensure consistent results, we run only on the Mica2 motes, therefore using only 46 out of 61 motes. Each Mica2 mote has an Atmel ATmega128L processor with 4 KB of RAM, 128 KB of flash, and a CC1000 433 MHz radio that modulates at 38.4 symbols per second using Manchester encoding. Moreover, each mote was attached to a Crossbow MIB6000 Ethernet interface board. The board provides power to the mote and allows remote reprogramming and data collection via Ethernet. We managed and controlled the entire testbed though a Motelab [3]-based web interface.

In all experiments, each mote was running the same version of Surge (TinyOS 1.1.0 release [7]). Surge transmits sensor readings at a fixed rate. We ran our experiments at several different data rates; we report here results where we send one packet every 10 seconds and one packet every 60 seconds, representing a high-load and a low-load scenario.

One packet every 10 seconds creates a high-contention situation even with no power-management scheme enabled. Polastre et al. [17] show that a 20-node Mica2 network can deliver (in aggregate) about 16 packets per second when running B-MAC. With 46 nodes each sending 1 packet every 10 seconds, with an average of node-depth of 3, the entire network sends 13.5 packets per second, which is close B-MAC maximum throughput capabilities. Following the trends shown by Polastre et al. [17], we expect our 46 node network to have somewhat less throughput than a 20 node network.

At a rate of 60 seconds per packet, we generate 2.25 packets per seconds on the network, clearly below the B-MAC throughput limits.

4.1 B-MAC

In our experiments with B-MAC we varied three different parameters: the routing protocol, the transmission rate and the preamble duration. We tested the latest version

Table 1. Performance usingz B-MAC and various routing protocols

B-MAC Always On				
High Data Rate (10 seconds period)				
Protocol	Throughput			
	Avg.	σ	Max.	Min.
MINT	56%	12%	72%	45%
/lib/Route	48%	2%	51%	46%
Reliable Route	47%	6%	54%	41%
Low Data Rate (60 seconds period)				
Protocol	Throughput			
	Avg.	σ	Max.	Min.
MINT	49%	5%	54%	43%
/lib/Route	61%	14%	82%	47%
Reliable Route	55%	10%	71%	45%
B-MAC LPL 100 ms				
High Data Rate (10 seconds period)				
Protocol	Throughput			
	Avg.	σ	Max.	Min.
MINT	37%	3%	41%	33%
/lib/Route	24%	7%	33%	17%
Low Data Rate (60 seconds period)				
Protocol	Throughput			
	Avg.	σ	Max.	Min.
MINT	40%	2%	43%	39%
/lib/Route	24%	11%	34%	8%

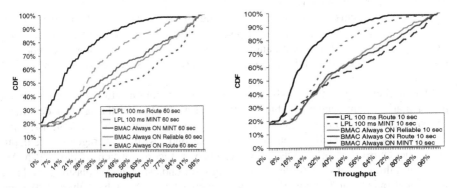

Fig. 1. On the left, CDF of the average throughput using various configurations of B-MAC and 60 sec data rate. Here, steeper, more convex curves indicate worse performance (as fewer nodes achieve high throughput), whereas more concave curves indicate better performance. On the right, CDF of the average throughput using various configurations of B-MAC and 10 sec data rate.

of B-MAC [17] using three different routing protocols: /lib/Route, MINTRoute, and ReliableRoute. We performed experiments at both high and low data rate. We used two variants of power management: in "always-on" mode and using low-power listening with the default preamble length of 100 ms. Unfortunately there is no existing implementation of ReliableRoute integrated with low-power listening.

Therefore, the combination ReliableRoute LPL is missing in Table 1. Each experiment ran for 60 minutes and was repeated 5-8 times.

We measured throughput by calculating the percentage of messages sent by the motes that were actually collected by the root node. Table 1 shows the results using different power-management schemes and traffic conditions. Here, avg. and σ represent the average throughput and the standard deviation of all trials, min and max represent the best and worst trial in the set.

From the results reported in Table 1 and Figure 1, we observe:

- In always-on mode and under high data rate conditions, there is no significant difference in performance among the different routing protocols. We believe this is due to frequent packets collisions that void the benefits that any particular routing metric provides.
- In always-on mode and under low-traffic conditions, /lib/Route performs better than MINTRoute and ReliableRoute. However, in always-on mode the throughput of the various protocols is not dramatically different; our results in Section 5.2 suggest that B-MAC may not be well suited to the particular application workload generated by Surge.
- Link-level retransmissions slightly improve throughput when medium contention is low, but decrease throughput when medium contention is high. Link-level retransmissions create a trade-off: on one hand they increase the probability that a particular packet is successfully received; on the other hand, they increase medium contention by increasing the average number of packets that need to be transmitted.

4.2 S-MAC

As with B-MAC, in our experiments with S-MAC we varied the routing protocol, the transmission rate and the duty cycle. We tested the latest version of S-MAC (version 1.2) using: /lib/Route and MINTRoute (we did not try ReliableRoute because S-MAC implements retransmissions at the link layer).

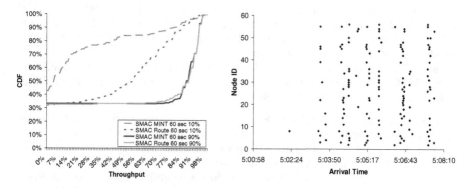

Fig. 2. On the left, average throughput CDF using various configurations of S-MAC with 60 sec data rate. On the right, arrival pattern of packets at the root node using S-MAC/Route with 10% duty cycle at 60 sec data rate.

Table 2. Performance of S-MAC at 90% duty cycle and various routing protocols

Table 3. Performance of S-MAC at 10% duty cycle and various routing protocols

S-MAC 90% duty cycle				
High Data Rate (10 seconds period)				
Protocol		Throughput		
	Avg.	σ	Max	Min
MINT	44%	13%	61%	26%
/lib/Route	31%	10%	40%	20%

Low Data Rate (60 seconds period)				
Protocol		Throughput		
	Avg.	σ	Max	Min
Route	90%	3%	92%	85%
/lib/Route	89%	2%	91%	87%

S-MAC 90% duty cycle (no retransmit)				
High Data Rate (10 seconds period)				
Protocol		Throughput		
	Avg.	σ	Max	Min
Route	32%	15%	45%	6%
/lib/Route	26%	7%	36%	19%

Low Data Rate (60 seconds period)				
Protocol		Throughput		
	Avg.	σ	Max	Min
Route	90%	1%	91%	88%
/lib/Route	85%	3%	87%	80%

S-MAC 10% duty cycle				
High Data Rate (10 seconds period)				
Protocol		Throughput		
	Avg.	σ	Max	Min
MINT	13%	7%	19%	2%
/lib/Route	20%	9%	36%	14%

Low Data Rate (60 seconds period)				
Protocol		Throughput		
	Avg.	σ	Max	Min
Route	36%	7%	45%	28%
/lib/Route	63%	10%	74%	50%

S-MAC 10% duty cycle (no retransmit)				
High Data Rate (10 seconds period)				
Protocol		Throughput		
	Avg.	σ	Max	Min
Route	16%	4%	21%	10%
/lib/Route	26%	7%	36%	19%

Low Data Rate (60 seconds period)				
Protocol		Throughput		
	Avg.	σ	Max	Min
Route	37%	4%	42%	31%
/lib/Route	84%	3%	88%	81%

We use the same high-rate and low-rate workloads as in the previous section. We tested S-MAC using two duty cycles: 90% and 10%. The latter is the default value for S-MAC and we picked 90% because is close to always-on mode but it still involves scheduling and neighborhood management.

Tables 2 and 3 show the results under different duty cycles and traffic conditions, with S-MAC with and without link-level retransmissions. From the results in Table 2 and 3 and from Figures 2 and 3, we observe:

- As in the case of B-MAC, link-level retransmissions do not always improve end-to-end throughput. At 90% duty cycle retransmissions slightly improve end-to-end throughput at both rates. However, at 10% duty cycle, when medium contention is higher, retransmissions consistently harm end-to-end throughput.
- At 90% duty cycle, MINTRoute performs slightly better than /lib/Route. However, at 10% duty cycle /lib/Route substantially outperforms MINTRoute.
- By studying the nodes routing tables, we determined that nodes using MINTRoute had difficulty finding a parent and tended to lose their parent once they found one. We believe this is because MINTRoute takes advantage of snooping to perform link-quality estimation and it is unable to cope with a MAC

layer that saves energy by turning off the radio to reduce idle-listening. On the other hand, the /lib/Route algorithm is based mainly on minimum hop count and is much more robust under low duty cycle operations.

- From Figures 3 we can see that increasing the S-MAC duty cycle creates instability in the parent selection algorithm. Figure 3 (left) shows stable parent selection when a 90% duty cycle is used. Figure 3 (right) shows that parent selection becomes unstable and parent switching more frequent with a 10% duty cycle.
- By looking at Figure 2 (right), we deduce that S-MAC duty cycling is able to spread in time packets that are simultaneously transmitted by all nodes and therefore take advantage of additional medium capacity.

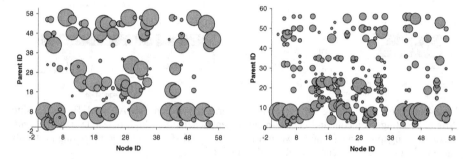

Fig. 3. On the left, parent distribution based on child's node ID using S-MAC with 90% duty cycle, Route and 60 sec. data rate. Circle size is proportional to the number of times a given node routed data via a given parent. On the right, parent distribution based on child's node ID using S-MAC with 10% duty cycle, Route and 60 sec. data rate.

5 Overall Performance

In this section, we compare the performance results from S-MAC and B-MAC to further study the source of many of the differences that we observed. Table 4 and Figure 4 summarizes our results.

Table 4. Best protocol combinations matrix with respective average throughput

POWER MANAGEMENT

		Enabled	Disabled
DATA RATE	**High**	MINTRoute B-MAC 37%	MINTRoute B-MAC 51%
	Low	Route S-MAC 84%	MINTRoute S-MAC 90%

In the low-contention scenario with a data rate of 1 packet per minute (Figure 4, right), S-MAC with Route clearly outperforms all the other combinations of MAC and routing protocols. S-MAC at 10% duty cycle with Route reaches a throughput nearly equivalent to S-MAC at 90% duty cycle and much higher than B-MAC in any configuration.

In the high data rate scenario (Figure 4, left), the best configuration was B-MAC in always-on mode with MINTRoute.

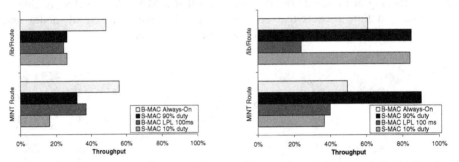

Fig. 4. *On the left*, average throughput comparison between S-MAC and B-MAC using different routing protocols and energy-management scheme and high data rate. *On the right*, average throughput comparison between S-MAC and B-MAC using different routing protocols and energy-management scheme and low data rate (60 sec).

5.1 Power Management

Looking at the results for low-power configurations in Figure 5, B-MAC Low Power Listening with a preamble of 100 ms and MINTRoute clearly outperformed S-MAC at 10% duty cycle, either with Route or MINTRoute. However, in the high-rate, low-power scenario, no configuration was able to exceed a 50% throughput (even with retransmissions), making all the studied protocols inappropriate for the majority of real-life applications.

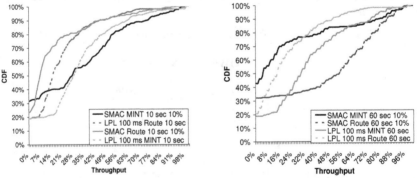

Fig. 5. On the left, CDF of throughput at high data rate (10 sec) using Low Power Listening with B-MAC or 10% duty cycle with S-MAC. On the right, CDF of throughput using Low Power Listening with B-MAC or 10% duty cycle with S-MAC and low data rate (60 sec).

Figure 5 (right) shows the CDF of the throughput for the experiment at 60 sec. data rate experiments with power management enabled. Notice that the curve corresponding to S-MAC with Route is much more concave than the others, suggesting that a large fraction of nodes is able to achieve relatively high throughputs, whereas other approaches performed quite poorly in this setting.

5.2   Inter-arrival Time of Send Requests

The application layer strongly influences the performance of the entire network. We varied the pattern of send requests across different nodes and studied how this variation impacts the performance of both B-MAC and S-MAC. In the standard case, nodes in Surge transmit data at the beginning of every time period with no randomization; since nodes begin running at about the same time, this leads many send requests occurring at the same time across many nodes . To study the effect of eliminating this bursty behavior, we forced nodes to be out of phase by having them delay by a time proportional to their node ID. Using B-MAC, the average throughput increased from 49% to 93% transmitting at 60 sec. per packet rate and from 56% to 91% transmitting at 10 sec. per packet rate (Figure 6).   With S-MAC, we see no benefits from using this technique, since S-MAC already spreads results in time (as shown in Figure 2, right).

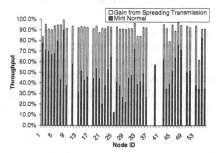

Fig. 6. Average throughput per node. MAC/MINT combination at data rate of 10 sec data rate with and without application-level delays between sending at different nodes ("spreading").

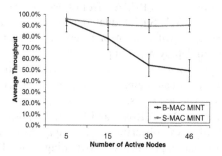

Fig. 7. Average throughput of B-MAC and S-MAC as network size varies. B-MAC is in always-on mode at 60 sec data rate, S-MAC is at 90% duty cycle and 60 sec data rate. Error bars are ±2σ.

5.3 Scaling Issues

Figure 7 shows the performance of S-MAC and B-MAC with networks of different sizes. From these experiments, it is clear that B-MAC does not scale as well as S-MAC since the end-to-end average throughput decreases as we increase the number of transmitting nodes in the network. Using B-MAC and MINTRoute and a data rate of 60 seconds per packet, we measured an average throughput of 78% when we had only 15 nodes operational and of 49% when we had 46 nodes operational. On the other hand, because S-MAC partitions the network into different schedules and spreads sending over time, it is able to scale much better – in fact, we did not see any performance degradation as we increased the network size.

6 Discussion

Here we briefly relate some observations derived from our performance analysis of the state of networking in TinyOS:

- Some power management schemes (and MAC layers) prohibit snooping on non-local radio traffic while some applications and routing layers rely on snooping for proper functioning. This is a fundamental issue that limits the ability to intermix different layer implementations. We discuss this issue in Section 6.1 in more details.
- Tuning power management settings (e.g., LPL preamble length and S-MAC sleep percentage) as well as other constants (e.g., link quality thresholds) is very hard for application designers, and making appropriate choices can dramatically affect application performance. For example, we saw that large, high-rate, power-managed networks with default power management settings in TinyOS perform poorly with any combination of MAC/routing layer, while small networks can perform quite well with default power management settings. Even when interfaces for tuning parameters are provided (as in B-MAC), it is often unclear how adjusting these settings will affect network performance.
- Application workload and type of traffic dramatically affect network throughput. For example, we saw how introducing delays at the application can increase network average throughput in B-MAC from 50% to 90%, but that such changes have little effect on S-MAC. Such hidden dependencies make it very difficult for application designers to switch from one network stack to another and can be quite frustrating when deploying an application.
- No MAC/routing combination wins in every possible situation. The choice of MAC layer, in particular, can dramatically affect the effective channel utilization of applications in unexpected ways.
- Aside from issues where MINTRoute and S-MAC's power management scheme interacted very badly, we observed surprisingly little sensitivity to routing protocol in any of our experiments. Switching from Route to MINTRoute increases overall throughput by about 5% (s=3.1%) (excluding the S-MAC at 10% duty-cycle case). In contrast, choosing the appropriate MAC for a given workload affects the overall throughput by about 16% on average.

- Link-level retransmissions do not always help and sometimes they hurt end-to-end throughput by increasing overall network contention. We discuss this issue in more detail in Section 6.2.
- Some protocols do not scale properly when run on larger networks. For example, B-MAC's performance with 46 transmitting nodes is 30% lower than with only 15 transmitting nodes. This effect is much less pronounced with S-MAC.

6.1 The Idle Listening vs. Snooping Trade-Off

Our experiments suggest that there is a fundamental tradeoff between reducing idle-listening and utilizing overhearing in sensor networks.

There appear to be two primary uses for overhearing: in in-network processing, with applications such as TinyDB [9] or monitoring diffusion phenomena [11], and in network protocols such as MINTRoute that use it to collect statistics about network performance. In the former case, overheard messages are used to improve performance but are not necessary for correctness; in the latter case, as in MINTRoute, overhearing is necessary for acceptable network performance. In cases when the ability to overhear is impaired (as when S-MAC shuts off the radio channel), very bad behavior can result.

In the literature there are several examples of successful link-quality estimation techniques that do not involve overhearing of unicast packets addressed to other nodes [15, 21]. Therefore, we believe that link-quality estimation can be performed without the need for overhearing, which suggests that building routing protocols that depend on it is probably a bad idea (since any power-conscious application will turn off the radio at least some of the time).

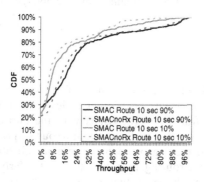

Fig. 8. Throughput CDF using S-MAC and varying the maximum number of link-level retransmissions and the data rate

6.2 Link-Level Retransmissions

Several proposals have claimed that link-level retransmissions substantially increase reliability of wireless sensor networks [13, 14, 17].

Our results show that this is not always the case. Link-level retransmissions present a trade-off between increasing the probability of end-to-end transmission success and decreasing overall medium-contention. From our results, we noticed that if the network is not congested, link-level retransmission tends to benefit the overall end-to-end throughput. However, in cases where the network is already congested, link-level retransmissions actually decrease overall throughput, as illustrated in Figure 8. This figure illustrates that at high duty cycles when medium-contention is low, link-level retransmissions improve throughput; on the other hand, at low duty cycle when medium-contention is high, link-level retransmissions decrease performance.

These observations suggest that network protocols need some facility to determine if losses are due to contention or simply transient external interference.

6.3 Cross-Layering

Others have noted the porosity of network layers and the extent of cross-layering optimization in sensor networks [10, 20]. We observed this as well; for example, different components of the routing layer choose to implement different parts of link-layer retransmissions in different layers. In the case of B-MAC, for example, the application implements duplicate suppression, the network layer implements retransmissions, and the MAC layer implements acknowledgements. This makes the job of application designers very difficult. Our experience suggests that this cross-layering is a source of incompatibility among protocols, since, as with the routing and link layers in B-MAC, it tends to create coupled sets of layers that depend on specific, non-standard cross-layer APIs. Though this coupling may help increase performance of a single application or network stack in the short-term, careless cross-layering limits the ability of protocol designers to innovate at different layers and will ultimately make developing solid implementations of sensor network protocols very hard. Hence, the sensor network community must converge on standard APIs and agree to abide by them.

7 Conclusion

By studying how different combinations of MAC, routing, and power management schemes interact with each other under several different application workloads, we have illustrated several issues with the current state of protocol implementations in TinyOS. First, and somewhat to our surprise, we found that no combination of MAC and routing protocols dominates all others, and that some combinations of MAC and routing protocols are particularly incompatible with one another. Second, we observed that some issues that we thought would dramatically affect performance (routing protocols, retransmissions) had little effect. Third, we observed (as others have), that cross-layer optimizations tend to blur lines between layers in sensor networks, and that this blurring makes the design of modular, interchangeable software components very difficult. We believe these lessons are an important step towards understanding the source of performance problems in sensor networks and that they will prove invaluable in our own and other's future work designing next generation protocol architectures for sensor networks.

References

1. P. Buonadonna, D. Gay, J. Hellerstein, W. Hong, and S. Madden: TASK: Sensor Network in a Box. European Workshop on Sensor Networks, January 2005.
2. Geoff Werner-Allen, Jeff Johnson, Mario Ruiz, Jonathan Lees, and Matt Welsh: Monitoring Volcanic Eruptions with a Wireless Sensor Network. European Workshop on Sensor Networks, January 2005.
3. M. Welsh, and G. Werner-Allen: G. Motelab webpage – http://motelab.eecs.harvard.edu.
4. V. Rajendran, K. Obraczka, and J.J. Garcia-Luna-Aceves: Energy-Efficient, Collision-Free Medium Access Control for Wireless Sensor Networks. ACM SenSys '03, November 2003.
5. T. van Dam, K. Langendoen: An Adaptive Energy-Efficient MAC Protocol for Wireless Sensor Networks. SenSys '03, November 2003.
6. B. Hohlt, L. Doherty and E. Brewer: Flexible Power Scheduling for Sensor Networks. In Proceedings of IPSN, April 2004.
7. TinyOS: http://webs.cs.berkeley.edu/tos/
8. W. Ye, J. Heidemann, and D. Estrin: An energy-efficient MAC protocol for wireless sensor networks. In INFOCOM, June 2002.
9. S. Madden, M. Franklin, J. Hellerstein, and W. Hong: TAG: a tiny aggregation service for ad-hoc sensor networks. In 5th Symposium on Operation System Design and Implementation, December 2002.
10. P. Levis, S. Madden, D. Gay, J. Polastre, R. Szewczyk, A. Woo, E. Brewer and D. Culler: The Emergence of Networking Abstractions and Techniques in TinyOS. In NSDI, March 2004.
11. L. Rossi, B. Krishnamachari, C. Kuo: Distributed Parameter Estimation for Monitoring Diffusion Phenomena Using Physical Models. In SECON, October 2004.
12. R. Szewczyk, J. Polastre, A. Mainwaring, and D. Culler: Lessons from a sensor network expedition. European Workshop on Sensor Networks, January 2004.
13. J. Zhao, and R. Govindanm: Understanding Packet Delivery Performance in Dense Wireless Sensor Networks. ACM SenSys '03, November 2003.
14. A. Woo, T. Tony, and D. Culler: Taming the Underlying Challenges of Reliable Multihop Routing in Sensor Networks. *ACM SenSys 2003*, November 2003.
15. D. De Couto, D. Aguayo, J. Bicket, and R. Morris: A High-Throughput Path Metric for Multi-Hop Wireless Routing. In Proceedings of. ACM MobiCom, September 2003.
16. W. Ye, J. Heidemann, and D. Estrin: Medium Access Control With Coordinated Adaptive Sleeping for Wireless Sensor Networks. In Transactions on Networking (2004) 493-506.
17. J. Polastre, J. Hill, and D. Culler: Versatile Low Power Media Access for Wireless Sensor Networks. ACM SenSys 2004, November 2004.
18. Crossbow: http://www.xbow.com
19. Crickets: http://www.nms.lcs.mit.edu/crickets
20. J. Polastre, J. Hui, P. Levis, J. Zhao, D. Culler, S. Shenker, and I. Stoica: A Unifying Link Abstraction for Wireless Sensor Networks. ACM SenSys 2005, November 2005.
21. M. Yarvis, W. Conner, L. Krishnamurthy, J.Chhabra, B. Elliott, and A. Mainwaring: Real-World Experiences with an Interactive Ad Hoc Sensor Network. IWAHN 2002, August 2002.

Results of Bit Error Measurements with Sensor Nodes and Casuistic Consequences for Design of Energy-Efficient Error Control Schemes

Andreas Willig[1] and Robert Mitschke[2]

[1] Telecommunication Networks Group, Technical University Berlin
awillig@ieee.org
[2] Hasso-Plattner-Institute, University of Potsdam
robert.mitschke@carmeq.com

Abstract. For the proper design of energy-efficient error control schemes some insight into channel error patterns is needed. This paper presents bit error and packet loss measurements taken with sensor nodes running the popular RFM TR 1001 wireless transceiver. Some key facts from the measurements are presented and it is evaluated, how energy-efficient selected combined forward error correction (FEC) and automatic repeat request (ARQ) schemes would be over the measured channel. One interesting result is that FEC schemes are less energy-efficient than schemes without FEC, even when the additional energy required to decode a packet is not considered. On the other hand, the energy-efficiency can be improved when retransmissions are postponed for a short time.

1 Introduction

A popular saying in the sensor networks community is that "Every bit transmitted brings a sensor node one moment closer to death"[1] and quiet sensor nodes potentially have the longest lifetime. However, from time to time communication is unavoidable. This communication takes place over inherently unreliable wireless channels, and error control schemes are needed to protect the data against the channel impairments [9, Chap. 6]. To properly design error control schemes in an energy-efficient way, a good understanding of channel error patterns is needed. While theoretical channel models like Gaussian noise [5] on the level of waveforms, or bit-level models like the binary symmetric channel [5] or the well-known Gilbert-Elliot model [7,4] may give useful insights during the early stages of the protocol design process, a realistic performance evaluation of such error control schemes requires incorporation of more realistic channel models. However, in the literature on wireless sensor networks only a few studies are available which present empirical data on channel errors and most performance evaluation studies of sensor network protocols resort to the theoretical models.

The aim of this paper is to fill this gap, to provide results from realistic measurements and to draw some conclusions on the effectiveness of different

---

[1] Greg Pottie, MIT Technology Review, Jul./Aug. 2003.

K. Römer, H. Karl, and F. Mattern (Eds.): EWSN 2006, LNCS 3868, pp. 310–325, 2006.
© Springer-Verlag Berlin Heidelberg 2006

error-control approaches when faced to the measured channels. Specifically, we present the results of a bit error measurement study carried out with the Scatterweb ESB (Embedded Sensor Board) nodes from the Computer Systems and Telematics Group at the Free University Berlin.[2] These nodes employ the popular RF Monolithics TR 1001 transceiver. The study took place on a publicly accessible floor within the building of the Hasso-Plattner-Institute at the University of Potsdam. The results indicate that not all of the different error-control mechanisms prove effective in reducing the energy consumption while ensuring reliable transmission. We have considered different combinations of forward-error correction (FEC) schemes with automatic repeat request (ARQ) schemes [12]. Our evaluations show that FEC schemes are less energy-efficient than schemes without FEC, even when the additional energy required to decode a packet is not considered. On the other hand, the energy-efficiency can be improved when retransmissions are postponed for a short time.

The paper is structured as follows: in the following Section 2 we describe our measurement setup and the approach to evaluation of measurement results. Following this, in Section 3 we survey the most interesting results of our measurements. The effectiveness and energy-efficiency of different (hybrid) forward error correction (FEC) and automatic repeat request (ARQ) schemes is investigated in Section 4. In Section 5 the related work is discussed and in Section 6 our conclusions are given.

2 Measurement Setup and Evaluation Method

2.1 The Sensor Node Platform

The ESB sensor nodes designed by the FU Berlin[3] use a 16 bit Texas Instruments MSP430F149 microcontroller offering 60 kbyte of flash memory and 2 kbytes of RAM, an instruction cycle time of 125 nsec, and several peripheral devices, including a UART to control a serial device.[4] The radio transceiver is an RF Monolithics RFM TR1001 module, which was configured to use a 19.200 bit per second OOK (on-off-keying) modulation scheme in the frequency range around 868 MHz at an output power of 0.75 mWatt (-0.28 dBm).[5]

2.2 Measurement Setup

We have used a setup consisting of a single transmitter and ten receivers, all arranged in an array on a plank, a schematics is shown in Figure 1. In the figure,

---

[2] See   http://www.inf.fu-berlin.de/inst/ag-tech/scatterweb_net/esb/index.shtml

[3] Scatterweb   project,   see   http://www.inf.fu-berlin.de/inst/ag-tech/scatterweb_net/esb/index.shtml

[4] The data sheet is provided here: http://www.inf.fu-berlin.de/inst/ag-tech/scatterweb_net/downloads/MSP430f149.pdf

[5] See   http://www.inf.fu-berlin.de/inst/ag-tech/scatterweb_net/downloads/TR1001.pdf

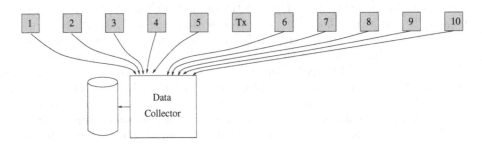

Fig. 1. Schematics of the measurement setup

the receivers are numbered from one to ten. The distance between any two sensor nodes (transmitter or receiver) on the plank is 30 centimeters. Please note that the transmitter is placed in the middle of the plank.

For a specific *measurement*, the transmitter sends a well-known sequence of packets (see below). The receivers try to capture the packets, timestamp each packet according to their local clock[6] and write the timestamp and the received data immediately onto their serial interface. The serial interface of all receivers is attached to a single central station, called the *data collector*, which writes the received data along with an identification of the receiver nodes into tracefiles on a harddisk. The evaluation of the stored measurement results is done offline. The serial interface of the transmitter is also attached to the data collector, in order to control start and stop the measurements.

To convince ourselves that the observed packet losses are really losses on the air interface and do not occur between the receivers and the data collector / harddisk, we have performed a stress test: each receiver generates data on the serial interface at the full rate of 115.2 kbit/s (i.e. at a much higher rate than used on the wireless interface). The data collector managed to collect all this data for half an hour without any losses. As a side effect, this test showed also that the serial links between the receivers and the data collector is working correctly.

We have performed a number of *measurements*. Within a single measurement the transmitter transmits a sequence of 9000 packets, all having the same size and well-known contents. For the next measurement, the plank was turned clockwise by 30 degrees, with the transmitter position being constant. The transmitter generates the packet at equidistant times (every 200 msec) without doing any carrier-sensing or running any kind of medium access control (MAC) protocol.

The packet format used for the measurements is quite simple: A packet starts with a PHY header of six bytes length, used to let the receiver acquire bit synchronization. The last byte of the PHY header is a fixed *start frame delimiter* (SFD). After sending the SFD byte the transmitter transmits the same 32-bit sequence number sixteen times, making up for a total packet size of 64 bytes (512 bits). The transmitter increments the sequence number before each new

---

[6] The local clock was incremented every 5 msec, but no attempt has been made to synchronize receivers clocks or to compensate different drift rates – this was done in the postprocessing stage.

packet. There are no separate MAC headers or MAC trailers like checksums. To help the receiver keeping synchronized, the transmitter must send each byte twice, the first time directly, and the second time as an inverted version.[7] The receiver waits for an incoming SFD. When this arrives, the receiver writes its current timestamp onto the serial interface and starts to output all the user bytes received from the wireless transceiver on the serial interface, the inverted bytes are dropped. The end of a frame is detected from time gaps.

2.3   Evaluation Approach

The data collector collects from all sensor nodes the received packets/bytes along with a timestamp, and stores this data in a tracefile (one packet per line and one file per receiver). As an example, we reproduce a few such (shortened) lines from the start of a tracefile (the initial line numbers are inserted for ease of reference):

```
1    25726.001A001A001A001A001A001A001A001A001A001A001A
2    25764.001B001B001B001B001B001B001B001B001B001B
3    25802.001C001C001C001C001C001C001C001C001C001C
4    25840.001D001D001D001D001D001D001D001D001D001D
5    25879.
6    25918.001F001F001F001F001F001F001F001F001F001F
7    25956.
8    25996.0021002100210021002100210021002100210021002100210021
9    26034.0022002200220022002200220022002200220022002200220022
10   26073.002300230023FFDCFFDCFFDCFFDCFFDCFFDCFFDCFFDCFFDC
11   26150.00250025002500250025002500250025002500250025
12   26187.0026002600260026002600260026002600260
```

The number before the dot is the timestamp assigned locally by the receiving sensor node, while the characters after the dot denote the received bytes in hexadecimal format. Please observe that different things can happen:

- Certain packets are entirely missing (what happened to sequence numbers 0001 to 0019?). We refer to this as *unobserved packets*.
- Occasionally a line does not have the full length (line 12). We refer to this as a *truncated packet*.
- Other lines contain a timestamp but not a single data byte (lines 5 and 7). These are referred to as *packet loss*.
- Finally, of course we can have full-length lines with bit errors (line 10).

A likely explanation for the first three phenomena has to do with bit synchronization. Remember that a packet begins with a PHY header (for acquisition purposes) and a start frame delimiter (SFD). An unobserved packet can occur when the receiver fails to acquire synchronization from the PHY header. A packet loss can occur when synchronization is acquired (and the receiver is thus aware of an incoming packet) but the SFD is missed. A packet truncation can occur when PHY header and SFD are acquired but synchronization gets lost in the

---

[7] This avoids too long runs of zeroes and ones and keeps the receiver DC-free.

middle of the packet. In other lines (like in line 10 of our example) the received data changes suddenly and the error patterns are not "sporadic" anymore. We suspect that due to synchronization errors the receiver looses or inserts a bit and back-inverts the bytes at wrong places.

The goal of the postprocessing is to figure out for each transmitted bit whether it is received correctly or not. Of course, this postprocessing cannot be applied to lost packets. We aim to create an *indicator sequence*, which marks correctly received bits by a zero and erroneously received bits by a one [17]. This requires to compare the received bits stored in the logfile with the transmitted bits. More precisely: the received bits are grouped into 32-bit words and compared with the transmitted sequence number. The main problem to solve is the following: given a line with received and noisy bytes, what could be the sequence number transmitted by the transmitter? This information cannot be derived directly from the timestamps, since no attempt has been made to synchronize the clocks of transmitter and receivers, and thus their clock offsets and drifts can be considered random. In a nutshell, our approach for guessing the transmitted sequence numbers for a given tracefile is as follows:

- In a first step, the data part of each line is split into groups of four characters, which are then converted into a 32 bit numbers.
- In a second step, for each line a histogram of the 32-bit values is computed and the most frequent value is called the *mode* of the line.
- In a third step, so-called *anchors* are identified: an anchor is constituted by four subsequent lines having modes i_0, i_0+1, i_0+2 and i_0+3. If such a group of lines is detected, their modes are accepted as their true (transmitted) sequence numbers and the lines are marked as *identified*.
- In the fourth step we check all the remaining unidentified lines. When the mode of such a line is truly within the sequence number range left free by neighbor anchors, the modes are accepted as the transmitted sequence numbers. For example, consider that line n with mode M_n is unidentified, that line $m < n$ with mode M_m is the largest identified line smaller tham n and line $o > n$ with mode M_o is the smallest identified line larger than n, and if furthermore $M_m < M_n < M_o$ holds, then line n is marked as identified with mode M_n. A second, quite heuristic criterion is applied to those lines which do not match this criterion: We have observed many lines in our traces which look quite similar to line 10 of our example: the first few 32 bit values are correct, while the remaining ones are impressingly wrong. If the first two 32-bit values are identical and belong to the sequence number range left free by the neighboring anchors, the first values are accepted as the true sequence number.
- It may happen that after the previous steps still some lines (i.e. their true sequence numbers) remain unidentified. Here, we analyze the timestamp of the packet with respect to timestamps of already identified neighbored packets and their respective sequence numbers to estimate the missing sequence number. Due to rounding to 5 msec intervals and for other reasons the timestamp values are noisy, too, and the possible presence of unobserved packets

adds further vaguery. Therefore, we have estimated a timestamp/sequence-number least-squares line through a number of neighbored and already identified timestamp/sequence number pairs. Suppose we are given this least-squares line, a range I of yet unidentified lines with timestamps t_1, t_2, t_k, and the timestamps and sequence number pairs (t_l, s_l), (t_u, s_u) of the identified lines surrounding I. The sequence numbers $s_l < s_1 < \ldots < s_k < s_u$ assigned to the timestamps $t_1, \ldots, t_n$ are chosen such that for all possible assignments of sequence numbers $s_l < s_1 = x_1 < s_2 = x_2 < \ldots < s_k = x_k < s_u$ to the present timestamps the sum-of-squared errors with respect to the estimated least-squares line is minimized.

Of course, we have applied consistency checks (like for example that the identified sequence numbers should be strictly monotonically increasing) after each of these steps, and indeed our evaluation passes these tests. After having determined the true sequence numbers it was straightforward to compute the per-packet indicator sequences. For packets with entirely missing contents (like in lines 5 and 7 of our example) no indicator sequence has been computed, since this would be meaningless.

3   Survey of Measurement Results

In this section we survey the results of our measurements. It should be noted that truncated packets have been removed from the traces, unless stated differently. This does not bias the results significantly, since the number of truncated packets was 647 out of 531968 recorded packets, amounting to $\approx 0.12\%$ of all packets.

3.1   Packet Losses

We first present results on the packet loss rates. Packet losses are an important kind of channel errors, because a priori they cannot be handled by any error-correcting FEC code, since FEC assumes the presence of (albeit) noisy data bytes. Packet losses are only correctable with the help of retransmissions carried out by an ARQ protocol. In this evaluation we are only interested in packet losses (like in lines 5 and 7 of our example), all other lines having the correct length are treated as "correct", even if they have bit errors.

In Table 1, we show the packet loss rates observed for all the measurements and each receiver. Each packet loss rate is computed as the fraction of lost packets out of the total of 9000 transmitted packets. It can be seen that the packet loss rate varies between 0.03% and up to 9.8%. Furthermore, there is no clear dependence of the packet loss rates on the position of the node on the plank. Taking all the measurements together, the average packet loss rate is about 3.8%.

We have investigated the statistics of packet losses a bit further. Specifically, we have investigated the lengths of *bursts* of subsequent packet losses and of loss-free periods (called *runs*) for all measurements at once (by simply concatenating the measurement traces). The observed range of run lengths is between one and

Table 1. Packet loss rates for the different receivers and the different angles of the plank

	0 deg	30 deg	60 deg	90 deg	120 deg	150 deg
Rcv. 1	0.0087	0.0187	0.07211	0.0452	0.0397	0.0253
Rcv. 2	0.0288	0.0533	0.09822	0.0843	0.0801	0.0583
Rcv. 3	0.0047	0.0088	0.009	0.0266	0.0398	0.0526
Rcv. 4	0.009	0.0172	0.06155	0.06	0.0473	0.0397
Rcv. 5	0.0003	0.0026	0.01522	0.0321	0.039	0.0544
Rcv. 6	0.0474	0.0587	0.02911	0.0234	0.0222	0.0203
Rcv. 7	0.0445	0.0534	0.08122	0.0831	0.0617	0.049
Rcv. 8	0.0048	0.0095	0.09533	0.0852	0.0576	0.0645
Rcv. 9	0.0131	0.0055	0.07244	0.0598	0.0322	0.0501
Rcv. 10	0.0015	0.003	0.002	0.0052	0.0048	0.0058

5039, the average run length is ≈ 25.3 packets, and the coefficient of variation (standard deviation divided by average) was approximately 3.56. The observed distribution function for the run lengths is shown in Figure 2. The 50% quantile is at ≈ 7 packets, the 90% quantile is at ≈ 46 packets. Stated differently: In 50% of all cases a run lasts for at most seven packets before the next packet is lost.

For the case of packet loss bursts we show in Figure 3 the relative frequencies of the observed packet loss burst lengths. It can be seen that the overwhelming majority ($\approx 98.4\%$) of loss bursts comprises of only a single lost packet, and in $\approx 99.9\%$ of all cases the burst length is no more than two packets. This

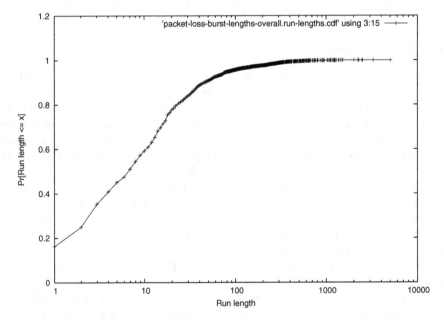

Fig. 2. Cumulative distribution function of the lengths of loss-free periods (runs), taken over all measurements

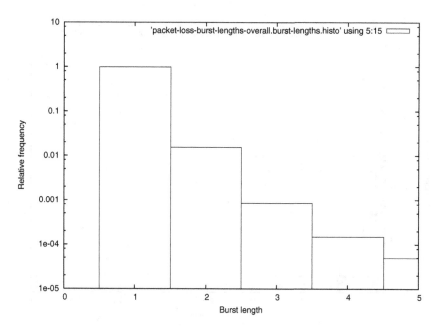

Fig. 3. Relative frequencies of the lengths of packet loss bursts, taken over all measurements

statistic is interesting for designing a retransmission strategy: if a receiver does not receive a packet due to packet loss, the transmitter can perform an immediate retransmission (with respect to the chosen interpacket duration) and enjoys a high probability that the next packet *is not* lost. The question, however, whether this next packet is really useful or has bit errors is answered in the following section.

3.2   Packet Failures

We denote as a *packet failure* a packet which is either a lost packet or which has at least one bit error and thus would need a retransmission when no FEC scheme is used. We have also looked into the statistics of *bursts* of subsequent packet failures and *runs* of subsequent failure-free packets.

The observed range of burst lengths varies between one and 393 packets, the average burst length is ≈ 1.77 packets, the coefficient of variation is ≈ 1.65, and more than 90% of all bursts have a length of three packets or less. Single-packet bursts make up for 72% of all bursts. The histogram with the relative frequencies of burst lengths is shown in Figure 4.

With respect to the successful runs, the following findings are interesting: The range of observed run lengths is between one and 2904 packets. The average run length is ≈ 9.3 packets, with a coefficient of variation of ≈ 3.8. Approximately 70% of all runs have a length of four packets or less, 90% of all runs have a length of 19 packets or less. Because of the larger range, we show the cumulative distribution function of run-lengths in Figure 5.

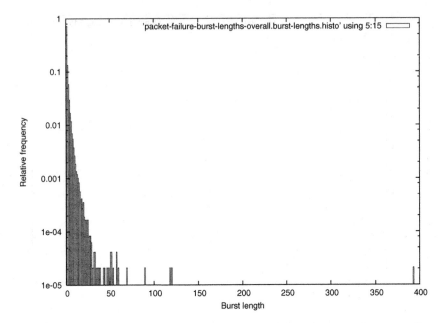

Fig. 4. Relative frequencies of the lengths of packet failure bursts, taken over all measurements

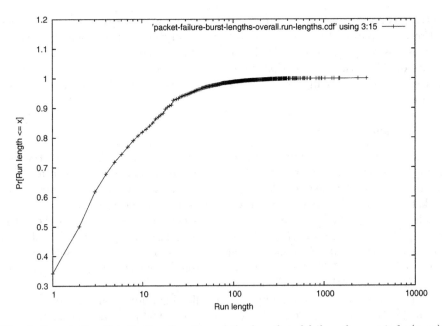

Fig. 5. Cumulative distribution function of the lengths of failure-free periods (runs), taken over all measurements

3.3   Per-Packet Bit Error Rate

In the next evaluation we have counted the number of bit errors in each packet. We have looked at all full-length packets from all the measurements, and we have counted the overall number of bit errors in each packet. Obviously, in the following statistics the lost packets are not included. The cumulative distribution function for the number of erroneous bits per packet is shown in Figure 6. The percentage of error-free packets is $\approx 87\%$, hence, about 13% of the non-lost packets have at least one bit error. The average number of bit errors per packet is ≈ 16.68, the coefficient of variation is ≈ 3.5. The average number of bit errors in an *erroneous packet* is ≈ 132.8 bits.

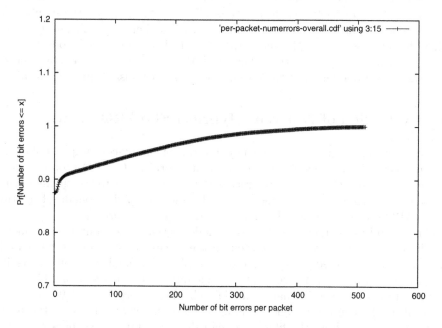

Fig. 6. Cumulative distribution function of the number of bit errors per packet, taken over all measurements

We can already conclude from this distribution some insights about the usefulness of practically realizable FEC codes. In general, FEC codes have the ability to correct a number of bit errors, but they come at a price: the overhead bits increase the on-times of the transmitter's transceiver[8], and the receiver has to spend a (sometimes significant) amount of energy to decode the packets (see [8,15,10,16,11] and [9, Chap. 6]). Let us for ease of exposition consider the case of block coding FEC schemes. The number t of reliably correctable bits in a block of length n bits depends on the actual coding scheme; however, an upper bound

---

[8] Conversely, when the on-times of the transmitter are kept fixed, fewer user data bits can be transmitted in a packet.

is imposed by the *Hamming bound*, which states that a block code with k user bits mapped to n channel bits can correct up to t bit errors only if the relation

$$2^{n-k} \geq \sum_{i=0}^{t} \binom{n}{i}$$

holds. The fact that a triple (n, k, t) satisfies this relation does not imply that a code with this properties really exists. However, let us assume for the moment that we live in a perfect world, and for each (n, k, t) satisfying the above relation there really exists a code. We are interested in the fraction of erroneous packets which can be corrected under different code strengths. Let us fix n to 512 and investigate different numbers of correctable bits t. After analyzing our data, we found that in order to correct 50% of all erroneous packets, the number of correctable bits must be $t = 105$. However, the numbers $n = 512$ and $t = 105$ allow for at most $k = 141$ user data bits, which amounts to a code rate of $\approx 27.54\%$. If we want to correct 90% of all erroneous packets, we would need $t = 312$ correctable bits, but then we are not able to transmit any data at all.

4   Evaluation of Different Hybrid FEC/ARQ Strategies

To get a deeper insight in the efficiency in terms of energy-consumption of error control methods, we have evaluated different hybrid FEC/ARQ protocols [12] running between a transmitter and receiver over a common wireless channel. The chosen protocols are either straightforward choices from the domain of hybrid FEC/ARQ protocols or have been suggested in the literature.

The "wireless channel" used in our model actually uses our measurement results directly: we have concatenated all the traces (after removing truncated packets) and extracted for each packet the observed number of bit errors in $n = 512$ bits. Lost packets are treated as having 512 bit errors. These bit error counts are fed into the simulation model. This list covers $N = 531968$ packets in total. Each time the channel is used for data packet transmission, the next number is fetched from the file and assigned to the transmitted packet as the number of bit errors that occur during transmission. For simplicity, we have assumed that acknowledgements are always transmitted correctly.

As for the ARQ protocol, we have chosen the alternating-bit protocol (ABP) as a basis. Since our interest is not in throughput issues and the channel delay is of no concern to this study, higher-level protocools like selective repeat need not be considered.

In the first investigated hybrid scheme (called *no adaptation*), ABP is combined with a constant FEC code, i.e. we apply the same coding scheme to each packet. The code is able to correct up to t bit errors in a packet of length $n = 512$ bits, where t is varied throughout the study. The number of user-bits k which can be transmitted in such a packet is again obtained from the Hamming bound. As our performance measure, we have taken the *goodput*, which is defined as the ratio of the total number of user bits which have been successfully received, to the total number of transmitted bits, after all the N packets have been exhausted. This goodput is a measure of the energy-efficiency achievable for transmitting user data (total bits per user bit), and no other sources of energy consumption like idle listening or collisions are taken into account. We made the advantageous assumption that the FEC decoding requires no extra energy as compared to the FEC-less case. Depending on the implementation, the decoding energy might actually be significant [15,16].

In the second scheme (called *fixed-switch-on*), the FEC strength (i.e. the number t of correctable bits in a packet of length $n = 512$ bits) is varied between two values: when the previous packet required zero retransmissions, t is set to zero for the next packet. When the previous packet required one or more retransmissions, t is set to a fixed value. This choice is made after each successfully transmitted packet, whereas during the retransmissions the code strength is kept fixed. Stated differently: once the transmission of a k-bits piece of user data has started, it is repeated without changing the FEC strength t until the transmitter receives an acknowledgement.[9]

In the third scheme, the FEC strength is varied according to an additive-increase-multiplicative-decrease (AIMD) scheme. Specifically, when the previous packet required zero retransmissions, the t-value is halved, when it required one retransmission, the t value is kept constant and when it required more than one retransmission, the t-value is increased by a specified increment.

Finally, in the *postponing scheme* (compare [1,2]) adaptation takes place when the transmitter has noticed the lack of an acknowledgement. Specifically, the transmitter postpones a retransmission by a specified amount of packet times. FEC is not used.

In Figure 7 we compare the three strategies no-adaptation, fixed-switch-on and AIMD against the baseline scheme where only ABP but no FEC is used. For each scheme the goodput is shown versus the number of correctable bits t. The t parameter corresponds in the no-adaptation scheme to the (constant) strength of FEC, in the fixed-switch-on scheme to the FEC strength used after switching FEC on, and in the AIMD scheme to the FEC strength by which the current FEC strength is increased after requiring two or more retransmissions for the previous packet. As a reference, we have drawn a horizontal line depicting the goodput of the baseline scheme. The figure confirms a conclusion that is already suggested from the statistics of the number of bit errors per packet seen in Section 3.3: FEC does not pay out energetically, because packets tend to be either correct or damaged well beyond the capabilities of practical FEC schemes.

In Figure 8 we investigate the postponing strategy as compared to the baseline scheme. Specifically, we display the goodput versus the number of packet slots a retransmission is postponed. It can be seen that postponing can potentially save energy. Of course, it depends on the details of a nodes energy consumption profile whether this promise can be kept. For example, the transmitter knows exactly about the fate of a packet trial and for how long it will postpone the

---

[9] This choice has practical reasons: it does not force the transmitter to re-packetize an in-transit packet, thus it can be kept in hardware buffers and retransmitted directly.

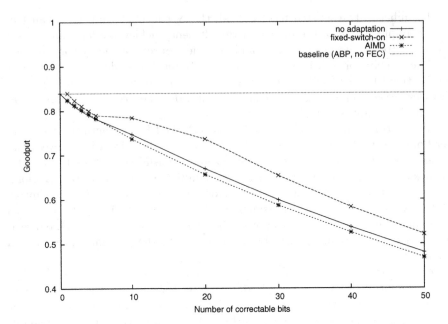

Fig. 7. Goodput vs. number of correctable bits t for the no-adaptation, switch-fixed-on and AIMD strategies, taken over all measurements

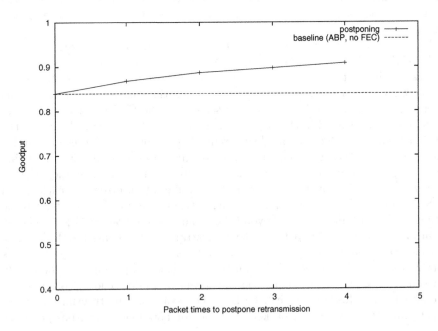

Fig. 8. Goodput vs. number of packet times to postpone retransmission, taken over all measurements

retransmission; it can readily exploit this waiting time by going into sleep mode. However, in order for the receiver to exploit a sleep mode, too, it must be absolutely sure about when the preceding trial ended and when it has to awake in order to receive the next trial. A more detailed investigation of practical and energy-efficient postponing schemes will be subject of future work.

5   Related Work

The quality of a wireless link can be measured at different levels. On the lowest level, certain characteristics of wave propagation like the rms delay spread or the path loss coefficient are measured for example from using channel sounders to obtain channel impulse responses [14]. However, for the design of protocols, the error characteristics on the level of bits or packets are more important. A number of studies have measured relevant information for wireless LAN technologies, for example [17,3,13].

To the best of our knowledge, so far only few studies have appeared that characterize link quality in wireless sensor networks. In [18] and [6] link quality is expressed in terms of packet loss rates, but there is no distinction between packet losses because of synchronization failure and packet losses due to checksum failures. In [6] link quality measurements in a 13×13 grid of 169 motes spaced two feets apart on an open parking place are presented. There is a single transmitter, all other motes are receivers. For a given transmit power there appears no deterministic relationship between distance and link quality; nodes at the same distance from the transmitter can experience widely varying packet loss rates. The region around a node having a certain packet loss rate does not have the shape of a circle, but is irregularly shaped. They have also shown that there is a significant degree of asymmetric links, where packets sent from node A to node B are received by B with small packet loss rates, while the packets from B to A experience a high packet loss rate. The fraction of asymmetric links grows with distance, reaching values between 5% and 15% of all links.

In [18] results of a measurement in a linear network are presented. The quality-vs-distance relationship (with quality measured as packet reception rate) shows three different regions: in the effective region receiving nodes have a distance of at most ten feet to the transmitter and receive consistently more than 90% of the packets. In the poor region the loss rates are consistently well beyond 90%. In the transitional region in between, the variance of the experienced loss rates for nodes at the same distance is significant. Another study considering packet losses on the physical, as well as on the MAC layer is [19].

6   Conclusions and Outlook

We believe that, despite the obvious limitations of this study like the usage of only a single type of transceiver and the investigation of just a single scenario, our results can give valuable input to the energy-efficient and channel-aware design of link-layer / error-control schemes in wireless sensor networks. Any scheme will quite likely be faced with environmental conditions such as ours, because it really was an almost randomly selected place in an office building, and not a clean-room laboratory environment.

Of course, much interesting further work can be done. This starts with a more detailed analysis of our results, looking at each receiver separately. A logical second step would be to devise a methodology that allows the identification and parameterization / estimation of suitable stochastic channel models, i.e. the identification of stochastic processes having only a few parameters but having enough degrees of freedom to approximate our results well. And finally, the incorporation of other transceiver types and environments would give more hints on how representative our results are.

References

1. Pravin Bhagwat, Partha Bhattacharya, Arvind Krishna, and Satish K. Tripathi. Using channel state dependent packet scheduling to improve TCP throughput over wireless LANs. *Wireless Networks*, 3(1):91–102, March 1997.
2. Richard Cam and Cyril Leung. Multiplexed ARQ for time-varying channels – part I: System model and throughput analysis. *IEEE Transactions on Communications*, 46(1):41–51, January 1998.
3. David A. Eckhardt and Peter Steenkiste. A trace-based evaluation of adaptive error correction for a wireless local area network. *MONET - Mobile Networks and Applications*, 4:273–287, 1999.
4. E. O. Elliot. Estimates of error rates for codes on burst-noise channels. *Bell Systems Technical Journal*, 42:1977–1997, September 1963.
5. Robert G. Gallager. *Information Theory and Reliable Communication*. John Wiley & Sons, New York, 1968.
6. Deepak Ganesan, Bhaskar Krishnamachari, Alec Woo, David Culler, Deborah Estrin, and Stephen Wicker. Complex behavior at scale: An experimental study of low-power wireless sensor networks. Technical Report UCLA/CSD-TR 02-0013, Computer Science Dept., University of California, Los Angeles (UCLA), 2002.
7. E. N. Gilbert. Capacity of a burst-noise channel. *Bell Systems Technical Journal*, 39:1253–1265, September 1960.
8. Manish Goel and Naresh R. Shanbhag. Low-Power Channel Coding via Dynamic Reconfiguration. In *Proc. International Conference on Acoustics, Speech and Signal Processing (ICASSP)*, Phoenix, Arizona, March 1999.
9. Holger Karl and Andreas Willig. *Protocols and Architectures for Wireless Sensor Networks*. John Wiley & Sons, Chichester, 2005.
10. Heikki Karvonen, Zach Shelby, and Carlos Pomalaza-Raez. Coding for energy efficient wireless embedded networks. In *Proc. International Workshop on Wireless Ad Hoc Networks (IWWAN)*, Oulu, Finland, June 2004.
11. Paul Lettieri, Curt Schurgers, and Mani B. Srivastava. Adaptive link layer strategies for energy-efficient wireless networking. *Wireless Networks*, 5(5):339–355, November 1999.
12. Hang Liu, Hairuo Ma, Magda El Zarki, and Sanjay Gupta. Error control schemes for networks: An overview. *MONET – Mobile Networks and Applications*, 2(2):167–182, 1997.

13. Giao T. Nguyen, , Randy H. Katz, Brian Noble, , and Mahadev Satyanarayanan. A trace-based approach for modeling wireless channel behavior. In *Proceedings of the Winter Simulation Conference*, Coronado, CA, December 1996.
14. Theodore S. Rappaport. *Wireless Communications – Principles and Practice*. Prentice Hall, Upper Saddle River, NJ, USA, 2002.
15. Y. Sankarasubramaniam, I.F. Akyildiz, and S.W. McLaughlin. Energy efficiency based packet size optimization in wireless sensor networks. In *Proc. 1st IEEE Intl. Workshop on Sensor Network Protocols and Applications (SNPA)*, Anchorage, AK, May 2003.
16. Eugene Shih, Benton H. Calhoun, Seong-Hwan Cho, and Anantha P. Chandrakasan. Energy-efficient link layer for wireless microsensor networks. In *Proc. Workshop on VLSI 2001 (WVLSI '01)*, april 2001.
17. Andreas Willig, Martin Kubisch, Christian Hoene, and Adam Wolisz. Measurements of a wireless link in an industrial environment using an IEEE 802.11-compliant physical layer. *IEEE Transactions on Industrial Electronics*, 49(6):1265–1282, 2002.
18. Alec Woo, Terence Tong, and David Culler. Taming the underlying challenges of reliable multihop routing in sensor networks. In *Proc. ACM SenSys 03*, Los Angeles, California, November 2003.
19. Jerry Zhao and Ramesh Govindan. Understanding packet delivery performance in dense wireless sensor networks. In *Proc. ACM SenSys 03*, Los Angeles, California, November 2003.

An Empirical Characterization of Radio Signal Strength Variability in 3-D IEEE 802.15.4 Networks Using Monopole Antennas

Dimitrios Lymberopoulos, Quentin Lindsey, and Andreas Savvides

Embedded Networks and Applications Lab, ENALAB,
Yale Univerisity, New Haven, CT 06520, USA
{dimitrios.lymberopoulos, quentin.lindsey, andreas.savvides}@yale.edu

Abstract. The wide availability of radio signal strength attenuation information on wireless radios has received considerable attention as a convenient means of deriving positioning information. Although some schemes have been shown to work in some scenarios, many agree that the robustness of such schemes can be easily compromised when low power IEEE 802.15.4 radios are used. Leveraging a recently installed sensor network testbed, we provide a detailed characterization of signal strength properties and link asymmetries for the CC2420 IEEE 802.15.4 compliant radio using a monopole antenna. To quantify the several factors of signal unpredictability due to the hardware, we have collected several thousands of measurements to study the antenna orientation and calibration effects. Our results show that the often overlooked antenna orientation effects are the dominant factor of the signal strength sensitivity, especially in the case of 3-D network deployments. This suggests that the antenna effects need to be carefully considered in signal strength schemes.

1 Introduction

The existence of radio connectivity and the attenuation of radio signal with distance are attractive properties that could potentially be exploited to estimate the positions of small-wireless devices featuring low-power radios. Radio signal strength indicator (RSSI), a standard feature in most radios, has attracted a lot of attention in the recent literature for obvious reasons. RSSI eliminates the need for additional hardware in small wireless devices, and exhibits favorable properties with respect to power consumption, size and cost. As a result, several RSSI based algorithms have been proposed that either assume a complete profiling of the network deployment area [1],[9][3],[15],[2],[8],[14],[16],[19] or a specific signal attenuation model that can provide distance or area information directly or indirectly from the raw RSSI data [21],[6],[7],[18],[11],[13],[12],[5].

Despite the increasing interest in signal strength localization using IEEE 802.14.5 radios, there is still a lack of detailed characterization of the fundamental factors contributing to large signal strength variability. To investigate these factors, and to get a better understanding of the asymmetries that arise in 3-D

K. Römer, H. Karl, and F. Mattern (Eds.): EWSN 2006, LNCS 3868, pp. 326–341, 2006.

schemarios, we present a detailed characterization of signal strength behaviors in an IEEE 802.15.4 sensor network with monopole antennas. Instead of proposing a specific algorithm, in this paper we focus on showing the sources of signal strength variability. We do so by collecting a large number of measurements from a 40-node testbed, both in an indoor and an open-field environment. This characterization differs from previous studies using IEEE 802.11 radios, since it examines a new radio technology with less powerful radio transmissions. Furthermore, a large fraction of the measurements are taken in a three-dimensional testbed deployment that emulates a realistic environment where sensor network deployments are likely to occur.

Our findings demonstrate that the relative antenna orientation between receiver-transmitter pairs is a major factor in signal strength variability, even in the absence of multipath effects. This suggests that many schemes using radio signal strength on similar radios should carefully consider these factors before going to actual deployments. The approximately 15,000 measurements collected for this study are available online at $http : //www.eng.yale.edu/enalab/rssidata/$.

Our presentation of this paper proceeds as follows: Section 2 provides an overview of other characterizations and schemes that use signal strength. This is followed by a discussion of the signal strength variability components and a detailed evaluation of our system.

2   Related Work

Some of the issues related with received signal strength ranging where presented by Whitehouse et. al. in an outdoor scenario characterization described in [20].

Three recent sensor network localization algorithms using low power sensor node radios are Ecolocation [21], MoteTrack[9] and Probability Grid [18]. Ecolocation determines the location of unknown nodes by examining the ordered sequence of received signal strength measurements taken at multiple reference nodes. The key idea of Ecolocation is that the distance-based rank order of reference nodes constitutes a unique signature for different regions in the localization space. Ecolocation reports a location error of $10ft$ for a very small outdoor network deployment area ($26ft$ x $49ft$) while Probability Grid reports a location error that is equal to the 70%-80% of the communication range for a $410ftx410ft$ outdoor network deployment. In the case of Probability Grid it is assumed that the goal of the sensor network deployment is to form a grid topology. Given this a priori knowledge, Probability Grid attempts to compute in a probabilistic way the one-hop distance and the number of hops that an unknown node is far away from an anchor node. MoteTrack is very similar to RADAR[1] but it does not require a back-end server where all the data have to be transferred and processed. Conversely, in Moterack the location of each mobile node is computed using a received radio signal strength signature from numerous beacon nodes to a database of signatures that is replicated across the beacon nodes themselves. The location error reported by Motetrack is approximately $13ft$ for an indoor network deployment area of $18751ft^2$.

Several schemes have also been presented using IEEE 802.11 radios. In [6] a comparative study of many RSSI based localization techniques using 802.11 cards is presented. According to the results of this study all the localization techniques produce approximately the same location error over a range of environments.

Other work on RSSI-based localization algorithms has been developed in the context of two broad categories: map based such as [1],[9],[3],[15],[2],[8],[14],[16], [19], and distance (or area) prediction based [21],[6],[7],[18],[11],[13],[12],[5].

3   Experimental Infrastructure

In the next sections we quantify the sources of RSSI variability using our Zigbee based infrastructure. A three dimensional, battery operated scalable testbed in our lab is used for indoor sensor network deployments. The testbed illustrated in Figure 1(b) is a 3-D structure measuring 4.5m(W) x 6m(L) x 3m(H) and it is designed to host a large number of static and mobile nodes to instrument a variety of application scenarios. The centerpiece of our infrastructure is the XYZ sensor node [10], an open-source general purpose sensing platform designed around the OKI ML67Q500x ARM/THUMB microprocessor and the IEEE 802.15.4 compliant CC2420 radio from Chipcon [4].

The communication subsystem of the XYZ sensor node was designed so that the correct operation of the radio chip is ensured. The radio chip is powered by the on-board voltage regulator and thus fluctuations in the battery voltage level do not affect the operation of the communication subsystem. In addition, the area under the chip on the PCB is used for grounding and it is well connected to the ground plane with several vias. The ground pins of the radio are connected to ground as close as possible to the package pin using individual vias and the microcontroller (as well as its support circuitry) was placed far away from the radio chip in order to avoid interference with the RF circuitry.

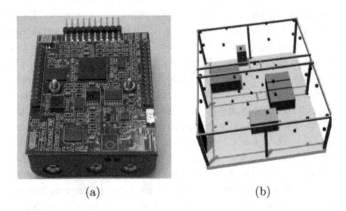

(a)   (b)

Fig. 1. a) The XYZ sensor node, b) Testbed node placement

The Chipcon CC2420 IEEE 802.15.4 radio transceiver operates in the 2.4GHz ISM band and includes a digital direct sequence spread spectrum (DSSS) modem providing a spreading gain of $9dB$ and an effective data rate of $250Kbps$. It was specifically designed for low power wireless applications and supports 8 discrete power levels: $0dBm$, $-1dBm$, $-3dBm$, $-5dBm$, $-7dBm$, $-10dBm$, $-15dBm$ and $-25dBm$ at which its power consumption varies from $29mW$ to $52mW$[10]. A built-in received signal strength indicator gives an 8-bit digital value: $RSSI_{VAL}$. The $RSSI_{VAL}$ is always averaged over 8 symbol periods ($128\mu s$) and a status bit indicates when the $RSSI_{VAL}$ is valid (meaning that the receiver was enabled for at least 8 symbol periods). The power P at the RF pins can be obtained directly from $RSSI_{VAL}$ using the following equation:

$$P = RSSI_{VAL} + RSSI_{OFFSET}[dBm] \tag{1}$$

where the $RSSI_{OFFSET}$ is found empirically from the front-end gain and it is approximately equal to $-45dBm$. In the next sections when we refer to the RSSI value we refer to the $RSSI_{VAL}$ and not the power P unless otherwise stated.

A straight piece of wire is used as a monopole antenna for our sensor node. The length of our antenna is equal to $1.1inch$, the optimal antenna length according to the CC2420's datasheet [4]. In all of the experiments described in the next sections, the length of the antenna on all the nodes was $1.1inch$ unless otherwise stated.

4   Sources of RSSI Variability

In addition to multipath, fading and shadowing of the RF channel, signal strength measurements are also affected by the following factors:

1. **Transmitter variability:** Different transmitters behave differently even when they are configured exactly in the same way. In practice, this means that when a transmitter is configured to send packets at a power level of d dBm then the transmitter will send these packets at a power level that is very close to d dBm but not necessarily exactly equal to d dBm. This can alter the received signal strength indication and thus it can lead to inaccurate distance estimation.
2. **Receiver variability:** The sensitivity of the receivers across different radio chips is different. In practice, this means that the RSSI value recorded at different receivers can be different even when all the other parameters that affect the received signal strength are kept constant.
3. **Antenna orientation:** Each antenna has its own radiation pattern that is not uniform. In practice, this means that the RSSI value recorded at the receiver for a given pair of communicating nodes and for a given distance between them varies as the pairwise antenna orientations of the transmitter and the receiver are changed.

4.1   Path Loss Prediction Model

The majority of RSSI localization algorithms that do not use full location profiling of the deployment environment make use of a signal propagation model
that maps RSSI values to distance estimates [17]. The most widely used signal
propagation model is the log-normal shadowing model:

$$RSSI(d) = P_T - PL(d_0) - 10\eta \log_{10} \frac{d}{d_0} + X_\sigma \qquad (2)$$

where, P_T is the transmit power, $PL(d_0)$ is the path loss for a reference distance
d_0, η is the path loss exponent and X_σ is a gaussian random variable with zero
mean and σ^2 variance, that models the random variation of the RSSI value.

Using the CC2420 radio we were able to verify the log-normal shadowing
model in an obstacle-free environment(basketball court). The effects of orientation and calibration were isolated by taking measurements with a single pair of
nodes, with the receiver and the transmitter on the same plane. Figure 5a shows
the RSSI vs Distance plots. Based on our measurements in the basketball court,
RSSI changes linearly with the log of the distance.

5   Variations Across Different Radios

In order to quantify the variability among different transmitter-receiver pairs
we conducted 2 different experiments. To characterize transmitter variations we
used a single receiver and 9 different transmitters. In all of our experiments the

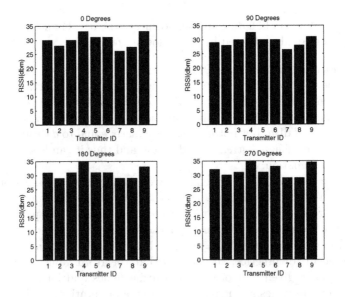

Fig. 2. Quantifying transmitter's variability

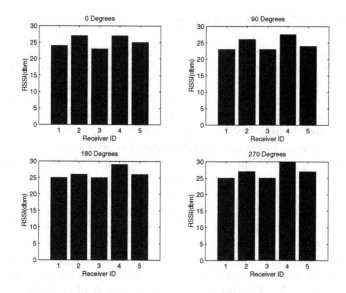

Fig. 3. Quantifying receiver's variability

receiver was exactly in the same position and with the same antenna orientation. One transmitter at a time was placed at a specific location that was $1.31ft$ far away from the receiver. Each transmitter was transmitting packets at $-15dBm$ while in 4 different orientations (0, 90, 180, and 270 degrees). The nodes under test were placed in the middle of a room without furniture in order to minimize the effect of the reflections in our measurements.

Figure 2 shows the RSSI values recorded at the receiver for all the transmitter and for all 4 orientations. For each orientation the average RSSI value and its standard deviation are computed. Averaging over all the average standard deviations for all different orientations we find that the overall standard deviation of the received RSSI value is equal to: $2.24dBm$. Using the log-normal signal propagation model shown in Figure 5a we find that the $2.24dBm$ RSSI standard deviation corresponds to $0.4ft$ distance standard deviation.

To quantify the variability in the receiver we used a similar setup using 1 transmitter and 5 different receivers. The transmitter was transmitting packets at $-15dBm$ while in 4 different orientations (0, 90, 180, and 270 degrees). Figure 3 shows the RSSI values recorded at the different receivers for all 4 orientations of the transmitter. For each orientation the average RSSI value and its standard deviation are computed. Averaging over all the average standard deviations for all different orientations we find that the overall standard deviation of the received RSSI value is equal to: $1.86dBm$. Using the log-normal signal propagation model shown in Figure 5a we find that the $1.86dBm$ RSSI standard deviation corresponds to $0.33ft$ distance standard deviation. The same experiment was performed several times with different transmitters in order to make sure that we were measuring the receiver variability and not something else that had to do with the specific transmitter.

6   Antenna Characterization

The XYZ sensor node, as most of the generic sensor node platforms, uses a simple wire as a monopole antenna. Ideally, the radiation pattern of this antenna should be uniform and it should look like a circle (2-D space) or a sphere (3-D space). Of course, this does not hold in practice. However, without knowing our antenna's radiation pattern it would be impossible to attempt inferring distance or location information directly from RSSI measurements.

We characterized our antenna in a basketball court measuring $79ft$ in length and $46ft$ in width. The ceiling of the court was at a height of $30ft$. In order to avoid the interference of the floor we attached our transmitter node to a string running from the one side of the court to the other. The transmitter node was at a height of approximately 8ft from the ground at the center of the court. Its antenna was vertical to the PCB board pointing down towards the floor.

We measured RSSI with a receiver node at 3 different heights from the floor: $1.25ft$, $3.5ft$, and $6.5ft$. For each one of these heights we measured the RSSI values for 8 different angles of the receiver with respect to the transmitter: 0, 45, 90, 135, 180, 215, 270, and 315 degrees. For each of these orientations we recorded the RSSI values on the receiver at a distance resolution of $2ft$. We stopped taking measurements for a given height and orientation only when the receiver was not able to receive any packets.

6.1   Antenna Length: Using a Suboptimal Antenna

According to the Chipcon's Zigbee radio chip datasheet [4] the optimal length of the monopole antenna should be 1.1inch. Therefore, in our first attempt to measure the antenna we used a wire with 1.1inch length as the monopole antenna. Both receiver and transmitter had exactly the same antenna.

Initially we tried to measure the antenna at the lowest power level $(-25dBm)$ of the radio. We noticed that even at the lowest power level, transmitter and receiver could communicate for almost any position of the receiver in the basketball court. In addition, we noticed that the RSSI values recorded at the receiver were changing dramatically with very small changes in the distance between transmitter and receiver even when the orientation of the nodes was kept constant. Therefore, it was impossible to infer any signal propagation model based on the RSSI data. Apparently, even at the lowest power level the 802.15.4 radio from Chipcon has a large communication range that is able to generate significant reflections even in the basketball court. Hence, the results in a real indoor environment with furniture and people would be much worse. By increasing the transmission power level of the radio we found out that even at slightly higher power levels two nodes could communicate over long distances even without line-of-sight. To reduce the effective communication range of the nodes we used a suboptimal antenna. Instead of using the recommended length (1.1inch) monopole antenna we used a 2.9inch wire as our monopole antenna. As it can be seen in Figure 5b, the communication range of the radio when using the suboptimal antenna is significantly reduced but the signal attenuation properties remain the same.

6.2   Antenna Orientation in Basketball Court

After replacing the 1.1inch antennas, on both the receiver and the transmitter, with 2.9inch antennas we repeated the same experiment. At the lowest transmission power level of the radio the communication range was 3.3-6.6ft. Despite the fact that changing the length of the antenna reduced the communication range, still we could not get any signal propagation model at the lowest power level. It was obvious that communication was totally unreliable at the lowest power level with the 2.9inch antenna.

However, we noticed that by using the next higher transmission power level we were getting consistent RSSI values on the receiver and we had reliable communication in a wide range of distances. The same was valid for all the other transmission power levels. Therefore, we decided to measure the 2.9inch antenna at the power level of $-15dBm$ using all the possible combinations described in the previous section.

Figures 4a, 4b, and 4c show the RSSI values versus distance for all the orientations and for the $6.5ft$, $3.5ft$, and $1.25ft$ receiver heights respectively. Note that when the receiver is at $1.25ft$ (Figure 4c) and $3.5ft$ (Figure 4b) height from the ground the raw RSSI data cannot be used to infer any distance information. The reason is that significantly different distances can produce the same or almost the same RSSI values. In addition, similar distances correspond to very different (even up to $11dBm$) RSSI values for different antenna orientations.

However, when the receiver is at $6.5ft$ height from the ground (Figure 4a) the RSSI versus distance plot can be easily fitted to the widely used log-normal signal propagational model. Note that as the distance between transmitter and receiver increases the variability in the RSSI value that corresponds to this distance also increases. In other words different ranges of RSSI values provide distance information with different levels of accuracy. This suggests that a probabilistic approach for translating RSSI values to distance information should be used. This can be easily implemented by computing the probability distribution of the raw RSSI values over the different distances. Using this prob-

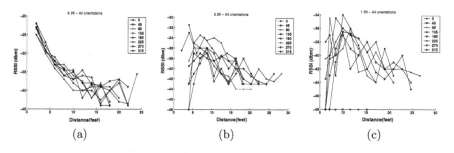

(a)   (b)   (c)

Fig. 4. RSSI vs. Distance plots at different heights a) 6.5ft, b) 3.5ft, c) 1.25ft. RSSI values equal to $-48dBm$ indicate absence of communication between receiver and transmitter

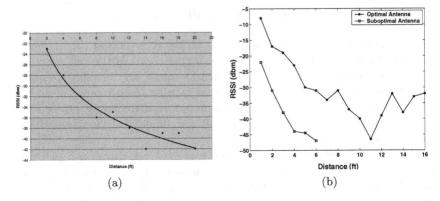

Fig. 5. a)RSSI vs Distance plots for an obstacle-free environment (basketball court). Each data point is the average RSSI value recorded for 20 packets, b) The effect of using a suboptimal antenna in an obstacle free indoor environment of size $24ft$ x $20ft$.

ability distribution we can map an RSSI value to a specific distance with a given probability. The higher the probability the higher the accuracy of the distance estimation.

Figures 4a, 4b, and 4c clearly show that different antenna orientations can produce different sets of RSSI values for the same distances between receiver and transmitter. In practice, this implies that the raw RSSI values cannot be directly translated to distance information. Extra knowledge about the specific antenna orientation that corresponds to this set of RSSI values is needed. Furthermore, our results show that even if we are able to map a set of RSSI values to a specific antenna orientation this does not necessarily mean that we can extract any useful distance information. The reason is that some antenna orientations do not provide a consistent signal attenuation.

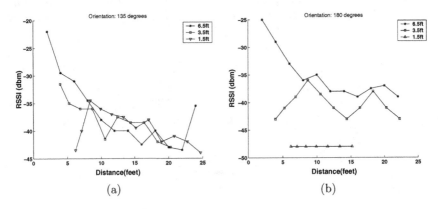

Fig. 6. a) The best angle between receiver and transmitter, b) One of the worst angles between the receiver and the transmitter. RSSI values equal to $-48dBm$ indicate absence of communication between receiver and transmitter.

Figures 6a and 6b provide some more insight to the antenna orientation effect. Figure 6 shows the best transmitter antenna orientation. Note that a single signal propagation model can be extracted that is independent of the height of the receiver.

On the other hand, Figure 6a shows the worst transmitter antenna orientation. It is obvious that any attempt to infer distance information directly from the RSSI values is impossible. Different heights of the receiver produce very different RSSI values. However, when the receiver is at $6.5ft$ height a signal propagation model can still be extracted. This implies that when the receiver is at $6.5ft$ the radiation pattern of the antenna seems to be very symmetric. This allows us to infer a signal propagation model independently of the antenna orientation of the transmitter. In other words, when the height difference between the transmitter and the receiver is small, antenna orientation does not affect the signal propagation model. But, as figure 6b shows, when the height difference between the transmitter and the receiver increases then the antenna orientation becomes a major factor that greatly affects the signal propagation model.

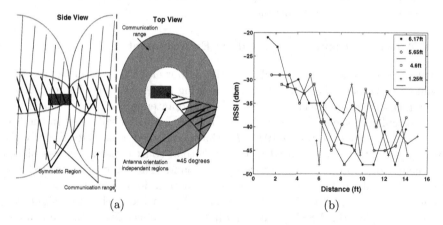

(a)   (b)

Fig. 7. a) Radiation Pattern of the monopole antenna, b) Indoors antenna characterization. RSSI values equal to $-48dBm$ indicate absence of communication between receiver and transmitter.

This can be seen in figure 7 where the radiation pattern of our monopole antenna is shown. The radiation pattern was constructed using all the measurements we collected in the basketball court. The shaded region of the antenna radiation pattern is the symmetric region for which a single signal propagation model can be extracted. Since the antenna orientation is not a major factor when the receiver and the transmitter are at the same height, the log-normal shadowing model is very accurate in the case of a 2-D sensor network deployment at an obstacle-free environment (outdoor deployment). However, the log-normal shadowing model is not able to capture the effect of the transmitter's antenna orientation in the case of a 3-D sensor network deployment even in an obstacle-free environment.

Consequently, a robust RSSI localization method should try to operate only in the shaded region of the antenna radiation pattern ,shown in Figure 7, where the log-normal shadowing model seems to hold. This requires isolating the shaded area from the rest of the communication region where the RSSI values are significantly affected by the antenna orientation of the transmitter and they cannot provide any reliable distance or location information. To demonstrate the difficulty of this task, consider the following case where a beacon is transmitting packets and a set of receivers listen the packets and record the RSSI values which are then send back to the beacon node. The beacon node is aware of a set of pairs of the following format: $< nodeID, RSSI >$. How can the beacon identify the nodes that were in the shaded area of its communication range? The only case where the beacon is able to identify those nodes is the case where the RSSI values recorded on the nodes that were in the shaded area of the communication range of the beacon node are unique. In other words, there is a unique set of RSSI values that can be recorded on the receiver only when the receiver is in the symmetric region of the communication range of the transmitter. Unfortunately, Figures 4 and 6 show that this unique set of RSSI values is very small and covers only a small range of short distances.

6.3   Antenna Orientation in Indoor Environments

In this section we focus on the effect of the indoor environment on the received signal strength between a pair of communicating nodes. Our first indoors experiment focused on the effect of reflections on the antenna radiation pattern. We tried to replicate the experiment that we run in the basketball court in the 3-D testbed ($15ft(W) \times 20ft(L) \times 10ft(H)$) that is installed in our lab. Exactly the same transmitter that was used in the basketball court experiment was placed at a height of approximately $7ft$ from the ground. The same receiver that was used in the basketball court experiment was placed in four different heights from the ground: $1.25ft$, $4.6ft$, $5.65ft$, and $6.17ft$. For each one of these heights the receiver recorded the RSSI values for different distances from the transmitter with a distance resolution of $1ft$(the transmitter was transmitting packets at the same power level as in the basketball court, $-15dBm$). In this experiment we focused only on a single transmitter antenna orientation, the one that gave us a single signal propagation model that was independent of the height of the receiver(Figure 6) in the obstacle-free environment.

The RSSI values that were recorded on the receiver for all the different distances and for all the different heights of the receiver can be seen in Figure 7b. When the receiver is at $6.17ft$ from the ground a clear log-normal signal propagation model can be derived as in the case of the obstacle-free environment. However, for the other three heights of the receiver the RSSI values seem totally random and no actual distance information can be extracted from these sets of RSSI values. What is even more interesting, is the fact that the randomness that the reflections introduce in the RSSI values directly affects the symmetric region of the antenna and makes it significantly narrower. Note that every RSSI value that is equal or smaller than $-30dBm$ can actually correspond to any distance that is larger than $1.6ft$ and smaller than the communication range. The only RSSI values that can be used to accurately estimate the distance between the nodes are the RSSI values that are higher than $-30dBm$. This range of RSSI values can only be produced by the symmetric region of the antenna and it is not affected by the reflections in the room or the height of the receiver. In addition, this range of RSSI values can be fitted to a linear signal propagation model and not to a log-normal signal propagation model. Unfortunately, the maximum distance that this region of RSSI values can cover is very small and approximately $3ft$ to $4ft$. This suggests that even for small rooms a very large number of sensor nodes is required in order to perform accurate RSSI localization.

6.4   Indoor Testbed Experiment

In order to verify the results of the previous section, we deployed 38^1 nodes with 2.9inch antennas on our 3-D testbed located inside our lab. The nodes were placed in 3-dimensions inside the testbed as shown in Figure 1b. The antennas of all the nodes on the floor were pointing to the ceiling and the antennas of the nodes on the testbed were pointing either towards the center of the testbed or towards the floor. In all cases, the antennas were vertical with respect to the PCB of the XYZ sensor node.

   In our experiment, each node broadcasts 10 packets at each one of the eight available power levels. All the nodes that hear a packet record the RSSI value for this packet and the sender id. At every time instant only one node is broadcasting packets. After a node has finished transmitting packets, a gateway node connected to a PC polls the recorded data from each node in the testbed separately. This process continues until all nodes transmit 10 packets at each power level. The experiment took place during the night when no people were in the lab.

Received Signal Strength Data. Figures 8a, 8b, 8c show the recorded RSSI values versus the true distances that they correspond to for different power levels and for all 38 nodes. It is obvious that no actual distance information can be extracted directly from the RSSI values. This is due to the reflections and the random placement of the nodes which created communicating pairs of nodes with random pairwise antenna orientations. Note, that as the transmitting power level used decreases, the RSSI data starts looking less random. The reason is that as the power level increases the reflections in the testbed also increase. However, even at the low power level it is very difficult to fit the RSSI data to a signal propagation model.

Connectivity and Link Symmetry. Our 38 node deployment also provided useful insight about the connectivity and the symmetry of the links in a real IEEE 802.15.4 sensor network. Figures 10a, 10b, and 10c show the connectivity achieved by the lowest, low and maximum power levels respectively.

---

[1] Initially we deployed 40 nodes. Unfortunately, as it can be seen in Figure 10, the batteries of nodes 20 and 21 were not full and therefore these nodes did not send/receive any packets.

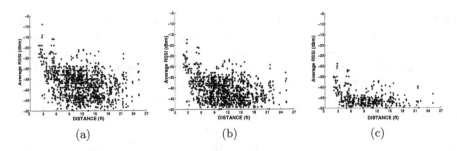

Fig. 8. RSSI vs Distance plots for the 38 node indoor sensor network deployment at different power levels: a) 0dBm, b) -5dBm, c) -15dBm

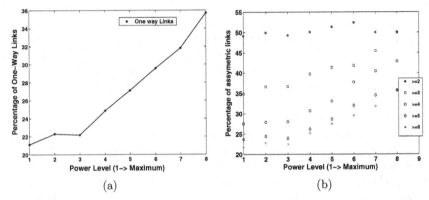

Fig. 9. Percentage of a) One-way links and b) asymmetric links

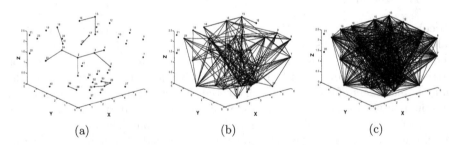

Fig. 10. Connectivity plots for the 38 node indoor sensor network a)-25dBm b) -15dBm, c) 0dBm. Nodes 20 and 21 were not equipped with fully charged batteries.

Figures 9a and 9b show the percentage of one-way links and the percentage of asymmetric[2] links respectively. As the power level of transmission decreases

---

[2] We call (A, B) link an asymmetric link if the RSSI value recorded at B when A is transmitting is different than the RSSI value recorded at A when B is transmitting. We call (A, B) link an one-way link if node A can reach node B but node B cannot reach node A. Asymmetric links include the one-way links.

the percentage of asymmetric links and their absolute difference as well as the percentage of one-way links increase. What is even more important, is the fact that the asymmetry of the links does not depend on the actual RSSI values. Our experimental data show that when node A transmits packets, node B might record a very high RSSI value that can be even equal to $-23dBm$ or $-25dBm$. However, when node B transmits packets, node A might record a very small RSSI value or it might not record any RSSI value at all because it is not able to receive any packets. Our experimental results, shown in Figure 9, show that the percentage of asymmetric links vary from 21% to 36% of the total number of links in the network depending on the power level used during transmission.

7 Discussion

Based on our detailed characterization we found that antenna orientation greatly impacts RSSI and link asymmetry in indoor and outdoor scenarios. This is especially the case in 3-D indoor deployments with random antenna orientations. These observations influence the assumptions of many node localization algorithms that utilize RSSI information. This includes RSSI distance prediction and profiling algorithms as well as other statistical approaches. Our results show that direct distance prediction from raw RSSI data in 3-D indoor environments is impossible. For profiling approaches, our measurements show that antenna orientation information should be included in the fingerprint. However, even if the antenna orientation that corresponds to a set of RSSI values is known it might be impossible to infer any distance information since some antenna orientations do not provide a consistent signal attenuation. This observation shows that modeling the antenna orientation effect as a random variable with gaussian distribution, as it is modeled in equation 1, is not realistic.

Our experiments also show that the antenna orientation has a great impact on the ordering of the RSSI values. The ordering of RSSI values is meaningful only when the communication takes place in the symmetric region of the antenna as it is shown in Figure 7(a). According to our findings this region of the antenna is only a small fraction of the communication range and therefore the ranking of the RSSI values provides little or no information in the case of 3-D deployments where the antenna orientations of the communicating nodes are almost random.

The antenna orientation effect has also implications on the statistical RSSI localization algorithms. In most probabilistic algorithms a probability distribution, usually gaussian, of the RSSI values is assumed. In general, such an assumption holds only in the symmetric region of the antenna. When the communication between two nodes takes place in the non-symmetric region of the antenna, which is generally the case in a 3-D network deployment, the variation in the RSSI values cannot be modeled by a gaussian distribution since, according to our experiments, there is a huge variation in the RSSI values. Consequently, our observations suggest that new probabilistic models that better capture RSSI variations need to be developed for 3-D environments.

In the case of indoor environments, reflections become the main problem in performing RSSI distance prediction. Only a very small range of RSSI values can be used for extracting distance information for up to $3 - 4ft$. In this region, RSSI changes linearly with distance. In addition, our findings show that 3-D indoor sensor network deployments suffer of a high degree of link asymmetry. This link asymmetry is due to the multipath and fading effects as well as due to the random pairwise antenna orientations used during communication.

8   Conclusions

We have conducted an empirical study of signal strength behavior using monopole antennas and the widely used Chipcon CC2420 radio. Our experiments in a large open space with minimal multipath effects have shown that antenna orientation corrupts signal strength. This significantly alters the quality of information that RSSI can provide for deriving spatial relationships. Our results and experience from this work show that signal strength localization will work in specially instrumented scenarios. In other scenarios and $3D$ deployments, signal strength localization remains an extremely challenging task. Statistical techniques and specific deployment scenarios will mitigate some of these challenges. However, the large amount of characterization needed will make the use of signal strength approaches with low power radios practically impossible. Our study also provides valuable insight into link asymmetry in indoor $3D$ deployments.

Acknowledgment

This work was supported in part by the National Science Foundation under award #0448082 and a gift from OKI Semiconductors. The authors would also like to thank Prof. Sekhar Tatikonda for his valuable feedback on this work.

References

1. P. Bahl and V. N. Padmanabhan. RADAR: An in-building RF-based user location and tracking system. In *Proc. IEEE Infocom*, pages 775–784, Tel-Aviv, Israel, April 2000.
2. M. Berna, B. Lisien, B. Sellner, G. Gordon, F. Pfenning, and S. Thrun. A learning algorithm for localizing people based on wireless signal strength that uses labeled and unlabeled data. In *Proceedings of IJCAI 03, pages 1427-1428*, 2003.
3. P. Castro, P. Chiu, T. Kremenek, and R. Muntz. A Probabilistic Location Service for Wireless Network Environments. *Ubiquitous Computing 2001*, September 2001.
4. Chipcon: CC2420 802.15.4 compliant radio. http://www.chipcon.com.
5. D.Niculescu and B. Nath. Vor base stations for indoor 802.11 positioning. In *Proceedings of Mobicom*, 2004.
6. E. Elnahrawy, X. Li, and R. M. Martin. The limits of localization using signal strength: A comparative study. In *Proceedings of Sensor and Ad-Hoc Communications and Networks Conference (SECON), Santa Clara California*, October 2004.

7. T. He, C. Huang, B. Blum, J. Stankovic, and T. Abdelzaher. Range-free localization schemes for large scale sensor networks. In *International Conference on Mobile Computing and Networking(Mobicom), September 14-19 San Diego California*, September 2003.

8. Jeffrey Hightower, Roy Want, and Gaetano Borriello. SpotON: An indoor 3d location sensing technology based on RF signal strength. UW CSE 00-02-02, University of Washington, Department of Computer Science and Engineering, Seattle, WA, February 2000.

9. Konrad Lorincz and Matt Welsh. Motetrack: A robust, decentralized aproachto rf-based location tracking. In *Proceedings of the International Workshop on Location- and Context-Awareness (Loca 2005)*, 2005.

10. D. Lymberopoulos and A. Savvides. Xyz: A motion-enabled, power aware sensor node platform for distributed sensor network applications. In *IPSN, SPOTS track*, April 2005.

11. D. Madigan, E. Elnahrawy, and R. Martin. Bayesian indoor positioning systems. In *Proceedings of INFOCOM 2005, Miami, Florida*, March 2005.

12. D. Niculescu and B. Nath. Localized positioning in ad hoc networks. In *Proceedings of the First IEEE International Workshop on Sensor Network Protocols and Applications*, San Diego, CA, May 2003.

13. N. Patwari and A. O. Hero III. Using proximity and quantized rss for sensor localization in wireless networks. In *WSNA03*, San Diego, CA, September 2003.

14. Prasithsangaree, P. Krishnamurthy, and P. K. Chrysanthis. On indoor position location with wireless lans. In *The 13th IEEE International Symposium on Personal, Indoor, and Mobile Radio Communications (PIMRC 2002)*, 2002.

15. S. Ray, W. Lai, and I. Pascalidis. Deployment optimization of sensornet-based stochastic location-detection systems. In *Proceedings of INFOCOM 2005, Miami, Florida*, March 2005.

16. S. Saha, K. Chaudhuri, D. Sanghi, and P. Bhagwat. Location determination of a mobile device using ieee 802.11 access point signals. In *IEEE Wireless Communications and Networking Conference (WCNC)*, 2003.

17. Scott Y. Seidel and Theodore S. Rapport. 914 MHz path loss prediction model for indoor wireless communications in multifloored buildings. *IEEE Transactions on Antennas and Propagation*, 40(2):207–217, February 1992.

18. R. Stoleru and J. Stankovic. Probability grid: A location estimation scheme for wireless sensor networks. In *Proceedings of Sensor and Ad-Hoc Communications and Networks Conference (SECON), Santa Clara California*, October 4-7 2004.

19. P. Myllymaki T. Roos and H. Tirri. A statistical modeling approach to location estimation. In *IEEE Trnsactions on Mobile Computing*, pages 1:59–69, 2002.

20. K. Whitehouse, A. Woo, C. Karlof, and D. Culler F. Jiang. The effects of ranging noise on multi-hop localization: An empirical study. In *Proceedings of Information Processing in Sensor Networks (IPSN), Los Angeles, CA*, April 2005.

21. K. Yedavalli, B. Krishnamachari, S. Ravula, and B. Srinivasan. Ecolocation: A technique for rf based localization in wireless sensor networks. In *Proceedings of Information Processing in Sensor Networks (IPSN), Los Angeles, CA*, April 2005.

Author Index

Lecture Notes in Computer Science

For information about Vols. 1–3772

please contact your bookseller or Springer

Vol. 3819: P. Van Hentenryck (Ed.), Practical Aspects of Declarative Languages. X, 231 pages. 2005.

Vol. 3818: S. Grumbach, L. Sui, V. Vianu (Eds.), Advances in Computer Science – ASIAN 2005. XIII, 294 pages. 2005.

Vol. 3817: M. Faundez-Zanuy, L. Janer, A. Esposito, A. Satue-Villar, J. Roure, V. Espinosa-Duro (Eds.), Nonlinear Analyses and Algorithms for Speech Processing. XII, 380 pages. 2006. (Sublibrary LNAI).

Vol. 3816: G. Chakraborty (Ed.), Distributed Computing and Internet Technology. XXI, 606 pages. 2005.

Vol. 3815: E.A. Fox, E.J. Neuhold, P. Premsmit, V. Wuwongse (Eds.), Digital Libraries: Implementing Strategies and Sharing Experiences. XVII, 529 pages. 2005.

Vol. 3814: M. Maybury, O. Stock, W. Wahlster (Eds.), Intelligent Technologies for Interactive Entertainment. XV, 342 pages. 2005. (Sublibrary LNAI).

Vol. 3813: R. Molva, G. Tsudik, D. Westhoff (Eds.), Security and Privacy in Ad-hoc and Sensor Networks. VIII, 219 pages. 2005.

Vol. 3810: Y.G. Desmedt, H. Wang, Y. Mu, Y. Li (Eds.), Cryptology and Network Security. XI, 349 pages. 2005.

Vol. 3809: S. Zhang, R. Jarvis (Eds.), AI 2005: Advances in Artificial Intelligence. XXVII, 1344 pages. 2005. (Sublibrary LNAI).

Vol. 3808: C. Bento, A. Cardoso, G. Dias (Eds.), Progress in Artificial Intelligence. XVIII, 704 pages. 2005. (Sublibrary LNAI).

Vol. 3807: M. Dean, Y. Guo, W. Jun, R. Kaschek, S. Krishnaswamy, Z. Pan, Q.Z. Sheng (Eds.), Web Information Systems Engineering – WISE 2005 Workshops. XV, 275 pages. 2005.

Vol. 3806: A.H. H. Ngu, M. Kitsuregawa, E.J. Neuhold, J.-Y. Chung, Q.Z. Sheng (Eds.), Web Information Systems Engineering – WISE 2005. XXI, 771 pages. 2005.

Vol. 3805: G. Subsol (Ed.), Virtual Storytelling. XII, 289 pages. 2005.

Vol. 3804: G. Bebis, R. Boyle, D. Koracin, B. Parvin (Eds.), Advances in Visual Computing. XX, 755 pages. 2005.

Vol. 3803: S. Jajodia, C. Mazumdar (Eds.), Information Systems Security. XI, 342 pages. 2005.

Vol. 3802: Y. Hao, J. Liu, Y.-P. Wang, Y.-m. Cheung, H. Yin, L. Jiao, J. Ma, Y.-C. Jiao (Eds.), Computational Intelligence and Security, Part II. XLII, 1166 pages. 2005. (Sublibrary LNAI).

Vol. 3801: Y. Hao, J. Liu, Y.-P. Wang, Y.-m. Cheung, H. Yin, L. Jiao, J. Ma, Y.-C. Jiao (Eds.), Computational Intelligence and Security, Part I. XLI, 1122 pages. 2005. (Sublibrary LNAI).

Vol. 3799: M. A. Rodríguez, I.F. Cruz, S. Levashkin, M.J. Egenhofer (Eds.), GeoSpatial Semantics. X, 259 pages. 2005.

Vol. 3798: A. Dearle, S. Eisenbach (Eds.), Component Deployment. X, 197 pages. 2005.

Vol. 3797: S. Maitra, C. E. V. Madhavan, R. Venkatesan (Eds.), Progress in Cryptology - INDOCRYPT 2005. XIV, 417 pages. 2005.

Vol. 3796: N.P. Smart (Ed.), Cryptography and Coding. XI, 461 pages. 2005.

Vol. 3795: H. Zhuge, G.C. Fox (Eds.), Grid and Cooperative Computing - GCC 2005. XXI, 1203 pages. 2005.

Vol. 3794: X. Jia, J. Wu, Y. He (Eds.), Mobile Ad-hoc and Sensor Networks. XX, 1136 pages. 2005.

Vol. 3793: T. Conte, N. Navarro, W.-m.W. Hwu, M. Valero, T. Ungerer (Eds.), High Performance Embedded Architectures and Compilers. XIII, 317 pages. 2005.

Vol. 3792: I. Richardson, P. Abrahamsson, R. Messnarz (Eds.), Software Process Improvement. VIII, 215 pages. 2005.

Vol. 3791: A. Adi, S. Stoutenburg, S. Tabet (Eds.), Rules and Rule Markup Languages for the Semantic Web. X, 225 pages. 2005.

Vol. 3790: G. Alonso (Ed.), Middleware 2005. XIII, 443 pages. 2005.

Vol. 3789: A. Gelbukh, Á. de Albornoz, H. Terashima-Marín (Eds.), MICAI 2005: Advances in Artificial Intelligence. XXVI, 1198 pages. 2005. (Sublibrary LNAI).

Vol. 3788: B. Roy (Ed.), Advances in Cryptology - ASIACRYPT 2005. XIV, 703 pages. 2005.

Vol. 3787: D. Kratsch (Ed.), Graph-Theoretic Concepts in Computer Science. XIV, 470 pages. 2005.

Vol. 3785: K.-K. Lau, R. Banach (Eds.), Formal Methods and Software Engineering. XIV, 496 pages. 2005.

Vol. 3784: J. Tao, T. Tan, R.W. Picard (Eds.), Affective Computing and Intelligent Interaction. XIX, 1008 pages. 2005.

Vol. 3783: S. Qing, W. Mao, J. Lopez, G. Wang (Eds.), Information and Communications Security. XIV, 492 pages. 2005.

Vol. 3782: K.-D. Althoff, A. Dengel, R. Bergmann, M. Nick, T.R. Roth-Berghofer (Eds.), Professional Knowledge Management. XXIII, 739 pages. 2005. (Sublibrary LNAI).

Vol. 3781: S.Z. Li, Z. Sun, T. Tan, S. Pankanti, G. Chollet, D. Zhang (Eds.), Advances in Biometric Person Authentication. XI, 250 pages. 2005.

Vol. 3780: K. Yi (Ed.), Programming Languages and Systems. XI, 435 pages. 2005.

Vol. 3779: H. Jin, D. Reed, W. Jiang (Eds.), Network and Parallel Computing. XV, 513 pages. 2005.

Vol. 3778: C. Atkinson, C. Bunse, H.-G. Gross, C. Peper (Eds.), Component-Based Software Development for Embedded Systems. VIII, 345 pages. 2005.

Vol. 3777: O.B. Lupanov, O.M. Kasim-Zade, A.V. Chaskin, K. Steinhöfel (Eds.), Stochastic Algorithms: Foundations and Applications. VIII, 239 pages. 2005.

Vol. 3776: S.K. Pal, S. Bandyopadhyay, S. Biswas (Eds.), Pattern Recognition and Machine Intelligence. XXIV, 808 pages. 2005.

Vol. 3775: J. Schönwälder, J. Serrat (Eds.), Ambient Networks. XIII, 281 pages. 2005.

Vol. 3774: G. Bierman, C. Koch (Eds.), Database Programming Languages. X, 295 pages. 2005.

Vol. 3773: A. Sanfeliu, M.L. Cortés (Eds.), Progress in Pattern Recognition, Image Analysis and Applications. XX, 1094 pages. 2005.